TOEFL® CBT

SUCCESS

SUPER PREP TEST

Bruce Rogers

THOMSON

PETERSON'S

Australia • Canada • Mexico • Singapore • Spain • United Kingdom • United States

About The Thomson Corporation and Peterson's

With revenues of US$7.2 billion, The Thomson Corporation (www.thomson.com) is a leading global provider of integrated information solutions for business, education, and professional customers. Its Learning businesses and brands (www.thomsonlearning.com) serve the needs of individuals, learning institutions, and corporations with products and services for both traditional and distributed learning.

Peterson's, part of The Thomson Corporation, is one of the nation's most respected providers of lifelong learning online resources, software, reference guides, and books. The Education Supersite℠ at www.petersons.com—the Internet's most heavily traveled education resource—has searchable databases and interactive tools for contacting U.S.-accredited institutions and programs. In addition, Peterson's serves more than 105 million education consumers annually.

About the Author

Bruce Rogers has taught English as a second language and test-preparation courses at the Economics Institute in Boulder, Colorado, since 1979. He has also taught in special programs in Indonesia, Vietnam, South Korea, and the Czech Republic. He is also the author of *The Complete Guide to TOEIC* and *The Complete Guide to TOEFL: Practice Tests*.

"TOEFL" is a registered trademark of Educational Testing Service (ETS). The author and the publisher are in no way affiliated with ETS, nor has ETS endorsed the contents of this text in any way. The test questions and all other testing information are provided in their entirety by the author and Peterson's.

TOEFL Success is adapted from *The Complete Guide to The TOEFL CBT*, CBT edition, by Bruce Rogers and published by Heinle & Heinle/Thomson Learning.

For more information, contact Peterson's, 2000 Lenox Drive, Lawrenceville, NJ 08648; 800-338-3282; or find us on the World Wide Web at www.petersons.com/about.

ISBN 0-7689-0951-1 (text and audiocassettes)
ISBN 0-7689-0950-3 (text with CD)
ISBN 0-7689-0949-X (text only)

Printed in the United States of America

10 9 8 7 6 5 4 3 2 1   04 03 02

CONTENTS

CONTENTS

Section 4: Essay Writing 257

Practice Test

Answer Keys and Audio Scripts

PREFACE

ABOUT THIS BOOK

If you are preparing for the TOEFL test, you are not alone. Almost a million people all over the world took the test last year. A high score on this test is an essential step in being admitted to graduate or undergraduate programs at almost all colleges and universities in North America. But preparing for this test can be a difficult, frustrating experience. Perhaps you haven't taken many standardized, multiple-choice tests such as the TOEFL. Perhaps you are not familiar with the format for the computer-based TOEFL. Maybe you've taken the TOEFL once but were not satisfied with your score, or maybe you've taken the test several times but can't seem to improve your score beyond a certain point.

In any of these cases, you need a guide. That's why this book was written—to help students preparing for this important exam to maximize their scores.

This is the most complete, accurate, and up-to-date TOEFL preparation book now available. It is based on years of classroom experience teaching TOEFL preparation classes in the United States and abroad and on years of research on the test. *TOEFL CBT Success* is simply written and clearly organized and is suitable for any intermediate or advanced student of English as a second or foreign language.

TOEFL CBT Success offers a step-by-step program that teaches you critical test-taking techniques, helps you polish the language skills needed for the exam, and generally makes you a smarter test-taker. And the guide is an efficient way to prepare for TOEFL; by concentrating only on the points that are actually tested, it lets you make the most of your preparation period and never wastes your time. If you have purchased the CD version of this book, you can access an online CBT practice test.

Good luck on the TOEFL CBT!

HOW TO USE THIS BOOK

Getting Started

The first section of the book serves as an introduction to the exam. The opening portion of this section, **Questions and Answers About the TOEFL CBT**, provides you with basic information about the format of the test, guides you through the process of registering for the exam, and helps you understand your scores. The next portion of this section, **Keys to High Scores**, presents the "secrets" of being a good test-taker—picking the right test date, arranging your preparation time, using the process of elimination, coping with test anxiety, pacing yourself during the test, and other important techniques. **What It's Like to Take the TOEFL CBT** provides a preview of the testing experience and lets you know what it will feel like to take the test at a testing center.

The main body of the book is divided into four sections, reflecting the main sections of the test: Listening, structure, reading comprehension, and essay. Each of these sections consists of the following components:

- An introduction containing basic strategies for that section of the test.
- A sample test to give you a feel for each part of the test and to provide a basis for understanding the lessons.
- Lessons that break down the knowledge and skills needed for each part of the test into comprehensible "bites" of information. Each of the lessons in the book contains sample items that illustrate exactly how the point brought up in that lesson is tested in TOEFL. Furthermore, each lesson contains one or more exercises for practicing the relevant points.
- Exercises that review the points brought up in the previous lessons. These put together the points practiced in isolation in the lessons and allow you to chart your progress.

Section 1: Listening

This section is divided into two parts: Part A: Dialogues and Part B: Longer Talks. The exercises and tests in this part of the book are intended to be used with the audio that accompanies this book.

Section 2: Structure

This section categorizes common grammatical points tested in structure problems and suggests ways to solve these problems.

Section 3: Reading

This section of the book prepares you for the third section of TOEFL test. The Reading portion of the book suggests reading attack skills, lists the various types of questions asked about the passages, and offers suggestions for answering each type of question. There are in-depth reading exercises to practice these techniques.

Section 4: Essay Writing

This part of the book introduces the essay writing section and presents the best methods for planning, writing, and checking the essay. There are model essays of strong essays, and there are practice questions.

Complete Practice Test

The practice test provides one of the best ways to get ready for TOEFL because it draws together all the points you have studied. The practice test in this book simulates as much as possible a computer-based test.

SUGGESTIONS FOR USING THIS BOOK

Whether working alone or in a group, you should begin your preparation for TOEFL test by reading the introductory Red Alert. You can then work through the book in the order in which it is written or begin with the section in which you are weakest (or in which the majority of the students in a class are weakest). Generally, you can make the fastest progress by working in your weakest area. You can determine which area is your weakest by looking at the scores from a previous test or by using one of the practice test as a diagnostic test.

The amounts of time required to cover each segment of this book are given below. Keep in mind that these times are approximate and do not include review sessions.

Getting Started. . . . . 1-3 hours
Listening. . . . . 12-16 hours
Structure. . . . . 20-25 hours
Reading. . . . . 15-20 hours
Essay Writing. . . . . 3-5 hours
Complete Practice Test. . . . . 4-6 hours

ACKNOWLEDGMENTS

I would like to thank the following professionals for their comments and suggestions during the development of this text:

Steven A. Stupak, Korea International Human Resources Development Center; Virginia Hamori, American Language Institute, American University of Paris; Jim Price, International Language Center, Bangkok; Stephen Thewlis, San Francisco State University; Connie Monroe, Queens College; Steven Horowitz, Central Washington University; Dan Douglas, Iowa State University; Frederick O'Connor, Washington State University, and Claire Bradin, Michigan State University.

I would like to thank Donald Pharr for his expert proofreading.

Thanks to Maggie Barbieri at Maxwell Macmillian and to David Lee and Ken Mattsson at Heinle & Heinle for their editorial help.

Special thanks to all of the students in my TOEFL Preparation Classes at the Economics Institute.

ACKNOWLEDGMENTS FOR THE SECOND EDITION

First, I would like to thank the many subscribers to the Material Writers branch of TESOL-L (an electronic bulletin board for teachers of English as a Second Language) who responded when I asked for suggestions on revising this text.

I would also like to thank the following for their reviews of an early draft of the manuscript:

Thanks also to the following for their painstaking reviews and proofreading of the "final" draft of the manuscript:

Ian Palmer, Seth Sycroft, University of California at Davis.

Domo arigato to Kayoko Otani, translator of the Japanese edition of *The Complete Guide to TOEFL*, for suggesting some of the vocabulary-in-context items in Section 3.

Thanks to my editors at Heinle & Heinle, David Lee and Eric Gunderson, and of course to Associate Editor Ken Mattsson for keeping the project on track.

And again, special thanks to the students in my TOEFL preparation courses at the Economics Institute.

RED ALERT

WHAT IS COMPUTER-BASED TOEFL?

In July 1998, Educational Testing Service (ETS) introduced the computer-based TOEFL test in the United States, Canada, Latin America, Europe, the Middle East, Africa, and selected Asian countries. According to ETS, the computer-based test will eventually completely replace the paper test. Some parts of the TOEFL will be a linear computerized test, which is scored the same way as a paper test. Other parts of the TOEFL will be a computer-adaptive test (CAT).

WHAT IS A COMPUTER-ADAPTIVE TEST?

A computer-adaptive test (CAT) is—as the title says—adaptive. That means that each time you answer a question the computer adjusts to your responses when determining which question to present next. For example, the first question will be of moderate difficulty. If you answer it correctly, the next question will be more difficult. If you answer it incorrectly, the next question will be easier. The computer will continue presenting questions based on your responses, with the goal of determining your ability level.

It is very important to understand that questions at the beginning of a section affect your score more than those at the end. That's because the early questions are used to determine your general ability level. Once the computer determines your general ability level, it presents questions to identify your specific ability level. As you progress farther into a section, it will be difficult to raise your score very much, even if you answer most items correctly. That's because the later questions affect your score less, as they are used to pinpoint your exact score once the computer has identified your general ability level. Therefore, take as much time as you can afford to answer the early questions correctly. Your score on each section is based on the number of questions you answer correctly, as well as the difficulty level of those questions.

You need only minimal computer skills to take the computer-based TOEFL. You will have plenty of time at the test center to work through a tutorial that allows you to practice such activities as answering questions, using the mouse, using the word processor (which you will need for your essay responses), and accessing the help function.

The computer-based tests are given at designated universities, bi-national institutes, ETS field offices, and Sylvan Technology Centers all over the world. The cost of the TOEFL CBT test is US$110.

WHAT KINDS OF QUESTIONS WILL BE ON THE COMPUTER-BASED TOEFL?

Like the paper test, the computer-based TOEFL will have three sections:

1. Listening (40–60 minutes, 30–50 questions, CAT)

2. Structure (15–20 minutes, 20–25 questions, CAT)

3. Reading (70–90 minutes, 44–60 questions, linear)

Some questions will be similar to those on the paper test while others will be very different. The Listening and Reading questions will include question types that are designed specifically for the computer. An essay will also be included that can be handwritten or typed on the computer.

HOW ARE THE COMPUTER-BASED TOEFL SCORES CALCULATED?

The computer-based TOEFL reports separate scores for each of the three test sections. The Listening is scored as a CAT. The Structure section is scored as a CAT and on the basis of the essay. The Reading section is scored as a linear test. The scores for all three sections are factored into a scaled total score, just like on the paper-based test.

The range of possible scores on each of the three multiple choice sections is from 0–30. The range for the entire test will be from 0–300. (The range on the paper version is from 200–667).

Test-Taking Tips for the CAT Sections of the Computer-Based TOEFL

The purpose of TOEFL CBT Success is to help you prepare for all forms of the test. You will increase your chances of scoring high on the TOEFL by being completely familiar with the content and format you will encounter on test day. The strategies and review sections of this book, as well as the practice tests, provide lots of opportunity to review relevant content. Keep in mind the following test-taking tips, most of which are unique to the CAT format.

- Understand the directions for each question type. Learn the directions for each type of question. The directions in this book are very similar to those on the actual test. Understanding the directions for each question type will save you valuable time on the day of the test.

- Focus on answering the questions at the beginning of sections 1 and 2 correctly. Remember that questions at the beginning of a section affect your score more than questions at the end. Be especially careful in choosing answers to questions in the first half of both the quantitative and verbal sections. Once the computer determines your general ability level with these initial questions, you will be unable to dramatically improve your score, even if you answer most of the questions toward the end correctly.

- In sections 1 and 2 be completely sure of each answer before proceeding. With a CAT, you must answer each question as it is presented. You cannot skip a difficult question and return to it later as you can with a paper test. Nor can you review responses to questions that you have already answered. Therefore, you must be confident about your answer before you confirm it and proceed to the next question. If you are completely stumped by a question, eliminate as many answer choices as you can, select the best answer from the remaining choices, and move on.

- Pace yourself. To finish all sections, you will need to work both quickly and accurately to complete each section within the time constraints. You will still receive a score, even if you do not complete all of the questions in a section.

QUESTIONS AND ANSWERS ABOUT TOEFL

Q: What is the TOEFL® test?

A: TOEFL stands for *Test of English as a Foreign Language*. The TOEFL® test is designed to measure the English-language ability of people who do not speak English as their first language and who plan to study at colleges and universities in North America. Educational Testing Service (ETS) of Princeton, New Jersey, prepares and administers the TOEFL® test. This organization produces many other standardized tests. Although there are other standardized tests of English, the TOEFL® test is by far the most important in North America. ETS has offered this exam since 1965. Each year, almost a million people take the TOEFL® test at testing centers all over the world.

Q: What format does the computer-based test follow? How long does it take to complete?

A: The computer-based test is divided into four sections: Listening, Structure, Reading, and Essay Writing, each with its own time limit. The four sections are always given in the same order. Before the actual test, you must take a tutorial that demonstrates the computer skills needed to take the test. This part is ungraded, of course, and untimed. Most test takers take about 40 minutes to complete this section. The first three sections consist mainly of multiple-choice questions while Essay Writing is a single essay-writing item.

Q: What are the main differences between the paper-based test and the computer-based test?

A: The first three sections of the computer-based test generally have fewer items. For example, on the most recent version of the paper-based test, there were 40 Structure items, while on the computer-based version there are 20 to 25. Another difference is the use of visuals in the Listening section. There are also some new "computer-unique" item-types in Listening and in Reading.

Computer-Based Format for the TOEFL® Test

Tutorial
Untimed—Average 40 minutes

1. Listening
40–60 minutes
30–50 questions (Computer adaptive)

   Part A: Dialogues 11–17 items
   Part B: Longer Talks 4–6
      talks/conversations 3–6 questions per talk

2. Structure
15–20 minutes
20–25 questions (Computer adaptive)

Sentence Completion and Error Recognition

Mandatory break—10 minutes

3. Reading
70–90 minutes
 4–5 readings
44–70 questions (Linear)

4. Essay Writing
1 essay prompt—30 minutes

   Total Time: Approximately 4 hours

Q: Are the computer-based test scores simply based on the number of correct answers?

A: No. Test-takers A and B may get the same number of correct answers on one section but test-taker A may get a higher score because he or she answered more difficult items correctly.

Q: When will I receive my test scores?

A: You will receive unofficial on-screen scores right after you take the test. The scores for Listening and Reading will be final scores, but the score for Structure and your overall score will be reported as a range of scores.

Here is an example of what these on-screen scores look like:

Listening   20
Structure   6–25
Reading   24
Overall   167–230

What your final scores will be depends on the score you receive on the Essay Writing section (which cannot be instantly graded). The Essay Writing score ranges from 0–6.

Here are some examples of scores you might receive, depending on your essay score:

Essay Score	Structure Score	Overall Score
0	6–7	167–170
1	9–10	177–180
3	15–16	198–201
5	22–23	220–223
6	24–35	227–230

You and the schools that you designate should receive final scores within two weeks if you word-process the essay. If you handwrite the essay, you should receive scores in 4–6 weeks.

Q: What is an Institutional TOEFL?

A: Institutional TOEFL tests are given by English language schools and other institutions. Sometimes they are used for placement in a school's English program or for testing a student's progress. Institutional tests are made up of items that previously appeared on tests administered by ETS.

Because ETS does not supervise these tests, some universities won't accept the results. However, many other universities will. You should check with the admissions offices of universities to see what their policy is. You must arrange for the institute where you took the exam to send the scores to the university.

Q: Has the format of the Institutional TOEFL® test also changed?

A: No, the Institutional TOEFL® test (a form of the test given by English language schools and other institutions) is still a paper-based test.

Q: What is TSE?

A: TSE (*Test of Spoken English*) tests your ability to communicate in spoken English. All of your responses are recorded on audiotape so that they can be evaluated later. The test takes about 20 minutes to complete and is given twelve times a year at various test centers. On TSE, you must answer questions about pictures or graphs, complete sentences, express your opinions on various topics, give short presentations, and so on. TSE is administered separately from TOEFL and must be paid for separately.

TSE is generally required only for students who are applying for positions as teaching assistants or for special programs or certificates.

Q: How do I register for the computer-based TOEFL® test?

A: There are a number of ways to register. You can register for the computer-based test by telephone if you have a credit card (Visa, MasterCard, or American Express). In North America, you can call Prometric TOEFL® Test Registration Center toll-free at 800-GO-TOEFL (800-468-6335) or you may call your local test center. There is a complete list of these in the *TOEFL® Information Bulletin*. Outside North America, call the Regional Registration Center for the country where you live. These are listed in the *Bulletin*. You will be given a confirmation number and be told when and where to report. You can also register by mail. If you are in North America, you can use the CBT Voucher Test Request Form found in the *Bulletin*. You can pay with credit card, check, or money order. You will receive a CBT voucher in several weeks. After that, you can call a center to schedule an appointment. If you live outside North America, you need to fill out the International Test Scheduling Form and mail it to your Regional Registration Center. Payment may be in the form of check, credit card, money order, bank draft, or UNESCO coupons. Outside North America, you may also register by faxing the International Test Scheduling Form to the Regional Registration Center for your country. Fax numbers for these centers are listed in the *Bulletin*. You can register in person by visiting the nearest testing site, and in the near future, you will probably be able to register on line by going to the TOEFL® Web site.

Q: What computer skills do I need to take the computer-based TOEFL® test?

A: The computer skills required are fairly basic. You only need to know how to point to and click on a choice with a mouse, how to scroll up and down through a document, and how to access help if you need it. If you choose to type your essay on the computer (rather than write it by hand), you will also need basic word-processing skills. Before you take the test at the center, you must complete a tutorial to make sure you have mastered the skills you need.

Q: Where is the computer-based test offered?

A: It is given at designated test centers, universities, bi-national institutes, and ETS field offices all over the world. There are two types of test centers, permanent and mobile. Tests are given at mobile centers only during certain months. A complete list of testing centers is given in the *Bulletin*. The computer-based test is not offered at nearly as many centers as the paper-based test was. Depending on where you live, you may have to travel a rather long distance to take the test.

Q: Can I choose whether to take the computer-based test or the paper-based test?

A: No. Once the computer-based test has been phased in, you will no longer have the option of taking the paper-based test.

Q: How much does the computer-based test cost?

A: It will cost US$110. (The paper-based version of the test had cost US$45.) If you need to reschedule the test, you will have to pay a US$40 rescheduling fee.

Q: What should I bring with me to the exam site?

A: You should bring the following:

- Your passport
- Your appointment confirmation number
- Your CBT voucher, if you are using one
- A list of the universities that you want your scores sent to

Don't bring any reference books, such as dictionaries or textbooks, or any electronic devices, such as translators, cellular phones, or calculators. You are not permitted to smoke, eat, or drink in the test center. You do not have to bring pencils or paper.

Q: Is every item on the test scored?

A: No, there is usually at least one unscored item in each part of the test. This is generally the last item in each part. For example, in Section 2, item 15 and item 40 are usually not scored. However, it's not recommended that you skip these items—ETS could always change its system!

Q: What is a passing score on the TOEFL® test?

A: There isn't any. Each university has its own standards for admission, so you should check the catalogs of universities you are interested in or contact their admission offices. Most undergraduate programs require scores between 173 and 213 (between 500 and 550 on the paper-based test) and most graduate programs ask for scores between 195 and 250 (between 525 and 600 on the paper-based test). Recently, there has a been a tendency for universities to raise their minimum requirements for the TOEFL® test.

Q: How are universities informed of my scores?

A: ETS reports your score to three institutions for free. For a charge, ETS will send your scores to additional institutions. There is a form for requesting this service in the *Bulletin*. Some universities will also accept photocopies of the test results that were mailed directly to you.

Q: If I feel I haven't done well on the TOEFL® test, can I cancel my scores?

A: Yes. Right after the test, you may either cancel your scores or view them. You may NOT cancel your scores once you have looked at them. However, if you are not satisfied with your unofficial scores, you can direct ETS to NOT send them on to any universities. Keep in mind that, even if you cancel your scores, you cannot take the test again until the next calendar month. It is generally NOT a good idea to cancel scores.

You may have done better on the test than you thought you did.

Q: Can I get my scores by phone?

A: Yes. Call 888-TOEFL-44 (toll-free) in North America and 609-771-7267 elsewhere 14 days after the test (4–5 weeks after the test if you handwrite the essay). ETS charges a fee for this service.

Q: How many times may I take the computer-based TOEFL® test?

A: There is no limit; you may take it as often as you like. However, you may not take the test more than once in any calendar month.

Q: Will there be other changes to the TOEFL® test in the near future?

A: Quite possibly. ETS has been working on a project called "TOEFL 2000" that could change the test even more dramatically within the next few years. For example, in the future, the test may routinely include a test of your speaking ability.

Q: How can I get more information about the TOEFL® test?

A: You can contact ETS via e-mail or get updated information about the test from their home page on the World Wide Web: E-mail: toefl@ets.org Web site: www.toefl.org

Q: Is it possible to improve one's score by cheating?

A: It is very difficult to have someone else take the exam for you. You must bring an official identification document with your picture on it. You are also required to bring a photo file record with a recent photo of yourself. ETS copies this photo and sends it with your scores to universities. If the person in the photo is not the same person who enrolls, that person may not be admitted.

The following are also considered cheating:

- Taking notes during the Listening section

- Talking to or signaling any other test takers

- Copying any test material

- Working on one section during the time allotted for another section

- Continuing to work on a section after time is called

Persons who are believed to be cheating will receive a warning for minor acts of cheating. For more serious matters, a person's scores will be canceled.

WHAT IT'S LIKE TO TAKE THE COMPUTER-BASED TOEFL® TEST

1. The first step is to call the closest testing center.* You should call at least a month before you need to take the test. There is typically a three-week waiting time, but this may vary by time of year and center. The waiting time for certain days—especially Saturdays—will be longer than for other days. If you have a credit card or have already purchased a CBT voucher, you can make an appointment over the phone to take the test. Otherwise, arrange to stop by the center. If you do make an appointment when you call, you will receive a confirmation number. Write this number down and keep it in a safe place.

2. A week after registering, you will receive directions to the center in the mail (including public transportation routes). Keep this card with your confirmation number. On the day before the test, get this card, your confirmation number, and your passport ready to take with you the following day.

3. Arrive at least a half-hour early for your appointment. At the time you arrive, you will be given a form to fill out.

4. At the time of your appointment, or whenever a computer is free, you will be taken into a room near the testing room and given a paragraph to copy and sign. This paragraph says that you really are who you say you are and that you promise not to tell anyone what is on the test. At this time, you will also have to show your passport and you will be photographed. Before you actually go into the testing room, you will have to sign a register. Center officials will then take you into the testing room and seat you at a computer. There may be a number of other people in the room taking tests—not only the TOEFL®. Your testing space will resemble a study carrel at a library.

5. Your computer will prompt you to answer some questions about yourself, your plans, and your reason for taking the test. After that, the tutorial will begin. This tutorial teaches you the basic computer skills required to take the test.

6. After you have finished the tutorial (which is not timed), you may begin the Listening section. You will have a chance to adjust the volume, read the directions, and answer a few practice items. Remember, you are NOT allowed to take notes during the Listening section.

7. After the Listening section, you may take a one-minute break or go directly on to the Structure section.

8. After completing the Structure section, there is a mandatory 10-minute break. You will have to sign out before you leave the testing area.

9. After the break, you will again have to sign in. You will be given six sheets of scrap paper and will be shown back to your computer. The next section of the test is Reading. Remember that this section of the test is NOT computer adaptive, and that you can move forward and backward through the readings. You can skip questions (although this is seldom a good idea), and go back and change your answers any time you want.

10. After you finish the Reading section of the test, you may take a one-minute break or proceed with the Essay Writing section. If you choose to word-process the essay, you will see a brief tutorial explaining *cut, paste, delete,* and other commands you need to write the essay on the computer. You may use the scrap paper you have been given to write a quick outline for your essay.

---

* Note: The testing experience may differ somewhat from center to center.

11. After you have written your essay, you will receive an unofficial grade report. You will then have a chance to choose from a pull-down menu the universities that will receive your scores. You may then be asked a number of questions about your experience taking the test. After that, you must hand in your scrap paper. You will then sign out.

12. If you word-process your essay, you will receive your final test scores in 2 weeks.

If you handwrite your essay, you will receive your final scores in 4-5 weeks.

Section 1:

LISTENING

RED ALERT

The Listening section of the TOEFL® test is always given first. The purpose of this section is to test your understanding of spoken English.

On the computer-based test, you will hear the Listening material through headphones, so the sound quality will be better than it was through loudspeakers. You will be able to control the rate at which you hear items and the volume. (NOTE: The TOEFL Sampler says that you can only change the volume before the test starts, but in fact, you can make volume changes by adjusting the on-screen volume icon at any time during the Listening section.)

The directions for this section are given on the tape as well as printed in your test book. There are four speakers, two men and two women. The speakers read the items at a normal speed. All four have standard North American accents. The tone of the items is conversational, much less formal than the items in the two other test sections.

Section I is divided into two parts. Part A consists of short dialogues with one question about each one. Part B consists of three types of longer listening stimuli with sets of multiple questions following them.

Here's what to expect during the Listening section:

1. As you listen to the dialogues and the longer talks and discussions, you will see photographs of the people involved or of things related to the discussion. There are two types of photographs. Most are context photos that merely set the scene for you. A few are content photos that clarify points made in the lectures or academic discussions.

2. Immediately after you hear the material, the photograph will disappear and a question will appear on the screen. At the same time, another speaker will read the question.

3. Immediately after hearing the question, the four answer choices will appear. Unfortunately, you cannot preview the answer choices as you listen to the Section 1 Guide to Listening dialogues or longer talks.) At this point you may click on the oval beside the answer choice that you think is correct.

4. After you have chosen an answer and are sure of it, you will click on the "Next" icon and then the "Confirm Answer" icon.

The directions for this section are spoken as well as visible on the screen. There are four speakers, two male and two female. All the speakers have standard North American accents and they read the items at a normal speed. The tone of the items is conversational, less formal than the items in the other test sections.

Listening Format

Part A: Dialogues 11-17 questions

Part B: Longer Talks

2-3 Conversations	2-3 questions	
2-3 Mini-Lectures	3-6 questions	
1-2 Academic Discussions	3-6 questions	
Total Listening Section	30-50 questions	40-60 minutes

Questions about Dialogues and Conversations are all multiple-choice problems. Mini-Lectures and Academic Discussions include both standard multiple-choice items and a number of other types of questions. These will be practiced in the lessons for Part B.

The Listening section actually tests both your listening ability and your reading skills since you must understand both the spoken material you hear through the headphones and the answer choices on the screen.

Many test takers find the Listening section the most difficult. Because it is given first, you may be more nervous during this part of the test. Furthermore, it is difficult to understand voices on tape (just as it is on the telephone or radio) because you can't see the speakers' gestures, facial expressions, or lip movements as you can during "live" listening. Finally, the test writers at ETS employ a number of "tricks" that make choosing the correct answer more difficult.

The exercises and tests in the Listening section of this text are designed to help you overcome these difficulties. You will become more comfortable listening to materials on tape or computer. You'll also become alert to many of the test writers' "tricks." If your copy of this book includes either audiocassette tapes or CDs, when you are taking the practice tests in the book, listen on headphones if they are available. Look only at the photo while you listen to the dialogue or talk. Then, when questions are being read, look only at those questions. Don't preview the answer choices (because you won't be able to do this during the actual test). Don't go back and change an answer once you have finished an item.

On the computer-based test, you control the speed at which you hear items. However, in the listening material for this book, items are separated by twelve-second pauses, as they were on the paper-based test.

You should spend some time working with the Listening sections of the audiocassettes or CDs in order to get used to controlling the speed at which you hear items.

Strategies for Section 1

- Familiarize yourself with the directions for each part before the exam. But remember, you are not permitted to turn the page to look over answer choices while the directions are being read. (No answer choices appear on the same page as the directions.)

- If you have any difficulties hearing the tape, inform one of the proctors during the introductory section. Once the test has begun, the proctors cannot stop the tape.

- Always answer promptly after the answer choices appear, not only to save time but also to keep the listening material fresh in your mind.

- Use your "power of prediction." While you are looking at the photo and listening to the spoken material, try to guess what the question or questions will be. Then, while you are listening to and reading the question, try to guess what the correct answer will be. Look for your predicted answer or something similar to it among the four choices.

- If you are not sure of an answer, try to eliminate unlikely choices and make your guess. If you have no idea which answer is correct, click on your guess answer and go on.

- Never spend too long on any one problem.

- Concentration is very important in this part of the test. Once you choose an answer, don't think about the last item—start thinking about the next one. Don't day-dream. Focus your attention on the tape and on the choices in your test book.

Begin your preparation for Section 1 by taking Preview Test 1: Listening on the following pages. This will familiarize you with the first section of the exam.

This section tests your ability to comprehend spoken English. It is divided into three parts, each with its own directions. You are *not* permitted to turn the page during the reading of the directions or to take notes at any time.

PART A

Directions: Each item in this part consists of a brief conversation involving two speakers. Following each conversation, a third voice will ask a question. You will hear the conversations and questions only once, and they will *not* be written out.

When you have heard each conversation and question, read the four answer choices and select the one—(A), (B), (C), or (D)—that best answers the question based on what is directly stated or on what can be inferred.

Here is an example.

You will hear:*

M1: Do you think I should leave this chair against the wall or put it somewhere else?

F1: Over by the window, I'd say.

M2: What does the woman think the man should do?

You will read:

What does the woman think the man should do?

(A) Open the window.
(B) Move the chair.
(C) Leave the room.
(D) Take a seat.

The correct answer is (B). From the conversation you find out that the woman thinks the man should put the chair over by the window. The best answer to the question "What does the woman think the man should do?" is choice (B), "Move the chair."

---

1. What can be said about Henry's bicycle?

   (A) It's brand new.
   (B) He just repaired it.
   (C) Someone painted it.
   (D) It's just been sold.

2. What will the man probably do next?

   (A) Give the woman cash.
   (B) Go to his car.
   (C) Purchase a book.
   (D) Use his credit card.

3. What does the woman tell Mark?

   (A) He should have listened to Professor Bryant's suggestions.
   (B) He doesn't have to read all the books.
   (C) All of the books on the list are important.
   (D) Some of the books are unavailable now.

4. What does the man mean?

   (A) The software isn't convenient to use.
   (B) He's not familiar with the software.
   (C) Using the software is simple.
   (D) He wishes he'd bought that software.

---

* Note: M1 = first male voice   M2 = second male voice   F1 = first female voice   F2 = second female voice

5. What does the man want to know?

    (A) What time his brother called
    (B) Where to meet his brother
    (C) Why his brother called
    (D) When to meet his brother

6. What does the man say about Howard?

    (A) He left on a long trip yesterday.
    (B) His letter arrived unexpectedly.
    (C) He seemed to be sad yesterday.
    (D) The letter he sent was very funny.

7. What can be inferred about Professor Welch from this conversation?

    (A) He'll probably give the man another grade.
    (B) He doesn't teach chemistry anymore.
    (C) He rarely changes his grades.
    (D) He'll probably retire soon.

8. What is the woman really saying to Allen?

    (A) His class has been canceled.
    (B) He shouldn't drop the class.
    (C) An earlier class would be better for him.
    (D) He doesn't need to study political science.

9. What does the man say about Professor Porter?

    (A) She mailed the grades to her students.
    (B) She left the students' tests in her office.
    (C) She can't get into her office.
    (D) She put a list of grades on the door.

10. What do the speakers imply about William?

    (A) He has a good excuse for being late.
    (B) No one has heard from him for a week.
    (C) He's still waiting to be contacted.
    (D) He doesn't take responsibility for errors.

11. What did the man think he had lost?

    (A) His wallet
    (B) An identification card
    (C) His job at the bookstore
    (D) A check

12. What can be inferred about the man?

    (A) He got on the wrong bus.
    (B) He's afraid he'll be late for his flight.
    (C) He's sorry he took a bus instead of flying.
    (D) He had to wait a long time for the bus.

13. What does the woman imply?

    (A) The meeting will have to be rescheduled.
    (B) She doesn't care whom the board picks as dean.
    (C) She's not sure where the meeting will be.
    (D) The board will not choose a dean this month.

14. What do they mean?

    (A) They wish they hadn't paid attention to Harvey.
    (B) They asked for some information about Harvey.
    (C) Harvey told them not to ignore him.
    (D) Only Harvey could give them any assistance.

15. What are the men probably discussing?

    (A) A hotel room
    (B) The man's family
    (C) A reasonable offer
    (D) The man's schedule

16. What can be inferred from Professor White's remark?

    (A) He must change his syllabus.
    (B) The woman cannot take his class.
    (C) He has extra copies of the syllabus.
    (D) Some students are not on his list.

17. What had the man originally assumed?

    (A) Peter wouldn't be favored in the match.
    (B) The match had already been played.
    (C) The match wouldn't be played.
    (D) Peter would win the match

PART B

Directions: This part of the test consists of extended conversations between two speakers. After each of these conversations, there are a number of questions. You will hear each conversation and question only once, and the questions are *not* written out.

When you have heard the questions, read the four answer choices and select the *one*—(A), (B), (C), or (D)—that best answers the question based on what is directly stated or on what can be inferred. Then fill in the space on your answer sheet that matches the letter of the answer that you have selected.

Don't forget: During actual exams, taking notes or writing in your test book is *not* permitted.

18. What course does Scott want to drop?

(A) Biochemistry
(B) Mathematics
(C) Language
(D) Music

19. What does Professor Lamont suggest that Scott do?

(A) Change majors.
(B) Study music.
(C) Get a tutor.
(D) Drop the class.

20. Which of the following best describes Professor Lamont's attitude toward Scott?

(A) Condescending
(B) Angry
(C) Encouraging
(D) Disappointed

21. According to the speaker, in what ways are Earth and Venus twins?
Choose two.

(A) They have similar surface conditions.
(B) They are about the same size.
(C) They spin in the same direction.
(D) They are relatively close together.

22. Which of the following can be seen through a telescope aimed at Venus?

(A) The phases of Venus
(B) The continents of Venus
(C) The moons of Venus
(D) The jungles of Venus

23. According to the speaker, which of the following were once common beliefs about the planet Venus?
Choose two.

(A) It was not a single object but two objects.
(B) Its surface temperatures were much colder than those on Earth.
(C) It had two moons: Phosphorous and Hesperus.
(D) There was life beneath its cloud cover.

24. Which of the following does the speaker say about the length of a day on Venus?

(A) It is shorter than an Earth day.
(B) It is longer than an Earth year.
(C) It is longer than a Venus year.
(D) It is the longest of any known planet.

25. In what order were these space probes sent to Venus?

Place the letter of the choice in the proper box. Use each choice only once.

(A) Mariner 2
(B) Venus Pioneer 2
(C) Magellan
(D) Venera 4

1.
2.
3.
4.

26. It can be inferred that the topic of the next student's presentation will be which of the following?

(A) The Moon
(B) The Sun
(C) The Earth
(D) The planet Mars

27. Why does Dana want to find a job?

(A) To pay for everyday expenses
(B) To pay for tuition
(C) To pay back a bank loan
(D) To pay for room and board

28. What job is Dana probably going to apply for?

(A) Selling gifts at a museum
(B) Directing an art gallery
(C) Working as a receptionist
(D) Working in a cafeteria

29. What must Dana do first to apply for the job she is interested in?

(A) Go to an interview with Dr. Ferrarra.
(B) Mail her application to the Financial Aid Office.
(C) Fill out some forms.
(D) Call the personnel office.

30. What is the main topic of this lecture?

(A) The role of religious music in Europe.
(B) Books of the colonial period.
(C) Domestic life in the nineteenth century in the United States.
(D) Eighteenth- and nineteenth-century music in the United States.

31. What does the speaker indicate about the song "Old Hundred"?

Choose two.

(A) It has a long history.
(B) It appeared in the Bay Psalm Book.
(C) It was extremely unusual.
(D) It was composed by Steven Foster.

32. Which of these is the best representation of the notational system used for Southern revival hymns?

(A)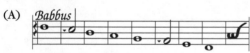

(B) ◆ ✚ ▲ ● ▼
(C) A-B♭-C-G-F♯

33. Which of these instruments was typically used to play minstrel songs?

(A)

(B)

(C)

(D)

34. Match the song with the correct musical category.

Place the letter of the choice in the proper box. Use each choice only once.

(A) Southern revival hymn

[ ]

(B) parlor song

[ ]

(C) minstrel song

[ ]

1. "Wayfaring Stranger"
2. "Dixie"
3. "The Old Arm Chair"

35. What does the speaker say about Stephen Foster?

(A) He didn't write songs; he adapted old melodies.
(B) His songs show a variety of influences.
(C) He composed only minstrel songs.
(D) His melodies are extremely complicated.

36. What is the main topic of this discussion?

(A) The choice of textbooks
(B) The students' final exam
(C) The students' final project
(D) The students' research paper

37. It can be inferred that Professor Hunter would approve of which of these methods of selecting subjects for groups?

Choose two.

(A) Letting the subjects pick their own group
(B) Having the subjects flip coins
(C) Using a computer program that makes random choices
(D) Allowing the experimenter to assign subjects to groups

38. In the experiment proposed by the student, what can be inferred about the people in the control group?

(A) Their grades will probably improve.
(B) They are not really necessary to the success of the experiment.
(C) Their grade performance will not be affected by exercise.
(D) They will exercise more than the people in the experimental group.

39. In what order should the students complete these tasks?

Place the letter of the choice in the proper box. Use each choice only once.

(A) Conduct the experiment.
(B) Analyze the results.
(C) Complete a detailed design and select subjects.
(D) Submit a hypothesis and summary.

1.
2.
3.
4.

40. When is the completed project due?

(A) Next week
(B) In November
(C) On the last day of class
(D) On the day of the final exam

This is the end of Preview Test 1: Listening.

Part A

ABOUT DIALOGUES

The first part of the Listening section consists of spoken dialogues (conversations) between two speakers. A third speaker asks a question about what was said or implied in the conversation. You must decide which of the four answer choices printed in your test book is the best answer for the question you hear and then mark that choice on your answer sheet. Between each of the dialogues is a 12-second pause.

The questions about dialogues are generally easier for most test takers to answer correctly than those about the longer talks. Remember, however, that this part of the test is computer adaptive, and if you are doing well, the last few dialogues you hear may be quite difficult.

Timing is important. Answer each item as soon as it appears. Sitting and thinking about the best answer will not help your score in this part. Don't forget: On the computer-based test, there is no time limit per item, but there is an overall time limit for the Listening section. To get a top score, you must answer most of the Listening questions.

Sample Item

You will hear:*

M1: Do you think I should leave this chair against the wall or put it somewhere else?

F1: Over by the window, I'd say.

M2: What does the woman think the man should do?

At the same time, you will see a photograph. Immediately after the dialogue is spoken, the photograph will disappear, and you will hear and read a question about the dialogue:

M2: What does the woman think the man should do?

The question about the dialogue will appear on your screen, and right after it is spoken, the four answer choices will also appear.

You will read:

What does the woman think the man should do?

(A) Open the window.
(B) Move the chair.
(C) Leave the room.
(D) Take a seat.

The correct answer is (B). The woman indicates that she thinks the man should put the chair over by the window rather than leave it where it is. In other words, he should move it.

---

* Note: M1 = first male voice   M2 = second male voice   F1 = first female voice   F2 = second female voice

THE DIALOGUES

Most of the dialogues in Part A involve a man and a woman. A few involve two men or two women. Each speaker usually speaks one or two sentences. Many dialogues (about 25 percent) are about facets of life at American universities: attending classes, talking to professors, writing research papers, and taking tests. Other dialogues are about more general activities: shopping in grocery stores, looking for housing, taking vacations, and going to meetings and parties. The tone of the dialogues is informal. Idioms, first names, contractions (*I'm, doesn't, can't*) are often heard. Some of the items test your ability to understand various language functions. For example, you must be able to determine if a speaker is agreeing or disagreeing with the other speaker or if one speaker is accepting or rejecting the other speaker's offer.

THE QUESTIONS

Most of the questions about the dialogues focus on what the second speaker says. However, it is usually necessary to understand the entire dialogue in order to choose the correct answer. For example, in the Sample Item, it is not clear what the woman means when she says "Over by the window" unless you understand what the man says first. One or two questions in each test may focus instead on what the first speaker says.

Common Part A Question Types	**Examples**
1. **Meaning questions** These are the most common questions (about 50 percent). They ask for a restatement of what the second speaker or both speakers say. They may be general questions or ask what the speakers say about some specific topic. They often follow dialogues that contain idioms.	"What does the man/woman mean?" "What do the speakers say about _____?"
2. **Inference questions** These are the second most common Part A questions (about 20 percent). The answers for these questions are not directly stated in the dialogue, but they can be inferred (concluded) from what the speakers say.	"What does the man/woman imply?" "What can be inferred from the conversation about _____?" "What can be concluded from the conversation about _____?"
3. **Questions about suggestions** In general, the first speaker talks about a problem or asks for advice. The second speaker makes a suggestion for solving the problem.	"What does the woman suggest the man do?" "What does the man suggest they do?" "What does the woman suggest?" "What does the woman think the man should do?"
4. **Questions about future actions** These ask what one or both of the speakers will do next or in the near future, or what one or both are planning to do.	"What will the man do?" "What will they probably do next?" "What are the speakers planning to do?"
5. **Topic questions** These ask about the subject of the dialogue.	"What are they talking about?" "What are they discussing?"
6. **Questions about opinions** These ask how one or both of the speakers feel about some topic.	"How does the man/woman feel about _____?" "What is their opinion of _____?"

7. **Questions about assumptions** These ask what the second speaker thought (assumed) before he or she spoke to the first speaker.

   "What had the man assumed about _____?"
   "What had the woman previously assumed?"

8. **Questions about questions** The first speaker makes a statement; the second speaker asks a question to get more information.

   "What does the man want to know?"

9. **Questions about reasons** These ask why one or both of the speakers did something.

   "Why did the man/woman _____?"
   "Why did they _____?"

10. **Questions about problems** These ask about some trouble one or both of the speakers are having.

    "What problem is the man having?"
    "What is the problem?"

THE ANSWER CHOICES

All four of the answer choices are logical answers for the question, but only one—the key—is correct according to the dialogue. However, as in all parts of TOEFL®, not all of the answer choices are equally attractive. You can often eliminate one or two choices easily even if you are not sure which answer is correct and so make a better guess.

Correct answers are seldom stated word for word by either of the speakers. Correct answers often contain synonyms (words with the same meaning) for words in the dialogues and use different sentence structures.

Grammatically, there are three types of answer choices:

1. Complete sentences (about 75 percent)

2. Incomplete sentences, usually beginning with verb forms—most often the simple form of the verb (about 20 percent)

3. Short noun or prepositional phrases (about 5 percent)

The form of the answer choice can sometimes help you guess what the question will be, and you can therefore focus your listening.

Question types and examples	Usual form of answer choice and examples
Meaning questions: "What does the man mean?"	Complete sentences: (A) He prefers coffee to tea. (B) He'd like some lemon in his tea.
Questions about inferences: "What does the woman imply about the article?"	Complete sentences: (A) She will probably read it today. (B) She wasn't able to find it in the library.
Questions about suggestions: "What does the woman suggest John do?" "What does the man suggest?"	Incomplete sentences beginning with simple forms of verbs or *-ing* forms (A) Call his cousin (B) Take his cousin home (A) Taking a bus to campus (B) Walking to class

Questions about future actions:

"What will the speakers probably do next?"

Incomplete sentences beginning with simple forms of verbs
(A) Park their car
(B) Get some gasoline

Topic questions:
"What are the speakers discussing?"

Noun phrases:
(A) The man's new schedule.
(B) A homework assignment.

Questions about opinions:
"What was their opinion of the play?"

Complete sentences or adjective phrases:
(A) They didn't enjoy it very much.
(B) They liked it more than they thought they would.

"How does the man feel about the announce-ment he heard?"

(A) Angry
(B) Enthusiastic

Questions about assumptions:

"What had the man assumed about Kathy?"

Complete sentences often containing the auxiliary verbs *would* or *had*:
(A) She had already finished the paper.
(B) She wouldn't finish the research on time.

Questions about questions:

"What does the woman ask about Professor Tolbert?"

"What does the man ask about the department store?"

Incomplete sentences beginning with the word *if* or one of the *wh-* words:
(A) If she is still in her office
(B) Where her office is

(A) Its location
(B) Its hours of operation

Questions about time:
"When will the man play the piano?"

Prepositional phrases of time:
(A) At the party
(B) Before the ceremony

Questions about reasons:

"Why did Jerry miss the party?"

"Why did Linda talk to Professor Delgado?"

Complete sentences or incomplete sentences beginning with infinitives (*to* + simple form):
(A) He didn't receive an invitation.
(B) He had other plans for the evening.

(A) To ask him about a grade.
(B) To explain why she missed class.

Questions about problems:
"What problem does the man have?"

Complete sentences:
(A) He didn't bring enough money for the tickets.
(B) There were no tickets available.

Questions about activities:
"What are they probably doing?"

Incomplete sentences beginning with *-ing* verbs:
(A) Buying groceries
(B) Cooking breakfast

The test writers sometimes make it more difficult to pick the correct answer by using soundalike words, homonyms, words with multiple meanings, and other techniques. You'll practice avoiding these traps in this part of the book.

Tactics for Dialogues

- Answer each question promptly and go on to the next dialogue as soon as possible.

- Be familiar with the directions for answering dialogue questions.

- Remember that the answer for the question is generally contained in the last line of the dialogue.

- If you are not sure of the answer, eliminate as many answer choices as you can.

- After you have chosen an answer, use the remaining time to preview the choices for the next item. If the answer choices are long, just skim over them quickly. Try to anticipate what the question will be by the form of the answer choices.

- If you don't understand all or part of a conversation, guess and go on.

- As soon as you click on the "Confirm Answer" icon, the next dialogue will begin automatically, so be ready.

Lesson 1

Some of the items in Part A involve a confusion between words that have similar sounds. Here's how they work: one of the speakers uses a word or phrase that sounds like a word or phrase in one or more of the answer choices. If you don't hear the word clearly, you might incorrectly choose an option with a soundalike word or phrase.

Sample Item

You will hear:*

M1: I've never had this type of fruit before. I don't even know what to do with it.

 F1: You just have to peel it and eat it.

M2: What does the woman mean?

You will read:

What does the woman mean?

(A) She doesn't feel like eating fruit.
(B) The man should take the pill before eating.
(C) The fruit shouldn't be eaten until it's been peeled.
(D) She isn't familiar with this type of fruit either.

The correct answer is (C). The word *feel* in choice (A) sounds like the word *peel* in the dialogue. In a different way, the word *pill* in choice (B) also sounds like the word *peel*. Notice that choice (C)—the correct answer—and choice (D) do not contain soundalike words.

Many soundalike expressions in Part A are **minimal pairs**. Minimal pairs are two words that are pronounced alike except for one vowel sound (*peel* and *pill*, *lack* and *lake*, *point* and *paint*) or one consonant sound (*peel* and *feel*, *vine* and *wine*, *mop* and *mob*).

Another sound problem involves two words that sound like one word, such as *mark it* and *market*, *sent her* and *center*, *in tents* and *intense*.

A third type of sound problem involves one word that sounds like part of a longer word, such as *nation* and *imagination*, *mind* and *remind*, *give* and *forgive*.

Hint: If an answer choice contains a word that sounds like a word in the spoken sentence, that choice is probably wrong. For example, if you hear the word *spell* and you read the word *spill* in an answer choice, you can usually eliminate that choice.

When you're taking Part A during an actual exam, you can use the **context** of the dialogues to help you solve problems with sound confusion. If you hear and understand all of the dialogue, you won't have much trouble eliminating choices involving soundalike words. However, if you only understand part of a dialogue or if you "mis-hear" one or two words, you may easily choose an incorrect answer.

---

* Note: M1 = first male voice   M2 = second male voice   F1 = first female voice   F2 = second female voice

EXERCISE 1.1

Focus: Discriminating between soundalike words in dialogues and answer choices

Directions: Listen to the dialogues. Decide which of the two choices, (A) or (B), best answers the question, and mark the appropriate blank.

Now start the listening program.

1. What does the woman suggest the man do?

_____ (A) Get in a different lane.

_____ (B) Stand in another line.

2. What did the children do?

_____ (A) Go down the slide

_____ (B) Play on the sled

3. What does the woman tell the man to do with the letters?

_____ (A) Put them in a file.

_____ (B) Throw them in a pile.

4. What is the man's problem?

_____ (A) He can't shut his suitcase.

_____ (B) His suitcase doesn't fit in the closet.

5. What is learned about Annie's bread?

_____ (A) It's made from whole wheat.

_____ (B) It's white bread.

6. What does the man say about the story?

_____ (A) Brenda is typing it.

_____ (B) It's being taped.

7. What is learned about Emily?

_____ (A) She recently moved.

_____ (B) She bought a new dress.

8. What does Dennis say about the coffee?

_____ (A) Its taste has improved.

_____ (B) It tastes slightly bitter.

9. What does the man ask Ellen?

_____ (A) How much the ticket cost

_____ (B) What she might win

10. What does the woman say about the bottle?

_____ (A) It's been chipped.

_____ (B) There's a ship inside it.

11. What happened to Jerry?

_____ (A) He tripped in the aisle.

_____ (B) He slipped in some oil.

12. Why is this area well known?

_____ (A) For its fast horses

_____ (B) For its natural resources

EXERCISE 1.2

Focus: Identifying soundalike expressions in answer choices and choosing correct answers

Directions: Listen to the dialogues. Each dialogue contains a word or phrase that sounds like a word or phrase in two of the answer choices.

Now start the listening program.

1. What is learned about Steven and Gloria?

(A) He went to the shopping mall with her.

(B) He wrote her an e-mail.

(C) He lent her some money.

(D) He plans to contact her later.

2. What does the woman say about Stuart?

(A) He has an appointment with the president.

(B) He was just appointed vice-president.

(C) He's unhappy because he lost the election.

(D) He's going to serve as president.

3. What does the woman say about the class she is going to take?

   (A) It is the study of living plants.
   (B) It is about life on other planets.
   (C) It concerns the breeding of cattle.
   (D) It deals with life on Earth.

4. What does Janet tell the man?

   (A) She won't leave until the rain is over.
   (B) Their drain has stopped up.
   (C) They shouldn't board the train until it completely stops.
   (D) She's been under a lot of strain lately.

5. What does the woman say about Sam?

   (A) He offered his help to Darlene.
   (B) He made an offer to Darlene's sister.
   (C) When Darlene was gone, he missed her.
   (D) He spoke to Darlene's assistant.

6. What does the man suggest the woman do?

   (A) Get a job at the hotel
   (B) Buy some cough drops
   (C) Get some copies made
   (D) Eat in the coffee shop

7. What does the woman say about Gus?

   (A) He has a pain behind his ear.
   (B) He didn't hear what the woman said.
   (C) He can lend the man a pen.
   (D) He has fallen behind in class.

Lesson 2

DIALOGUES WITH HOMONYMS AND WORDS WITH MULTIPLE MEANINGS

Two words are **homonyms** if they have the same pronunciation but are spelled differently and have different meanings. The words *flour* and *flower* are homonyms, as are *bare* and *bear*. In some dialgoues one or more incorrect answer choices refer to a homonym of a word that is used on the listening program, as in the example below.

Sample Item

You will hear:*

M1: Eugene missed a lot of classes last week.
 F1: That's because he was sick. I think he had the flu.
M2: What is learned about Eugene?

You will read:

What is learned about Eugene?

(A) He has been feeling weak for a long time.
(B) Because of sickness, Eugene was absent.
(C) Eugene's eyesight isn't very strong, so he needs glasses.
(D) Eugene flew to another city this week.

The correct answer is (B). The dialogue contains the word *week*, meaning a seven-day period. Choices (A) and (C) refer to a homonym of that word, *weak*, which means *not strong*. The dialogue also contains the word *flu*, an illness similar to a bad cold. Choice (D) refers to a homonym of that word, *flew* (took a trip by plane).

The dialogues may also contain **words with multiple meanings**. In these items, one or two of the answer choices refer to another definition of a word as it is used in the dialogue.

---

* Note: M1 = first male voice   M2 = second male voice   F1 = first female voice   F2 = second female voice

Sample Item

You will hear:*

F1: Are you sure this is how Lois spells her last name?
M1: It doesn't look right, does it? In fact, I'm not even sure it starts with that letter.
M2: What does the man mean?

You will read:

What does the man mean?

(A) The letter to Lois was incorrectly addressed.
(B) Lois' last name may be incorrectly spelled.
(C) Lois' name appeared on the right side of the page.
(D) Lois hasn't begun writing the letter yet.

The correct answer is (B). The dialogue contains the words *right*, meaning "correct," and the word *letter*, meaning a character in the alphabet. Choices (A) and (D) also contain the word *letter*, but in those choices the word has another definition—a message sent through the mail. Choice (C) also contains the word *right*, but in that choice, it refers to a direction—the opposite of left.

You won't be confused by these items if you understand the entire sentence. Again, the **context** of the sentence can help you choose the correct answer. But if you focus only on single words, like *week* and *flu* or *letter* and *right* in the two samples, you can easily make mistakes.

EXERCISE 2.1

Focus: Using the context of dialogues to identify homonyms
Directions: Listen to the dialogues. Decide which of the pair of homonyms appears in the dialogues and mark the appropriate answer, (A) or (B).
Now start the listening program.

1. _____ (A) presence
   _____ (B) presents

2. _____ (A) overdue
   _____ (B) overdo

3. _____ (A) pain
   _____ (B) pane

4. _____ (A) where
   _____ (B) wear

5. _____ (A) fined
   _____ (B) find

6. _____ (A) right
   _____ (B) write

7. _____ (A) board
   _____ (B) bored

8. _____ (A) brakes
   _____ (B) breaks

9. _____ (A) sail
   _____ (B) sale

___
* Note: M1 = first male voice   M2 = second male voice   F1 = first female voice   F2 = second female voice

EXERCISE 2.2

Focus: Using the context of dialogues to identify the definitions of words with multiple meanings

Directions: Listen to the dialogues. One word from the dialogue is given, along with two possible definitions of the word. Choose the definition of the word as it is used in the dialogue and mark the appropriate answer, (A) or (B).

Now start the listening program.

1. cold

   _____ (A) minor illness

   _____ (B) chilly weather

2. kind

   _____ (A) type

   _____ (B) considerate

3. light

   _____ (A) not heavy

   _____ (B) not dark

4. wing

   _____ (A) part of an airplane

   _____ (B) part of a building

5. tables

   _____ (A) charts

   _____ (B) furniture

6. coat

   _____ (A) layer

   _____ (B) warm clothing

7. field

   _____ (A) outside the classroom

   _____ (B) area of study

EXERCISE 2.3

Focus: Using the context of dialogues to answer questions involving both homonyms and words with multiple definitions

Directions: Listen to the statements. Decide which of the two choices best answers the question and mark the appropriate answer, (A) or (B).

Now start the listening program.

1. What does the woman suggest Tom do?

   (A) Look for mistakes
   (B) Complete his research
   (C) Write a check
   (D) Read the newspaper

2. What are they discussing?

   (A) Events in the historic past
   (B) The man's performance in class
   (C) A physical exam
   (D) A historical study

3. What does the man mean?

   (A) He'd never heard of that park before.
   (B) That was the first herd he'd ever seen.
   (C) He'd never heard buffaloes before.
   (D) He wanted to go to the park but he couldn't.

4. What does the woman tell the man to do?

   (A) Sign his name on this line
   (B) Follow the directions on the sign
   (C) Sign up for another class
   (D) Stand in another line

5. What does the man mean?

   (A) He can't carry the luggage by himself.
   (B) The handle on one of the suitcases is broken.
   (C) He bought his luggage in that store.
   (D) There isn't enough room for his luggage there.

6. What does the woman think John should do?

    (A) Close the window right away
    (B) Take a quick shower
    (C) Go for a swim
    (D) Put on some other clothes

7. What does Patrick mean?

    (A) The class had a better opinion of him.
    (B) He had to stand in front of the class.
    (C) No one in the class understands him.
    (D) He wasn't hurt in the accident.

Lesson 3

DIALOGUES WITH IDIOMS

On many TOEFL exams, up to half the dialogues in Part A contain idiomatic expressions. Many of the idiomatic expressions are two- or three-word verbs, such as *call off* and *look out for*.

Sample Item

You will hear:*

F1: I wonder where Mike is.

M1: He'll show up as soon as the work is done, I bet.

M2: What does the man say about Mike?

You will read:

What does the man say about Mike?

(A) He probably won't arrive until the work is finished.
(B) He went to a show instead of going to work.
(C) He can show them how to do the work.
(D) He'll probably work late today.

The correct answer is (A). The idiom *show up* means "arrive." Choices (B) and (C) contain the word *show*, but it is not used in the idiomatic sense.

In most dialogues, the second speaker uses the idiomatic expression. Most questions about this type of dialogue are questions about meaning ("What does the man mean?" for example), but some are inference questions or other types of questions. The correct answer often contains a synonym for the idiom (*arrive* for *show up* in choice (A) of the Sample Item). Incorrect choices often contain references to the literal meaning of idioms, as in choices (B) and (D).

Memorizing these phrases does not guarantee that you will recognize all the idiomatic expressions that you will hear in the Listening section. There are, after all, thousands of these expressions in English. You must develop "a good ear" for guessing the meaning of idioms. The context of the sentence will help you understand the expression, even if you're unfamiliar with it.

---

* Note: M1 = first male voice   M2 = second male voice   F1 = first female voice   F2 = second female voice

EXERCISE 3.1

Focus: Recognizing synonyms for idiomatic expressions

Directions: Listen to the spoken statements. Each contains an idiomatic or figurative expression that is written out. First decide which of the two choices best answers the question, and mark the appropriate answer, (A) or (B). Then underline the phrase in the correct answer that has the same meaning as the idiom.

Now start the listening program.

1. bumped into

   What does the man mean?

   _____ (A) He met Caroline unexpectedly at the cafeteria.

   _____ (B) He and Caroline had an accident.

2. got into hot water

   What does Rita mean?

   _____ (A) She was in trouble.

   _____ (B) She took a warm bath.

3. hit it off

   What does the man mean?

   _____ (A) He and Chuck argued as soon as they met.

   _____ (B) He and Chuck quickly became friends.

4. piece of cake

   What does the woman mean?

   _____ (A) The exam was simple.

   _____ (B) She had a snack after the test.

5. at the drop of a hat

   What does Robert imply?

   _____ (A) He can't leave until he finds his hat.

   _____ (B) He's ready to leave immediately.

6. under the weather

   What does the man imply about Julie?

   _____ (A) She didn't want to practice because of the bad weather.

   _____ (B) She wasn't there because she felt a little sick.

7. takes after

   What does the man say about Albert?

   _____ (A) He looks like his grandfather.

   _____ (B) He takes care of his grandfather.

EXERCISE 3.2

Focus: Understanding dialogues involving idiomatic and figurative expressions

Directions: Look over the idiomatic expressions listed before each set of items. The dialogues each contain one of the listed expressions. Listen to the dialogues and mark the one answer choice, (A) or (B), that best answers the question.

Now start the listening program.

Set A

believe one's eyes   short for
push one's luck   music to one's ears
get off the ground   turn in
run of the mill   over one's head
lend a hand   what the doctor ordered

1. What does the man mean?

    _____ (A) He's not sure Max's business will succeed.

    _____ (B) He doesn't know if Max is on the plane.

2. What does the woman imply?

    _____ (A) Gary shouldn't drive his car much further.

    _____ (B) It's time for Gary to get some new tires.

3. What will the man do next?

    _____ (A) Go to bed

    _____ (B) Turn on the television

4. What does Alice mean?

    _____ (A) She didn't understand all the jokes.

    _____ (B) She left before the performance was over.

5. What does the woman mean?

    _____ (A) Ice water sounds perfect.

    _____ (B) The doctor told her to drink a lot of water.

6. What is learned from this conversation?

    _____ (A) Elizabeth is taller than Liz.

    _____ (B) Elizabeth's nickname is "Liz."

7. What does the man say about the restaurant?

    _____ (A) The service is very fast there.

    _____ (B) It's just an average restaurant.

8. What does the woman mean?

    _____ (A) She enjoys the sound of nature.

    _____ (B) She wishes she'd brought a radio.

9. What does the woman offer to do?

    _____ (A) Lend the man some books

    _____ (B) Help the man with the boxes

10. What does the woman mean?

    _____ (A) She doesn't think the man is telling the truth.

    _____ (B) She was surprised to see the snow.

Set B

by heart	chip in
call it a day	get in one's blood
look who's talking	take a lot of nerve

11. What does Karen mean?

_____ (A) Skiing can be a dangerous sport.

_____ (B) It's easy to get into the habit of skiing.

12. What does the woman imply about Norman?

_____ (A) She has to look for him.

_____ (B) He doesn't study much himself.

13. What does the man mean?

_____ (A) They'll all pay for the gasoline.

_____ (B) There will be plenty of room in the van.

14. What does the man say about Donna?

_____ (A) She seemed too nervous.

_____ (B) She took a bold approach.

15. What does Dan mean?

_____ (A) He doesn't want to do any more painting today.

_____ (B) He'll phone the woman later today.

16. What does the woman mean?

_____ (A) She is going to speak the lines in an emotional way.

_____ (B) She's already memorized the scene.

EXERCISE 3.3

Focus: Using the context of dialogues to understand the meaning of idioms
Directions: Listen to the following dialogue.
Now start the listening program.

1. What is the woman going to do next?

(A) Go to work with Jim
(B) Go out for coffee
(C) Get some exercise
(D) Study for a test

2. What does the man want to know?

(A) If the woman will go to the party with him
(B) If the red tie looks good with his shirt
(C) If he should wear a tie to the party
(D) If the party is already over

3. What does the woman imply?

(A) They both missed class because they were sailing.
(B) The man should take better notes during Professor Morrison's class.
(C) She missed Friday's class, too.
(D) She dropped Professor Morrison's class.

4. What can be concluded about Ron?

(A) He cut himself while he was preparing food.
(B) He doesn't want to work in a restaurant.
(C) He's planning to open up his own restaurant.
(D) He's not going to eat at a restaurant tonight.

5. What does the man mean?

(A) He wants to know if the woman is joking.
(B) He wants the woman to leave him alone.
(C) He'd like to know what the quiz will be about.
(D) He needs a doctor to look at his injured leg.

6. What does Brian mean?

   (A) The program was canceled.
   (B) The shuttle was launched yesterday.
   (C) The weather was better than expected.
   (D) The launch was delayed.

7. What does the man say about Jennifer?

   (A) She stood up and left the lecture.
   (B) It was too warm for her to wear a sweater in the lecture hall.
   (C) Her sweater made her easy to spot.
   (D) Her notes on the lecture were easy to read.

8. What does the woman say about Phil?

   (A) He deserved to get a speeding ticket.
   (B) He was going to a good restaurant.
   (C) He probably wasn't speeding.
   (D) His ticket was no longer valid.

9. What does the woman imply about George?

   (A) He's out of breath.
   (B) He'll be glad to help.
   (C) If he helps, it will save the man some money.
   (D) He won't be very cooperative.

10. What is learned about Jill from this conversation?

   (A) The man didn't get her a watch.
   (B) The weather won't be warm when she graduates.
   (C) She won't be graduating.
   (D) She isn't going to watch the graduation.

11. What does the man say about Dora?

   (A) She ordinarily works in a florist's shop.
   (B) In the end, she won't have a problem.
   (C) She wears too much perfume to work.
   (D) She can always anticipate problems at work.

12. What does Roy tell the woman?

   (A) He doesn't have any questions for her.
   (B) He won't be able to take a trip.
   (C) He can't study during spring break.
   (D) He hasn't decided if he can take a trip.

13. What is learned about Mick from this conversation?

   (A) His father told him to go to medical school.
   (B) His father studied medicine.
   (C) He and his father walked to the school.
   (D) He surprised his father with his decision

Lesson 4

ANSWERING INFERENCE QUESTIONS ABOUT DIALOGUES

Sometimes the answer to a question about a dialogue is not directly stated in the dialogue. How can you answer this type of question? You must be able to make an **inference** about the dialogue. In other words, information in the dialogue will indirectly provide you with the answer to the question.

This type of question can be phrased in two ways:

- What does the man/woman imply?

- What can be inferred from the conversation?

Some inference questions involve **overstatement**, or exaggeration.

F: Are you interested in selling your car?
M: Sure—if someone has a million dollars!

Because of the exaggeration, we can infer that the man doesn't want to sell his car at all.

Sample Item

You will hear:*

M1: Can I take this bus to the art museum?

F1: No, this bus goes north to Bank Street. You want a bus that goes the opposite way.

M2: What can be inferred from this conversation?

You will read:

What can be inferred from this conversation?

(A) The man needs to take a south-bound bus.
(B) There is no bus to the museum.
(C) It takes a long time to get to the museum by bus.
(D) The art museum is on Bank Street.

The correct answer is (A). This information can be inferred, because the first bus is going north, but the man must take a bus going in the opposite direction to get to the art museum. Choice (B) is incorrect; it IS possible to get to the museum by bus. There is no information about choice (C). Choice (D) can't be true because Bank Street is where the first bus is going.

---

* Note: M1 = first male voice   M2 = second male voice   F1 = first female voice   F2 = second female voice

EXERCISE 4

Focus: Listening to dialogues that are followed by inference questions and identifying the best answers

Directions: Listen to the following dialogues.
Now start the listening program.

1. What can be inferred about the man?

   (A) He's not related to Larry.
   (B) He doesn't think Larry won the contest.
   (C) He's not a very good dancer.
   (D) He has never believed Larry.

2. What can be inferred from this conversation?

   (A) The man doesn't like the way the suit looks.
   (B) The suit costs a lot of money.
   (C) The man dresses as if he were very wealthy.
   (D) The man already owns an expensive suit.

3. What does the man imply?

   (A) There is just enough food.
   (B) Many uninvited guests will come.
   (C) The woman has prepared too much food.
   (D) The party will be moved to another location.

4. What can be inferred about the man?

   (A) He took a physics test tonight.
   (B) He has a class every evening.
   (C) He was studying by himself tonight.
   (D) He's concerned about his grade.

5. What does the woman imply about Greg?

   (A) He's changed his major often.
   (B) He hasn't really changed his major.
   (C) He won't do well in his new major.
   (D) He was changed by his experience.

6. What can be inferred from this conversation about Professor Sutton?

   (A) His lectures put his students to sleep.
   (B) He's a middle-aged man.
   (C) He lectures about history.
   (D) His lectures are very difficult to follow.

7. What does the woman imply?

   (A) She hasn't been to the dentist for years.
   (B) She wasn't able to see the dentist yesterday.
   (C) She had a long wait before she saw the dentist.
   (D) She was quite late for her dental appointment.

8. What does the man imply about the experts and the plan?

   (A) They have agreed on it.
   (B) They have different opinions about it.
   (C) It depends on their cooperation.
   (D) It doesn't require their attention.

9. What does the woman imply about Louis?

   (A) His new boss shouldn't have been promoted.
   (B) He and his old boss argued.
   (C) He should get a better job.
   (D) His boss has helped him a lot.

10. What does the woman imply?

    (A) There's not enough snow to cause a cancellation yet.
    (B) It will probably snow all night.
    (C) The university has already decided to cancel classes.
    (D) It has already stopped snowing.

11. What does the man imply?

    (A) He has been interested in folk dancing for a long time.
    (B) He's interested in making new friends.
    (C) He wants to form a new folk dancing club.
    (D) He'll never learn how to dance.

12. What can be inferred from the woman's remark?

    (A) She didn't enjoy the music.
    (B) She couldn't see the concert very well.
    (C) She had a good seat near the stage.
    (D) She found her seat uncomfortable.

13. What does the man imply?

    (A) Last summer was even hotter.
    (B) This is the hottest summer he can remember.
    (C) He didn't live here last year.
    (D) The weather is cooler than usual.

14. What can be inferred from this conversation?

    (A) Students must pay a fee to swim in the pool.
    (B) The public cannot use the pool on campus.
    (C) The swimming pool is temporarily closed.
    (D) The pool can be used by students for free.

15. What can be inferred about the speakers?

    (A) They can't see the stars clearly.
    (B) They're not in the city tonight.
    (C) They are looking at the lights of the city.
    (D) They've never seen each other before tonight.

16. What does Mike imply?

    (A) He generally works on Saturday.
    (B) He doesn't know many people at work.
    (C) He isn't allowed to get phone calls at work.
    (D) He wasn't expecting a phone call.

REVIEW TEST A: DIALOGUES

Directions: Each item in this part consists of a brief dialogue involving two speakers. After each dialogue, a third voice asks a question.

When you have heard each dialogue and question, read the four answer choices and select the one that best answers the question based on what is directly stated or on what can be inferred. Don't look at the questions until they are read on the listening program.

Now start the listening program.

1. What does the man imply about Wanda?

    (A) He met her during the winter.
    (B) He's never liked her very much.
    (C) He warned her of a problem.
    (D) His impression of her has changed.

2. What does the woman imply about the movie?

    (A) She's never seen it.
    (B) She thinks it is very unusual.
    (C) She likes it a lot.
    (D) She hasn't seen it for a long time.

3. What does the woman mean?

    (A) The glasses are stacked on the shelf.
    (B) The juice is no worse than the other brands.
    (C) The new glasses are quite attractive.
    (D) She plans to stock up on this juice.

4. What does Adam imply?

    (A) He hasn't finished working on the bookshelves.
    (B) The tools have been misplaced.
    (C) He hates working with tools.
    (D) The tools have already been returned.

5. What can be inferred from this conversation?

    (A) There is no charge for drinks here.
    (B) The first woman wants some ice water.
    (C) The man is not the woman's waiter.
    (D) The iced tea isn't very good here.

6. What does the man want to do?

    (A) Review the last point
    (B) Go on to the next chapter
    (C) Leave the classroom
    (D) Point out the teacher's mistake

7. What does the woman think the man should do?

    (A) Meet a friend of hers
    (B) Keep a budget
    (C) Increase his income
    (D) Get some exercise

8. What can be inferred from the man's comment?

   (A) The woman should clean out her closet.
   (B) The lamp will look better in a small space.
   (C) He doesn't like the lamp very much.
   (D) The living room is the best place for the lamp.

9. What does the man mean?

   (A) He certainly likes Ernie's red car.
   (B) The man in the red car resembles Ernie.
   (C) Ernie has a car just like that red one.
   (D) He can't see the man in the red car.

10. What does the man say about John?

    (A) He hurt his hand when he was scuba diving.
    (B) He hasn't gone scuba diving in a long time.
    (C) He's not too old to go scuba diving.
    (D) He's an experienced scuba diver.

11. What can be inferred from this conversation?

    (A) The man would like to use Becky's computer.
    (B) Becky will need the computer for a long time.
    (C) The computers in the library are already in use.
    (D) Becky wants the man to go to the library.

12. What do the speakers mean?

    (A) The ring is quite attractive.
    (B) Laura got a bargain on the ring.
    (C) The ring was probably expensive.
    (D) Laura had to sell her ring.

13. What does the man imply by his remark?

    (A) Professor Clayburn is going to speak some other night.
    (B) He's never heard of Professor Clayburn.
    (C) He didn't realize Professor Clayburn was speaking tonight.
    (D) Professor Clayburn is giving his speech in this room.

14. What can be concluded from this conversation?

    (A) Joe has been making too much noise.
    (B) Dogs are not allowed in the dorm.
    (C) No one understands the parking regulations.
    (D) Joe is not allowed to leave his room.

15. What can be inferred from this conversation?

    (A) The woman didn't realize Bill had to work.
    (B) Bill has not finished his work.
    (C) The break has not lasted long enough.
    (D) The work didn't take long to complete.

16. What can be inferred from this conversation?

    (A) The woman has just begun to collect rocks.
    (B) Paul is unwilling to help.
    (C) The box is very heavy.
    (D) There's nothing in the box.

This is the end of Review Test A.

Lesson 5

DIALOGUES INVOLVING AGREEMENT AND DISAGREEMENT

To answer questions about some of the dialogues in Part A, it is necessary to understand if the second speaker agrees or disagrees with the first speaker's ideas or proposals.

There are many ways to express agreement and disagreement:

Agreement

So do I.
Me too.
Neither do I.*
I don't either.*
Who wouldn't?
Isn't he/she/it though! (Didn't he/
    Wasn't she/Hasn't it though!)

I'll second that.
I'll say!
You can say that again.
Is/Has/Was it ever!
You bet!
I couldn't agree with you more.
I feel the same way you do about it.

* These two expressions show agreement with a negative statement:

    I don't really like my schedule this term.
    I don't either. *OR* Neither do I.

Disagreement

I don't think so.
That's not what I think.
That's not the way I see it.
I can't say I agree.
I couldn't agree with you less.
I'm afraid I don't agree.

Probably not.
Not necessarily.
Not really.
I'm afraid not.
I'm not so sure.

There are, of course, other expressions that show agreement and disagreement. Some are practiced in the exercises.

Sample Items

You will hear:*

M1: Howard certainly is a talented journalist.

F1: Isn't he though!

M2: What does the woman mean?

You will read:

What does the woman mean?

(A) She doesn't know if Howard is a journalist.
(B) She agrees that Howard is talented.
(C) She read Howard's journal.
(D) She doesn't think Howard is talented.

The correct answer is (B). Although the woman's reply seems negative in form, it actually signals agreement.

You will hear:*

F1: I thought Cheryl's photographs were the best at the exhibit.

F2: I didn't really see it that way.

M1: What does the second woman mean?

You will read:

What does the second woman mean?

(A) She thought Cheryl's photos were the best.
(B) She didn't look at Cheryl's photos.
(C) She thought other photos were better than Cheryl's.
(D) She didn't go to the exhibit.

The correct answer is (C). The woman's response, "I didn't really see it that way," means that she disagreed with the first woman's opinion that Cheryl's photographs were the best.

EXERCISE 5.1

Focus: Determining if one speaker agrees or disagrees with the other speaker

Directions: Listen to the following dialogues. Decide if the second speaker agrees or disagrees with the first speaker, and mark the appropriate blank.

Now start the listening program.

1. _____ (A) Agrees
   _____ (B) Disagrees

2. _____ (A) Agrees
   _____ (B) Disagrees

3. _____ (A) Agrees
   _____ (B) Disagrees

4. _____ (A) Agrees
   _____ (B) Disagrees

5. _____ (A) Agrees
   _____ (B) Disagrees

6. _____ (A) Agrees
   _____ (B) Disagrees

* Note: M1 = first male voice   M2 = second male voice   F1 = first female voice   F2 = second female voice

7. _____ (A) Agrees

_____ (B) Disagrees

8. _____ (A) Agrees

_____ (B) Disagrees

9. _____ (A) Agrees

_____ (B) Disagrees

EXERCISE 5.2

Focus: Listening to dialogues that involve agreement and disagreement and answering questions about them

Directions: Listen to the following dialogues.
Now start the listening program.

1. What does the man mean?

(A) He prefers taking a final exam.
(B) He thinks an exam takes too much time.
(C) He'd rather write a research paper.
(D) He has plenty of time to work.

2. How does the woman feel about the first chapter?

(A) It was difficult, but she understood it.
(B) She hasn't had a chance to read it yet.
(C) She doesn't think it is as useful as some chapters.
(D) It's probably easier than the other chapters.

3. How does the man feel about the woman's idea?

(A) He completely disagrees with it.
(B) He doesn't believe the university will accept it.
(C) He thinks it's a good one.
(D) He wants more information about it.

4. What was the woman's opinion of Jack's story?

(A) She doesn't think that Jack wrote it.
(B) She thought it was quite funny.
(C) She thinks it had too many details.
(D) She found it well-written.

5. What does the man mean?

(A) He has the perfect bicycle.
(B) He thinks it's a good day for bike riding, too.
(C) He doesn't agree with the woman's opinion of the weather.
(D) He didn't hear what the woman said.

6. What does the woman mean?

(A) She thinks Arthur wasn't doing well in the class.
(B) She's not sure why Arthur dropped the class either.
(C) She believes Arthur dropped the class for no reason.
(D) She's decided to drop the class too.

7. What does the woman say about Tom's plan?

(A) It's very impractical.
(B) It's never been tried before.
(C) It's unnecessary.
(D) It might work.

8. What was the man's *initial* reaction to the editorial?

(A) He didn't understand it.
(B) It made him angry.
(C) He agreed with it.
(D) He thought it was depressing.

9. What does the woman say about the library?

(A) She's never been there during final exam week.
(B) It's not crowded now, but it soon will be.
(C) It's crowded because students will be taking exams soon.
(D) It will be closed right after the final exams.

10. What does the man mean?

(A) He likes the costumes Madeleine made.
(B) He's not sure who designed the costumes.
(C) He recommends the play.
(D) He doesn't think the costumes are attractive.

Lesson 6

DIALOGUES INVOLVING SUGGESTIONS, INVITATIONS, OFFERS, AND REQUESTS

A number of dialogues in Part A involve a speaker making and/or responding to **suggestions**, **invitations**, **offers**, and **requests**. There are many ways to express these language functions. Some are listed in the charts in this lesson, while others are practiced in the exercises.

SUGGESTIONS

These are pieces of advice that one speaker gives another. In most dialogues, the first speaker poses a problem and the second speaker suggests a possible solution to that problem. In some dialogues, the first speaker makes a suggestion, and the second speaker responds to that suggestion positively or negatively.

Making Suggestions

Why don't you/we . . .
Why not . . .
Have you ever thought of . . .
You/We might want to . . .
You/We could always . . .
Maybe you/we could . . .
Try . . .

If I were you . . .
If I were in your shoes . . .
You/We should . . .
Shouldn't you/we . . .
What about . . .
What if you/we . . .
How about . . .

Positive Responses

Why not!
Good idea!
That's an idea.
Sounds good to me.
By all means!
Why didn't I think of that?
That's worth a try.
Thanks, I'll give that a try.

Negative Responses

I don't think so.
I don't believe so.
I already thought of that.
I don't think that will work.
Don't look at me!
Can I take a rain check?*

* This means, "Could we do this some other time?"

Sample Item

You will hear:*

M1: I'm doing so poorly in physics class, I think I'm going to have to drop it.

F1: You know, Frank, you should talk to Professor de Marco before you do anything. He's given special help to lots of students who were having trouble.

M2: What does the woman suggest Frank do?

You will read:

What does the woman suggest Frank do?

(A) Study with a group of students
(B) Drop his mathematics course
(C) Discuss the problem with the professor
(D) Take no action at this time

The correct answer is (C). The woman suggests that the man talk to Professor de Marco because the professor has helped many students in the past.

INVITATIONS

These are requests for someone to come somewhere or to take part in some activity. The first speaker may invite the second speaker to do something, and the second speaker responds, or the second speaker may invite the first speaker to do something.

Making Invitations

Shall we . . .
Would you like to . . .
Would you care to . . .
Would you be able to . . .
Want to . . .

Let's . . .
Do you want to . . .
Could you . . .
Can you . . .

Positive Responses

Yes, let's.
Sure, thanks.
Sounds good.
All right, I'd love to.
I'd like that.
What a great idea!
Sure. Thanks for inviting me.
If you want me to.
Don't mind if I do.

Negative Responses

I'm sorry, but . . .
I'd like to, but . . .
I'd love to, but . . .
Thanks a lot, but . . .
That sounds nice, but . . .
I'll pass.
Thanks for the invitation, but . . .
I don't think I'll be able to make it this time.

---

* Note: M1 = first male voice   M2 = second male voice   F1 = first female voice   F2 = second female voice

Sample Item

You will hear:*

M1: Would you like to join us on Sunday? We're going to go on a picnic at the lake.
F1: I'd love to, but I have a test Monday, and I have to get ready for it.
M2: What will the woman probably do on Sunday?

You will read:

What will the woman probably do on Sunday?

(A) Study for a test
(B) Go on a picnic
(C) Take an exam
(D) Join a club

The correct answer is (A). The man invites the woman to come to a picnic. The woman says that she'd love to go, but that she must study for a test she is taking Monday. (If the woman had accepted the man's invitation, choice (B) would have been correct.)

OFFERS

These are proposals to help someone or allow someone to do something. Either speaker in the dialogue may make an offer.

Making Offers

Let me . . .	Can I . . .
Shall I . . .	May I . . .
Would you like me to . . .	Should I . . .
Do you want me to . . .	I could . . .

Positive Responses

That would be nice.
Yes, please.
Please do.
Sure, thanks.

Negative Responses

I don't think so.
I'm afraid not.
That won't be necessary.
Thanks anyway.
Please don't.

---

* Note: M1 = first male voice   M2 = second male voice   F1 = first female voice   F2 = second female voice

Sample Item

You will hear:*

F1: Should I make reservations for dinner Friday night?
M1: Thanks anyway, but I've already made them.
M2: What does the man mean?

You will read:

What does the man mean?

(A) He can't go to dinner Friday night.
(B) Reservations won't be required.
(C) He made reservations earlier.
(D) He'd like the woman to make reservations.

The correct answer is (C). The woman offers to make reservations, but the man replies that he's already made them.

REQUESTS

To make a request is to ask someone to do something, or to ask for help or information.

Making Requests

Would you . . .   Will you . . .
Could you/I . . .   May I . . .
Do you mind if . . .   Can you/I . . .
Would you mind if . . .

Positive Responses

I'd be glad to.
I'd be delighted.
Sure thing.
Certainly.
Why not?
If you want to.
If you'd like.
You bet.
*Not at all.
*Of course not.

Negative Responses

Sorry, but . . .
I'm afraid not.
I'd like to, but . . .
I wish I could, but . . .
*Actually, I do/would.
*I'm afraid I do/would.
*As a matter of fact, I do/would.

* Responses for "Do you mind if . . ." or "Would you mind if . . ."

---

* Note: M1 = first male voice   M2 = second male voice   F1 = first female voice   F2 = second female voice

Sample Item

You will hear:*

M1: I have to make one more phone call before I go.

F2: Take your time. Would you just lock the door when you finish?

M2: What does the woman want the man to do?

You will read:

What does the woman want the man to do?

(A) Lock the office.
(B) Finish his phone call quickly.
(C) Tell her what time it is.
(D) Look up a phone number.

The correct answer is (A). The woman requests that the man lock up the office.

EXERCISE 6.1

Focus: Identifying suggestions, invitations, offers, and requests and responses to them

Directions: Listen to the following dialogues. Decide which of the two choices best completes the sentence, and mark the appropriate space.

Now start the listening program.

1. The man is

_____ (A) declining an offer.

_____ (B) making a suggestion.

2. The woman is

_____ (A) accepting an invitation.

_____ (B) making an offer.

3. The woman is

_____ (A) declining an offer.

_____ (B) making a suggestion.

4. Mark is

_____ (A) rejecting a request

_____ (B) agreeing to a request.

5. The woman is

_____ (A) giving an invitation.

_____ (B) making a suggestion.

6. The man is

_____ (A) agreeing to a request.

_____ (B) turning down an offer.

7. Ed is probably going to

_____ (A) receive a suggestion.

_____ (B) make an offer.

8. The woman is

_____ (A) suggesting a solution.

_____ (B) offering help.

9. Cynthia is

_____ (A) giving an invitation.

_____ (B) accepting an offer.

10. The woman is

_____ (A) declining an offer.

_____ (B) making a request.

_____
* Note: M1 = first male voice   M2 = second male voice   F1 = first female voice   F2 = second female voice

11. The man will probably

_____ (A) do what the woman suggests.

_____ (B) turn down the woman's invitation.

12. Bob is

_____ (A) agreeing to an offer.

_____ (B) refusing a request.

13. The man is

_____ (A) making a suggestion.

_____ (B) accepting an invitation.

EXERCISE 6.2

Focus: Listening to dialogues involving suggestions, invitations, offers, and requests and answering questions about them

Directions: Listen to the following dialogue. Decide which choice—(A), (B), (C), or (D)—best answers the question about the dialogues, and mark the appropriate answer.

Now start the listening program

1. What does the man mean?

(A) He would like a cigarette.
(B) The woman can smoke if she likes.
(C) He doesn't want the woman to smoke.
(D) He thinks he smells smoke.

2. What does the woman say about the gray suit?

(A) The man wears it too often.
(B) It needs to be cleaned.
(C) It's not as nice as the blue one.
(D) The man could wear it tonight.

3. What does the man say about Cathy?

(A) She could plan the trip.
(B) She may not feel well.
(C) She can go on the class trip.
(D) She has some other plans.

4. What does the man mean?

(A) He doesn't want more coffee.
(B) He doesn't want to use his credit card.
(C) He hasn't had enough coffee.
(D) He doesn't want to make coffee.

5. What does the woman mean?

(A) She doesn't think it's warm.
(B) She'll open the window herself.
(C) She wants the window closed.
(D) She's going to turn down the heat.

6. What will the man probably do?

(A) Go somewhere else for lunch
(B) Order another type of sandwich
(C) Skip lunch today
(D) Have some soup for lunch

7. What does the woman imply?

(A) The kitchen also needs cleaning.
(B) The living room doesn't have to be cleaned.
(C) The man shouldn't do the cleaning.
(D) There's not enough time to clean both rooms.

8. What does the man offer to do for the woman?

(A) Give her some information about classes
(B) Go with her to the registrar's office
(C) Help her find her way to the registrar's office
(D) Tell her where to get her own map

9. What does the woman suggest they do?

(A) Work on their statistics homework
(B) Have breakfast
(C) Stop studying for a little while
(D) Go to work on the math problems

10. What does the man suggest that Lisa do?

(A) Buy a new toaster
(B) Replace her old shoes
(C) Have repairs done
(D) Make another piece of toast

11. What does the man tell the woman?

(A) It's time for her to go now.
(B) She can read his magazine if she wants.
(C) He hasn't finished reading the magazine.
(D) She should finish writing the article.

12. What does the woman think the man should do?

(A) Buy an antique desk
(B) Get a new computer
(C) Sit down and get to work
(D) Use another computer disk

Lesson 7

DIALOGUES INVOLVING CONTRADICTIONS, ASSUMPTIONS, AND QUESTIONS

CONTRADICTIONS

These involve the second speaker correcting what the first speaker says, as in the samples below:

Sample Item

You will hear:*

F2: Amy didn't work overtime last week.
M1: As a matter of fact, she *did*.
M2: What does the man say about Amy?

You will read:

What does the man say about Amy?

(A) She is always late for work.
(B) She never works overtime.
(C) She worked extra hours last week.
(D) She hasn't had her job very long.

The correct answer is (C). The man's emphatic use of the auxiliary verb *did* shows that he is contradicting what the woman said.

You will hear:*

M1: Martin always talks about how he loves to dance.
F1: Yes, but you don't see him out on the dance floor very often, do you?
M2: What does the woman say about Martin?

You will read:

What does the woman say about Martin?

(A) He is an excellent dancer.
(B) He doesn't like dancing very much.
(C) He doesn't talk about dancing very often.
(D) He goes dancing four times a week.

The correct answer is (B). The woman's use of the word *but* and the tag question (". . . do you?") suggest that she doesn't believe that Martin really loves to dance.

---

* Note: M1 = first male voice   M2 = second male voice   F1 = first female voice   F2 = second female voice

Sample Items (Continued)

You will hear:*

F1: All of the students voted for the proposal to expand the Student Council.

M1: Well, most of them did, anyway.

M2: What does the man mean?

You will read:

What does the man mean?

(A) All of the students voted.
(B) Some of the students opposed the proposal.
(C) The proposal was defeated.
(D) The Student Council voted.

The correct answer is (B). The man says that most of the students voted for the proposal, contradicting the idea that all of them did. Therefore, some of the students must have opposed the proposal.

In some dialogues, such as the third Sample Item, the second speaker does not completely contradict what the first speaker says but rather limits the first speaker's idea.

ASSUMPTIONS

These are the beliefs that one speaker has until he or she receives information from a second speaker. You will generally hear dialogues involving assumptions near the end of Part A. These questions are considered difficult, but once you understand how they work and practice answering them, you should find them no more difficult than any other type of question. In this type of dialogue, the first speaker makes a statement. The second speaker is surprised because the first statement contradicts what he or she believes to be true. The second speaker's response often begins with the word "Oh" and ends with the phrase ". . . after all." The answer to assumption questions is the reverse of what the second speaker thinks, and so what is "true" according to the first speaker is not the correct choice.

Sample Item

You will hear:*

F1: No, Judy's not here right now. She's at her economics class.

M1: Oh, so she decided to take that course after all.

M2: What had the man assumed about Judy?

You will read:

What had the man assumed about Judy?

(A) She wouldn't take the course.
(B) She had already completed that course.
(C) She was busy studying economics.
(D) She wouldn't find economics difficult.

The correct answer is (A). The man is surprised that Judy is in economics class because he thought that she had decided not to take the course. Therefore, he had obviously assumed that Judy was not going to take the course before he spoke to the woman.

---

* Note: M1 = first male voice   M2 = second male voice   F1 = first female voice   F2 = second female voice

QUESTIONS

The second speaker in a dialogue sometimes asks about what the first speaker says. The third speaker then asks what the second speaker wanted to know.

Sample Item

You will hear:*

F1: Professor Petrakis said that Mark Twain was his favorite writer.

M1: When did he say that?

M2: What does the man want to know?

You will read:

What does the man want to know?

(A) When Mark Twain lived
(B) What the professor said about Mark Twain
(C) When the professor made his remark
(D) What books Mark Twain wrote

The correct answer is (C). The man asks when Professor Petrakis called Mark Twain his favorite author.

Two question phrases that may give you trouble are *What . . . for?* and *How come . . .?* Both mean *Why . . . ?*

EXERCISE 7

Focus: Answering questions about dialogues involving contradictions, assumptions, and questions
Directions: Listen to the following dialogues.
Now start the listening program.

1. What does the man say about Ginny?

    (A) She is definitely coming to dinner.
    (B) She likes fish more than chicken.
    (C) She may invite them to dinner.
    (D) She doesn't mind eating chicken.

2. What had the man assumed about Mona?

    (A) She had already moved.
    (B) She hadn't found a new apartment yet.
    (C) She'd already made an appointment.
    (D) She was no longer planning to move.

3. What does the woman want to know?

    (A) What the man's name is
    (B) Who told the man to see the dean
    (C) Where the dean's office is
    (D) Who the dean is

4. What does the man mean?

    (A) He wants to take part in the election.
    (B) He's not interested in being president.
    (C) He wants to get more facts from the president.
    (D) He'll have to run to get to class on time.

5. What had the man assumed about Carol?

    (A) She didn't need to do any research for this paper.
    (B) She wasn't going to word-process the paper.
    (C) She hadn't completed all the research.
    (D) She had finished the final draft a long time ago.

---

* Note: M1 = first male voice   M2 = second male voice   F1 = first female voice   F2 = second female voice

6. What does the woman imply about Bert?

(A) He doesn't really like horseback riding.
(B) He rides horses whenever possible.
(C) He doesn't talk about riding very much.
(D) He loves to watch people ride horses.

7. What does the woman want to know?

(A) When her travel agent called
(B) What time her flight will leave
(C) How far she will be flying
(D) If her flight has been canceled

8. What had the woman assumed about Cliff?

(A) He was working full time.
(B) He was eating in the cafeteria.
(C) He couldn't make a decision.
(D) He didn't want a job.

9. What does the woman want to know?

(A) When they returned
(B) Who went hiking
(C) Where they hiked
(D) How long their hike was

10. What does the man mean?

(A) He thinks the clothes at that store are expensive.
(B) He doesn't think the clothes at that store are very nice.
(C) He thinks the woman is being unreasonable.
(D) He's never been to the store on Collins Street.

11. What does the woman ask the man?

(A) Where the meeting will be held
(B) When the meeting will start
(C) Where the recreation center will be built
(D) What has been proposed

12. What had the woman assumed?

(A) Joy did not want to study abroad.
(B) The overseas program had been canceled.
(C) Joy was already living overseas.
(D) Joy would study overseas this year.

13. What does the woman ask the man?

(A) If the party was at Ben's house
(B) What time the party ended
(C) If the man enjoyed the party
(D) Who attended the party

14. What does the man mean?

(A) All of Ted's answers were incorrect.
(B) Most of the problems were done correctly.
(C) Ted doesn't have to solve the problems.
(D) Ted has had a few good jobs.

15. What does the man ask the woman?

(A) How she got to the grocery store
(B) Why she went to the grocery store
(C) How much she paid for groceries
(D) What street the grocery store is on

Lesson 8

ANSWERING QUESTIONS ABOUT PLANS, TOPICS, AND PROBLEMS

QUESTIONS ABOUT PLANS

These questions follow dialogues in which two speakers discuss what one or both of them are going to do in the future.

Sample Item

You will hear:*

F2: Are you going to go to Boston with Michael this summer?
M1: Wish I could, but if I want to graduate next year, I've got to stay here and take a couple classes.
M2: What does the man plan to do this summer?

You will read:

What does the man plan to do this summer?

(A) Graduate
(B) Attend classes
(C) Visit Michael
(D) Go to Boston

The correct answer is (B). The man indicates that he must stay where he is and take classes in order to graduate next year.

---

* Note: M1 = first male voice   M2 = second male voice   F1 = first female voice   F2 = second female voice

QUESTIONS ABOUT TOPICS

The third speaker asks what the other two speakers are talking about. The topic is not usually mentioned directly in the dialogue; it must be inferred from a general understanding of the dialogue. The topic can be a person, a thing, or an activity.

Sample Item

You will hear:*

F1: Have you seen this letter from the bursar's office?

F2: Oh, no! Not another increase! If you ask me, we're already spending too much to go to school here.

M2: What are these speakers talking about?

You will read:

What are these speakers talking about?

(A) Higher tuition costs
(B) A poor grade
(C) Higher postage rates
(D) A letter from a relative

The correct answer is (A). The fact that the letter comes from the bursar's office (the financial office of a university) and that the second woman is upset about an increase and feels they are spending too much to go to school, it is clear that they are talking about an increase in tuition.

QUESTIONS ABOUT PROBLEMS

These questions follow dialogues in which the speakers are discussing some trouble one or both of them are having. The third speaker asks what the problem is.

Sample Item

You will hear:*

M2: Gordon, what happened to your window?

M1: When I was painting the window last week, I hit it with the ladder.

F1: What problem does Gordon probably have?

You will read:

What problem does Gordon probably have?

(A) His house needs painting.
(B) He broke his ladder.
(C) He spilled some paint.
(D) His window is broken.

The correct answer is (D). Gordon, the second speaker, says that he hit the window with the ladder when he was painting the house. The logical result—a broken window.

---

* Note: M1 = first male voice   M2 = second male voice   F1 = first female voice   F2 = second female voice

EXERCISE 8

Focus: Answering questions about plans, topics, and problems
Directions: Listen to the dialogues and the questions about them.
Now start the listening program.

1. What are they talking about?

   (A) Road conditions
   (B) A weather report
   (C) A motel reservation
   (D) Highway repairs

2. What are they probably going to do this afternoon?

   (A) Go to a party
   (B) Move Beth's belongings
   (C) Get ready to have a party
   (D) Clean up Beth's apartment

3. What is the problem?

   (A) The man's car is not running.
   (B) The man isn't going to the party.
   (C) No one knows where the party will be.
   (D) The car isn't big enough for four people.

4. What are they probably talking about?

   (A) A shopping center
   (B) A bridge
   (C) A street
   (D) An office

5. What are the speakers probably planning to do tomorrow?

   (A) Shop for groceries
   (B) Go on a camping trip
   (C) Go to a circus
   (D) Leave on a business trip

6. What does Brian intend to do?

   (A) Get some medicine for his headaches
   (B) Buy some new frames for his eyeglasses
   (C) Find another doctor
   (D) Get different lenses for his glasses

7. What are these people discussing?

   (A) Clothing
   (B) Hair styling
   (C) Painting
   (D) Cooking

8. What is the man going to do next?

   (A) Take a trip
   (B) Watch television
   (C) Examine some documents
   (D) Go to sleep

9. What problem did the man have with the book?

   (A) He lent it to someone else.
   (B) It was ruined in the rain.
   (C) He forgot where he left it.
   (D) One of the pages was torn.

10. What are the speakers probably discussing?

    (A) A car
    (B) A magazine
    (C) A computer
    (D) A piano

11. What will Shirley probably do right after she finishes her undergraduate program?

    (A) Go to business school
    (B) Look for a job with a big company
    (C) Start her own business
    (D) Take a trip around the world

12. What is Dave's problem?

    (A) He doesn't have Phyllis's address.
    (B) He doesn't like any of the postcards.
    (C) He can't find the post office.
    (D) He doesn't have a stamp.

Lesson 9

DIALOGUES WITH SPECIAL VERBS

CAUSATIVE VERBS

These verbs indicate that someone causes someone else to do something. When a dialogue contains a causative verb, you must understand who performs the action. The verbs *have*, *get*, *make*, and *let* are the most common causative verbs.

They are used in the following patterns:

Have

have someone do something	Dave had the mechanic fix his car.
have something done	Dave had his car fixed.

The causative verb *have* indicates that one person asks or pays another to do something. The subject of this sentence, *Dave*, does not perform the action. In the first sentence, the mechanic does. In the second sentence, an unnamed person does.

Get

get someone to do something	Jerry got his cousin to cut his hair.
get something done	Jerry got his hair cut.

The causative verb *get* usually means to persuade someone to do something. Again note that the subject, *Jerry*, does not perform the action.

Make

make someone do something	She made her son do his homework.

The causative verb *make* means to force someone or compel someone to do something.

Let

let someone do something	The boss let us go home.

The verb *let* means permit or allow.

Sample Item

You will hear:*

M1: Did you speak to the head of the department.

F1: No, she had her assistant meet with me.

M2: What does the woman mean?

You will read:

What does the woman mean?

(A) She spoke to the head of the department.

(B) The head of the department had a meeting with her assistant.

(C) She met with the assistant to the head of the department.

(D) The assistant will soon become head of the department.

The correct answer is (A). According to the dialogue, the head of the department directed her assistant to meet with the woman.

USED TO

The expression *used to* has two forms, each with a different meaning:

    used to + simple form

I used to live in New York.   means ⟶ I once lived in New York (but now I don't).

               + gerund (*-ing* verb)

  be/get + *used to*

               + noun phrase

I'm not used to driving on the left side of the road.   means ⟶ I'm not accustomed to driving on the left side.

I've finally gotten used to my new job.   means ⟶ I've finally become accustomed to my new job.

The dialogues in Part A sometimes take advantage of these two functions of *used to*.

---

* Note: M1 = first male voice   M2 = second male voice   F1 = first female voice   F2 = second female voice

Sample Items

You will hear:*

F2: What does Hank's father do for a living?

M1: He's a salesman now, but he used to be a truck driver.

M2: What does the man say about Hank's father?

You will read:

What does the man say about Hank's father?

(A) He once drove trucks.
(B) He sells used trucks.
(C) His truck is still useful.
(D) He's accustomed to his job.

The correct answer is (A). The man says that Hank's father used to be a truck driver. In other words, Hank's father once drove trucks, but he no longer does so.

You will hear:*

F1: Nancy is working late again today?

M1: Yeah, she must be getting used to it by now.

M2: What does the man say about Nancy?

You will read:

What does the man say about Nancy?

(A) She probably has a more difficult job now.
(B) She once worked later than she does now.
(C) She seldom comes to work late.
(D) She is becoming accustomed to late hours at work.

The correct answer is (D). The second speaker indicates that Nancy has probably adjusted to working late.

EXERCISE 9

Focus: Listening to dialogues that contain causative verbs or expressions with *used to*
Directions: Listen to the dialogues and the questions about them. Then decide which of the two answer choices—(A) or (B)—best answers the question, and mark the appropriate blank.
Now start the listening program.

1. What does the man say?

_____ (A) Doug is happy to be Rose's friend.

_____ (B) Doug and Rose are no longer good friends.

2. What does the woman tell Roger?

_____ (A) He can do the job as well as a professional.

_____ (B) He should hire an electrician to do the job.

3. What does the man say about the radio station?

_____ (A) It now plays classical music.

_____ (B) It doesn't broadcast anything but news.

_____
* Note: M1 = first male voice   M2 = second male voice   F1 = first female voice   F2 = second female voice

4. What can be inferred from Lynn's remark?

_____ (A) Changing the oil was easy for her.

_____ (B) The oil didn't need to be changed.

5. What does the man mean?

_____ (A) He's not accustomed to early classes yet.

_____ (B) His classes are difficult, too.

6. What does Peggy mean?

_____ (A) She's finally accustomed to skating.

_____ (B) She doesn't go skating as often as she once did.

7. What does Kenny mean?

_____ (A) He's going to clean his tie.

_____ (B) He's going to take his tie to the cleaner's.

8. What does the man mean?

_____ (A) He moved the poster.

_____ (B) He no longer likes the sofa and desk.

9. What does the woman mean?

_____ (A) She will take a vacation in August no matter what her boss says.

_____ (B) She'll probably be too busy to go on vacation in August.

10. What did Greg's teacher do?

_____ (A) She asked Greg to explain the point.

_____ (B) She explained the point to Greg.

11. What do the speakers say about Carter?

_____ (A) He isn't accustomed to his glasses.

_____ (B) He looks quite different without glasses.

12. What does Nick tell the woman?

_____ (A) This type of weather is not new to him.

_____ (B) He once lived in a very different climate.

13. What does Sally mean?

_____ (A) She's going to take a picture of the members of her club.

_____ (B) Someone is going to photograph her club.

REVIEW TEST B: DIALOGUES

Directions: Listen to the conversations and the questions about them. Decide which of the four answer choices—(A), (B), (C), or (D)—is the best answer to the question.

Now start the listening program.

1. What are they discussing?

(A) Books
(B) Clothing
(C) Candy
(D) Songs

2. What does the woman suggest?

(A) Looking for a new apartment
(B) Getting more sleep
(C) Turning up his stereo
(D) Discussing the problem with his neighbor

3. What does the man tell Sonya about the seminar?

(A) Professor Osborne probably won't lead it.
(B) It is not a required course for her.
(C) It is being offered now, not next semester.
(D) She doesn't need Professor Osborne's permission to take it.

58

4. What does Adam imply?

    (A) He hasn't finished working on the bookshelves.
    (B) The tools have been misplaced.
    (C) He can't work with his hands very well.
    (D) He didn't really need the tools to build the bookshelf.

5. What does the man imply?

    (A) He doesn't like the woman's suggestion very much.
    (B) His sister needs several new roommates.
    (C) He didn't really want the woman to give him advice.
    (D) Grace is the perfect roommate for his sister.

6. What does the woman ask Mark?

    (A) What he is writing
    (B) Where he is living now
    (C) Why he doesn't want to go
    (D) Why he is in a hurry

7. What does the woman mean?

    (A) She doesn't know where his hat is.
    (B) It's not very cold today.
    (C) She likes the way the hat looks.
    (D) The man ought to wear his hat.

8. What does the man mean?

    (A) He doesn't believe what his friend told him.
    (B) He thinks the team was unprepared, too.
    (C) He disagrees with his friend's idea.
    (D) He isn't ready to go to the game either.

9. What problem is Richard having?

    (A) His shoes hurt his feet.
    (B) He was injured in a skiing accident.
    (C) His shoes are old and in bad shape.
    (D) He walked so far that his legs hurt.

10. What are these people discussing?

    (A) A television commercial
    (B) A history class
    (C) The woman's field of study
    (D) Some famous artists

11. What does the woman mean?

    (A) She was about to suggest the same thing.
    (B) She doesn't feel like giving a party.
    (C) She's completely surprised by the man's suggestion.
    (D) She isn't hungry right now.

12. What do the speakers imply about Victor?

    (A) He doesn't go out as often as he once did.
    (B) He doesn't always tell the truth.
    (C) He isn't as friendly as he once was.
    (D) He hasn't always been so sociable.

13. What does the man mean?

    (A) The woman may see his painting.
    (B) He'd like the woman to visit him.
    (C) The woman should draw a picture herself.
    (D) He's going to take a guess.

14. What does the woman tell the man?

    (A) The weather will probably improve by tomorrow.
    (B) She doesn't listen to the news on the radio anymore.
    (C) Tomorrow probably won't be such a nice day.
    (D) She heard about a big new store on the radio.

15. What does the second woman want to know?

    (A) Where the medical center is located
    (B) Which office Dr. Norton is in
    (C) What Dr. Norton told the first woman
    (D) Why the first woman went to see Dr. Norton

16. What had the man assumed about Angela?

    (A) She liked chemistry.
    (B) She would graduate in May.
    (C) She didn't have to repeat a course.
    (D) She hadn't completed the required courses.

This is the end of Review Test B.

Part B

EXTENDED CONVERSATIONS

ABOUT EXTENDED CONVERSATIONS

The second part of the Listening section consists of longer conversations between a man and a woman or (sometimes) between two men or two women. Each conversation lasts from 30 to 90 seconds. It is preceded by brief introductory comments. After each of the conversations, there are from three to five questions. The questions are separated by a 12-second pause. You must decide which one of the four answer choices in your test book is the best answer for the question, then mark that answer on your answer sheet. You're not permitted to take notes. There are two longer conversations on the standard form, three or four on the long form.

THE INTRODUCTORY COMMENTS

These comments tell you which questions the conversation refers to and provides some brief information about the conversation:

"Questions 31 to 34. Listen to two students talk about their psychology class."
"Questions 31 to 35. Listen to a conversation about plans for a class trip."
"Questions 35 to 38. Listen to two friends discussing a performance that they attended."
"Questions 36 to 39. Listen to a conversation in a student housing office."
"Questions 35 to 39. Listen to a conversation between two teaching assistants."

Not only do these introductory comments tell you to get ready to listen, they also tell you how many questions in your test book to preview at one time. Moreover, they give you a general idea of what to expect as you listen.

Sample Item

You will hear:*

M2: Listen to a conversation between two students.

F1: Bill, you're a physics major, aren't you?

M1: That's right.

F1: I need some advice. I want to take an introductory physics class and I have to choose between two teachers, Professor Hunter and Professor McVey. Do you know much about them?

M1: I've taken classes from both of them. To tell you the truth, I don't really like Hunter's style of teaching. He doesn't seem to care if his students understand or not, and his lectures are pretty dry.

F1: Well then, what about McVey? I've heard his course is difficult.

M1: It's not easy, but you'll learn a lot, and he always encourages his students to ask questions and join in discussions.

You will then hear:*

M2: What does the woman ask Bill to do?

You will read:

What does the woman ask Bill to do?

(A) Give her information about two teachers
(B) Help her with a physics assignment
(C) Speak to a professor for her
(D) Lead a discussion

The correct answer is (A). The woman asks Bill for some advice about the two professors who are teaching basic physics courses.

You will then hear:*

M2: What does Bill imply that the woman should do?

You will read:

What does Bill imply that the woman should do?

(A) Change her major to physics
(B) Discuss her problem with Professor Hunter
(C) Sign up for an easy class
(D) Take Professor McVey's class

The correct answer is (D). Bill speaks critically of Professor Hunter's teaching methods, but favorably of Professor McVey's, so he would probably advise her to take McVey's course.

---

* Note: M1 = first male voice   M2 = second male voice   F1 = first female voice   F2 = second female voice

CONVERSATIONS

The extended conversations are similar to the Part A dialogues in style, but are longer. They frequently take place in a campus setting between two students or between a professor and a student.

THE QUESTIONS

The questions may be overview questions or detail questions. The first question after the conversation is often an overview question. Overview questions require a broad understanding of the entire conversation. To answer them correctly, you must understand what BOTH speakers say. There are several types of overview questions:

Type of Overview Question	Sample Question
Topic question	"What are the speakers discussing?"
Questions about settings (time and location)	"Where did this conversation take place?" "When did this conversation take place?"
Questions about the speakers	"Who are the speakers?" "What is the probable relationship between the speakers?"

It's important to listen carefully to the first few lines of an extended conversation to answer overview questions because this part of the talk often sets the scene. It often establishes the time and location of the conversation, the identity of the speakers, and the main idea of the rest of the conversation.

Detail questions ask about specific points in the conversation. The answer will usually be contained in what ONE speaker says. Detail questions follow the order of information in the conversation. In other words, the first of these questions refers to a point made early in the conversation, and the last asks about a point made near the end of the conversation. Most detail questions are factual questions; the answers are directly stated in the conversation. Many factual questions begin with these phrases:

According to the conversation, . . .
According to the man, . . .
According to the woman, . . .

A few of the detail questions are inference questions. In other words, the information is not directly given by the speakers; it can be concluded from the information that IS stated, however.

What can be inferred from the man's comment about . . . ?
What does the man imply about . . . ?
What will the speakers probably try to do?

THE ANSWER CHOICES

The four choices are all plausible answers for the question. Usually the answer choices are mentioned in some way in the conversation; but, only one, the key, answers that particular question correctly.

Some people prefer to close their eyes or look away while listening to the extended conversations in order to concentrate on the voices on the tape. However, it is better if you read over the answer choices in the test book while listening. This technique is difficult, but it has several advantages:

- It allows you to get an overall sense of what the topic of the conversation will be.

- It enables you to anticipate what the questions will be, then concentrate on listening for those points.

- It permits you to confirm some of the details that you hear by comparing them with the answer choices in the test book.

In the next section of this book, you will practice previewing answer choices, listening to Part B conversations, and answering both overview and detail questions about the conversations.

Tactics for Extended Conversations

- Be familiar with the directions, but remember that you cannot turn the page to look over answer choices while the directions are being read.

- Pay attention to the introductory sentence for each talk. These will tell you which items each talk refers to and may give you an idea of what the talks will be about.

- Preview the answer choices while the talks are being read and during the pauses between questions. Try to guess what the questions will be.

- Listen for overall concepts:

    - Who is taking part in the conversation?

    - Where and when does the conversation take place?

    - What is the main topic of the conversation?

    The answers to these questions are often suggested in the first few lines of the talks.

- You are not permitted to take written notes, but try to take "mental notes" on specific details: facts, figures, dates, places, and so on. You can sometimes check the information you think you hear against information you read in the answer choices while you are previewing.

- Answer items right away.

- Always guess.

Lesson 10

ANSWERING MAIN IDEA/MAIN TOPIC QUESTIONS ABOUT EXTENDED CONVERSATIONS

After each extended conversation in Part B, there are four to five questions. Usually the first and sometimes the last question are **overview questions**. To answer these questions, you need an understanding of the whole lecture or conversation rather than of any specific point.

Overview questions for the Extended Conversations:

- What is the main topic of this conversation?

- What are these people primarily discussing?

- Where does this conversation take place?

- When does this conversation take place?

- What is the relationship between the speakers?

- What is the man's/woman's occupation?

- What is one speaker's attitude toward the other speaker?

Main topic questions must correctly summarize the talk. Incorrect answers for these questions are too general, too specific, or incorrect according to the conversation.

Although these questions require an overall understanding of the conversations, the first few sentences often "set the scene." In other words, the opening lines of the talk establish the time, place, and main topic. Read the opening lines of the extended conversation given below:

M1: (Answering phone) Hello?

F1: Hi, Rod, this is Rita—I'm in your nine o'clock class. I missed class because of a cold, and I was wondering if I could borrow your notes.

M1: I don't know if you could read my notes—I have terrible handwriting. But I can tell you what happened. Professor Phillips went over the material in Chapter 4, about different types of stars in our galaxy. And she talked about what the midterm exam is going to be like.

F1: Uh-oh, you better tell me all about the midterm—I really need to do well on it.

From this portion of a conversation, we learn that:

. . . both of the speakers are students

. . . they are probably taking a course in astronomy

. . . the class is about halfway over (because they are taking midterm exams)

. . . the rest of the talk will probably deal with the material that will be on the examination

Not all conversations begin with so much detail. However, it is important to concentrate on the opening lines to learn this kind of information.

EXERCISE 10

Focus: Listening to the opening lines of extended conversations and answering overview questions about the topics, settings, and speakers

Directions: Listen to the conversations and the questions about them.

Now start the listening program.

1. What will the main topic of this conversation probably be?

   (A) Methods of predicting earthquakes
   (B) Ways to improve the man's presentation
   (C) The many new uses of computer graphics
   (D) The role of statistics in geology

2. What are the main purposes of this discussion?

   Choose two.

   (A) To explain the reason for higher rents
   (B) To review a reading assignment
   (C) To contrast two forms of taxation
   (D) To discuss the need for sales taxes

3. What will the main subject of this conversation probably be?

   (A) Professor Quinn's approach to teaching
   (B) The process of getting a student identification card
   (C) Procedures for checking out reserve materials
   (D) Several recent articles in sociology journals

4. What will the rest of this talk mainly be about?

   Choose two.

   (A) The disadvantages of being in the program
   (B) The physical rewards of dancing
   (C) The importance of the program to the university
   (D) The procedures for arranging a tryout

5. What will the two speakers probably discuss?

   (A) Their plans for the coming school year
   (B) Tina's volunteer position
   (C) Tina's trip to Europe
   (D) An archaeology class that they both took

6. What are the speakers mainly discussing?

   (A) Reading experiments at Duke University
   (B) Reasons why scientists don't believe ESP is valid
   (C) The accomplishments of Professor Rhine
   (D) The failure of recent experiments in parapsychology

7. What is this lecture primarily going to concern?

   (A) The historical record contained in shipwrecks
   (B) The role of the State Historical Society
   (C) The history of New England
   (D) The leading causes of shipwrecks

8. What will the rest of the lecture probably concern?

   (A) Problems of the tobacco industry in the United States
   (B) Government regulation of advertisers
   (C) Tactics involved in deceptive advertisements
   (D) Self-regulation of the advertising industry

Lesson 11

ANSWERING DETAIL AND INFERENCE QUESTIONS ABOUT EXTENDED CONVERSATIONS

Most of the questions in Part B are **detail questions** that require an understanding of specific points in the conversation. A majority of these questions are **factual questions**, asking what, where, when, why, and how much. To answer the question, you need to listen carefully.

Other questions are **inference questions**. As previously explained, the answers to inference questions are not directly stated, but are suggested by information in the lecture. Many of these questions begin, "What do the speakers imply about . . ." or "What can be inferred from the conversation about . . ."

Remember that the order of detail questions follows the order of the conversation. In other words, the first detail question will be about something mentioned early in the conversation while the last one is about something mentioned near the end of the conversation.

If anything in the conversation is emphasized, it will probably be asked about. In other words, if something one speaker says is repeated by the second speaker, or if one speaker talks about something in an emphatic tone of voice, there will probably be a question about that information, as in this section of a conversation:

M1: My project for my filmmaking class took me six weeks to finish.
F1: Six weeks! I can hardly believe it. Doesn't the teacher realize you have other classes too?

You can be fairly sure that there will be a question, "How long did the man's project take to complete?"

EXERCISE 11

Focus: Answering detail and inference questions based on specific points in short portions of extended conversations

Directions: You will hear three extended conversations, each one divided into several short portions. After each portion, there will be a number of questions based on that part of the talk.

Now start the listening program.

1. Why is Steve tired?

   (A) He stayed up most of the night.
   (B) He had to take a test last night.
   (C) He's been studying all morning.
   (D) He's been too nervous to sleep well lately.

2. How did Steve feel about the grade he received?

   (A) It was an improvement.
   (B) It was disappointing.
   (C) It was unfair.
   (D) It was a surprise.

3. Who teaches the seminars at the Study Skills Center?

   Choose two.

   (A) Undergraduate students
   (B) Professors
   (C) Graduate students
   (D) Librarians

4. What seminar will Steve probably take?

   (A) Basic scientific research
   (B) Business management
   (C) Test-taking skills
   (D) Chemistry

5. Where is the main office of the Study Skills Center?

   (A) In the library
   (B) In the Physics Tower
   (C) In a dormitory
   (D) In Staunton Hall

6. What does the woman think Steve should do next?

   (A) Study for his next exam
   (B) Go to the Study Skills Center
   (C) Talk to his chemistry professor
   (D) Get some sleep

7. When did orbital debris first appear?

   (A) In the 1950s
   (B) In the 1960s
   (C) In the 1980s
   (D) In the 1990s

8. What happens to most pieces of orbital debris?

   (A) They fly off into deep space.
   (B) They remain in orbit forever.
   (C) They collide with other pieces.
   (D) They burn up in the atmosphere.

9. How many orbital bodies are being monitored today?

   (A) Three to four hundred
   (B) Three to four thousand
   (C) About eight thousand
   (D) Half a million

10. Why is it impossible to monitor most pieces of orbital debris?

    (A) They are too small.
    (B) They are too far away.
    (C) They are moving too fast.
    (D) They are made of reflective material.

11. Which of the following types of orbital debris are probably most dangerous to astronauts on a spacecraft?
    Choose two.

    (A) A large booster rocket
    (B) A piece of metal the size of an aspirin
    (C) A lost tool
    (D) A tiny fleck of paint

12. What makes orbital debris such a danger to spacecraft?

    (A) Its high speed
    (B) Its jagged shape
    (C) Its gigantic size
    (D) Its unusual composition

13. Assume that this is a representation of a satellite equipped with a collector. Where would the space debris be stored? Circle the letter of the correct response.

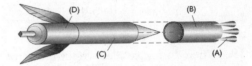

14. In which ways could the collector be used to solve the problem of orbital debris?
    Choose two.

    (A) It could be used to track even very small pieces of orbital debris.
    (B) It could serve as a protective device for manned spacecraft.
    (C) It could be mounted on unmanned spacecraft to find and trap pieces of debris.
    (D) It could burn up large pieces of orbital debris.

15. What can be inferred about the collector described in the talk?

    (A) It has already been tested on Earth.
    (B) It is no longer in common use.
    (C) It has already been installed on spacecraft.
    (D) It has not been built yet.

16. Where is the town of San Juan Capistrano located? (Circle the letter of the correct response.)

17. What were the professor's main reasons for going to San Juan Capistrano?

    Choose two.

    (A) To visit a friend
    (B) To see the swallows arrive
    (C) To help a colleague
    (D) To see a parade

18. What can be inferred about the swallows?

    (A) They are a type of insect.
    (B) They are a kind of fish.
    (C) They are a type of bird.
    (D) They are a type of mammal.

19. When do the swallows return to San Juan Capistrano?

    (A) In March
    (B) In early summer
    (C) In October
    (D) In mid-winter

20. How far do the swallows migrate?

    (A) About 200 miles
    (B) About 1,000 miles
    (C) About 3,000 miles
    (D) About 7,000 miles

21. According to the professor, how was the mission church in San Juan Capistrano damaged?

    (A) By a storm
    (B) By a fire
    (C) By an earthquake
    (D) By the swallows

22. According to the professor, why are the swallows popular with the people of San Juan Capistrano?

    Choose two.

    (A) They eliminate insect pests.
    (B) They help bring money into the community.
    (C) They are believed to bring good luck.
    (D) They are extremely beautiful creatures.

23. When is the guided tour of the campus given?

    (A) Before the semester begins
    (B) Only during the first week of the semester
    (C) Whenever students ask for them
    (D) Only in the afternoon

24. What did the man have trouble locating the week before?

    (A) A tour guide
    (B) A classroom
    (C) A map
    (D) A pamphlet

25. Where does the self-guided tour start?

    (A) In the Science Building
    (B) In the Student Center Building
    (C) In the University Recreation Center
    (D) In the planetarium

Lesson 12

ANSWERING MATCHING AND ORDERING QUESTIONS ABOUT LONGER TALKS

These two types of items are unique to the computer-based TOEFL® test. They did not appear on the paper-based form of the test. They require understanding not just single details but a large portion of the talk. It would be much easier to answer these questions if you could take notes on paper, but this is not permitted. You'll have to try to take "mental notes" to remember what you hear.

For most test takers, matching and ordering items are probably the most difficult parts of the Listening section.

Ordering questions require you to put four events or four steps of a process in the correct order. Any time you hear the lecturer or speakers discussing a sequence of events, a biography of a person, the steps of a process, or a ranking of things according to their importance, there will probably be an ordering question. Listen for words that signal a sequence, such as next, then, after that, later, or before that, previously, earlier. Try to keep track of the events or steps. They may not be given in the talk in the order in which they are listed in the questions.

To answer these questions on the computer, you must first click on one of the four words, phrases, or sentences in the top half of the screen and then click on the appropriate box (labeled 1, 2, 3, and 4) in the lower half of the screen. The expression from the top will then appear in the box that you clicked on. Do this for all four boxes.

You really have to put only three answers in their proper positions because the fourth answer must of course go in the remaining position.

Matching questions require you to connect three words, phrases, or sentences with three other words or phrases somehow related to them. If the lecturer or speaker lists three or more concepts and then gives definitions, examples or characteristics or uses of those concepts, you can expect to hear a matching question.

To answer a matching question, you must click on one of the three expressions in the top half of the screen and then on the box above the expression that you think is related to it. That word or phrase will then appear in the box. Do this for all three boxes.

You really have to correctly match two pairs of answers because the one remaining pair of answers must be matched.

EXERCISE 12

Focus: Listening to portions of Mini-Lectures and Academic Discussions and answering matching and ordering questions about them

Directions: Write the letters of the words or phrases in the appropriate boxes. (Note: There are no letters by the choices in the computer version. You simply click on the choice and then on the box where you think it belongs.)

Now start the listening program.

1. The lecturer discusses the steps involved in the creation of coal. Summarize this process by putting the events in the proper order.

   Place the letters in the proper boxes.

   (A) During the process of decomposition, plants lose oxygen and hydrogen.
   (B) Layers of sand and mud put pressure on the peat.
   (C) Plants grow in swampy areas.
   (D) Plants die and fall into swampy waters.

1.
2.
3.
4.

2. Match the form of coal with the type of industry that primarily uses it.

   Place the letters in the proper boxes.

   (A) coal tar

   (B) bituminous coal

   (C) coke

   1. Electric utilities
   2. Plastic manufacturers
   3. Steelmakers

3. Match the accounting principle with the appropriate description of it.

   Place the letters in the proper boxes.

   (A) cost principle

   (B) business entity

   (C) matching principle

   1. Owner's accounts must be kept separate from business accounts.
   2. Firm must record sales expenses in period in which they were made.
   3. Costs must be recorded at their original price.

4. The lecturer mentions four types of crops that are grown in Harrison County. Rank these four crops in their order of economic importance, beginning with the MOST important.

   Place the letters in the proper boxes.

   (A) Wheat
   (B) Organic fruit
   (C) Corn
   (D) Soy beans

1.
2.
3.
4.

5. Match the type of wheat with the product that is most often made from it.

Place the letters in the proper boxes.

(A) Hard red

[   ]

(B) Soft white

[   ]

(C) Durum wheat

[   ]

1. Pasta
2. Bread flour
3. Breakfast cereals

6. The professor discusses some of the history of Antarctic exploration. Summarize this history by putting these expeditions in the order in which they began.

Place the letters in the proper boxes.

(A) Amundson's
(B) Scott's
(C) Byrd's
(D) Shackleton's

1. [   ]
2. [   ]
3. [   ]
4. [   ]

7. Match these Antarctic explorers with the countries from which they came.

Place the letters in the proper boxes.

(A) Scott

[   ]

(B) Amundson

[   ]

(C) Byrd

[   ]

1. United States
2. Norway
3. Britain

8. Match the performance with its maximum decibel level.

Place the letters in the proper boxes.

(A) The first violin's solo

[   ]

(B) The Metropolitan

[   ]

(C) The Creatures' concert

[   ]

1. 60 decibels
2. 90 decibels
3. 115 decibels

REVIEW TEST C: LONGER TALKS

Directions: This part involves longer talks: conversations, discussions, and lectures. You will hear the talks only once. After each of these talks, there are a number of questions.

When you have read and heard the questions, read the answer choices and select the best answer or answers based on what is directly stated or on what can be inferred.

Don't forget: During actual exams, taking notes during the Listening section is not permitted.

Now start the listening program.

1. Why did Martha come to the library?

(A) To look up some terms
(B) To meet Stanley
(C) To get a snack
(D) To prepare for an exam

2. What did Stanley lose?

(A) His library card
(B) A statistics book
(C) Some index cards
(D) A notebook

3. According to Stanley, what does the term "stacks" refer to?

    (A) The part of the library where journals are stored

    (B) Piles of note cards

    (C) The part of the library where books are shelved

    (D) A place to get something to eat in the library

4. What are the main purposes of the lecture?

    Choose two.

    (A) To talk about the hunter-gatherer stage of humankind

    (B) To outline the process of domestication in general

    (C) To discuss the domestication of dogs

    (D) To describe the various tasks dogs have been given

5. According to the lecturer, how did early humans adapt dogs to different tasks?

    (A) By crossing wolves with other animals

    (B) By careful training

    (C) By selective breeding

    (D) By rewarding dogs with pieces of food

6. Why does the lecturer mention Idaho?

    (A) The first dogs were domesticated there.

    (B) A famous mural of a dog was painted there.

    (C) The remains of an early specimen of domesticated dog were found there.

    (D) It was there that dogs first learned how to help humans to hunt.

7. The lecturer mentions a number of roles that dogs have played since they were first domesticated. List these roles in the correct chronological order.

    Place the letters in the proper boxes.

    (A) Hunter

    (B) Herder

    (C) Companion

    (D) Guard

1.
2.
3.
4.

8. Circle the part of the picture that represents the herders' "best friend."

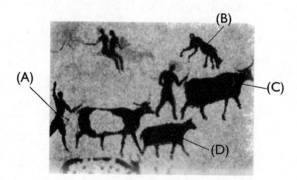

9. Why does Professor Kemp NOT want to stage the play *Our Town* this spring?

    (A) It is a play usually produced by high school drama classes.

    (B) It would not involve any work for students interested in costumes and scenery.

    (C) She doesn't have the necessary background to direct this play.

    (D) She has never liked this play.

10. Professor Kemp and her students discuss a number of plays. Match the characteristics of the play with the title of the play.

    Place the letters in the proper boxes.

    (A) A Shakespearean comedy
    (B) A play about the Salem witch trials
    (C) A musical

    [   ]

    The Tempest

    [   ]

    A Chorus Line

    [   ]

    The Crucible

11. In what time period is the play *The Crucible* set?

    (A) In medieval times
    (B) In the seventeenth century
    (C) In the 1950s
    (D) In the present

12. Which of these plays does Professor Kemp show the most enthusiasm for staging?

    (A) *Our Town*
    (B) *The Crucible*
    (C) *A Chorus Line*
    (D) *The Tempest*

13. What does Professor Kemp ask the students to do before their next class?

    (A) Get a book
    (B) Attend a play
    (C) Learn their lines
    (D) Make a decision

14. What does the article that Nicole is reading say about Hambleton College?

    (A) Its tuition rates are going up faster than the ones at Babcock University.
    (B) It has the highest tuition rates in the state.
    (C) Its tuition rates are still lower than those at Babcock University.
    (D) It has actually lowered its tuition rates recently.

15. Who is Penny Chang?

    (A) The president of the Student Council
    (B) A member of the Board of Regents
    (C) A spokesperson for the administration
    (D) A journalist for the campus newspaper

16. What can be inferred from the remark made by the spokesperson for the administration?

    (A) The new dormitory will not be built.
    (B) The proposal to increase student services will not be adopted.
    (C) The tuition will not be raised.
    (D) New computers will be bought.

17. According to the speaker, when did Webster graduate from Yale University?

    (A) Before the Revolutionary War
    (B) During the Revolutionary War
    (C) After American independence
    (D) After publication of his books

18. What is Noah Webster mainly remembered for today?

    (A) His military service
    (B) His political philosophy
    (C) His dictionary
    (D) His unusual spellings

19. According to the speaker, what kind of book was the "blue-backed book"?

    (A) A history book
    (B) A dictionary
    (C) An autobiography
    (D) A spelling book

20. Which of the following are spellings that Benjamin Franklin would probably have approved of?

    Choose two.

    (A) T-H-E-A-T-R-E instead of T-H-E-A-T-E-R
    (B) F-O-T-O-G-R-A-F instead of P-H-O-T-O-G-R-A-P-H
    (C) L-A-B-O-U-R instead of L-A-B-O-R
    (D) N-I-F instead of K-N-I-F-E

This is the end of Review Test C.

Section 2:

STRUCTURE

ABOUT STRUCTURE

The second section of the TOEFL® test examines your understanding of English grammar and usage. There are two types of questions in this section of the test: Sentence Completion and Error Identification. On the paper-based test, these two types of items were presented in separate parts of the section, but on the computer version, the two types of items are intermingled. Except for that fact, this section of the test has changed very little from the paper-based format.

There are 20 to 25 items in this section, and the time limit is from 15 to 20 minutes. On the average, you have about 45 seconds in which to answer each item. For most test takers, this is plenty of time.

Remember that your grade on the fourth section of the test, Essay Writing, counts for about half of your grade in Structure. If you have problems with writing essays, it is especially important that you do well on this part of the test to pull up your Structure grade.

Although a wide range of grammar points are tested, there are certain points that appear again and again, and you can master these points with the information and practice this book provides.

Section 2 should be less stressful for you than Section 1 because you don't have to divide your attention between the spoken material and the information on the screen. It may also seem less stressful than Section 3 because it is easier to finish all the items in the amount of time allotted.

Like Listening, Structure is computer adaptive. The first items you see will be of medium difficulty. Don't rush through these items, however, because the first half of the section is very important to your score. If you keep answering the questions correctly, the items will become progressively more difficult.

Structure sentences are generally about academic subjects: the physical sciences (such as astronomy or geology), the social sciences (such as anthropology or economics), or the humanities (such as music or literature). You will NOT see sentences that deal with "controversial" subjects such as abortion, illegal drugs, or sensitive political issues.

Any cultural references in the sentences are to the culture of the United States or Canada. Many of the sentences contain references to people, places, and institutions that you will not be familiar with. (In fact, many North Americans are not familiar with these either!) It's not necessary to know these references; you should simply concentrate on the structure of the sentences. It's also not necessary to understand all the vocabulary in a sentence; you can often answer a question correctly without a complete understanding of the sentence.

There are two possible approaches to Section 2 problems: an analytical approach and an intuitive approach. A test-taker who uses the analytical approach quickly analyzes the grammar of a sentence to see what element is missing (in Sentence Completion items) or which element is incorrect (in Error Identification items). Someone who uses the second approach simply chooses the answer that "sounds right" (in Sentence Completion items) or the one that "sounds wrong" (in Error Identification items). Although this book emphasizes the first approach, the second can be useful too, especially for people who learned English primarily by speaking it and listening to it rather than by studying grammar and writing. You can also combine the two approaches: if you get "stuck" using one method, you can switch to another.

SENTENCE COMPLETION

This type of item consists of an incomplete sentence. Some portion of the sentence has been replaced by a blank. Under the sentence, four words or phrases are listed. One of these completes the sentence grammatically and logically.

Sample Item

Pepsin _____ an enzyme which is used in digestion.

(A) that
(B) is
(C) of
(D) being

The correct answer is (B). The sentence consists of an incomplete main clause (*Pepsin _____ an enzyme*) and an adjective clause (*which is used in digestion*). Each clause must contain a subject and a verb. There is a subject but no verb in the main clause. Only choices (B) and (D) are verbal forms. However, an *-ing* verb can never be used alone as a sentence verb. Only choice (B), the verb *is*, supplies a verb for the main clause.

What Is the Best Way to Answer Sentence Completion Items?

If the answer choices are fairly short, you should begin by taking a quick look at the answer choices to get an idea of what is missing from the sentence. A glance at the answer choices can often tell you that you are looking at a problem involving verb forms, word order, parallel structure, misplaced modifiers, and others.

If the answer choices are long or complicated, begin by reading the stem. Don't analyze it word for word, but as you are reading, try to form a picture of the sentence's overall structure. How many clauses will there be in the complete sentence? Does each clause have a complete subject and verb? Is there a connecting word to join clauses? Are any other elements obviously missing? If you can't find the answer immediately, try to eliminate as many distractors as possible. Distractors for Sentence Completion items are generally incorrect for one of the following reasons:

- A necessary word or phrase is missing, so the sentence is still incomplete.

- An unnecessary word or phrase is included.

- Part of the answer choice is ungrammatical when put into the stem.

Don't click on an answer until you've read the sentence completely; sometimes an option seems to fit in the sentence unless you read every word.

After you have eliminated as many answer choices as possible, read the sentence quickly to yourself with the remaining choice or choices in place of the blank. If an answer doesn't "sound right," it probably isn't. If you still can't decide, guess and go on.

Error Identification

This type of item consists of a sentence in which four expressions—single words or two- or three-word phrases—are underlined. Your job is to identify which of these phrases must be rewritten (it can't simply be omitted) in order for the sentence to be correct. All the errors involve grammar or usage—never punctuation or spelling.

Sample Items

Music, dramatic, and art contribute to
        A   B
the culture of any community.
      C   D

The correct answer is (A). This sentence should correctly read, "Music, *drama*, and art contribute to the culture of any community." Choice (A) would have to be rewritten to correct the sentence, and so that is the best answer.

Lenses may having either concave or
          A   B   C
convex shapes.
    D

The correct answer is (A). The correct verb form after a modal auxiliary is the simple form *have*. This sentence should read, "Lenses may have either concave or convex shapes," so the best answer is choice (A), *having*.

What Is the Best Way to Answer Error Identification Items?

You should begin with a quick reading of each sentence to find any obvious errors. **Don't** simply read the underlined portions, because in most items, the underlined expression is incorrect only in the context of the sentence. **Don't** answer the question until you've read the entire sentence.

Easy questions can be answered after the first reading; click on the answer and go on to the next problem. If you can't find the error immediately, reread the sentence, now concentrating on the underlined expressions. You can't use the same techniques for reading these items as you would to read other materials, such as newspapers or magazine articles. Usually, a person's eyes move very quickly over "little words" like articles and prepositions because these words don't contain much information. However, in this part of the test, these expressions may be used incorrectly. You should train your eyes to move slowly and pronounce the sentences in your mind as if you were speaking them.

If you haven't identified the error after a careful reading of the sentence, go through a mental checklist of the most common errors: word form, word choice, and verb error. Do the underlined expressions seem to fit into any of these categories?

If you still can't find an error, eliminate expressions that seem to be used correctly, then make the best guess you can from any items that remain.

COMPUTER SKILLS FOR THE STRUCTURE SECTION

Answering Structure items on the computer is easy. For Sentence Completion items, you simply click on either the oval by the choice that you think is the best answer or on any part of the answer itself. As in all parts of the test, it is easier to click on the answer choice itself than on the oval. To answer an Error Identification item, you must click on some portion of the answer that you think is best. You can click anywhere within the underlined portion. (There are no ovals to click on when answering this type of item.) When you click on an underlined phrase, it will become highlighted, indicating that this is your choice. The easiest way to

change an answer is to click on another underlined word or phrase. That choice will then be highlighted, and the highlight will disappear from the first choice. And that's all there is to it!

STRATEGIES FOR STRUCTURE

In General

- Be familiar with the directions for Structure. As soon as this section starts, click on *Dismiss Directions*.

- You can spend an average of about forty-five seconds on each item. If an item seems difficult, eliminate unlikely items and make the best guess that you can. Don't spend too much time working on items you find difficult.

- Never answer any item too quickly, even if it seems easy. Always consider all four answer choices. It is easy to make mistakes in Structure because of carelessness.

- Pace yourself carefully through this section by keeping an eye on the *Time Remaining* indicator and the item number indicator. Don't work so slowly that there will still be unanswered problems when time expires, but don't work so quickly that you finish long before the time expires.

Sentence Completion

- If the answer choices are short, look them over before you read the sentence. Try to get an idea of what type of problem you are working with.

- Read the sentence, trying to determine which elements are missing. Never choose an answer until you have read the entire sentence; sometimes an answer will seem to fit until you have read the last few words of the sentence.

- Mark your choice immediately if the answer is obvious. If you're not sure, try to eliminate incorrect answers.

- Read the sentence with the remaining answer choices in place of the blank. Choose the option that sounds best.

- Save yourself time by clicking on the answer itself rather than on the oval.

- If you are still unable to decide on an answer, guess and go on.

Error Identification

- Skim each sentence, looking for obvious errors.

- If you haven't found the error, read the sentence again carefully, concentrating on the underlined parts. Go through a mental checklist of the most common types of errors (word form, word choice, verb error) to see if any of the underlined expressions seem to fall into those categories.

- If you are still unable to find an error, try eliminating options that seem to be correct. If more than one option remains, take a guess and go on.

Now begin your preparation for Section 2 by taking the Preview Structure Test. Be sure to observe the 20-minute time limit.

Directions: This section tests your ability to recognize both correct and incorrect English structures. There are two types of items in this section.

One type involves a sentence that is missing a verb or phrase. Four words or phrases appear below the sentence. You must choose the one that best completes the sentence.

Example I

_____ large natural lakes are found in the state of South Carolina.

(A) There are no
(B) Not the
(C) It is not
(D) No

The correct answer is (D). This sentence should properly read, "No large natural lakes are found in the state of South Carolina."

The other type of item involves a sentence in which four words or phrases have been underlined. You must identify the one underlined word or phrase that must be changed for the sentence to be considered correct.

Example II

When painting a fresco, an artist is applied paint directly to the damp plaster of a wall.
    A   B   C   D

The correct answer is (B). This sentence should read, "When painting a fresco, an artist applies paint directly to the damp plaster of a wall." Keep in mind that on the CBT, letter choices will not appear below the answer choices. We have included them here in order to make it easier to discuss the questions in the Answer Keys.

As soon as you understand the directions, begin work on this Preview Test.
There are 25 questions.

1. Martha Graham, _____ of the pioneers of modern dance, didn't begin dancing until she was twenty-one.

   (A) who, as one
   (B) she was
   (C) one
   (D) was one

2. There are thousand of different types of
         A   B   C   D
   roses.

3. Sponges have neither heads or separate
                 A   B   C
   body organs.
          D

4. Tiger moths _____ wings marked with stripes or spots.

   (A) have
   (B) with
   (C) their
   (D) whose

5. The first recorded use of natural gas to light
                    A   B
   street lamps it was in the town of Freder-
               C   D
   ick, New York in 1825.

6. Most of Annie Jump Cannon's career as an astronomer involved the observation, classification, and _____.

   (A) she analyzed stars
   (B) the stars' analysis
   (C) stars were analyzed
   (D) analysis of stars

7. The French Quarter is the most famous and
   _____ A _____ B
   the most old section of New Orleans.
   ___ C _____ D

8. Liquids take the shape of any container
   _____ A ____ B
   which in they are placed.
   ____ C _____ D

9. There are several races of giraffes, but there
   ___ A _____ B _____ C
   are only one species.
   ___ D

10. Platinum is harder than copper and is almost as pliable _____.

    (A) gold
    (B) than gold
    (C) as gold
    (D) gold is

11. Many communities are dependent on groundwater _____ from wells for their water supply.

    (A) that obtained
    (B) obtained
    (C) is obtained
    (D) obtain it

12. Boolean algebra is most often used
    _____ A
    to solve problems in logic, probability, and
    ___ B _____ C
    engineer.
    ___ D

13. There were _____ federal laws regulating mining practices until 1872.

    (A) none
    (B) not
    (C) no
    (D) nor

14. A number of the materials used in manufac-
    ___ A
    turing paint are potential dangerous
    ___ B ___ C
    if mishandled.
    ___ D

15. _____ experimental studies of the aging process, psychologist Ross McFarland determined that people could work productively much longer than had previously been thought.

    (A) In that
    (B) Through
    (C) Since
    (D) Into

16. Despite they are small, ponies are strong
    ___ A _____ B _____ C
    and have great stamina.
    ___ D

17. Physical therapists help patients relearn
    _____ A
    how to use their bodies after disease or
    ___ B _____ C
    injure.
    ___ D

18. Designed by Frederic Auguste Bartholdi,
    _____.

    (A) the United States was given the Statue of Liberty by the people of France
    (B) the people of France gave the Statue of Liberty to the United States
    (C) the Statue of Liberty was given to the United States by the people of France
    (D) the French people presented the United States with a gift, the Statue of Liberty

19. In 1791 Quebec was divided into two sections, Upper Canada and Lower Canada, _____ were ruled by elected assemblies.

    (A) they both
    (B) both of them
    (C) in which both
    (D) both of which

20. _____ quicksand can be found all over the world, little was known about its composition until recently.

    (A) Except
    (B) Although
    (C) Even
    (D) Despite

21. _____ are a form of carbon has been known since the late eighteenth century.

    (A) Diamonds
    (B) Because diamonds
    (C) That diamonds
    (D) Diamonds, which

22. In the late nineteenth century many public
                      A
buildings, especially that on college
                          B
campuses, were built in the Romanesque
                        C
Revival style of architecture.
                 D

23. Not only _____ places of beauty, they serve scientific and educational purposes as well.

    (A) are botanical gardens
    (B) botanical gardens to be
    (C) botanical gardens are
    (D) to be botanical gardens

24. Since 1908 breeders set out to produce
          A   B
chickens that could survive anada's
                     C
cold climate.
      D

25. There was once a widespread believe that
               A   B
all lizards were poisonous.
      C   D

This is the end of Preview Test 2: Structure

Lesson 13

INDEPENDENT CLAUSES

The structures practiced in this lesson are the ones that are most often tested in the Structure section. About 20 percent of all problems in the section (usually three or four per test) involve incomplete main clauses.

ABOUT CLAUSES

All sentences consist of one or more clauses. A **simple sentence** consists of one clause.

People need vitamins.
The man took a vitamin pill.
Judy lives in northern California.
In the summer, Tom walks to his office.

A **compound sentence** consists of two independent clauses joined by a coordinating conjunction (such as *and* and *but*).

The man took a vitamin pill, and he drank a glass of orange juice.
Judy lives in northern California now, but she was raised in Ohio.

A **complex sentence** consists of an independent clause (called the main clause) and a subordinate (dependent) clause. Subordinate clauses may be adverb clauses, noun clauses, or adjective clauses. In the sentences below, the independent clauses are italicized.

The man took a vitamin pill because he had a cold. (independent clause + adverb clause)
I didn't realize that Nancy was here. (noun clause)
Tom walks to his office, which is located on Broadway, *every day during the summer*.
     (independent clause + adjective clause)

All three types of subordinate clauses are commonly seen in the Structure part of the test, and each is considered in separate lessons (Lessons 14, 15, and 16). The emphasis in this chapter, however, is on the basic components of independent clauses.

MISSING SUBJECTS, VERBS, OBJECTS, AND COMPLEMENTS

All clauses have a **subject** and a **verb**. Clauses with an action verb often take a **direct object** as well.

Subject	Verb	Object
People	need	vitamins.

The verb missing from an independent clause may be a single-word verb (*need, was, took, had, walked*) or a verb phrase consisting of one or more auxiliary verbs and a main verb (*will need, has been, should take, would have had, had walked*). The verbs may be active (*need, take*) or passive (*was needed, is taken*).

The missing subject and direct object may be a noun (*people, vitamins, Tom*), a noun phrase (*some famous people, a vitamin pill, my friend Tom*), or a pronoun. (*He, she, it,* and *they* are subject pronouns; *him, her, it,* and *them* are object pronouns.)

After the verb *to be* and certain other nonaction verbs, a **subject complement** is used rather than a direct object. (Subject complements are also known as predicate nominatives and predicate adjectives.)

Subject	*Verb*	*Complement*
She	is	an architect.
The teacher	seemed	upset.

In the Structure section of TOEFL, it is common for any of these elements or a combination of two or more of these elements to be missing from the stem. The most common problem in structure involves a missing verb. A missing subject and a missing subject-verb combination are common as well. The missing element may also be part of rather than all of the verb or noun phrase.

Sample Items

The art of storytelling _____ almost as old as humanity.

(A) that is
(B) is
(C) it is
(D) being

The correct answer is (B). It supplies the missing verb. Choice (A) is incorrect because the word *that* is used to connect a relative clause to a main clause; in this sentence, there is only one verb, so there can only be one clause. Choice (C) is incorrect because there is an unnecessary repetition of the subject (*The art of storytelling it . . .*). Choice (D) is not correct because an *-ing* form (*being*) cannot be the main verb of a clause.

_____ a few of the sounds produced by insects can be heard by humans.

(A) Only
(B) There are only
(C) That only
(D) With only

The correct answer is (A). It completes the noun phrase that is the subject of the sentence. The expletive *There* in choice (B) is incorrectly used. In choice (C), the word *That* creates a noun clause, but each clause must have its own verb. (*Produced* is used as a participle, not a main verb, in this sentence.) Choice (D) is incorrect because a preposition may not be used directly before the subject.

_____ when lava cools very rapidly.

(A) Because pumice is formed
(B) To form pumice
(C) Pumice is formed
(D) Forming pumice

The correct answer is (C). It supplies an independent clause to join to the adverb clause *when lava cools very rapidly*. Choice (A) consists of an adverb clause; two adverb clauses cannot be joined to form a complete sentence. Choices (B) and (D) are incorrect because they do not contain main verbs, and an independent clause must contain a main verb. (*To form* and *forming* are not main verbs.) Only choice (C) could serve as an independent clause because it contains a subject (*Pumice*) and a full verb; the passive verb *is formed*.

Sample Items (Continued)

Duke Ellington wrote _____ during his career.

(A) that over a thousand songs
(B) over a thousand songs
(C) over a thousand songs were
(D) there were over a thousand songs

The correct answer is (B). The direct object is missing from this sentence. In choice (A), the connecting word *that* is used unnecessarily. In choice (C), the verb *were* is used unnecessarily because there is only one clause and it has a verb (*wrote*). In choice (D), the phrase *there were* is not needed between a verb and its direct object.

Before the invention of the printing press, books _____.

(A) that were very rare
(B) were very rarely
(C) were very rare
(D) as very rare

The correct answer is (C). Choice (A) incorrectly forms an adjective clause; an adjective must be joined to a main clause. Choice (B) contains an adverb; after the verb *to be*, an adjective is required. Choice (D) lacks a verb. Choice (C) correctly supplies a verb (*were*).

CLAUSES WITH *THERE* AND *IT*

Some clauses begin with the introductory words *there* or *it* rather than with the subject of the sentence. These introductory words are sometimes called **expletives**.

The expletive *there* shows that someone or something exists, usually at a particular time or place. These sentences generally follow the pattern *there* + verb *to be* + subject.

There are many skyscrapers in New York City.
There was a good movie on television last night.

The expletive *it* is used in a number of different situations and patterns:

It is important to be punctual for appointments. (with the verb *to be* + adjective + infinitive)
It was in 1959 that Alaska became a state. (with the verb *to be* + adverbial + noun clause)
It takes a long time to learn a language. (with the verb *to take* + time phrase + infinitive)
It was David who did most of the work. (with the verb *to be* + noun + relative clause)

It and *there*, along with the verb and other sentence elements, may be missing from the stem.

Sample Items

In Michigan, _____ over six hundred feet deep.

(A) salt deposits
(B) where salt deposits are
(C) having salt deposits
(D) there are salt deposits

The correct answer is (D). Choice (D) correctly supplies an introductory word (*there*), a verb, and a subject. Choice (A) lacks a verb. Choice (B) contains a subordinator, used to introduce a clause; there is only one verb, however, so there can only be one clause. Choice (C) also lacks a main verb.

_____ a tomato plant from seventy-five to eighty-five days to develop into a mature plant with ripe fruit.

(A) It takes
(B) To take
(C) That takes
(D) By taking

The correct answer is (A). Choice (A) correctly completes the sentence with the introductory word *It* and a verb. Choices (B) and (D) do not supply main verbs. Choice (C) incorrectly creates a noun clause.

EXERCISE 13

Focus: Completing structure problems involving incomplete independent clauses. (Note: Three or four items in this exercise do NOT focus on missing subjects, verbs, complements, or introductory words; these items are marked in the answer key with asterisks.)

Directions: Choose the one option—(A), (B), (C), or (D)—that correctly completes the sentences.

1. In the United States, _____ is generally the responsibility of municipal governments.

   (A) for water treatment
   (B) water treatment
   (C) where water treatment
   (D) in which water treatment

2. Crop rotation _____ of preserving soil fertility.

   (A) it is one method
   (B) one method
   (C) a method is one
   (D) is one method

3. _____ the dollar as its monetary unit in 1878.

   (A) Canada adopted
   (B) Adopted by Canada,
   (C) It was adopted by Canada
   (D) The Canadian adoption of

4. _____ almost impossible to capture the beauty of the aurora borealis in photographs.

   (A) Being
   (B) It is
   (C) There is
   (D) Is

5. _____ two major art museums, the Fogg and the Sadler.

   (A) Harvard University has
   (B) At Harvard University
   (C) Harvard University, with its
   (D) There at Harvard University

6. American actress and director Margaret Webster _____ for her production of Shakespearean plays.

   (A) who became famous
   (B) famous as she became
   (C) becoming famous
   (D) became famous

7. _____ gas tanks connected to welding equipment, one full of oxygen and the other full of acetylene.

   (A) It is two
   (B) Of the two
   (C) There are two
   (D) Two

8. _____ is more interested in rhythm than in melody is apparent from his composi-tions.

   (A) That Philip Glass
   (B) Philip Glass, who
   (C) Philip Glass
   (D) Because Philip Glass

9. _____ by cosmic rays.

   (A) The Earth is constantly bombarded
   (B) Bombarded constantly, the Earth
   (C) Bombarding the Earth constantly
   (D) The Earth's constant bombardment

10. _____ primary colors are red, blue, and yellow.

   (A) There are three
   (B) The three
   (C) Three of them
   (D) That the three

11. _____ who was elected the first woman mayor of Chicago in 1979.

   (A) It was Jane Byrne
   (B) Jane Byrne
   (C) That Jane Byrne
   (D) When Jane Byrne

12. Every computer consists of a number of systems _____ together.

   (A) by working
   (B) work
   (C) they work
   (D) that work

13. On the Moon, _____ air because the Moon's gravitational field is too weak to retain an atmosphere.

   (A) there is no
   (B) where no
   (C) no
   (D) is no

14. The Glass Mountains of northwestern Oklahoma _____ with flecks of gypsum, which shine in the sunlight.

   (A) they are covered
   (B) covered them
   (C) that are covered
   (D) are covered

15. In some cases, _____ to decide if an organism is a plant or an animal.

   (A) difficult if
   (B) it is difficult
   (C) the difficulty
   (D) is difficult

16. The first American novelist to have a major impact on world literature _____.

   (A) who was James Fenimore Cooper
   (B) James Fenimore Cooper was
   (C) it was James Fenimore Cooper
   (D) was James Fenimore Cooper

Lesson 14

ADJECTIVE CLAUSES

As mentioned in the previous lesson, there are three types of dependent clauses, all of which are tested in structure.

Adjective clauses—also called **relative clauses**—are the most commonly tested of the three. You will see one or two items involving adjective clauses on most tests.

Adjective clauses are a way of joining two sentences. In the joined sentence, the adjective clause modifies (describes) a noun (called the **head noun**) in another clause of the sentence. It begins with an **adjective clause marker**.

I wanted the book. The book had already been checked out.
The book *that I wanted* had already been checked out.

The adjective clause in this example begins with the marker *that* and modifies the head noun *book*.

Adjective clause markers are relative pronouns such as *who, that,* or *which* or the relative adverbs *when* or *where*.

Adjective Clause Marker	Use	Example
who	Subject (people)	A neurologist is a doctor *who* specializes in the nervous system.
whom	Object (people)	This is the patient *whom* the doctor treated.
whose	Possessive (people/things)	Mr. Collins is the man *whose* house I rented.
which	Subject/Object (things)	That is a topic *which* interests me. (*which* as subject)
		That is the topic *on which* I will write. (*which* as object of preposition)
that	Subject/Object (people/things)	Art *that* is in public places can be enjoyed by everyone. (*that* as subject)
		The painting *that* Ms. Wallace bought was very expensive. (*that* as object)
where	Adverb (place)	Here is the site *where* the bank plans to build its new headquarters.
when	Adverb (time)	This is the hour *when* the children usually go to bed.

Like all clauses, adjective clauses must have a subject and a verb. In some cases, the adjective-clause marker itself is the subject; in some cases, there is another subject.

The painting was very expensive. Ms. Wallace bought it.
The painting *which Ms. Wallace bought* was very expensive.

The adjective-clause marker in the joined sentence replaces *it,* the object of the verb *bought.* In the joined sentence, the adjective clause keeps the subject—*Ms. Wallace*—that it had in the original sentence.

This is a topic. It interests me.
This is a topic *that interests me.*

The adjective-clause marker in the joined sentence replaces *it,* the subject of the second original sentence. In the joined sentence, the marker itself is the subject of the adjective clause. Notice that the inclusion of the pronoun *it* in the joined sentences above would be an error.

Incorrect:
    *The painting which Ms. Wallace bought *it* was very expensive.
    *This is a topic which *it* interests me.

This type of mistake is sometimes seen in distractors.

When the markers *which*, *that*, and *whom* are used as objects in relative clauses, they can correctly be omitted.

The painting Ms. Wallace bought is very expensive. (*which* omitted)

The adjective-clause markers *which* and *whom* can also be used as objects of prepositions:

That is the topic. I will write on it.
That is the topic *on which I will write*.

You may also see sentences with adjective clauses used in this pattern:

quantity word + *of* + relative clause

He met with two advisers. He had known both of them for years.
He met with two advisers, *both of whom he had known for years*.

I read a number of articles. Most of them were very useful.
I read a number of articles, *most of which were very useful*.

Any part of a relative clause can be missing from the stem of Structure items, but most often, the marker and the subject (if there is one) and the verb are missing. Any word or phrase from another clause—usually the head noun—may also be missing from the stem.

Sample Items

Cable cars are moved by cables _____ underground and are powered by a stationary engine.

(A) they run
(B) that they run
(C) run
(D) that run

The correct answer is (D). Choice (A) is incorrect because the pronoun *they* cannot be used to join two clauses. Choice (B) is not appropriate because the subject *they* is not needed in the adjective clause; the marker *that* serves as the subject of the clause. Choice (C) is incorrect because there is no marker to join the adjective clause to the main clause.

Sample Items (Continued)

The melting point is the temperature _____ a solid changes to a liquid.

(A) which
(B) at which
(C) which at
(D) at

The correct answer is (B). Choice (A) is incorrect because a preposition is needed before the adjective clause. Choice (C) is incorrect because the relative pronoun comes before the preposition. Choice (D) is incorrect because the relative pronoun has been omitted.

There are six types of flamingos, all _____ have long legs, long necks, and beaks that curve sharply downward.

(A) of them
(B) that
(C) of which
(D) they

The correct answer is (C). Choices (A) and (D) do not contain connecting words needed to join clauses. Choice (B) does not follow the correct pattern of relative clauses after a quantity word (*all*). The correct pattern needed to complete this sentence is quantity word + *of* + marker. Only (C) follows this pattern.

EXERCISE 14

Focus: Answering structure problems involving incomplete adjective clauses. (Note: One or two items in this exercise do NOT focus on adjective clauses; these items are marked in the answer key with asterisks.)

Directions: For Sentence Completion items, mark the answer choice—(A), (B), (C), or (D)—that correctly completes the sentence. For Error Identification items, circle the underlined portion of the sentence that would not be considered correct.

1. Most folk songs are ballads _____ have simple words and tell simple stories.

   (A) what
   (B) although
   (C) when
   (D) that

2. After its introduction in 1969, the float process _____ the world's principal method of manufacturing flat sheets of glass.

   (A) by which it became
   (B) it became
   (C) became
   (D) which became

3. Dolphins lack vocal cords but they have a
                  A
   large, oil-filled organ called the "melon"
                  B
   which with they can produce a wide
          C   D
   variety of sounds

4. In 1850, Yale University established Sheffield Scientific School, _____ .

   (A) engineers were educated there
   (B) where engineers were educated
   (C) in which were engineers educated
   (D) where were engineers educated

5. There are thousands of kinds of bacteria,
                      A
   many of whom are beneficial.
    B   C   D

6. The Ringling Brothers were five brothers

which built a small group of performers
<u>A</u>   <u>B</u>
into the world's largest circus.
    <u>C</u>   <u>D</u>

7. Most beans _____ are a form of
kidney bean.

(A) that are cultivated in the United States
(B) their cultivation in the United States
(C) are cultivated in the United States they
(D) they are cultivated in the United States

8. In addition to being a naturalist, Stewart E.
White was a writer _____ the struggle
for survival on the American frontier.

(A) whose novels describe
(B) he describes in his novels
(C) his novels describe
(D) who, describing in his novels

9. Diamonds are often found in rock formations called pipes, _____ the throats of
extinct volcanoes.

(A) in which they resemble
(B) which resemble
(C) there is a resemblance to
(D) they resemble

10. William Samuel Johnson, who helped write
                        <u>A</u>   <u>B</u>
the Constitution, become the first president
                    <u>C</u>   <u>D</u>
of Columbia University in 1787.

11. Seals appear clumsy on the land, _____
are able to move short distances faster than
most people can run.

(A) but they
(B) which they
(C) they
(D) which

12. The Pritzker Prize is given every year to
                              <u>A</u>
architects their work benefits humanity
        <u>B</u>   <u>C</u>
and the environment.
    <u>D</u>

13. The instrument panel of a light airplane has
at least a dozen instruments _____ .

(A) the pilot must watch
(B) what the pilot must watch
(C) which the pilot must watch them
(D) such that the pilot must watch them

14. A keystone species is a species of plants or
animals _____ absence has a major
effect on an ecological system.

(A) that its
(B) its
(C) whose
(D) with its

15. Active stocks are <u>stocks</u> <u>they</u> are <u>frequently</u>
                        <u>A</u>   <u>B</u>   <u>C</u>
bought and sold.
    <u>D</u>

16. Pipettes are glass tubes, open at <u>both ends</u>,
                                    <u>A</u>
which chemists use them to transfer small
<u>B</u>   <u>C</u>
volumes of liquid.
    <u>D</u>

17. The size and shape of a nail depends
primarily on the function _____ intended.

(A) which it is
(B) for which it is
(C) which it is for
(D) for which is

18. Gene Krupa had one of <u>the few big band</u>
                              <u>A</u>   <u>B</u>
that was <u>centered around</u> a drummer.
<u>C</u>   <u>D</u>

19. In geometry, a tangent is a straight line
_____ a curve at only one point.

(A) it touches
(B) whose touching
(C) its touching
(D) that touches

20. There are <u>many species</u> of plants and
            <u>A</u>   <u>B</u>
animals <u>that they</u> are <u>peculiar</u> to Hawaii.
        <u>C</u>   <u>D</u>

Lesson 15

FULL ADVERB CLAUSES

An **adverb clause** consists of a connecting word, called an **adverb clause marker** (or subordinate conjunction), and at least a subject and a verb.

The demand for economical cars increases *when gasoline becomes more expensive.*

In this example, the adverb clause marker *when* joins the adverb clause to the main clause. The adverb clause contains a subject (*gasoline*) and a verb (*becomes*).

An adverb clause can precede the main clause or follow it. When the adverb clause comes first, it is separated from the main clause by a comma.

When gasoline becomes more expensive, the demand for economical cars increases.

The following markers are commonly seen in the Structure section:

Adverb Clause Marker	Use	Example
because	cause	*Because* the speaker was sick, the program was canceled.
since	cause	*Since* credit cards are so convenient, many people use them.
although	opposition (contrary cause)	*Although* he earns a good salary, he never saves any money.
even though	opposition (contrary cause)	*Even though* she was tired, she stayed up late.
while	contrast	Some people arrived in taxis *while* others took the subway.
if	condition	*If* the automobile had not been invented, what would people use for basic transportation?
unless	condition	I won't go *unless* you do.
when	time	Your heart rate increases *when* you exercise.
while	time	Some people like to listen to music *while* they are studying.
as	time	One train was arriving *as* another was departing.
since	time	We haven't seen Professor Hill *since* she returned from her trip.
until	time	Don't put off going to the dentist *until* you have a problem.
once	time	*Once* the dean arrives, the meeting can begin.
before	time	*Before* he left the country, he bought some traveler's checks.
after	time	She will give a short speech *after* she is presented with the award.

In structure items, any part of a full adverb clause—the marker, the subject, the verb, and so on—can be missing from the stem.

CLAUSE MARKERS WITH *-EVER*

Words that end with *-ever* are sometimes used as adverb clause markers. (In some sentences, these words are actually noun-clause markers, but they are seldom used that way in structure items.)

The three *-ever* words that you are likely to see in the Structure section are given in the chart below:

Adverb clause marker with *-ever*	Meaning	Example
wherever	any place that . . .	Put that box *wherever* you can find room for it.
whenever	any time that . . .	They stay at that hotel *whenever* they're in Boston.
however	any way that . . .	*However* you solve the problem, you'll get the same answer.

REDUCED ADVERB CLAUSES

When the subject of the main clause and the subject of the adverb clause are the same person or thing, the adverb clause can be reduced (shortened). Reduced adverb clauses do not contain a main verb or a subject. They consist of a marker and a participle (either a present or a past participle) or a marker and an adjective.

When astronauts are orbiting the Earth, they don't feel the force of gravity. (full adverb clause)
When orbiting the Earth, astronauts don't feel the force of gravity. (reduced clause with present participle)

Although it had been damaged, the machine was still operational. (full adverb clause)
Although damaged, the machine was still operational. (reduced clause with a past participle)
Although he was nervous, he gave a wonderful speech. (full adverb clause)
Although nervous, he gave a wonderful speech. (reduced clause with an adjective)

You will most often see reduced adverb clauses with the markers *although*, *while*, *if*, *when*, *before*, *after*, and *until*. Reduced adverb clauses are NEVER used after *because*.

PREPOSITIONAL PHRASES WITH THE SAME MEANING AS ADVERB CLAUSES

There are also certain prepositions that have essentially the same meaning as adverb-clause markers but are used before noun phrases or pronouns, not with clauses.

Preposition	Related marker	Example
because of	because/since	He chose that university *because of* its fine reputation.
due to	because/since	The accident was *due to* mechanical failure.
on account of	because/since	Visibility is poor today *on account of* air pollution.
in spite of	although/even though	He enjoys motorcycle riding *in spite of* the danger.
despite	although/even though	*Despite* its loss, the team is still in first place.
during	when/while	Her father lived in England *during* the war.

In structure items where the correct answer is an adverb-clause marker, one of these words often appears as a distractor.

Sample Items

No one knows what color dinosaurs were _____ no sample of their skin has survived.

(A) because of
(B) because that
(C) it is because
(D) because

The correct answer is (D). Choice (A) is incorrect; *because of* can only be used before nouns or pronouns. In choice (B), *that* is unnecessary. In choice (C), the phrase *it is* is used unnecessarily.

_____ rises to the surface of the Earth, a volcano is formed.

(A) Liquid magma
(B) Whenever liquid magma
(C) Liquid magma, which
(D) That liquid magma

The correct answer is (B). Choice (A) creates two clauses, but there is no connecting word to join them. Choice (C) creates a sentence with a main clause and an adjective clause, but the main clause has two subjects (*liquid magma* and *a volcano*). Choice (D) creates a noun clause. In a correct sentence, when a noun clause begins a sentence, the clause itself is the subject of the verb in the main clause, but this sentence already has a subject (*volcano*).

_____ invisible to the unaided eye, ultraviolet light can be detected in a number of ways.

(A) Although is
(B) Despite
(C) Even though it
(D) Although

The correct answer is (D). It completes a reduced adverb clause. In choice (A), the adverb clause lacks a subject and is not a correct reduction because it contains a verb. In choice (B), *despite* cannot be used with an adjective (only with a noun phrase or pronoun). Choice (C) does not supply a verb for the adverb clause and is not a correct reduction because it contains a subject.

Because _____, alabaster can be easily carved.

(A) is soft
(B) softness
(C) of its softness
(D) of soft

The correct answer is (C). Choice (A) lacks a subject in the adverb clause. Choice (B), a noun, could only be used with *because of*. In choice (D), *because of* is followed by an adjective; to be correct, it must be followed by a noun phrase or pronoun.

EXERCISE 15

Focus: Completing structure problems involving adverb clauses, reduced adverb clauses, and prepositional expressions. (Note: Two or three items do NOT focus on one of these structures. These items are marked in the answer key with an asterisk.)

Directions: For Sentence Completion items, mark the answer choice—(A), (B), (C), or (D)—that correctly completes the sentence. For Error Identification items, circle the underlined portion of the sentence that would not be considered correct.

1. Small sailboats can easily capsize _____ they are not handled carefully.

   (A) but
   (B) which
   (C) if
   (D) so

2. _____ they are tropical birds, parrots can live in temperate or even cold climates.

   (A) Despite
   (B) Even though
   (C) Nevertheless
   (D) But

3. Despite cats cannot see in complete
       A
   darkness, their eyes are much more
          B   C
   sensitive to light than humans' eyes.
        D

4. _____ added to a liquid, antifreeze lowers the freezing temperature of that liquid.

   (A) That
   (B) As is
   (C) It is
   (D) When

5. Because of cheese is essentially a
       A   B
   concentrated form of milk, it contains
        C
   the same nutrients as milk.
      D

6. In spite of their frightening appearance, the
       A   B   C
   squid is shy and completely harmless.
                    D

7. _____ advertising is so widespread in the United States, it has had an enormous effect on American life.

   (A) Why
   (B) The reason
   (C) On account of
   (D) Since

8. _____ toward shore, its shape is changed by its collision with the shallow sea bottom.

   (A) During a wave rolls
   (B) As a wave rolls
   (C) A wave rolls
   (D) A wave's rolling

9. Snakebirds were not given their name
                        A
   because they eat snakes, but because of
           B   C   D
   their long, slender necks resemble snakes.

10. _____ people are increasingly linked over long distances by electronic communications, but many of them still prefer face-to-face encounters.

    (A) Although
    (B) Despite
    (C) Today
    (D) The fact that

11. _____ together in one place, they form a community.

    (A) When people who live
    (B) When people living
    (C) Whenever people live
    (D) Whenever living people

12. _____ managed by an independent governor and board of directors, the Bank of Canada is owned by the Canadian government.

(A) And yet
(B) In spite of it
(C) Although
(D) It is

13. In the sixteenth century, it was thought
A   B
that a compass needle pointed north
                          C
because some mysterious influence of the
    D
stars.

14. During lava cools exceptionally fast,
A   B
it forms a natural glass called obsidian.
  C   D

15. _____, the seeds of the Kentucky coffee plant are poisonous.

(A) Until they have been cooked
(B) Cooking them
(C) They have been cooked
(D) Cooked until

16. Although Adlai Stevenson was never elected
A   B
president, he was one of the preeminent
American politics of the mid-twentieth
           C
century.
  D

17. Natural silk is still highly prized _____ similar artificial fabrics.

(A) although is available
(B) despite there are available
(C) in spite of the availability of
(D) even though an availability of

18. Cattle ranches are found almost _____ in Utah.

(A) wherever
(B) everywhere
(C) overall
(D) somewhere

19. Since its acute sense of smell, the blood-
A   B   C
hound is often used in tracking.
       D

20. _____ through a prism, a beam of white light breaks into all the colors of the rainbow.

(A) When shines
(B) It shines
(C) It is shone
(D) When shone

Lesson 16

NOUN CLAUSES

Noun clauses are the third type of subordinate clause. They begin with **noun-clause markers**. Noun clauses that are formed from statements begin with the noun-clause marker *that*. Noun clauses formed from *yes/no* questions begin with the noun-clause markers *whether* or *if*. Those formed from information questions begin with *wh-* words: *what*, *where*, *when*, and so on.

Dr. Hopkins' office is in this building. (statement)
I'm sure *that* Dr. Hopkins' office is in this building.
Is Dr. Hopkins' office on this floor? (yes/no question)
I don't know *if* (*whether*) Dr. Hopkins' office is on this floor.
Where is Dr. Hopkins' office? (information question)
Please tell me *where* Dr. Hopkins' office is.

Notice that the word order in direct questions is not the same as it is in noun clauses. The noun clause follows statement word order (subject + verb), not question word order (auxiliary + subject + main verb). Often one of the distractors for noun-clause items will incorrectly follow question word order.

*I don't know what *is her name*. (incorrect use of question word order)
    I don't know what *her name is*. (correct word order)
*She called him to ask what time *did his party start*. (incorrect use of question word order)
    She called him to ask what time *his party started*. (correct word order)

Noun clauses function exactly as nouns do: as subjects, as direct objects, or after the verb *to be*.

When the meeting will be held has not been decided. (noun clause as subject)
The weather announcer said *that there will be thunderstorms*. (noun clause as direct object)
This is *what you need*. (noun clause after *to be*)

Notice that when the noun clause is the subject of a sentence the verb in the main clause does not have a noun or pronoun subject.

In structure items, the noun-clause marker, along with any other part of the noun clause—subject, verb, and so on—may be missing from the stem, or the whole noun clause may be missing.

Sample Items

_____ was caused by breathing impure air was once a common belief.

(A) Malaria
(B) That malaria
(C) Why malaria
(D) Because malaria

The correct answer is (B). Choice (A) is incorrect because there are two verbs (*was caused* and *was*) but only one subject. Choice (C) is incorrect because *Why* is not the appropriate noun-clause marker in this sentence; the noun clause is based on a statement, not on an information question. Choice (D) is incorrect because it forms an adverb clause, but the main clause lacks a subject. In the correct answer the noun clause itself (*That malaria was caused by breathing impure air*) is the subject of the verb *was* in the main clause.

One basic question psychologists have tried to answer is _____ .

(A) people learn
(B) how do people learn
(C) people learn how
(D) how people learn

The correct answer is (D). Choice (A) is incorrect; there is no connector between the first clause and the second. Choice (B) incorrectly follows question word order. Choice (C) is incorrect because *how* is in the wrong position.

EXERCISE 16

Focus: Completing structure problems involving incomplete noun clauses. (Note: Two or three items in this exercise do NOT focus on noun clauses. These items are marked in the answer key with asterisks.)

Directions: For Sentence Completion items, mark the answer choice—(A), (B), (C), or (D)—that correctly completes the sentence. For Error Identification items, circle the underlined portion of the sentence that would not be considered correct.

1. _____ begin their existence as ice crystals over most of the earth seems likely.

(A) Raindrops
(B) If raindrops
(C) What if raindrops
(D) That raindrops

2. Scientists cannot agree on _____ related to other orders of insects.

(A) that fleas are
(B) how fleas are
(C) how are fleas
(D) fleas that are

3. It was in 1875 _____ joined the staff of the astronomical observatory at Harvard University.

(A) that Anna Winlock
(B) Anna Winlock, who
(C) as Anna Winlock
(D) Anna Winlock then

4. A test pilot tries out new kinds of aircraft
   A   B
   to determine if are they safe.
   C   D

5. _____ is a narrow strip of woods along a stream in an open grassland.

(A) Ecologists use the term "gallery forest"
(B) What do ecologists call a "gallery forest"
(C) "Gallery forest" is the term ecologists use
(D) What ecologists call a "gallery forest"

6. _____ developed so rapidly in Alabama primarily because of its rich natural resources.

(A) That heavy industry
(B) Heavy industry
(C) Heavy industry that was
(D) When heavy industry

7. _____ so incredible is that these insects successfully migrate to places that they have never even seen.

(A) That makes the monarch butterflies' migration
(B) The migration of the monarch butterflies is
(C) What makes the monarch butterflies' migration
(D) The migration of the monarch butterflies, which is

8. Art critics do not all agree on what
           _____
                A
are the qualities that make a painting great.
_____   _____   _____
        B   C   D

9. In order to grow vegetables properly, gardeners must know _____.

(A) what the requirements for each vegetable are
(B) that the requirements for each vegetable
(C) what are each vegetable's requirements
(D) that is required by each vegetable

10. Exactly when was the wheel invented is not
          A   _____ _____ ___
                           B   C   D
known.

11. For many years people have wondered _____ exists elsewhere in the universe.

(A) that life
(B) life which
(C) whether life
(D) life as it

12. Although geologists have a clearly under-
                              _____
                                     A   B
standing of why earthquakes occur, they
                              _____
                                   C
cannot reliably predict when they will take
                                 _____
                                       D
place.

Lesson 17

PARALLELISM

In certain structure items, the correct use of **parallel structures** is tested. Parallel structures have the same grammatical form and function. Look at the following sentences:

She spends her leisure time *hiking*, *camping*, and *fishing*.
He *changed* the oil, *checked* the tire pressure, and *filled* the tank with gas.
Nancy plans to either *study* medicine or *major* in biology.
Nancy plans to study either *medicine* or *biology*.

All of the structures in italics are parallel. In the first, three gerunds are parallel; in the second, three main verbs; in the third, two simple forms; and in the fourth, two nouns. Many other structures must be parallel in certain sentences: adjectives, adverbs, infinitives, prepositional phrases, noun clauses, and others.

The most common situation in which parallel structures are required is in a sequence (*A*, *B*, and *C*) as in the first two sentences above. Parallel structures are also required with correlative conjunctions such as *either . . . or* or *not only . . . but also*. (Correlative conjunctions are presented in Lesson 30.)

SENTENCE COMPLETION

Many types of structures may be involved in this type of Sentence Completion item: adjectives, noun phrases, prepositional phrases, clauses, and others.

Sample Item

San Francisco has a pleasant climate, _____ and many fascinating neighborhoods.

(A) exciting scenery,
(B) has exciting scenery
(C) that the scenery is exciting
(D) the scenery is exciting,

The correct answer is (A). This sentence contains a series of three objects after the verb *has*: the first and third are noun phrases (*a pleasant climate* and *many fascinating neighborhoods*). To be parallel, the second object must also be a noun phrase. Choices (B), (C), and (D) are not parallel.

ERROR IDENTIFICATION

Error Identification items involving parallelism usually feature noun phrases, adjectives, verbs, prepositional phrases, gerunds, and infinitives.

Some problems with parallelism are actually word form problems similar to those in Lesson 18.

Sample Items

As a young <u>man</u>, George Washington liked <u>boating</u>, <u>to hunt</u>, and <u>fishing</u>.
$\qquad$ A $\qquad\qquad\qquad\qquad$ B $\quad$ C $\qquad$ D

The correct answer is (C). Choice (C), *to hunt*, is an infinitive, while choice (B), *boating*, and choice (D), *fishing*, are gerunds.

EXERCISE 17.1

Focus: Identifying errors involving parallelism

Directions: If the underlined form is parallel to other forms in the sentence, mark the sentence *C*. If the underlined form is not parallel, mark the sentence *X* and write a correction for the underlined form in the blank at the end of the sentence.

_____ 1. Steel is alloyed with manganese to increase its strength, hardness, and <u>resistance</u> to wear.

_____

_____ 2. The type of plant and animal life living in and around a pond depends on the soil of the pond, <u>what the quality of the water is</u>, and the pond's location.

_____

_____ 3. Philosophers are concerned with questions about nature, <u>human behavior</u>, society, and reality.

_____

_____ 4. When taking part in winter sports, one should wear clothing that is lightweight, <u>warmth</u>, and suitable for the activity.

_____

_____ 5. Folklore consists of the beliefs, customs, traditions, and <u>telling stories</u> that people pass from generation to generation.

_____

_____ 6. Major sources of noise pollution include automobiles and other vehicles, industrial plants, and <u>heavy construction equipment</u>.

_____

_____ 7. Because of their hardness, industrial diamonds can be used for cutting, <u>grind</u>, and drilling.

_____

_____ 8. Scholar John Fiske wrote on history, <u>religious</u>, and social issues.

_____

_____ **9.** Electricity is used to light, <u>hot</u>, and cool buildings.

_____

_____ **10.** ^{T.} S. Eliot was equally distinguished as a poet, <u>he wrote criticism</u>, and a dramatist.

_____

EXERCISE 17.2

Focus: Completing structure problems involving parallelism. (Note: One or two items in the exercise do NOT focus on items involving parallel structures. These items are marked in the answer key with asterisks.)

Directions: For Sentence Completion items, mark the answer choice—(A), (B), (C), or (D)—that correctly completes the sentence. For Error Identification items, circle the underlined portion of the sentence that would not be considered correct.

1. The bellflower is a wildflower that <u>grows</u> <u>in</u>
                              A   B
shady fields, in <u>marshes,</u> and <u>mountain</u>
                    C   D
slopes.

2. Insects provide many beneficial services, such as _____, breaking down dead-wood, and pollinating plants.

  (A) they condition soils
  (B) to condition soil
  (C) conditioning the soil
  (D) soil conditioned

3. Computers are <u>often used</u> to control,
                      A
<u>adjustment,</u> and <u>correct</u> complex <u>industrial</u>
   B   C   D
operations.

4. Eggs may be <u>boiling in the shell</u>, <u>scrambled,</u>
                   A   B
<u>fried</u>, and cooked in countless <u>other</u> ways.
  C   D

5. Frozen orange juice must be packed, _____, and stored when the fruit is ripe.

  (A) be frozen
  (B) must be frozen
  (C) frozen
  (D) it must be frozen

6. In 1900 electrically powered cars were more popular than gasoline powered cars because they were quiet, operated smoothly, and _____ .

  (A) handled easily
  (B) ease of handling
  (C) handling easily
  (D) easy to handle

7. Many places of <u>history</u>, scientific, <u>cultural,</u>
                 A   B
or <u>scenic</u> importance have been designated
    C
<u>national</u> monuments.
    D

8. Roger Williams was a clergyman, _____ the colony of Rhode Island, and an outspoken advocate of religious and political freedom.

  (A) founded
  (B) the founder of
  (C) was the founder of
  (D) he founded

9. <u>Modern</u> motorcycles are <u>lighter</u>, faster,
   A   B
and <u>specialized</u> than <u>motorcycles</u> of 25
     C   D
years ago.

10. Paint can be applied to a surface with rollers, _____, or spray guns.

  (A) brushes
  (B) brushes can be used
  (C) with brushes
  (D) by brush

11. Many people who live near the ocean

    depend on it as a source of food,
    _____
         A   B
    recreation, and to have economic opportu-
    _____   _____
        C   D
    nities.

12. The use of labor-saving devices in homes,
    _____, and in factories added to the
    amount of leisure time people had.

    (A) at office
    (B) used in offices
    (C) offices
    (D) in offices

13. Throughout history, trade routes have
    increased contact between people,
    _____, and greatly affected the growth
    of civilization.

    (A) have resulted in an exchange of ideas
    (B) an exchange of ideas has resulted
    (C) resulted in an exchange of ideas
    (D) resulting in an exchange of ideas

14. Large commercial fishing vessels are

    equipped to clean, packaging, and freeze
    _____   _____   _____
         A   B   C
    the fish that they catch at sea.
    _____
                D

15. As a breed, golden retrievers are intelligent,
    _____   _____
       A   B
    loyally, and friendly dogs.
    _____   _____
       C   D

16. Mathematics can be considered a language,
                                   _____
                                        A
    an art, a science, a tool, or playing a game.
    _____ _____   _____   _____
       B   C   D
    (continuation under A: language; under D: playing a game)

17. Photographers' choice of a camera depends
    on what kind of pictures they want to take,
    how much control they want over expo-
    sure, and _____ they want to spend.

    (A) the amount of money
    (B) what money
    (C) how much money
    (D) so much money that

18. Barbara Jordan was the first woman in the
    South to win an election to the House of
    Representatives, _____ as Congress-
    woman from Texas from 1973 to 1979.

    (A) to serve
    (B) served
    (C) serving
    (D) has served

19. Paper may contain mineral, vegetables, or
                       _____ _____
                          A   B
    man-made fibers.
    _____
           D
    (vegetables underlined B; or... C)

20. R. Buckminster Fuller was a design,
                                 _____
                                    A
    an architect, an inventor, and an engineer.
    _____ _____   _____
          B   C   D

REVIEW TEST D: STRUCTURE

Directions: For Sentence Completion items, select the answer choice—(A), (B), (C), (D)—that correctly completes the sentence. For Error Identification items, select the answer choice—(A), (B), (C), (D)—that corresponds to the underlined portion of the sentence that would not be considered correct.

1. _____ by Anna Baldwin in 1878.

    (A) The invention of the vacuum milking
        machine
    (B) That the vacuum milking machine was
        invented
    (C) The vacuum milking machine, which
        was invented
    (D) The vacuum milking machine was
        invented

2. Dry cleaning is the process _____
    clothes are cleaned in liquids other than
    water.

    (A) by
    (B) which through
    (C) by which
    (D) through

3. Jaguars that resemble leopards but they are
            _____   _____
                   A   B
    larger and are marked with rosettes
                   _____
                      C
    rather than spots.
    _____
          D

4. Job specialization takes place _____ of production is separated into occupations.

   (A) whenever the work is
   (B) when the work
   (C) is when the work
   (D) whenever working

5. Despite most mushrooms are edible, some
   ‾‾‾‾‾A   ‾‾‾‾B
   species cause serious poisoning.
   ‾‾‾‾‾C   ‾‾‾‾‾‾‾D

6. Judges in dog shows rate dogs on
                    ‾‾‾‾‾A
   such points as their colorful, posture,
   ‾‾‾‾‾‾B   ‾‾‾‾‾‾‾C
   shape, and size.
         ‾‾‾‾D

7. _____ are hot is a common misconception.

   (A) All deserts
   (B) All deserts which
   (C) Of all deserts
   (D) That all deserts

8. Medical researchers are constantly looking for ways to control, _____, and cure diseases.

   (A) prevention
   (B) preventing
   (C) prevent
   (D) to prevent

9. _____ pieces of rope are of different thicknesses, the short bend, or weaver's knot, can be used to join them.

   (A) Two of
   (B) What two
   (C) Two such
   (D) If two

10. _____ imaginative stories about the origin of the game of chess.

    (A) Many
    (B) So many
    (C) There are many
    (D) Of the many

11. Storks constantly rearrange their nests to
    ‾‾‾‾‾A   ‾‾‾‾‾B
    keep their eggs safety, dry, and warm.
              ‾‾‾‾‾C   ‾‾‾‾D

12. The Loop, that is the commercial heart of
                ‾‾‾A   ‾‾‾‾‾B
    hicago, is enclosed within a rectangular
    ‾‾‾‾‾C   ‾‾‾‾‾‾D
    loop of elevated train tracks.

13. Judge Francis Hopkinson is probably best known as a signer of the Declaration of Independence, but he also excelled as a poet, _____, and an orator.

    (A) as a musician
    (B) by playing music
    (C) a musician
    (D) he played music

14. _____ relatively inexpensive, the metal pewter can be fashioned into beautiful and useful objects.

    (A) Even it is
    (B) Despite
    (C) Nevertheless, it is
    (D) Although

15. Owls can hunt in total darkness
             ‾‾‾‾A
    because their remarkably keen sense of
    ‾‾‾‾‾‾B   ‾‾‾‾‾‾‾C
    smell.
    ‾‾‾D

16. _____ about four years for a new aircraft model to move from the preliminary design stage to the full production stage.

    (A) It takes
    (B) Taking
    (C) That takes
    (D) To take

17. Nathaniel Hawthorne wrote four novels, _____ *The Scarlet Letter,* became an American literary classic.

    (A) of which one,
    (B) which one
    (C) one of which,
    (D) one was

18. An auger is a tool that a carpenter uses it
    $\qquad\qquad\qquad\qquad\qquad\quad \underset{A}{} \qquad\qquad \underset{B}{}$
    to bore holes in wood.
    $\underset{C}{} \qquad \underset{D}{}$

19. _____ is a general category that
    includes all mental states and activities.

    (A) What do psychologists call cognition
    (B) Psychologists call it cognition
    (C) What psychologists call cognition
    (D) Cognition, as it is called by psychologists, which

20. The medicine of prehistoric people
    $\qquad\qquad\qquad\quad \underset{A}{}$
    probably consisted of a mixture of scientific
    $\qquad\qquad\qquad\qquad\qquad \underset{B}{}$
    practices, superstitious, and religious
    $\qquad\qquad\qquad \underset{C}{}$
    beliefs.
    $\underset{D}{}$

Lesson 18

WORD FORMS

By far the most common type of written expression error involves word forms. As many as eight or nine items per test may be word form problems. Most errors of this type involve using one part of speech in place of another. Both the incorrect word and the correction come from the same root *(rapid* and *rapidly,* for example, or *inform* and *information).* The four parts of speech generally involved are verbs, nouns, adjectives, and adverbs. The most common problems are adjectives in place of adverbs and adverbs in place of adjectives. Nouns in place of adjectives and adjectives in place of nouns are also commonly seen. In some word form problems, different forms of the same form of speech may be involved. For example, a noun that refers to a person *(leader)* may be used in place of the field *(leadership).* A gerund (a verbal noun) may also be used in place of an ordinary noun *(judging* and *judgment,* for example).

Parts of speech can often be identified by their suffixes (word endings).

Common Noun Endings

-tion	information		*-ery*	recovery
-sion	provision		*-ship*	scholarship
-ence	independence		*-tude*	multitude
-ance	acceptance		*-ism*	capitalism
-ity	creativity		*-cracy*	democracy
-hood	childhood		*-logy*	biology
-dom	wisdom		*-ness*	happiness
-th	health		*-ment*	experiment

Endings for nouns that refer to persons

-er	explorer		*-ee*	employee
-or	sailor		*-ic*	comic
-ist	psychologist		*-ian*	technician
-ent	student		*-ant*	attendant

Common Verb Endings

-ize	realize		*-ify*	justify
-en	shorten		*-ate*	incorporate
-er	recover			

Common Adjective Endings

-ate	moderate		*-y*	sunny
-ous	dangerous		*-ic*	economic
-al	normal		*-ical*	logical
-ial	remedial		*-ory*	sensory
-able	comfortable		*-less*	hopeless
-ible	sensible		*-ive*	competitive
-ish	sluggish		*-ly*	friendly
-ant	resistant		*-ful*	colorful

Common Adverb Endings

-ly	quickly		*-ally*	historically

ADJECTIVE/ADVERB ERRORS

The most common type of word form problem involves the use of an adverb in place of an adjective or an adjective in place of an adverb. A few points to keep in mind:

- Adjectives modify nouns, noun phrases, and pronouns.

  - Adjectives often come before nouns.

  an *important* test
  a *quiet* evening
  a *long* letter

  - They often answer the question *What kind?*

  She is a *brilliant* doctor. (What kind of a doctor is she? *A brilliant one.*)

- Adjectives also follow the verb *to be* and other linking verbs.

  The glass was *empty*.
  That song sounds *nice*.
  They look *upset*.

- Adverbs may modify verbs, participles, adjectives, prepositions, adverb clause markers, and other adverbs.

  Ann *eagerly* accepted the challenge. (adverb modifying the main verb *accepted*)
  It was a *rapidly* changing situation. (adverb modifying the present participle *changing*)
  She wore a *brightly* colored scarf. (adverb modifying the past participle *colored*)
  Ted seemed *extremely* curious about that topic. (adverb modifying the adjective *curious*)
  We arrived at the airport *shortly* before our flight left. (adverb modifying the adverb-clause marker *before*)
  We arrived at the airport *shortly* before noon. (adverb modifying the preposition *before*)
  The accident occurred *incredibly* quickly. (adverb modifying the adverb *quickly*)

  - Sometimes adverbs are used at the beginning of sentences, usually followed by a comma. These adverbs sometimes modify the entire sentence rather than one word in the sentence.

  Generally, I like my classes.
  Usually, Professor Ingram's lectures are more interesting.

  - Most adverbs tested in this section are adverbs of manner. They are formed by adding the suffix -*ly* or -*ally* to an adjective.

  quick quickly
  comic comically
  comfortable comfortably
  historic historically

  - Adverbs of manner answer the question *How?*

  She treated her employees *honestly*. (How did she treat her employees? *Honestly.*)

  - A few adverbs (*fast, hard, high*, for example) have the same form as adjectives.

  He bought a *fast* car. (adjective)
  He was driving so *fast* that he got a speeding ticket. (adverb)

  - *Well* is the irregular adverb form of the adjective *good*.

  Juan is an exceptionally *good* student.
  He did very *well* on the last test.

  - Some adjectives also end in -*ly*: *friendly, yearly, costly,* and *lively*, for example.

  That was a *costly* mistake.
  I found Houston a very *friendly* city.

Sample Items

The Black Hills of South Dakota are covered with densely pine forests.
A   B   C   D

The correct answer is (D). An adjective, *dense*, not an adverb is required to modify the noun phrase *pine forests*.

Crows and ravens are members of a family of birds that includes exact 100 species.
                 A   B   C   D

The correct answer is (C). The adverb *exactly* is needed in place of the adjective *exact*.

INCORRECT FORMS OF WORDS CONNECTED WITH CERTAIN FIELDS

This error involves a confusion between the names of fields (*biology*, for example) and the name of a person who practices in that field (*biologist*), or between one of those terms and the adjective that describes the field (*biological*).

Sample Item

First specializing in industrial photography, Margaret Bourke-White later became a famous
       A   B

news photographer and editorial.
    C   D

The correct answer is (D). The adjective *editorial* is used to describe the field of editing. However, a noun referring to a person (*editor*) is needed in this sentence.

OTHER WORD FORM PROBLEMS

There are many other word form problems. Some examples are given here:

Sample Items

Corn played an important role in the cultural of the cliff-dwelling Indians of the Southwest.
               A   B   C   D

The correct answer is (C). The noun *culture*, not the adjective *cultural* is needed.

The galaxy Andromeda is the most distance object visible to observers in the Northern
      A   B   C   D
Hemisphere.

The correct answer is (B). The adjective *distant* is needed in place of the noun *distance*.

Scientists belief that the continents once formed a single continent surrounded by an
            A   B   C
enormous sea.
   D

The correct answer is (A). In this sentence, the verb *believe* is needed in place of the noun *belief*.

Bunsen burners are used to hot materials in a chemistry lab.
                  A   B   C   D

The correct answer is (B). The verb *heat* is needed in place of the adjective *hot*.

A sudden freezing can destroy citrus crops.
A   B   C   D

The correct answer is (B). Rather than the gerund (*-ing*) form, the noun *freeze* is required.

EXERCISE 18.1

Focus: Correctly providing word forms for different parts of speech are commonly confused in written expression problems

Directions: Fill in the lines in the blanks below with the appropriate word forms. In some cases, there may be more than one correct answer. The first one is done as an example.

Verb	Noun	Adjective	Adverb
1. differ	difference	different	differently
2. compete	competence	competent	competently
3. deep	deeperence	deeperent	deeply
4. decision	decision	decisional	decisionate
5. beautify			
6. prohibit	prohibition	prohibi	
7. empatize	empathcy	emphatic	empathic
8.		inconvenient	
9. glorify	glory		
10. mystify			
11. generaly	general	general	
12.		simpl.	simply

EXERCISE 18.2

Focus: Providing word forms related to the names of fields, to adjectives describing those fields, and to people involved in those fields

Directions: Fill in the blanks in the chart below with the appropriate form. The first one is done as an example.

Field	Person	Adjective
1. music	musician	musical
2.	surgeon	
3.		poetic
4.	architect	
5. administration		
6.		financial
7.	photographer	
8. theory		
9.		athletic
10. grammar		
11.	philosopher	
12.	criminal	

EXERCISE 18.3

Focus: Identifying errors and recognizing correct use of adjectives and adverbs
Directions: Underline the form that correctly completes the sentence.

1. In any animal community, herbivores (great/greatly) outnumber carnivores.

2. Floods cause billions of dollars worth of property damage (annual/annually).

3. (Regular/Regularly) airmail service in the United States began in 1918.

4. Writer Ernest Hemingway was known for his (simple/simply) language and his lively dialogue.

5. The tiny coral snake is (beautiful/beautifully) but deadly.

6. (General/Generally), bauxite is found near the surface, so it is relatively (simple/simply) to mine.

7. The colony of New Hampshire was (permanent/permanently) separated from the Massachusetts Bay Colony in 1692.

8. The most numerous and (wide/widely) distributed of all insectivorous animals are the shrews.

9. The endocrine system functions in (close/closely) relationship with the nervous system.

10. A gap in the Coast Range of California provides (easy/easily) access to the San Francisco Bay Area.

11. Mushrooms are found in an (incredible/incredibly) range of sizes, colors, and shapes.

12. Some airplanes have an automatic pilot that is connected to the airplane's controls and (automatic/automatically) keeps the plane on course.

EXERCISE 18.4

Focus: Identifying which parts of speech are appropriate in sentences
Directions: Underline the form that correctly completes the sentence. Then identify the parts of speech of the words in parentheses. You can use these abbreviations for parts of speech:

N = noun	G = gerund (-ing) noun
V = verb	ADJ = adjective
PN = "person" noun	ADV = adverb

The first one is done as an example.

1. Sinclair Lewis' novel *Babbitt* is set in the (fiction/<u>fictional</u>) town of Zenith. (__N__ / __ADJ__)

2. By-products from chicken eggs are used by (industry/industrial) in manufacturing such (produces/products) as soap and paint. (_____/_____) (_____/_____)

3. The daylily is an attractive, (fragrance/fragrant) flower. (_____/_____)

4. An equation is a (mathematics/mathematical) statement that says that two expressions are (equal/equality). (_____/_____) (_____/_____)

5. The Richter scale measures the (severely/severity) of earthquakes. (_____/_____)

6. Justin Winsom promoted the (developing/development) of libraries throughout the United States in the nineteenth century. (_____/_____)

7. Scientists (differ/different) in their opinions of how snow crystals (originate/origin).

   (_____/_____) (_____/_____)

8. Harry Blackstone was a famous (magic/magician). (_____/_____)

9. Glass sponges are found in oceans at a (deep/depth) of 300 feet or more. (_____/_____)

10. Colorado shares with Wyoming the (distinction/distinctly) of having four (perfect/perfectly) straight

    borders. (_____/_____) (_____/_____)

11. Rose Han Lee wrote a number of (scholar/scholarly) accounts about the effects of (immigrant/

    immigration) on mining towns in the western United States. (_____/_____)

    (_____/_____)

12. Most snails venture out to look for (feed/food) only after sunset or on (rain/rainy) days.

    (_____/_____) (_____/_____)

13. Hats may (symbolic/symbolize) social status or (occupation/occupational) as well as being fashion

    items. (_____/_____) (_____/_____)

14. Analgesics are used to (relieve/relief) pain and reduce fever. (_____/_____)

15. A (member/membership) of the Paiute tribe of Nevada, Sarah Winnemuca worked as a guide and

    (interpret/interpreter). (_____/_____) (_____/_____)

16. The Earth's (out/outer) shell is divided into sections called plates, which are (constant/constantly) in

    motion. (_____/_____) (_____/_____)

EXERCISE 18.5

Focus: Identifying errors involving word form problems. (Note: One or two items in this exercise do not focus on word form errors. These are marked in the answer key with an asterisk.)

Directions: Decide which of the four underlined words or phrases —(A), (B), (C), or (D)—would not be considered correct, and write the letter of the expression in the blank at the beginning of the sentence. Then, on the line following the sentence, write the correction for the underlined phrase.

_____ 1. Liberal arts colleges cultivate general intellectually abilities rather than technical or
                             A   B   C
   professional skills.
           D

   _____

_____ 2. Goats are extremely destruction to natural vegetation and are often responsible for soil erosion.
                             A   B   C   D

_____ **3.** Wild plants were of considerable important to early settlers, and many are still used
             A   B   C

medicinally and as foods.
     D

_____ **4.** One important branch of linguistics is semantics, which analysis the meaning of words.
                     A   B   C   D

_____ **5.** Unlike folk dancers, which are the product of a single culture, ballet is an international art form.
                    A   B   C   D

_____ **6.** The strong of a rope is directly proportional to its cross-sectional area.
         A   B   C   D

_____ **7.** Black bears can move rapidly when necessary and are skillful tree-climbers for their size
                         A   B   C

and weigh.
   D

_____ **8.** In an arboretum, trees are cultivated for scientific and educational purpose.
                       A   B   C   D

_____ **9.** In most Western states, the first major industry was mining, which was gradually
                                 A   B

supplemented by ranches.
   C   D

_____ **10.** Peach trees grow good in a variety of soil types, but do best in sandy loam.
              A   B   C   D

_____ **11.** The unit of measuring called the foot was originally based on the length of the human foot.
               A   B   C   D

_____ **12.** Philosopher Theodore A. Langerman was interested in the fields of literary and music.
            A   B   C   D

_____ **13.** A chemical react that absorbs heat is called endothermic.
            A   B   C   D

_____ 14. One characteristic of the poems of Emily Dickinson is the sharp of her images.
                          A   B   C   D

_____ 15. Luther Gulick was a teacher and physician who spent much of his live promoting
                                 A   B   C

physical fitness.
   D

_____ 16. A dog should be checked regularly by a veterinarian to ensure that it remains in good healthy.
                                       A   B   C   D

_____ 17. Southwestern Boston is made up of Hyde Park, West Roxbury, and other pleasant residential
                  A   B   C

neighbors.
  D

_____ 18. Pure nitric acid is colorless, but it acquires a yellow color when it is exposed of air.
      A   B   C   D

_____ 19. Hunting and fishing techniques were highly developed among the North American Indians,
                                          A

particularly in regions where agriculture was less success.
   B   C   D

_____ 20. Science requires the careful collect and organization of data.
       A   B C   D

Lesson 19

Word choice errors involve the incorrect use of one word in place of another. These two words may be related forms (*other* and *another*, for example) or they may be completely different (*do* and *make*, for example).

Descriptions of some of the most common word choice errors are given below:

WRONG CHOICE OF *MAKE* OR *DO*

The verb *to do* is often used in place of *to make*, and *to make* in place of *to do*. In its basic sense, *to make* means to produce, to create, to construct, while *to do* means to perform, to act, to accomplish. These verbs are also used in a number of set expressions:

Common Expressions with *Make*

make advances in	make an investment
make an attempt	make a plan
make a comparison	make a prediction
make a contribution	make a profit
make a decision	make a promise
make a distinction	make an offer
make a forecast	make a suggestion
make a law	make a sound/noise
make a point	

be made of (= be composed of)
make up (= compose)

To make is also used in this pattern: *make* + someone + adjective (The gift *made* her happy.)

Common Expressions with *Do*

do an assignment	do a job (errand, chore)
do business with	do research
do one's duty	do one's work
do someone a favor	

The auxiliary verb *do* is used rather than repeat main verbs: (My computer doesn't operate as fast as theirs *does*.)

Anytime you see the verb *make* or *do* underlined in the Structure section, suspect a word choice error.

Sample Items

Cement is done from varying amounts of limestone, clay, and gypsum.
      A   B   C   D

The correct answer is (A). The verb *done* is incorrect in this sentence. The correct word choice is *made*.

Small town newspapers often urge readers to make business with local merchants.
            A   B   C   D

The correct answer is (C). The phrase should read *do business with*.

WRONG CHOICE OF *SO, SUCH, TOO,* AND *AS*

The words *so, such,* and *too* are used in the following patterns:

so + adjective + *that* clause
>   These boxes are *so* heavy that we can't lift them.

(*So* is also used with *many . . . that* and *much . . . that.*)
>   There were *so* many people in the auditorium that we could barely get in the front door.

such + adjective + noun + *that* clause
>   It was *such* a pretty view that he took a photograph.

too + adjective + infinitive
>   It's *too* cold to go swimming today.

Notice that *so* and *such* are both followed by *that* clauses, but *too* is followed by an infinitive.

The words *as* and *so* are also sometimes confused:

>   Jane did *so* well as I did on the economics exam. (INCORRECT)
>   The coffee was *as* hot that I couldn't drink it. (INCORRECT)

In the first sentence, the word *as* should be used in place of *so*; in the second, *so* should be used in place of *as*.

Also look for *so much* or *too much* used in place of *so* or *too*.

Sample Items

>   The sun is so bright to look at directly.
> $\overline{\text{A}}$ $\quad$ $\overline{\text{B}}$ $\quad$ $\overline{\text{C}}$ $\overline{\text{D}}$

The correct answer is (B). The correct pattern *too* + adjective + infinitive.

>   In much of Alaska, the growing season is as short that crops can't be raised.
> $\overline{\text{A}}$ $\quad$ $\overline{\text{B}}$ $\quad$ $\overline{\text{C}}$ $\quad$ $\overline{\text{D}}$

The correct answer is (C). The correct pattern is *so* + adjective + *that* clause.

>   The giant squid is so an elusive animal that at one time it was believed to be purely mythical.
> $\overline{\text{A}}$ $\quad$ $\overline{\text{B}}$ $\quad$ $\overline{\text{C}}$ $\quad$ $\overline{\text{D}}$

The correct answer is (A). Before an adjective + noun + *that* clause, the word *such* should be used.

>   The mineral grains in basalt are so much small that they cannot be seen with the unaided eye.
> $\overline{\text{A}}$ $\quad$ $\overline{\text{B}}$ $\quad$ $\overline{\text{C}}$ $\quad$ $\overline{\text{D}}$

The correct answer is (B). The phrase should read *so small* rather than *so much small*.

WRONG CHOICE OF *ANOTHER* OR *OTHER*

	Another	Other
Used as an adjective	*another* + singular noun (Have *another* sandwich.)	*other* + plural noun (I wonder if there is life on *other* planets.) determiner + *other* + noun (There may be life on some *other* planets.)
Used as a pronoun	*another* (Thanks. I'll have *another*.)	determiner + *other* ("I have one book." "I have the *other*.")

Another means "one more, an additional one." It can be used as an adjective before a singular noun or alone as a pronoun.

He needs *another* piece of paper.
I have one class in that building and *another* in the building across the quadrangle.

Other is used as an adjective before a plural noun. It is also used as an adjective before a singular noun when preceded by a determiner such as *the*, *some*, *any*, *one*, *no*, and so on. It can also be used alone as a pronoun when preceded by a determiner.

There are *other* matters I'd like to discuss with you.
One of the books was a novel; the *other* was a collection of essays.
There's no *other* place I'd rather visit.

Sample Items

Willa Cather is known for *My Antonia* and another novels of the American frontier.
      A   B   C   D

The correct answer is (B). Before a plural noun, *other* must be used.

An understudy is an actor who can substitute for other actor in case of an emergency.
A   B   C   D

The correct answer is (C). *Other* is used incorrectly in place of *another* before a singular noun.

WRONG CHOICE OF *BECAUSE* OR *BECAUSE OF;* *IN SPITE OF/DESPITE* OR *ALTHOUGH;* *DURING* OR *WHEN/WHILE*

Certain expressions, such as *because*, are adverb clause markers and are used only before clauses. Other expressions, such as *because of*, are prepositions and are used before noun phrases or pronouns.

Adverb-clause Markers (Used with clauses)	Prepositions (Used with noun phrases)
because	because of
although	despite
	in spite of
when	
while	during

Sample Items

Because migration to the suburbs, the population of many large American cities declined
‾‾‾‾‾‾‾‾‾‾A‾‾‾‾‾‾‾‾‾‾ ‾‾‾‾‾‾‾‾‾‾B‾‾‾‾‾‾‾‾ ‾‾‾C‾‾‾ ‾‾‾‾‾‾‾‾D‾‾‾‾‾‾‾
between 1950 and 1960.

The correct answer is (A). efore a noun phrase (*migration*), the preposition *because of* must be used.

Despite most people consider the tomato a vegetable, botanists classify it as a fruit.
‾‾A‾‾ ‾‾‾‾‾‾‾B‾‾‾‾‾‾‾ ‾‾‾C‾‾‾ ‾‾‾D‾‾‾

The correct answer is (A). Before a full clause (*most people consider the tomato a vegetable*), the adverb marker *although* must be used.

WRONG CHOICE OF *MUCH* OR *MANY* AND SIMILAR EXPRESSIONS

Certain expressions can only be used in phrases with plural nouns; others can be used in expressions only with uncountable nouns.

Used with plural nouns	Used with uncountable nouns
many	much
few, a few	little, a little
fewer, the fewest	less, the least
number	amount

Sample Items

Pearls are found in <u>much</u> colors, including cream, blue, lavender, and black.
        A   B   C   D

The correct answer is (B). Many must be used with a plural noun (*colors*).

Even <u>during</u> economic booms, there is a small <u>number</u> of <u>unemployment</u>.
    A   B   C   D

The correct answer is (C). The word *amount* must be used to refer to an uncountable noun such as *unemployment*.

OTHER WORD FORM PROBLEMS

Other pairs of words are sometimes confused in written expression, including those listed below. (NOTE: If one of the words appears in *italics*, that word is generally used incorrectly in Structure sentences; the other word is the correction for the error.) All of the starred sentences are examples of errors and are INCORRECT.

no   Used as an adjective before nouns; means "not any"; also used in the expression *no longer*
not   Used to make all other words negatives

               * *Not* gasoline was left in the tank.
               * This is *no* the station I usually listen to.
               * I *not* longer listen to that station.

most   Used in superlative adjective phrases; also used to mean "the majority"
almost   Used as an adverb to mean "nearly"

               * This is the *almost* interesting chapter in the book.
               * I've read *almost* of the chapters in the book.
               * I've solved *most* all of the problems in the book.

twice   Used as an adjective to mean "two times"
double   Used as an adjective to mean "make twice as large"

               * Henry has *double* as much money as he did before he invested it.
               * Henry *twice* his money.

earliest   Used as a superlative adjective to mean "most distant in time"
soonest   Used as a superlative adverb to mean "most promptly"

               * These are the *soonest* examples of the artist's works.

(You will probably not see *earliest* used incorrectly in place of *soonest*.)

percent   Used after a number
percentage Not used after a number

               * Fifty *percentage* of the people voted in favor of the initiative.
               * The *percent* of people who approve of the initiative has been steadily growing.

after   Used as a preposition before a noun or as an adverb-clause marker before a clause
afterward   Used as an adverb, means "after that"

               * We'll go to dinner *afterward* the play.
               * We'll go to dinner *afterward* the play is over.
               * First the performer played the guitar and *after* she played the flute.

ago	Used to talk about a time earlier than the present
before	Used to talk about a time earlier than some other point in time

      * Harold won a gold medal in the Olympics last year, and four years *ago* that, he won a silver medal.

(You will probably not see *before* used incorrectly in place of *ago*.)

tell	Used with an object; also used in certain set expressions: *tell a story*, *tell the truth*, *tell a secret*
say	Used without an object

      *Mr. Hunter *said* us that he'd had a good trip.
      *Joe *said* a wonderful story.
      *Mr. Hunter *told* that he'd had a good trip.

ever	Means "at any time"; used with *not* to mean "never"; also used in some set expressions such as *ever since* and *hardly ever*
never	Means "at no time"; not used with a negative word

      *He hardly *never* goes to that club.

(You will probably not see *ever* used incorrectly in place of *never*.)

alive	Used after a verb
live	Used before a noun

      * Sue likes to have *alive* plants in her apartment.
      * Although she forgot to water it for a week, the plant was still *live*.

around	Used as a preposition to mean "in a circular path"
round	Used as an adjective to mean "circular in shape"

      * The new office building will be an *around* glass tower.

(You will probably not see *round* used incorrectly in place of *around*.)

age	Used as a noun, often in these patterns: at the age of 21, 21 years of age
old	Used as an adjective, often in this pattern: 21 years old

      * Harriet will be thirty years *age* next week.
      * Operators of motor vehicles must be thirty years of *old* in this state.

near	Used as an adjective; means "close to"
nearly	Used as an adverb; means "almost"

      * Lynn is looking for an apartment *nearly* the Medical Center.
      * The two-bedroom apartment she looked at cost *near* a thousand dollars a month.

some	Used as a determiner before a noun to mean "an indefinite amount"
somewhat	Used as an adverb to mean "slightly"

      * This bicycle is *some* more expensive that the one I looked at yesterday.

(You will probably not see *somewhat* used incorrectly in place of *some*.)

    NOTE: The distinctions between words such as *desert* and *dessert*, *stationary* and *stationery*, *capital* and *capitol*, which are really spelling problems, are NOT tested on TOEFL. (One reason is that native-speakers of English often make mistakes with these words!)

EXERCISE 19.1

Focus: Correctly choosing between *do* and *make*
Directions: Underline the word that correctly completes each sentence below.

1. The tips of high-speed dental drills are (done/made) of tungsten steel and often contain diamonds.

2. A cottage industry is a form of manufacturing (done/made) at home.

3. Margaret Mead (did/made) fundamental contributions to both the theory and fieldwork of anthropology.

4. Many universities receive grants to (do/make) research for the federal government.

5. Research in genetics in the early nineteenth century (did/made) much to improve agriculture.

6. Futurologists study current trends to (do/make) predictions about the future.

7. Filmmaker George Lucas has (done/made) many advances in the production of motion pictures, especially in the use of special effects.

8. The distinction between wildflowers and weeds is one that is often difficult to (do/make).

EXERCISE 19.2

Focus: Correctly choosing between *so, such, too,* and *as*
Directions: Underline the word that correctly completes each sentence below.

1. The mineral talc is (so/such) soft that it can be scratched with a fingernail.

2. Oceanographers use robots and unmanned submarines to explore parts of the ocean that are (so/too) deep for people to explore safely.

3. (So/As) much paper money was printed during the Revolutionary War that it became almost worthless.

4. The walking stick is an insect with (so/such a) close resemblance to a twig that it escapes the notice of its enemies.

5. At present, solar cells are (so/too) expensive and inefficient to be used in the commercial generation of electricity.

6. Acrylic plastics are very hard and are (so/as) clear as glass.

7. Founded in 1682, Norfolk developed (so/such a) prosperous sea trade that it quickly became the largest town in the colony of Virginia.

8. Continental islands are (so/so much) close to continents that their plant and animal life are identical to life on the mainland.

EXERCISE 19.3

Focus: Correctly choosing between *other* and *another*
Directions: Underline the word that correctly completes each sentence below.

1. Lightning is a rush of electrical current from a cloud to the ground or from one cloud to (another/ other).

2. A ballet dancer's techniques and skills are very different from those of (another/other) dancers.

3. The commercial center of New York City, the island of Manhattan is joined to the (another/other) boroughs by bridges and tunnels.

4. The legal surrender of a criminal suspect from one state or country to (another/other) is called extradition.

5. Life expectancy for both males and females is higher in Hawaii than it is in any (another/other) state.

6. Rocky Mountain spotted fever is one type of disease that is carried by ticks, and Colorado tick fever is (another/other).

7. The art of photography has often been influenced by—and has influenced—(another/other) fine arts.

8. (Another/Other) than the cheetah, all cats have retractable claws.

9. Few (another/other) Supreme Court justices have had as much impact on American law as William O. Douglas did during his thirty-six years on the bench.

EXERCISE 19.4

Focus: Correctly choosing between *much* or *many* and similar words
Directions: Underline the words that correctly complete each sentence below.

1. (Many/Much) industrial products can be made from soybeans.

2. Desert plants compete fiercely for the (few/little) available water.

3. The American designer Louis Comfort Tiffany took (many/much) of his inspiration from nature.

4. A (few/little) simple precautions can prevent accidents at home and on the job.

5. In a formal debate, the same (number/amount) of persons speak for each team, and both teams are granted an equal (number/amount) of time in which to make their arguments.

6. Bats do (few/little) damage to people, livestock, or crops.

7. Even small (numbers/amounts) of zinc can have a significant effect on the growth of plants.

8. The adrenal glands, one on top of each kidney, secrete (many/much) important hormones.

EXERCISE 19.5

Focus: Correctly choosing between other commonly confused words
Directions: Underline the words that correctly complete each sentence below.

1. In 1941, nylon was first used to make stockings, and the year (ago/before), it was first used to make toothbrush bristles.

2. The Missouri River is about (double/twice) as long as the Colorado River.

3. Catherine Esther Beacher established schools in Connecticut and Ohio, and (after/afterward) founded the American Women's Educational Association.

4. (Most/Almost) antibiotics are antibacterial agents, but some are effective against fungal, protozoal, or yeast infections.

5. At eight weeks of (age/old), red foxes begin to get their adult markings.

6. Chuck Berry was one of the (soonest/earliest) and most influential performers of rock music.

7. Long before Columbus, various thinkers believed that the Earth was (around/round).

8. Apricots, (some/somewhat) smaller than peaches, are known for their delicate taste.

9. Huge radio telescopes aimed into space may someday (say/tell) us whether intelligent life exists elsewhere in the universe.

10. Except for humans and apes, all mammals can produce vitamin C in their livers, so they (ever/never) suffer from a lack of it.

11. One of Canada's most beautiful botanical gardens is Butchart Gardens (near/nearly) Victoria, British Columbia.

12. When the Hopi Indians perform the Snake Dance, the dancers handle (alive/live) rattlesnakes.

13. Around 85 (percentage/percent) of the bauxite produced in the United States is mined in Arkansas.

14. Artist Clementine Hunter continued to paint until she was more than 100 years (age/old).

15. The period immediately (after/afterward) the Civil War is known as Reconstruction.

16. The (most/almost) familiar type of pump in use today is the piston pump.

EXERCISE 19.6

Focus: Identifying a variety of word choice errors. (Note: One or two items in this exercise do not focus on word choice errors. These are marked in the answer key with an asterisk.)

Directions: Decide which of the four underlined words or phrases—(A), (B), (C), or (D)—would not be considered correct, and write the letter of the expression in the blank.

_____ 1. One should <u>never</u> <u>throw</u> water on an <u>alive</u> <u>electrical</u> fire.
                A   B   C   D

_____ 2. The University of Chicago is <u>unlike</u> <u>most other</u> U.S. universities in that it has emphasized
                                        A   B
        graduate student programs <u>so much</u> as undergraduate programs <u>ever since</u> it opened.
                           C   D

_____ 3. The mass <u>production</u> of paper bags cut costs <u>so much</u> that a bag <u>soon</u> became a routine part
                       A   B   C
        of <u>near</u> every purchase.
          D

_____ 4. A person <u>must be</u> at least thirty <u>years</u> <u>age</u> in order to <u>serve</u> as a U.S. senator.
                    A   B   C   D

_____ 5. No other state receives <u>as</u> <u>few</u> rainfall <u>as</u> the state <u>of</u> Nevada.
                            A B   C   D

_____ 6. Because of refraction, the water in a tank <u>ever</u> looks <u>as deep</u> as it <u>actually</u> is.
                  A   B   C   D

_____ 7. The *lei*, which is <u>made of</u> flowers, shells, and <u>other</u> materials, is presented to visitors <u>as a</u>
                         A   B   C
        <u>symbolize</u> of Hawaiian hospitality.
        D

_____ 8. The botanists Katherine Hunter and Emily Fose <u>spent</u> <u>many</u> difficult months <u>making</u> research
                                      A   B   C
        <u>in the</u> Rocky Mountains.
        D

_____ 9. Oysters are <u>today</u> grown and harvested <u>much</u> <u>like</u> any <u>another</u> crop.
                      A   B C   D

Lesson 20

VERBS

Whenever the verb is underlined in a Structure problem, you should check for the common verb errors outlined in this lesson:

ERRORS IN SUBJECT/VERB AGREEMENT

If a subject is singular, the verb must be singular. If the subject is plural, the verb must be plural. Most problems involving subject-verb agreement on TOEFL are simple, but a few are tricky.

Sample Items

Minerals in seawater exists in the same proportions in all of the oceans of the world.
  A   B   C   D

The correct answer is (B). The plural subject *minerals* requires a plural verb, *exist*. You might have found this question tricky because the singular noun *seawater* comes between the subject and the verb, and you may have mistaken that word for the true subject.

Bowling, one of the most popular indoor sports, are popular all over the United States and in
  A   B   C
other countries.
D

The correct answer is (C). The subject of the sentence is *bowling*, not *sports*. The singular verb form *is* should therefore be used.

There are some special rules about subject-verb agreement that you should be familiar with:

- A sentence with two subjects joined by *and* takes a plural verb.

    The chemistry lab and the physics lab *are* . . .

- Some words end in *-s* but are singular in form. Many of these words are the names of fields of study (*economics, physics,* and so on). *News* is another word of this kind.

    Economics *is* . . .
    The news *was* . . .

- Irregular plurals (*children, feet, mice,* and so on) do not end in *-s* but take plural verbs.

    The women *were* . . .
    His feet *are* . . .

- When a clause begins with the expletive *there*, the verb may be singular or plural, depending on the grammatical subject.

    There *was* a loud noise . . .
    There *were* a few problems . . .

- Subjects with *each* and *every* take singular verbs. (This includes compound words like *everyone* and *everything*.)

> Each state *has* . . .
> Each of the representatives *was* . . .
> Every person *was* . . .
> Everyone *wants* . . .

- The verb in relative clauses depends on the noun that the relative pronoun refers to.

> The house that *was* built . . .
> The students who *were* selected . . .

- The phrase *the number of* + plural noun takes a singular verb. The phrase *a number of* + plural noun takes a plural verb.

> The number of trees *is* . . .
> A number of important matters *have* . . .

- Singular subjects used with phrases such as *along with*, *accompanied by*, *together with*, *as well as*, and *in addition to* take singular verbs.

> The mayor, along with the city council, *is* . . .
> Together with his friends, Mark *has* . . .

- Quantities of time, money, distance, and so on usually take a singular verb.

> Five hundred dollars *was* . . .
> Two years *has* . . .
> Ten miles *is* . . .

ERRORS INVOLVING TENSE

Most tense errors involve the simple present tense, the simple past tense, and the present perfect tense.

- The simple present tense is a general-time tense. It usually indicates that a condition is always true or that an action always occurs. It may also indicate that an action regularly occurs.

> The atmosphere *surrounds* the Earth.
> Dana often *stays* at this hotel.
> Generally, the lectures in this class *are* very interesting.

- The simple past tense indicates that an action took place at a specific time in the past.

> They *moved* to Phoenix five years ago.
> This house *was built* in the 1920s.
> Dinosaurs *lived* millions of years ago.

- The present perfect tense usually indicates that an action began at some time in the past and continues to the present. It may also indicate that an action took place at an unspecified time in the past.

> Mr. Graham *has worked* for this company since 1990.
> She *hasn't been* to a doctor for a year.
> Jennifer *has* recently *returned* from Europe.

Sample Items

> The <u>most important</u> period of physical <u>growth</u> in humans <u>occurred</u> during <u>their</u> first two years.
>   A   B   C   D

The correct answer is (C). The simple present tense, not the past tense, should be used because the situation described in this sentence always occurs.

> <u>Personal</u> taxes for Americans <u>rose</u> <u>sharply</u> <u>since</u> 1945.
>   A   B   C   D

The correct answer is (C). The time phrase *since 1945* means *from 1945 until now.* Therefore, the present perfect (*have risen*) is required in place of the past tense.

INCORRECT VERB FORMS

Some of the verb errors are errors in form. Most verb form problems involve main verb forms: An *-ing* form may be used in place of a past participle, a past participle in place of a past tense form, a simple form in place of an *-ing* form, an infinitive in place of a simple form, and so on. Some involve irregular verbs that have different forms for the past tense and the past participle—*took* and *taken*—for example. The following information may help you chose the correct form of the main verb.

- The simple form follows all modal auxiliaries.

might be	can remember	should study
must know	could go	may follow

  (Certain similar auxiliary verbs require infinitives.)

ought to attend	used to play	have to hurry

- The past participle is used after a form of *have* in all perfect forms of the verb.

has done	had called	should have said
have run	will have read	could have made

- The *-ing* form is used after a form of *be* in all progressive forms of the verb.

is sleeping	has been writing	should have been wearing
was working	had been painting	will be waiting

- The past participle is used after a form of *be* in all passive forms of the verb.

is worn	has been shown	would have been lost
is being considered	had been promised	might have been canceled
were told	will have been missed	

Verb form problems may also involve auxiliary verbs: *has* may be used in place of *did, is* in place of *does,* and so on.

Sample Item

The first bicycle race on record in the United States <u>taken place</u> in 1883.
     A   B   C   D

The correct answer is (C). The correct verb is the past tense form (*took*), not a past participle.

The Michigan Dunes, <u>located</u> on Lake Michigan's eastern shore, <u>may</u> <u>to reach</u> a <u>height</u> of 200 feet.
                 A   B   C   D

The correct answer is (C). After a modal auxiliary, the simple form of the verb (*reach*) should be used in place of the full infinitive (*to reach*).

Dextrose does not <u>taste</u> as <u>sweet</u> as table sugar <u>is</u>.
      A   B C   D

The correct answer is (D). The correct auxiliary verb in this sentence is *does*, not *is*. The auxiliary *does* replaces the present tense verb *tastes*.

EXERCISE 20.1

Focus: Structure problems involving subject-verb agreement

Directions: Underline the form that correctly completes each sentence. Then circle the subject with which the underlined verb agrees. The first one is done as an example.

1. Ethics (is/are) the study of moral duties, principles, and values.

2. The first bridge to be built with electric lights (was/were) the Brooklyn Bridge.

3. There (is/are) two types of calculus, differential and integral.

4. George Gershwin, together with his brother Ira, (was/were) the creator of the first musical comedy to win a Pulitzer Prize.

5. In a chess game, the player with the white pieces always (moves/move) first.

6. The Earth and Pluto (is/are) the only two planets believed to have a single moon.

7. A number of special conditions (is/are) necessary for the formation of a geyser.

8. Each of the Ice Ages (was/were) more than a million years long.

9. The battery, along with the alternator and starter, (makes/make) up the electrical system of a car.

10. Teeth (is/are) covered with a hard substance called enamel.

11. The more-or-less rhythmic succession of economic booms and busts (is/are) referred to as the business cycle.

12. The number of protons in the nucleus of an atom (varies/vary) from element to element.

EXERCISE 20.2

Focus: Recognizing and correcting errors in verb tense and form
Directions: If the underlined form is correct, mark the sentence *C*. If the underlined form is incorrect, mark the sentence *X*, and write a correction for the underlined form in the blank following the sentence.

_____ 1. Coal, grain, steel, and other products are often <u>shipping</u> by barge on inland waterways.

_____

_____ 2. The first cotton mill in Massachusetts <u>has built</u> in the town of Beverly in 1787.

_____

_____ 3. Physician Alice Hamilton <u>is known</u> for her research on industrial diseases.

_____

_____ 4. When scientists search a site for fossils, they begin by examining places where the soil has <u>wore</u> away from the rock.

_____

_____ 5. The popularity of recreational vehicles <u>has been grown</u> over the last few decades.

_____

_____ 6. Experts have estimated that termites cause as much property damage every year as fire <u>has</u>.

_____

_____ 7. In music, a chord is the sound of two or more notes that <u>are playing</u> together.

_____

_____ 8. The white pine <u>is</u> the most commercially important forest tree in North America until the beginning of the twentieth century.

_____

_____ 9. In 1846, the Swiss naturalist Louis Agassiz <u>come</u> to the United States to give a series of lectures.

_____

_____ 10. Parrots and crows <u>are considered</u> the most intelligent birds.

_____

_____ 11. The first experimental telegraph line in the United States <u>run</u> from Baltimore to Washington, D.C., a distance of forty miles.

_____

_____ 12. Portable fire extinguishers generally <u>containing</u> liquid carbon dioxide.

_____

_____ 13. The first seven American astronauts <u>were chose</u> in 1959.

_____

EXERCISE 20.3

Focus: Structure problems involving verbs. (Note: Several items in this exercise do not focus on verbs. These sentences are marked in the answer key with asterisks.)

Directions: For Sentence Completion items, mark the answer choice that correctly completes the sentence. For Error Identification items, decide which of the four underlined words or phrases—(A), (B), (C), or (D)—would *not* be considered correct, and circle that letter.

1. Medical students must to study both the
   A   B
   theory and practice of medicine.
   C   D

2. R. M. Bartlett of Philadelphia _____ the first private business college in the United States in 1843.

   (A) founding
   (B) founded
   (C) was founded
   (D) has founded

3. The seal, like the sea lion and the walrus, is
        A   B
   a descendant of ancestors that once live on
        C   D
   the land. _____

4. In 1989 the space probe Voyager 2 _____ by the planet Neptune.

   (A) fly
   (B) having flown
   (C) flying
   (D) flew

5. The top layer of the ocean stores as much
              A   B
   heat as does gases in the atmosphere.
   C   D

6. A cupful of stagnant water may _____ millions of microorganisms.

   (A) contains
   (B) to contain
   (C) contain
   (D) containing

7. Sarah Knight _____ a fascinating account of a journey she made from Boston to New York in 1704.

   (A) written
   (B) writes
   (C) wrote
   (D) writing

8. Every one of the body's billions of cells
                               A
   require a constant supply of food and
   B   C   D
   oxygen.

9. In Colonial times, flax and wool required
   A   B
   months of preparation before they could be
                                      C
   dyed and spin into cloth.
            D

10. Although some people find bats terrifying,
                            A
    they are actually beneficial because they ate
    B   C   D
    harmful insects.

11. All animals _____ on other animals or plants.

    (A) feed
    (B) feeds
    (C) fed
    (D) feeding

12. Chromium _____ in the manufacture of stainless steel.

    (A) using
    (B) is used
    (C) uses
    (D) is using

13. Each of the four types of human tooth
                                      A   B
    are suited for a specific purpose.
    C   D

14. The Masters, one of the most important of all golf tournaments, _____ every year in Augusta, Georgia since 1934.

    (A) has held
    (B) held
    (C) is held
    (D) has been held

15. Porous rocks such as chalk and sandstone allow water_____ through them.

    (A) soaks
    (B) is soaked
    (C) to soak
    (D) can soak

16. Electric <u>milking</u> machines <u>have made</u> dairy
           A   B
<u>farming</u> a much easier job than it once <u>did</u>.
 C   D

17. Playwright Frank Shin <u>has often</u> <u>describes</u>
                  A   B
<u>the lives</u> of Chinese Americans in his
  C
dramas.
 D

18. Weavers are social birds that _____ complex nests housing hundreds of families.

    (A) build
    (B) are built
    (C) are building
    (D) built

19. Cans of paint must be <u>shaking</u> to <u>mix</u> the
                          A   B
pigments with the medium <u>in which</u> they
                            C
<u>are suspended</u>.
   D

20. The American dancer Maria Tallchief first _____ prominent in Europe.

    (A) to become
    (B) become
    (C) has become
    (D) became

Lesson 21

PARTICIPLES

Participles are verbal adjectives. Two kinds of participles are tested: present participles and past participles. The present participle always ends in *-ing*. The past participle of regular verbs ends in *-ed*, but many verbs have irregular past participles.

Participles are tested in both types of Structure problems.

SENTENCE COMPLETION

Sentence Completion items usually test the use of **participial phrases** (a participle and related words) after nouns. Participial phrases used this way are actually **reduced** (shortened) **adjective clauses.** Present participles are used to reduce adjective clauses that contain active verbs.

> Minnesota, *which joined the Union in 1858,* became the thirty-second state.
>   (full adjective clause with active verb)
> Minnesota, *joining the Union in 1858,* became the thirty-second state.
>   (participial phrase with a present participle)

Past participles are used to reduce adjective clauses with passive verbs.

> The College of William and Mary, *which was founded in 1693,* is the second oldest college in the United States.
>   (full adjective clause with a passive verb)
> The College of William and Mary, *founded in 1693,* is the second oldest college in the United States.
>   (participial phrase with a past participle)

Participial phrases can also come before the subject of a sentence.

> *Joining the Union in 1858,* Minnesota became the thirty-second state.
> *Founded in 1693,* the College of William and Mary is the second oldest college in the United States.

Usually, the participle itself is missing from this type of Structure item, but any part of a participial phrase as well as parts of a main clause may be missing.

Sample Item

Natural resources provide the raw materials _____ to produce finished goods.

(A) needed
(B) are needed
(C) which need
(D) needing

The correct answer is (A). Choice (B) is a passive verb; the sentence cannot contain two main verbs (*are needed* and *provide*) in the same clause. Choice (C) creates an adjective clause, but the verb in the clause is active and a passive verb is needed. (However, a relative clause with a passive verb (*which are needed*) would be a correct answer. Choice (D) is a present participle and has an active meaning; a past participle is needed.

ERROR IDENTIFICATION

Error Identification items most often test participles used before nouns as one-word adjectives. When used before a noun, present participles have an active meaning; past participles have a passive meaning.

It was an *exhausting* ten-kilometer race. (present participle)
The *exhausted* runners were too tired to move after the race. (past participle)

In the first sentence, the race exhausts the runners. The race "performs" the action. In the second sentence, the runners are exhausted by the race. They receive the action.

Error Identification items may also test the use of participles in phrases after nouns as reduced (shortened) relative clauses. Again, present participles imply an active idea, past participles a passive one.

The man *stealing* the money was arrested. (present participle; means "who stole")
The money *stolen* from the bank was recovered. (past participle; means "which was stolen")

In Error Identification items, you may see past participles used incorrectly for present participles or present participles used incorrectly for past participles.

You may also see a main verb used when a participle is required.

EXERCISE 21.1

Focus: Identifying errors and correct forms of participles
Directions: Underline the form that best completes each sentence.

1. The largest (knowing/known) insects are found in tropical rain forests.

2. A hummingbird's heart beats at the (astonished/astonishing) rate of 615 beats per minute.

3. A bill of lading is a (writing/written) receipt for goods that are sent by public transportation.

4. At the peak of his jump, a pole vaulter performs a series of (twisting/twisted) body motions to clear the bar.

5. Anyone (working/worked) under conditions that cause a heavy loss of perspiration can suffer heat exhaustion.

6. A mosquito (filled/is filled) with blood is carrying twice its own body weight.

7. The state of Wisconsin has seventy-two counties, many (naming/named) after Indian tribes.

8. Sun spots occur in cycles, with the greatest number generally (appearing/are appearing) every eleven years.

EXERCISE 21.2

Focus: Structure problems involving incomplete or missing participial phrases. (Note: One or two items in this exercise do NOT focus on participial phrases; these items are marked on the answer key with asterisks.)

Directions: Choose the one option—(A), (B), (C), or (D)—that correctly completes the sentence. For Error Identification items, circle the underlined portion of the sentence that would not be considered correct. Then mark the appropriate blank.

1. Aerodynamics is the study of the forces _____ on an object as it moves through the atmosphere.

    (A) acting
    (B) act
    (C) are acting
    (D) acted

2. Most candles are <u>made of</u> paraffin wax
    A
    <u>mixing</u> with compounds that have higher
    B
    <u>melting</u> points <u>to keep</u> them from melting
    C   D
    in hot weather.

3. _____ for their strong fiber include flax and hemp.

   (A) Plants are grown
   (B) Plants grown
   (C) Plants that grow
   (D) To grow plants

4. _____, methane can be used as a fuel.

   (A) It's produced by the fermentation of organic matter
   (B) Produced by the fermentation of organic matter
   (C) The production by fermentation of organic matter
   (D) The fermentation of organic matter is produced

5. Ralph Blakelock <u>specialized in</u> <u>painting</u>
                  A   B
   wild, lonely nighttime <u>landscapes</u>, usually
                         C
   with black trees <u>were silhouetted</u> against
                  D
   the Moon.

6. Elfreth's Alley in Philadelphia is the oldest residential street in the United States, with _____ from 1728.

   (A) houses are dated
   (B) the dates of the houses
   (C) the dating of houses
   (D) houses dating

7. The Farallon Islands are <u>a group of</u>
                         A
   <u>uninhabited</u> islands <u>lying</u> about <u>40 mile</u>
      B   C   D
   west of San Francisco.

8. In 1821, the city of Indianapolis, Indiana, was laid out in a design _____ after that of Washington, D.C.

   (A) patterned
   (B) was patterned
   (C) a pattern
   (D) that patterned

9. The <u>crushing</u> leaves of yarrow plants
        A
   <u>can serve</u> as a <u>traditional</u> medicine for
      B   C
   <u>cleansing</u> wounds.
     D

10. _____ in front of a camera lens changes the color of the light that reaches the film.

    (A) Placed a filter
    (B) A filter is placed
    (C) A filter placed
    (D) When a filter placed

11. The Massachusetts State House, _____ in 1798, was the most distinguished building in the United States at that time.

    (A) completing
    (B) which was completed
    (C) was completed
    (D) to be completed

12. Checkerboard Mesa in Utah <u>features</u> a
                        A
    <u>strangely</u> <u>cracking</u> expanse of <u>stone</u>.
       B   C   D

13. Barbara McClintock _____ for her discovery of the mobility of genetic elements.

    (A) known
    (B) who knows
    (C) knowing
    (D) is known

14. <u>Throughout</u> the long career, Pete Seeger
            A
    has been a <u>leading</u> figure in <u>reviving</u> folk
       B   C   D
    music.

15. The solitary scientist _____ by himself has in many instances been replaced by a cooperative scientific team.

    (A) to make important discoveries
    (B) important discoveries were made
    (C) has made important discoveries
    (D) making important discoveries

16. Geometry is the branch of mathematics _____ the properties of lines, curves, shapes, and surfaces.

    (A) that concerned with
    (B) it is concerned with
    (C) concerned with
    (D) its concerns are

Lesson 22

GERUNDS, INFINITIVES, AND SIMPLE FORMS

The use of verbal forms—gerunds, infinitives, and (for the purposes of this lesson) simple forms—are tested in both types of Structure problems.

Gerunds are verbal nouns: *being, going, giving, building*. Like present participles, gerunds end in *-ing*. Gerunds are often followed by objects: *giving directions, building a house*. Together, a gerund and its object form a **gerund phrase.**

Gerunds are used as any other noun is used. You will see gerunds as subjects, as the objects of certain verbs (see the list on page 135), and as the objects of prepositions.

> *Dancing* is good exercise. (gerund as subject)
> He enjoys *going* to good restaurants. (gerund as object of a verb)
> You can solve this problem by *using* a calculator. (gerund as object of a preposition)

Gerunds are also used after verb + preposition combinations.

> Michael's father didn't approve of his *changing* his major from accounting to acting. (gerund after verb + preposition)

This is true even after phrases that contain the word *to*.

> Ruth is looking forward to *taking* a long vacation.

Infinitives consist of the word *to* and the simple form of the verb: *to be, to go, to give, to build*. Infinitives are often followed by an object: *to give directions, to build a house*. Together, an infinitive and its object form an **infinitive phrase.** Like gerunds, infinitives can be the subjects of verbs and the objects of certain verbs (see the list on page 134).Unlike gerunds, infinitives can NEVER be the objects of prepositions.

> *To help* others is rewarding. (infinitive as subject)
> He attempted *to swim* across the river. (infinitive as object of a verb)

Infinitives are used in several other ways:

* *To* show purpose (to explain *why* an action takes place)

  > He took lessons *to learn how to dance*. (Why did he take lessons? To learn how to dance.)

  These infinitive phrases often come at the beginning of a sentence, and are set off by commas.

  > *To learn how to dance*, he took lessons.

  The phrase *in order* + infinitive also shows purpose.

  > *In order to learn how to dance*, he took lessons.

* After certain adjectives

  > It's important *to change* the oil in your car frequently.

* After nouns

  The first person *to walk* on the moon was Neil Armstrong.

  > You will often see this after noun phrases containing the word *first, last, only,* and other ranking words.

You may also see items that focus on **passive infinitives.** A passive infinitive consists of the words *to* + *be* + past participle.

> Nancy Hong was the only person *to be asked* to speak at the ceremony.

Simple forms are the base forms of verbs; they consist of the infinitive without the word *to*: *be, go, give, build*.

Simple forms are used after the causative verbs *have, make,* and *let* and after the phrase *would rather*.

Mark had the carpenter *repair* the door.
His father makes him *study* hard.
Penny let her son *go* on the trip.
She'd rather *go* jogging than *use* the exercise machines.

COMMON VERBS THAT TAKE VERBAL OBJECTS

Verbs Used with Gerunds	Verbs Used with Infinitives	Verbs Used with Simple Forms
admit	agree	have
anticipate	aim	let
avoid	allow	make
consider	appear	would rather
deny	arrange	
delay	ask	
discuss	attempt	
dislike	cause	
enjoy	choose	
finish	claim	
justify	convince	
postpone	decide	
practice	deserve	
resist	enable	
resume	expect	
risk	hope	
quit	instruct	
recommend	know (how)	
suggest	learn (how)	
understand	need	
	permit	
	persuade	
	prepare	
	promise	
	require	
	seem	
	teach (how)	
	tell	
	tend	
	use	
	vote	
	warn	

SENTENCE COMPLETION

Most often, the gerund or infinitive itself is missing from the sentence. In some cases a complete gerund or infinitive phrase or some other portion of the sentence phrase may be needed to correctly complete the sentence.

Sample Items

_____ the eggs of most birds must be kept warm.

(A) Proper development
(B) By properly developing,
(C) They develop properly
(D) To develop properly,

The correct answer is (D). The only one of these four phrases listed here that can show purpose is choice (D), an infinitive. This expression means, *In order to develop properly.*

In 1959 the political philosopher Hannah Arendt became the first woman _____ a full professor at Princeton University.

(A) to appoint
(B) was appointed
(C) to be appointed
(D) an appointment as

The correct answer is (C). After a noun phrase such as *the first woman* an infinitive is used as an adjective phrase. Because a passive form is needed (Hannah Arendt receives the action; she doesn't perform the action), choice (A) is not the correct infinitive form. Choice (C), a passive infinitive, is best.

The ear is the organ of hearing, but it also plays a role in _____ balance.

(A) maintaining
(B) it maintains
(C) to maintain
(D) maintained

The correct answer is (A). A gerund is used correctly after a preposition. Choices (B), (C), and (D) would not be appropriate after a preposition.

EXERCISE 22.1

Focus: Identifying errors and correct forms of gerunds, infinitives, and simple forms
Directions: Underline the form that best completes each sentence.

1. Sports parachutes are relatively easy (controlling/to control).

2. Sleeve bearings let pistons (to move/move) back and forth.

3. One of the most important steps in (producing/to produce) a motion picture is film editing.

4. An opera singer is required (having/to have) a powerful and beautiful voice.

5. The Wampanoag Indians taught the Pilgrims how (growing/to grow) corn.

6. Frogs and certain kinds of birds use their tongues (to catch/catch) insects.

7. Modems permit computers (communicating/to communicate) with one another over telephone lines.

8. Smells can be more effective than any other sensory stimuli in vividly (bringing/bring) back memories.

9. Isadora Martinez invented a knee transplant that allows people with severe arthritis (to bend/bend) their knees easily.

10. A sudden sound can make a golfer (to miss/miss) a shot.

11. Heavy spring snows may cause the branches of trees (snap/to snap).

12. Modern race cars store fuel in rubber bladders that are almost impossible (rupturing/to rupture).

EXERCISE 22.2

Focus: Completing structure problems involving infinitive and gerund phrases. (Note: One or two of the items in this exercise do NOT focus on infinitives or gerunds. These items are marked in the answer key with asterisks.)

Directions: For Sentence Completion items, mark the answer choice that correctly completes the sentence. For Error Identification items, decide which of the four underlined words or phrases—(A), (B), (C), or (D)—that correctly completes the sentence.

1. The most <u>widely used</u> material for <u>package</u>
   A   B   C
   consumer goods <u>is</u> cardboard.
         D

2. _____ for a career in dance generally begins at an early age.

   (A) People train
   (B) That people train
   (C) If training
   (D) Training

3. A baby's first teeth _____ are generally the lower incisors.

   (A) appearance
   (B) appear
   (C) to appear
   (D) in appearing

4. One of the latest <u>methods</u> of <u>quarrying</u>
               A   B
   stone is <u>to cutting</u> the stone <u>with a jet</u>
          C   D
   torch.

5. In 1944 biologist Charles Michener <u>devised</u>
                                A
   a system for <u>to classify</u> the <u>approximately</u>
              B   C
   20,000 <u>species</u> of bees.
          D

6. A climbing helmet _____ protection for a rock-climber's head from falling rocks and other hazards.

   (A) to provide
   (B) provides
   (C) providing
   (D) that provides

7. Power tools require careful handling _____ injuries.

   (A) by avoiding
   (B) they avoid
   (C) to avoid
   (D) that avoid

8. Geothermal <u>energy</u> is energy <u>obtaining</u> by
              A   B
   <u>using</u> heat from <u>the Earth's interior</u>.
     C   D

9. An electromagnet is created _____ electrical current through a coil of wire.

   (A) by passing
   (B) passes by
   (C) to be passed
   (D) passed

10. _____ at home requires only three types of chemicals, several pieces of simple equipment, and running water.

    (A) For the development of film
    (B) To develop film
    (C) When film is developed
    (D) In developing film

11. Brown lung is a <u>respiratory</u> <u>disease</u> <u>caused</u>
                      A   B
    by <u>inhaling</u> dust from cotton or some
         C
    another fiber.
      D

12. The purpose of cost accounting is _____ involved in producing and selling a good or service.

    (A) as a determination of its costs
    (B) the costs determined
    (C) that determines the costs
    (D) to determine the costs

13. _____ was one of the most difficult tasks pioneers faced on their journeys west.

    (A) Crossing rivers
    (B) While crossing rivers
    (C) Rivers being crossed
    (D) By crossing rivers

14. It is the facets cut into a diamond that make
    ___   ___   ___
     A   B   C
    it to sparkle.
    __
     D

15. Bathe in mineral water has long been
    ____   _____
     A   B
    believed to have beneficial effects.
    _____   _____
           C   D

16. Energy can be defined as the ability _____ .

    (A) do working
    (B) to do work
    (C) doing work
    (D) work to be done

17. The process of _____ by hand has changed little since the fifteenth century.

    (A) to bind books
    (B) binding books
    (C) books are bound
    (D) bound books

18. Robert A. Moog developed an electronic
                _____
                       A
    device that could be used for play
                    _____   ___
                       B   C
    synthesized music.
    _____
        D

19. _____ often obtain funds from the sale of stocks.

    (A) For corporations to operate
    (B) The operation of corporations
    (C) Corporations operate by
    (D) To operate, corporations

20. A crescent wrench has adjustable jaws for _____ a nut, bolt, or pipe.

    (A) to grip
    (B) they grip
    (C) gripping
    (D) gripped

REVIEW TEST E: STRUCTURE

Directions: For Sentence Completion items, select the answer choice—(A), (B), (C), (D)—that correctly completes the sentence. For Error Identification items, select the answer choice—(A), (B), (C), (D)—that corresponds to the underlined portion of the sentence that would not be considered correct.

1. _____, an organism must be able to adapt to changing factors in its environment.

    (A) If survival
    (B) For surviving
    (C) To survive
    (D) It survives

2. Bricks can be made from many difference
   _____   ____ _____
     A   B   C
   types of clay.
   _____
     D

3. The narrow blades of speed skates allow _____ speeds of up to 30 miles per hour.

    (A) for skaters maintaining
    (B) skaters to maintain
    (C) skaters maintain
    (D) maintenance by skaters

4. The game backgammon has been playing
   _____   ___ ____ _____
          A   B   C
   since ancient times.
   _____
          D

138

5. The Mummers' Parade has _____ every year in Philadelphia on New Year's Day since 1901.

   (A) holding
   (B) been holding
   (C) held
   (D) been held

6. Before the late eighteenth century, most
   <u>A</u>
   textiles <u>were</u> <u>done</u> at <u>home</u>.
   B   C   D

7. Political science, <u>alike</u> the <u>other</u> social
                      A   B
   sciences, <u>is</u> not <u>an exact</u> science.
              C   D

8. _____ on barren slopes can help prevent erosion.

   (A) Planting trees
   (B) For trees to be planted
   (C) In order to plant trees
   (D) Trees are planted

9. Animals that hibernate <u>usually</u> eat <u>large</u>
                           A   B
   <u>numbers</u> of food <u>in</u> the autumn.
    C   D

10. <u>Lightly</u>, sandy soil <u>absorbs</u> water more
     A   B
    <u>quickly</u> than clay or <u>loam</u>.
     C   D

11. In 1870 Hiram R. Revels _____ the first black to be elected to the U.S. Senate.

    (A) becoming
    (B) became
    (C) to have become
    (D) has become

12. During the Depression of the 1930s, <u>many</u>
    <u>A</u>   B
    artists <u>were giving</u> jobs by the Federal Arts
             C   D
    Project.

13. Sand dunes are made of loose sand _____ up by the action of the wind.

    (A) it builds
    (B) builds
    (C) is building
    (D) built

14. A <u>feeding</u> animal will usually permit
        A
    competitors <u>approaching</u> only within a
                 B
    certain area, the <u>boundaries of which</u> are
                       C
    called its feeding <u>territory</u>.
                        D

15. It is a <u>chemical called</u> capsaicin <u>that gives</u>
             A   B
    hot peppers <u>their</u> <u>spice</u> flavor.
                 C   D

16. Amber is a hard, yellowish-brown _____ from the resin of pine trees that lived millions of years ago.

    (A) substance formed
    (B) to form a substance
    (C) substance has formed
    (D) forming a substance

17. The University of Wisconsin was the <u>first</u>
                                         A
    school to make a serious <u>effort</u> to <u>teaching</u>
                              B   C
    students public <u>administration</u>.
                     D

18. Diaries and journals <u>writing</u> during Colonial
                          A   B
    times provide the <u>best</u> records of that <u>era</u>.
                       C   D

19. Snowshoes let a person <u>to walk</u> on snow
                            A
    without <u>sinking</u> into it because <u>they</u>
             B   C
    distribute the person's weight <u>over a wide</u>
                                    D
    area.

20. Beams of ultrasonic <u>sound waves</u> can be
                         A
    <u>send</u> through <u>pieces</u> of metal <u>to detect</u>
     B   C   D
    flaws.

21. A deep-tissue massage is a type of massage therapy _____ on one part of the body, such as the lower back.

    (A) its concentration is
    (B) concentrating
    (C) why it concentrates
    (D) to be concentrated

22. Some plants and insects exhibit so high
                                         A   B

    degree of interdependence that the

    elimination of one results in the elimination
                                  C

    of the other.
        D

23. Founded in 1620, Plymouth was the
         A

    soonest of the five colonies established by
      B   C   D

    the Pilgrims in Massachusetts.

24. Trucks can be used to transport a wide
            A   B   C

    various of cargoes.
       D

25. The astronomer George Hale was a pioneer
             A   B

    in the art of photograph the sun.
       C   D

Lesson 23

PRONOUNS

Pronoun errors in written expression involve several types of pronouns:

- **Personal pronouns**
  (*he*, *she*, *it*, *they*, and so on)
- **Reflexive pronouns**
  (*himself*, *herself*, *itself*, *themselves*, and so on)
- **Relative pronouns** (adjective-clause markers)
  (*who*, *whose*, *which*, *that*, and so on)
- **Demonstrative pronouns**
  (*this*, *that*, *these*, *those*)

For the purposes of this lesson, possessive adjectives (*his* house, *their* bicycles) are considered personal pronouns, and demonstrative adjectives (*that* book, *those* horses) are considered demonstrative pronouns.

The greatest number of errors involve personal pronouns.

ERRORS IN PRONOUN/NOUN AGREEMENT

A pronoun must agree with the noun to which it refers (the pronoun's **referent**).

Most agreement errors with personal pronouns, reflexive pronouns, and demonstrative pronouns consist of a singular pronoun referring to a plural noun or a plural pronoun referring to singular nouns.

Agreement errors with relative pronouns usually involve the use of *who* to refer to things or *which* to refer to persons. (Note: The relative pronoun *that* can be used in certain sentences to refer to both persons and things.)

Another error involves the use of *this* or *these* in place of *that* and *those*. (*This* and *these* are used to refer to things that are perceived as close in time or space; *that* and *those* are used to refer to things that are perceived as distant in time or space.)

Sample Items

Jackrabbits have powerful rear legs that enable it to leap long distances.
      A   B   C   D

The correct answer is (C). The pronoun referring to the plural noun *Jackrabbits* must be plural.

The best way for children to learn science is for them to perform experiments himself.
        A   B   C   D

The correct answer is (D). The referent is plural (*children*), so the reflexive pronouns must also be plural (*themselves*) to agree with it.

The Canadian Shield is a huge, rocky region who curves around Hudson Bay like a giant
                        A   B   C   D

horseshoe.

The correct answer is (B). The referent for the pronoun *who* is *region*. To agree with the referent, the relative pronoun *that* must be used. The pronoun *who* can refer only to a person.

Trademarks enable a company to distinguish its products from these of another company.
         A   B   C   D

The correct answer is (C). The demonstrative *these* cannot be used to refer to the products of another company. The demonstrative *those* should be used instead.

ERRORS IN PRONOUN FORM

These errors involve personal pronouns. A subject form like *he* might be used in place of an object form like *him*, or a possessive pronoun like *hers* might be used in place of a possessive adjective like *her*. This type of pronoun error is usually easy to spot.

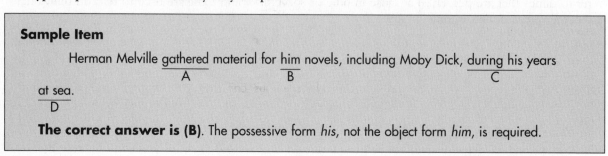

Sample Item

Herman Melville gathered material for him novels, including Moby Dick, during his years
                    A   B   C

at sea.
 D

The correct answer is (B). The possessive form *his*, not the object form *him*, is required.

INCORRECT TYPE OF PRONOUN

In some sentences, the wrong type of pronoun is used. For example, a reflexive pronoun might be used when a personal pronoun is needed, or a personal pronoun used when a relative pronoun is required.

Sample Items

As larvae, barnacles are free-swimming, but as adults they attach them to stones, docks, and
　　　　　　　　　A　　　　　　　　　　　　　　　B　　　　C

hulls of ships.
　　D

The correct answer is (C). The reflexive pronoun is required because the subject and object are the same entity: *they attach themselves.*

A barometer is a device it is used to measure atmospheric pressure.
　　A　　　　　B　　　　　C　　　　　　　　　D

The correct answer is (B). A personal pronoun (*it*) cannot be used to connect an adjective clause to the rest of the sentence. A relative pronoun (*which* or *that*) must be used instead.

INCORRECT INCLUSION OF PRONOUNS

Some errors involve the unnecessary use of pronouns. Often, this type of error occurs when a personal pronoun is used as a subject in a sentence that already has a noun subject. Or it may involve a personal pronoun used unnecessarily in a relative clause.

In a few items, a relative pronoun is used unnecessarily.

Sample Items

Block Island in Long Island Sound it is surrounded by cold, dangerous waters.
　　A　　　　　　　　　　　　　B　　C　　　　　　　　D

The correct answer is (B). The subject of the sentence is *Block Island*; the personal pronoun *it* is an unnecessary repetition of the subject.

Dutch elm disease, which it is caused by a fungus, can destroy a tree within four weeks.
　　　　　　　　　A　B　　　　　　　　　　C　　　　　　D

The correct answer is (A). The relative pronoun *which* is the true subject of the relative clause; the personal pronoun *it* is not needed.

Certain types of turtles that may live as long as 100 years.
　　　　A　　　　B　　　　C　　　　　D

The correct answer is (B). The relative pronoun *that* is unnecessary in this sentence because there is only one verb (*may live*). A sentence that contains a relative clause must have a verb in each clause.

EXERCISE 23.1

Focus: Identifying and correcting pronoun agreement

Directions: If the underlined form is correct, mark the sentence *C*. If the underlined form is incorrect, mark the sentence *X,* and write a correction for the underlined form in the blank following the sentence. Then circle the referent (the noun to which the pronoun refers).

_____ 1. Unlike other marsupial animals, the opossum does not transport <u>their</u> babies in a pouch.

_____

_____ 2. A talus is an accumulation of rock fragments found at the base of a cliff or on a slope beneath <u>them</u>.

_____

_____ 3. Investment banking is concerned with the sale of government bonds, and <u>they</u> also deals with corporate stocks and bonds.

_____

_____ 4. Compared to the fossil record of animals, <u>that</u> of plants is relatively skimpy.

_____

_____ 5. The emerald gets <u>their</u> beautiful green color from titanium and chromium impurities in the stone.

_____

_____ 6. The viola is larger and heavier than the violin, and <u>she</u> has a darker, somewhat nasal tone.

_____

_____ 7. Storms on the planet Saturn may be larger than the planet Earth <u>itself</u>.

_____

_____ 8. The molecules of a liquid are held together tighter than <u>that</u> of a gas.

_____

_____ 9. Ducks make nests out of leaves and <u>its</u> own feathers.

_____

EXERCISE 23.2

Focus: Identifying and correcting errors involving incorrect types and forms of pronouns
Directions: If the underlined form is correct, mark the sentence *C*. If the underlined form is incorrect, mark the sentence *X*, and write a correction for the underlined form in the blank following the sentence.

_____ **1.** Artist Margaret Leng Tan combined dance and piano-playing in <u>her</u> performances.

_____

_____ **2.** Years of breeding domestic rabbits has given <u>their</u> softer, finer fur than wild rabbits.

_____

_____ **3.** New England poet Edwin A. Robinson moved to New York City in 1896 and devoted <u>himself</u> to his writing.

_____

_____ **4.** There are between 100 and 400 billion stars in <u>ours</u> galaxy, the Milky Way.

_____

_____ **5.** The atoms of a crystal always arrange <u>them</u> into a specific array, called a lattice.

_____

_____ **6.** Fred Astaire and Gene Kelly were basically tap dancers, but <u>their</u> both added some ballet movements to their dance steps.

_____

_____ **7.** Attorney Clarence Darrow was known for <u>him</u> defense of unpopular persons and causes.

_____

_____ **8.** Savannah, Georgia, has preserved to a remarkable degree <u>it</u> historic houses and famous gardens.

_____

EXERCISE 23.3

Focus: Identifying errors involving pronoun problems. (Note: One or two items in this exercise do NOT focus on pronoun errors. These are marked in the answer key with an asterisk.)
Directions: Decide which of the four underlined words or phrases—(A), (B), (C), (D)—would not be considered correct and circle that expression.

1. A beaver uses its strong front <u>teeth</u> to cut down trees and <u>peel off</u> <u>its</u> bark.
      A   B   C D

2. "Sprung" wood floors, used in <u>top quality</u> basketball courts <u>and</u> dance studios, <u>they are</u> the safest
                                      A   B   C
surfaces for indoor <u>exercise</u>.
                  D

3. Ants cannot see red light, so <u>it</u> is possible to observe <u>themselves</u> in an artificial nest <u>without</u> disturb-
                                     A   B   C
ing <u>their</u> activities.
    D

4. The glaciers in Olympia National Park are <u>unusual</u> because <u>they</u> are found at altitudes lower than
                                A   B
   <u>these</u> at <u>which</u> glaciers are usually found.
    C   D

5. In his novels, Sinclair Lewis <u>drew</u> critical portraits of Americans <u>who</u> thought of <u>them</u> as model
      A   B   C   D
   citizens.

6. Elizabeth Peabody, <u>founder</u> of the first American kindergarten, <u>she</u> helped gain <u>acceptance</u> of that
                       A   B   C
   institution <u>as</u> a regular part of public education.
             D

7. <u>Almost</u> bacteria <u>have</u> strong cell walls <u>much like</u> <u>those</u> of plants.
     A   B   C   D

8. Bees <u>collect</u> pollen, <u>which</u> <u>furnishes</u> protein for <u>its</u> diet.
          A   B   C   D

9. A small business often limits <u>their</u> operations <u>to</u> a single <u>neighborhood</u> or a group of neighboring
                               A   B   C
   communities.
      D

10. A caricature is a picture <u>in which</u> the subject's <u>distinctive</u> features <u>they are</u> deliberately <u>exaggerated</u>.
                             A   B   C   D

11. The <u>principles</u> used in air conditioning are <u>basically</u> the same as <u>those</u> used by the human body to
          A   B   C
    cool <u>himself</u>.
        D

12. In that age of computers, it is difficult to imagine how tedious the work of bookkeepers and clerks
      A   B   C
    must have been in the past.
        D

Lesson 24

PLURAL NOUNS IN PLACE OF SINGULAR NOUNS AND SINGULAR NOUNS IN PLACE OF PLURAL NOUNS

Underlined nouns in the Structure section may be incorrect because they are plural but should be singular, or because they are singular but should be plural.

Sometimes it is clear that a singular subject is incorrectly used because the verb is plural, or that a plural noun is used incorrectly because the verb is singular. In this type of item, the verb will NOT be underlined, because this is not a verb error.

Sometimes it is obvious that a plural or a singular noun is needed because of the determiners that precede the noun. Certain determiners are used only before singular nouns while other determiners are used only before plural nouns.

Determiners used with singular nouns	Determiners used with plural nouns
a/an	two, three, four, etc.
one	dozens of
a single	hundreds of
each	thousands of
every	a few (of)
this	many (of)
that	a number of
	the number of
	a couple (of)
	every one of
	each one of
	each of
	one of
	these
	those

Each *contestant* won a prize.
Each of the *contestants* won a prize.
This *flower* is a yellow rose.
These *flowers* are yellow roses.
I only attended one *game* this season.
It was one of the most exciting *games* that I ever attended.

Sample Items

Several of Washington Irving's story have become classics in American literature.
         A   B   C   D

The correct answer is (B). In this item, both the determiner before the noun (*Several of*) and the plural verb (*have*) indicate that a plural noun (*stories*) should be used.

Mauna Loa, an active volcano on the island of Hawaii, usually has one eruptions every
               A   B   C   D

three years.

The correct answer is (D). A singular noun must be used after the determiner *one*.

One of the most beautiful state capitol is the Utah Sate Capitol, located in Salt Lake City.
     A   B   C   D

The correct answer is (C). The pattern is *one of the* + superlative adjective + plural noun. The plural noun *capitols* must therefore be used.

ERRORS INVOLVING IRREGULAR PLURALS

Most plural nouns in English end in *-s*, but a few are irregular. Only the most common irregular plurals are tested on TOEFL test. (Irregular plurals that come to English from Latin or Greek—*data, cacti, alumnae,* or *phenomena,* for example—will NOT be tested on TOEFL.)

Common Irregular Plural Nouns

Singular Noun	Plural Noun
child	children
man	men
woman	women
foot	feet
tooth	teeth
mouse	mice
fish	fish

Sample Item

As childs grow older, their bones become thicker and longer.
     A   B C   D

The correct answer is (A). The plural form of *child* is *children*.

ERRORS WITH PLURAL FORMS OF NON-COUNT NOUNS

In some items a non-count noun (such as *furniture, research, sunshine, information, bread,* and so on) is incorrectly given as a plural noun.

Sample Item

Some encyclopedias deal with specific fields, such as music or philosophy, and provide
<u>A</u>   <u>B</u>   <u>C</u>

<u>informations</u> only on subject.
<u>D</u>

The correct answer is (D). *Information* is an uncountable noun and cannot be pluralized.

ERRORS WITH PLURAL COMPOUND NOUN

Compound nouns consist of two nouns used together to express a single idea: *grocery store, travel agent, dinner party,* and *house cat* for example. Only the second noun of compounds is pluralized: *grocery stores, travel agents, dinner parties,* and *house cats.*

(There are rare exceptions to this rule—*sports cars* and *women doctors,* for example—but these won't be tested.)

Sample Item

Raymond Chandler's <u>detectives stories</u> are <u>admired</u> both by critics and general <u>readers</u>.
            <u>A</u>   <u>B</u>   <u>C</u>   <u>D</u>

The correct answer is (A). The plural form of this compound noun is *detective stories.*

ERRORS INVOLVING PLURAL FORMS OF NUMBERS AND MEASUREMENT

Some errors involve numbers + measurements:

   They went for a *6-mile* walk.
   They walked *6 miles.*

In the first sentence, the number + measurement is used as an adjective, and the measurement is singular. In the second, the measurement is a noun, and is therefore plural.

Numbers like *hundred, thousand,* and *million* may be pluralized when they are used indefinitely—in other words, when they do not follow other numbers:

seven thousand   thousands
five million dollars   millions of dollars

Sample Items

The U.S. president serves a maximum of two four-years terms.
 A   B   C   D

The correct answer is (D). When used before a noun, a number + measurement is singular.

Thousand of antibiotics have been developed, but only about thirty are in common use today.
   A   B   C   D

The correct answer is (A). The plural form *thousands* should be used.

EXERCISE 24

Focus: Identifying and correcting errors involving singular and plural nouns. (Note: One or two items in this exercise do not focus on singular-plural errors. These are marked in the answer key with an asterisk.)

Directions: Decide which of the four underlined words or phrases—(A), (B), (C), or (D)—would not be considered correct, and write the letter of the expression in the blank.

_____ 1. The male mandril baboon is one of the most colorful of all mammal.
              A   B   C   D

_____ 2. Zoonoses are diseases that can be transmitted to humans beings by animals.
                        A   B   C   D

_____ 3. Many championship automobiles and motorcycle races take place in Daytona Beach, Florida.
              A   B   C   D

_____ 4. The Newberry Award is granted every years to the authors of outstanding books for children.
                                        A   B   C   D

_____ 5. The major source of air pollution vary from city to city.
              A   B   C   D

_____ 6. Around 75 percents of the earth's surface is covered by water.
              A   B   C   D

_____ 7. All college and universities get their funds from a variety of sources.
              A   B   C   D

_____ 8. Russell Cave in northeastern Alabama was the home of cliff-dwelling Indians thousand of
                          A   B   C
           years ago.
           D

_____ 9. The Federalist Papers are a 500-pages collection of eighteenth century newspaper articles
                                        A   B   C
           written to support the Constitution.
           D

_____ 10. The mathematician and astronomer David Rittenhouse was one of the first man of science in
                                A   B   C   D
            the American colonies.

_____ 11. Insurance underwriter insure people against many types of risks.
                        A   B   C   D

_____ 12. The electric toaster was one of the earliest appliance to be developed for the kitchen.
              A   B   C   D

_____ **13.** Tornadoes can pick up objects as heavy as automobiles and carry them for hundreds of foot.
                                       A   B   C   D

_____ **14.** Many kinds of vegetables are growth in California's Imperial Valley.
                A   B   C D

_____ **15.** In typical pioneers settlements, men, women, and children worked from morning until night
                         A   B   C

at farm and household tasks.
   D

_____ **16.** Few of the doctors practicing in the thirteen North American colonies had formal training in
                  A   B   C

the field of medicines.
           D

_____ **17.** The pine tree is probably the more important lumber tree in the world.
         A   B   C   D

Lesson 25

PREPOSITIONS

Errors with **prepositions** are among the most difficult errors to catch. Preposition use in English is very complex. For every rule, there seems to be an exception. Recently, there have been more errors involving prepositions in the Structure part of TOEFL test, and the errors have been more difficult to spot.

Prepositions are used in the following ways:

- In adverbial phrases that show time, place, and other relationships.

  in the morning   on Pennsylvania Avenue   to the park
  by a student

- After certain nouns.

  a cause of   a reason for   a solution to

- After certain adjectives and participles

  different from   aware of   disappointed in

- After certain verbs

  combine with   rely on   refer to

- In phrasal prepositions (two- or three-word prepositions)

  according to   together with   instead of

- In certain set expressions

  by far   in general   on occasion   at last

There are two main types of preposition errors that you may see in the Structure part of the test, errors in preposition choice and incorrect inclusion or omission of prepositions.

ERRORS IN PREPOSITION CHOICE

The wrong preposition is used according to the context of the sentence.

There are two particular situations involving preposition choice that are often tested in Structure:

- Errors with *from . . . to* and *between . . . and*

Both these expressions are used to give the starting time and ending time. They can also be used to show relationships of place and various other relationships.

> He lived in Seattle *from* 1992 *to* 1997.
> He lived in Seattle *between* 1992 *and* 1997.
>
> Route 66 ran *from* Chicago *to* Los Angeles.
> Route 66 ran *between* Chicago *and* Los Angeles.

Errors usually involve an incorrect pairing of those words, or the incorrect use of other prepositions:

* *between* A *to* B   * *from* X *and* Y
* *between* A *with* B   * *since* X *to* Y

- Errors with *since*, *for*, and *in*

Since is used before a point in time with the present perfect tense—but never with the past tense. *For* is used before a period of time with the present perfect and other tenses. *In* is used before certain points in time (years, centuries, decades) with the past tense and other tenses—but never with the present perfect tense.

> He's lived here *since* 1995.
> He's lived here *for* two years.
> He moved here *in* 1995.

Errors involve the use of one of these prepositions for another:

> * He's lived here *in* 1995.
> * He's lived here *since* two years.
> * He moved here *since* 1995.

Sample Items

The pitch of a <u>tuning</u> fork <u>depends of</u> the size <u>and</u> shape of <u>its</u> arms.
          A   B   C   D

The correct answer is (B). The preposition after the verb *depend* is *on*, not *of*.

The Alaskan Pipeline <u>runs</u> <u>between</u> Prudhoe Bay on the Arctic Coastal Plain to the <u>port</u> of
                       A   B   C
Valdez, a <u>distance</u> of 789 miles.
         D

The correct answer is (B). The pattern is *from . . . to*.

Candles were mankind's chief <u>source</u> of illumination <u>since</u> <u>at least</u> 2,000 years.
          A   B   C   D

The correct answer is (C). Before a period of time (*2,000 years*) the preposition *for* should be used.

INCORRECT INCLUSION OR OMISSION OF PREPOSITIONS

A preposition is used when one is not needed, or not used when one is needed.

Sample Items

According many critics, Mark Twain's novel *Huckleberry Finn* is his greatest work and is
_____ A _____   B

one of the greatest American novels ever written.
____ C ____   D

The correct answer is (A). The preposition *to* has been omitted from the phrase *according to.*

Some of the most of spectacular waterfalls in the eastern United States are found in the Pocono
____ A ____ B ____   C   D

Mountains of Pennsylvania.

The correct answer is (B). The preposition *of* should not be used in this phrase. (When *most* means "majority," it can be used in the phrase *most of the.* "Most of the people agree . . . ," for example. However, in this sentence, *most* is part of the superlative form of the adjective *spectacular,* and so cannot be used with *of.*)

EXERCISE 25.1

Focus: Identifying correct and incorrect preposition choice
Directions: Underline the prepositions that correctly complete the sentences below.

1. Wage rates depend (in/on) part (from/on) the general prosperity (of/for) the economy.

2. (For/To) an injection to be effective (on/against) tetanus, it must be administered (by/within) 72 hours (of/for) the injury.

3. The invention (of/for) the hand-cranked freezer opened the door (for/to) commercial ice-cream production, and (for/since) then, the ice-cream industry has grown (in/into) a four-billion-dollar-a-year industry.

4. (At/On) the time (of/in) the Revolutionary War, the North American colonies were merely a long string (with/of) settlements (along/among) the Atlantic Coast (between/from) Maine and Georgia.

5. The probability (of/for) two people (in/on) a group (of/for) ten people having birthdays (in/on) the same day is about one (in/of) twenty.

6. Showboats were floating theaters that tied up (at/to) towns (in/on) the Ohio and Mississippi Rivers to bring entertainment and culture (to/at) the people (on/in) the frontier.

7. Scrimshaw, the practice (of/for) carving ornate designs (in/on) ivory, was first practiced (by/of) sailors working (by/with) sail needles while (in/on) long sea voyages.

8. Assateague Island, (off/of) the coast (off/of) Virginia, is famous (for/to) its herds (of/with) wild ponies.

9. (In/On) order (for/to) an object to be visible, light must travel (from/for) that object (at/to) a person's eyes.

10. (In/On) the 1930s and 1940s, when train travel was (on/at) its peak, passengers could look forward (for/to) wonderful meals (on/at) trains.

11. (In/Since) the 1960s, op art, which was based (in/on) scientific theories (of/for) optics, employed patterns (of/in) lines and colors that seemed to change shape as the viewer looked (on/at) them.

12. The first national convention devoted (for/to) the issue (of/with) women's rights, organized partly (of/by) Elizabeth Cady Stanton, was held (in/on) her hometown (in/of) Seneca Falls, New York, (in/on) 1848.

EXERCISE 25.2

Focus: Identifying and correcting errors involving the inclusion or omission of prepositions

Directions: If there is a preposition unnecessarily included in a sentence, mark that sentence *X,* and underline the preposition. If there is a preposition incorrectly omitted from a sentence, mark that sentence *X,* underline the words before and after the missing preposition, and write the correct preposition on the line following the sentence. If the sentence is correctly written, mark that sentence *C.*

_____ 1. According polls taken throughout the twentieth century, Lincoln and Washington are the preeminent American presidents.

_____

_____ 2. Today, many varieties of fruit are available all year thanks improved storage and shipping techniques.

_____

_____ 3. The origin of the Moon remains a mystery.

_____

_____ 4. Traffic jams can cause of pollution, delays, and short tempers.

_____

_____ 5. The Sun's rays heat the Earth's surface, on which then radiates the heat into the air.

_____

_____ 6. A warm-blooded animal is one that keeps the same body temperature regardless the air temperature.

_____

_____ 7. Charlie Parker, considered by many the greatest improviser in the history of jazz, influenced many other jazz musicians.

_____

_____ 8. Most the people are aware of the need to visit dentists regularly.

_____

_____ 9. Muscle fibers are attached bones by tendons.

_____

_____ 10. In his essay "Self Reliance," Ralph W. Emerson told to his readers why they should not depend on the ideas of others.

_____

_____ 11. The crayfish is a freshwater crustacean related the lobster.

_____

_____ 12. Charles Goren was an expert the game of bridge.

_____

_____ 13. Stomata are the tiny openings in the leaves of plants through which oxygen and carbon dioxide pass.

_____

_____ 14. Ducks have small oil glands by which keep their feathers oily and repel water.

_____

_____ 15. The tail of a comet always points away the Sun.

_____

_____ 16. Lichens grow in extreme environments in where no other plant can exist.

_____

_____ 17. Not all of waterfalls are formed in the same way.

_____

EXERCISE 25.3

Focus: Identifying and correcting preposition errors. (Note: One or two items in this exercise do not focus on preposition errors. These are marked in the answer key with an asterisk.)

Directions: For Sentence Completion items, mark the answer choice—(A), (B), (C), or (D)—that correctly completes the sentence. For Error Identification items, circle the underlined portion of the sentence that would not be considered correct.

1. _____ seed of a flowering plant is covered by a dense protective coat.

   (A) On each
   (B) Each
   (C) Each of
   (D) That each

2. Dynamite is ordinarily detonated _____ called a blasting cap.

   (A) a device is used
   (B) that a device
   (C) with a device
   (D) the use of a device

3. Water polo is a game <u>in which is played</u>
                           A
   <u>in the water</u> by two teams, <u>each</u> with <u>seven</u>
      B   C   D
   players.

4. _____ 1900 there were some 300 bicycle factories in the United States which produced over a million bicycles.

   (A) In
   (B) Because in
   (C) It was in
   (D) That in

5. A thick layer of fat called blubber keeps whales warm even _____ coldest water.

   (A) though the
   (B) in the
   (C) the
   (D) of the

6. Many <u>of</u> radio stations <u>began</u> broadcasting
        A   B   C
   baseball games <u>during</u> the 1920s.
                D

7. _____ the United States, the general movement of air masses is from west to east.

   (A) Across
   (B) To cross
   (C) They cross
   (D) It's across

8. The economy of Maine is based to a great
   $\underset{A}{}$ $\underset{B}{}$
   extent in its forests, which cover 80
   $\underset{C}{}$
   percent of its surface area.
   $\underset{D}{}$

9. The removal of waste materials is
   $\underset{A}{}$ $\underset{B}{}$
   essential to all forms of live.
   $\underset{C}{}$ $\underset{D}{}$

10. The bark of a tree thickens _____.

    (A) with age
    (B) it gets older
    (C) as older
    (D) by age

11. John Diefenbaker, Prime Minister of Canada
    during 1957 to 1963, is given much of the
    $\underset{A}{}$ $\underset{B}{}$ $\underset{C}{}$
    credit for the adoption of the Canadian Bill
    $\underset{D}{}$
    of Rights.

12. A substance that is harmless to a person who has no allergies can cause mild to serious reactions in a person _____ allergies.

    (A) has
    (B) which having
    (C) can have
    (D) with

13. The first stage on the manufacturing of all
    $\underset{A}{}$ $\underset{B}{}$
    types of clothing is the cutting of the
    $\underset{C}{}$ $\underset{D}{}$
    material.

14. All of the wheat grown throughout the
    $\underset{A}{}$ $\underset{B}{}$
    world belongs one of fourteen species.
    $\underset{C}{}$ $\underset{D}{}$

15. In 1886 a number of national unions formed the American Federation of Labor _____.

    (A) Samuel Gompers was its leader
    (B) under the leadership of Samuel Gompers
    (C) which, under Samuel Gompers' leadership
    (D) Samuel Gompers led it

16. Harmonicas and autoharps _____ folk instruments.

    (A) are examples
    (B) for example
    (C) are examples of
    (D) as examples of

17. There are approximately 600 different
    $\underset{A}{}$ $\underset{B}{}$
    species of trees native of the continental
    $\underset{C}{}$ $\underset{D}{}$
    United States.

18. _____ industries, such as banking and travel, in which computers are not a convenience but a necessity.

    (A) Where some
    (B) In some
    (C) Some
    (D) There are some

19. Waterwheels, which appeared on the fourth
    $\underset{A}{}$ $\underset{B}{}$
    century B.C., were probably the first
    $\underset{C}{}$
    machines not powered by humans or
    $\underset{D}{}$
    animals.

20. Since centuries, Southwestern Indian tribes
    $\underset{A}{}$
    have valued turquoise and have used it
    $\underset{B}{}$ $\underset{C}{}$
    in jewelry.
    $\underset{D}{}$

Lesson 26

ARTICLES

Articles are specifically tested only in Error Identification items.

Like errors with prepositions, errors with articles are sometimes hard to catch. This is partly because of the complexity of the article system in English, and partly because articles, like prepositions, are "small words," and one's eye tends to skip over errors involving these words.

The basic uses of articles are explained in the chart:

Indefinite Articles *a* and *an*	Definite Article *the*	No Article

A or *an* is used before singular nouns when one does not have a specific person, place, thing, or concept in mind:
  an orange
  a chair
	The is used before singular, plural, and noncount nouns when one does not have a specific person, place, thing, or concept in mind:
	  the orange
	  the oranges
	  the fruit
	  the chair
	  the chairs
	  the furniture
		No article is used before noncount nouns or plural nouns when one does not have specific persons, places, concepts, or things in mind:
		  orange
		  oranges
		  fruit
		  chair
		  chairs
		  furniture

The indefinite article *a* is used before words that begin with a consonant sound (*a chair, a book*); *an* is used before words that begin with a vowel sound (*an orange, an ocean liner*). Before words that begin with the letters *h-* and *u-*, either *a* or *an* can be used, depending on the pronunciation of the words.

Vowel Sounds	Consonant Sounds
an honor	a hat
an umbrella	a university

There are also some specific rules for using (or not using) articles that you should be aware of.

- An indefinite article can be used to mean "one." It is also used to mean "per."

    a half, a quarter, a third, a tenth
    a mile a minute (one mile per minute)
    an apple a day (one apple per day)

- A definite article is used when there is only one example of the thing or person, or when the identity of the thing or person is clear.

    The Moon went behind some clouds. (There's only one moon.)
    Please open *the door*. (You know which door I mean.)

- A definite article is usually used before these expressions of time and position.

the morning	the front	the beginning
the afternoon	the back	the middle
the evening*	the center	the end
	the top	
the past	the bottom	
the present		
the future		

---

* No article is used in the expression "at night."

- A definite article comes before a singular noun that is used as a representative of an entire class of things. This is especially common with the names of animals, trees, inventions, musical instruments, and parts of the body.

    The tiger is the largest cat.
    My favorite tree is *the oak*.
    The Wright bothers invented *the airplane*.
    The oboe is a woodwind instrument.
    The heart pumps blood.

- A definite article is used before expressions with a ordinal number. No article is used before expressions with cardinal numbers.

the first	one
the fourth chapter	Chapter Four
the seventh volume	Volume Seven

- A definite article is used before decades and centuries.

the 1930s	the 1800s
the fifties	the twenty-first century

- A definite article is usually used before superlative forms of adjectives.

the widest river	the most important decision

- A definite article is used in quantity expressions in this pattern: quantifier + *of* + *the* + noun.

many of the textbooks	not much of the paper
some of the water	most of the students
all of the people	a few of the photographs

    These expressions can also be used without the phrase *of the*.

many textbooks	not much paper
some water	most students
all people	a few photographs

- A definite article is used before the name of a group of people or a nationality. No article is used before the name of a language.

    The Swedish are proud of their ancestors, *the Vikings*.
    She learned to speak *Swedish* when she lived in Stockholm.

- A definite article is used when an adjective is used without a noun to mean "people who are. . . ."

    Both the *young and the old* will enjoy this movie.
    The poor have many problems.

- A definite article is used before a noncount noun or a plural noun when it is followed by a modifier. No article is used when these nouns appear alone.

    The rice that I bought today is in the bag.
    Rice is a staple in many countries.
    Trees provide shade.
    The trees in this park are mostly evergreens.

- A definite article is used before the name of a field of study followed by an *of* phrase. If a field is used alone, or is preceded by an adjective, no article is used.

the literature of the twentieth century	literature
the history of the United States	American history

- Definite articles are used before the "formal" names of nations, states, and cities. (These usually contain *of* phrases.) No articles are used before the common names of nations, states, and cities.

the United States of America	America
the state of Montana	Montana
the city of Philadelphia	Philadelphia

- Definite articles are used before most plural geographic names: the names of groups of lakes, mountains, and islands. No article is used before the names of individual lakes, mountains, and islands.

the Great Lakes	Lake Powell
the Rocky Mountains	Mount Washington
the Hawaiian Islands	Long Island

In the Structure section, there are three main types of errors involving articles:

INCORRECT ARTICLE CHOICE

One of the most common errors is the use of *a* in place of *an* or vice versa. Fortunately, this is also the easiest type of error to detect. Another error is *a* or *an* used in place of *the*, or *the* in place of *a* or *an*.

Sample Items

A eclipse of the sun may be either total or partial.
  A   B   C   D

The correct answer is (A). *An* must be used before a noun beginning with a vowel sound such as *eclipse*.

Rose Bird was a first woman in the history of California to serve on the State Supreme Court.
              A   B   C   D

The correct answer is (A). In a phrase with an ordinal number (such as *first*) the definite article *the* must be used.

INCORRECT OMISSION OR INCLUSION OF AN ARTICLE

Sometimes an article is used when none is needed, or one is omitted when one is required.

Sample Items

Slag consists of waste materials and impurities which rise to top of melted metals.
                    A   B   C   D

The correct answer is (C). The definite article *the* should not be omitted from the phrase *the top of*.

The most asteroids are beyond the orbit of the planet Mars.
 A   B   C   D

The correct answer is (A). Definite articles are used only before quantity expressions that contain *of* phrases. (*Most asteroids* or *Most of the asteroids* are both correct in this sentence.

USE OF A DEFINITE ARTICLE IN PLACE OF A POSSESSIVE

A definite article may be incorrectly used in place of a possessive word—*its*, *his*, *her*, or *their*.

Sample Item

The Ozark Mountains of Arkansas are famous for the rugged beauty.
$\overline{\quad}$ A $\qquad\qquad$ B $\;$ C $\qquad$ D

The correct answer is (D). The should correctly read *their* because the sentence refers to the beauty belonging to the Ozark Mountains.

EXERCISE 26.1

Focus: Identifying the correct and incorrect use of articles
Directions: Underline the forms that correctly complete the sentence.

1. Only about (the one/one) percent of (the water/water) on Earth is (the fresh/fresh) water.

2. (The mineral/Mineral) phosphate is (the most/most) common ingredient of all types of (the fertilizers/fertilizers).

3. (The/A) process of refining minerals requires (a/an) huge amount of (an electrical/electrical) energy.

4. (A humor/Humor) runs through (the American/American) literature from (the earliest/earliest) times until (the present/present).

5. (The ozone/Ozone) layer acts as (a/an) umbrella against (the most/most) of (the Sun's/Sun's) dangerous rays.

6. In (the early/early) 1800s, Sequoia, (a Cherokee/Cherokee) leader, created (the/a) first written form of (a North/North) American Indian language.

7. (The Goddard/Goddard) family of (the New/New) England produced some of (the/a) finest furniture made in (the United/United) States in (the seventeenth/seventeenth) century.

8. (The popcorn/Popcorn) has (a/the) same food value as any other kind of (a corn/corn).

EXERCISE 26.2

Focus: Identifying and correcting errors with articles. (Note: One or two items in this exercise do not focus on article errors. These are marked in the answer key with an asterisk.)
Directions: Decide which of the four underlined words or phrases—(A), (B), (C), or (D)—would not be considered correct, and write the letter of the expression in the blank.

_____ 1. The most butterfly eggs are coated with a sticky substance that holds them to plants.
A $\qquad\qquad$ B $\qquad\qquad$ C $\quad$ D

_____ 2. A number of large insurance companies have the headquarters in Hartford, Connecticut.
A $\qquad\qquad$ B $\quad$ C $\qquad$ D

_____ 3. To be effective, an advertisement must first attract an attention.
A $\;$ B $\qquad\qquad$ C $\qquad$ D

_____ 4. Virgin Islands National Park features a underwater preserve with coral reefs and colorful
A $\qquad\qquad$ B $\qquad\qquad$ C
tropical fish.
D

_____ 5. Arthritis, a painful swelling of the joints, is often associated with elderly people, but can
                            A   B   C
afflict young as well.
       D

_____ 6. Wilmington is an only large city in the state of Delaware.
                  A   B C   D

_____ 7. About the third of the Earth's land surface is covered by relatively flat plains.
                  A   B   C

_____ 8. In the 1920s, gasoline companies began giving away free road maps to the customers.
           A   B

_____ 9. The Tropic of Cancer is imaginary line that marks the northern boundary of the Earth's
           A   B   C   D
tropical zone.

_____ 10. Hereford cows are one of most common breeds of cattle raised for beef.
            A   B   C   D

_____ 11. American soprano Kathleen Battle taught music in elementary school before beginning
                                              A   B
the career as a professional singer.
       C   D

_____ 12. In 1891, first state law to help local communities pay for highways was passed in New Jersey.
                A   B   C   D

_____ 13. Lumber is dried and seasoned in an heated chamber called a dry kiln.
            A   B   C   D

_____ 14. Grandfather Mountain, a highest mountain in the Blue Ridge mountain range, is in North
                              A   B   C   D
Carolina.

_____ 15. The eardrum is the only organ in a human body that is capable of detecting changes in air
                  A   B   C   D
pressure.

_____ 16. It was around 1925 that accurate, convenient system for recording the choreography of
                 A   B   C
ballet was developed.
       D

Lesson 27

WORD ORDER

Word order is tested in both types of Structure items.

SENTENCE COMPLETION

All of the answer choices for a Sentence Completion item involving word order contain more or less the same words, but they are arranged in four different orders. The word order is "scrambled" in three choices; in one it is correct. Most items involve three or four words.

- (A) X Y Z
- (B) Y X Z
- (C) Z Y X
- (D) X Z Y

Word order problems are easy to identify because the answer choices are exactly—or almost exactly—the same length, so the answer choices form a rectangle.

- (A) so far away from
- (B) away so far from
- (C) from so far away
- (D) away from so far

Many different types of structures are used in word order problems. One of the most common is a phrase with a superlative adjective or adverb.

Word order items are the only Sentence Correction items in which the distractors may be ungrammatical. In other types of Sentence Correction problems, distractors are always correct in some context. However, at least two of the choices may be grammatical. The correct choice depends on the context of the sentence. See the first Sample Item on page 164 for an example of this.

It is sometimes easy to eliminate distractors in word order items by making sure they "fit" with the rest of the sentence. If you are not sure which remaining answer is correct, use your ear. Say the sentence to yourself (silently) to see which sounds best. Sometimes in word order problems, the answer that looks best doesn't always sound best when put into the sentence.

A special type of word order problem involves **inversions.** This type of sentence uses question word order (auxiliary + subject + main verb) even though the sentence is not a question.

When Are Inversions Used?

- When the negative words listed below are placed at the beginning of a clause for emphasis

not only	rarely
never	at no time
not until	scarcely
seldom	by no means
nowhere	no sooner

Seldom *have I heard* such beautiful music.

Not only *did the company* lose profits, but it also had to lay off workers.

- When a clause begins with one of these expressions with the word *only,* an inversion is used in that clause.

> only in (on, at, by, etc.)   only recently   only once

Only in an emergency *should you use* this exit.

Only recently *did she return* from abroad.

Only by asking questions *can you learn.*

- When sentences begin with these expressions with the word *only,* the subject and verb of the second clause are inverted

> only if   only after
> only when   only until
> only because

Only if you have a serious problem *should you* call Mr. Franklin at home.

Only when you are satisfied *is the sale* considered final.

- When clauses begin with the word *so* + an adjective or participle

So rare *is this coin* that it belongs in a museum.

So confusing *was the map* that we had to ask a police officer for directions.

- When clauses begin with expressions of place or order, the subject and verb are inverted (but auxiliary verbs are not used as they would be in questions)

In front of the museum *is a statue.*

Off the coast of California *lie the Channel Islands.*

First *came a police car,* then *came an ambulance.*

Sample Items

Andromeda is a galaxy containing millions of individual stars, but it is _____ Earth that it looks like a blurry patch of light.

(A) so far away from
(B) away so far from
(C) from so far away
(D) away from so far

The correct answer is (A). It has the correct word order for this sentence. The word order in choices (B) and (D) be incorrect in any sentence. Choice (C) might be correct in certain sentences, but is not correct here.

Not only _____ shade and beauty, but they also reduce carbon dioxide.

(A) do trees provide
(B) trees provide
(C) provide trees
(D) trees do provide

The correct answer is (A). It correctly uses question word order after *not only.* Choices (B) and (C) do not use an auxiliary verb, which is required here. Choice (D) does not follow the correct word order: auxiliary + subject + main verb.

ERROR IDENTIFICATION

Most word order errors in written expression consist of two words in reverse order. Some of the most common examples of this type of error are given below:

Error	Example	Correction
Noun + adjective	drivers careful	careful drivers
Noun + possessive	clothing women's	women's clothing
Main verb + auxiliary	finished are	are finished
Adjective + adverb	a basic extremely idea	an extremely basic idea
Verb + subject (in an indirect question or other *wh*- clause)	Tell me where is it. I spoke to John when was he here.	Tell me where it is. I spoke to John when he was here.
Preposition/adverb clause marker + adverb	after immediately	immediately after
Participle + adverb	baked freshly bread	freshly baked bread
Relative pronoun + preposition	the house which in she lives	the house in which she lives
adverb, adjective, or quantifier + *almost*	totally almost, late almost, all almost	almost totally, almost late, almost all
enough + adjective*	enough good	good enough

* *Enough* can correctly be used before nouns: *enough money, enough time. Enough* may also be used before an adjective when the adjective comes before a noun. (There weren't *enough good seats* at the concert.)

Sample Items

Goods such as flowers fresh and seafood are often shipped by air.
     A   B   C   D

The correct answer is (B). The adjective *fresh* must come before the noun *flowers: fresh flowers.*

Visitors to Vancouver often comment on how beautiful its setting is and on how clean is it.
           A   B   C   D

The correct answer is (D). The correct word order is subject + verb: *it is.*

EXERCISE 27.1

Focus: Identifying and correcting word order in sentences

Directions: If the word order of the underlined form is correct, mark the sentence *C*. If the word order is incorrect, mark the sentence *X*, and write a correction in the blank following the sentence.

_____ 1. The Douglas fir is the <u>source chief</u> of lumber in the state of Oregon.

_____

_____ 2. The painted turtle is a <u>colored brightly</u>, smooth-shelled turtle.

_____

_____ 3. Trained in Europe, John Sargent became <u>an extremely successful</u> portrait painter in the United States.

_____

_____ 4. For thousands of years, humankind has asked the question, "How old <u>the Earth is</u>?"

_____

_____ 5. For thousands of years, humankind has wondered how old *is the Earth*.

_____

_____ 6. Ammonia, a compound of nitrogen and hydrogen, has many <u>industrial uses</u>.

_____

_____ 7. The Atlantic coastline of the United States is about 400 <u>longer miles</u> than the Gulf coastline.

_____

_____ 8. Identical colors may appear to be quite different when <u>are they</u> viewed against different backgrounds.

_____

_____ 9. Zoos provide an opportunity to study a wide range of animals, often in their <u>habitats natural</u>.

_____

_____ 10. The development of transistors made <u>possible it</u> to reduce the size of many electronic devices.

_____

_____ 11. The air of the upper atmosphere is just <u>enough dense</u> to ignite meteors by friction.

_____

_____ 12. Monterey, California, has <u>long been</u> a center for artists and artisans.

_____

_____ 13. Cirrus clouds are composed <u>entirely almost</u> of ice crystals.

_____

_____ 14. Many sailboats are equipped with small engines for times when there is not <u>enough wind</u>.

_____

_____ 15. Prior to the 1940s, most runways were <u>too much</u> short for long distance airplanes to take off from, so many long distance aircraft <u>were seaplanes</u>.

_____

_____ 16. Margaret Wise Brown was a successful writer of <u>books children's</u>.

_____

EXERCISE 27.2

Focus: Identifying errors involving word-order. (Note: One or two items in this exercise do not focus on word order errors. These are marked in the answer key with an asterisk.)

Directions: For Sentence Completion items, mark the answer choice—(A), (B), (C), (D)—that correctly completes the sentence. For Error Identification items, circle the underlined portion of the sentence that would not be considered correct.

1. Hills known as land islands, or salt domes, are _____ Louisiana's marshlands.

   (A) extremely interesting features of
   (B) of extremely interesting features
   (C) interesting extremely features of
   (D) extremely interesting of features

2. During pioneer times, the Allegheny
   A
   Mountains were a barrier major
   B   C
   to transportation.
   D

3. An umbra is a shadow's darkest
   A
   central part where is light totally excluded.
   B   C   D

4. _____ of chamber music is the string quartet.

   (A) The famous most form
   (B) The most famous form
   (C) The form most famous
   (D) Most the form famous

5. In Philadelphia's Franklin Institute, there is
   A
   a working model of a human heart
   B   C
   enough large for visitors to walk through.
   D

6. Not until the seventeenth century _____ to measure the speed of light.

   (A) did anyone even attempt
   (B) anyone did even attempt
   (C) did anyone attempt even
   (D) did even attempt anyone

7. Alfalfa is _____ for livestock.

   (A) a primarily grown crop
   (B) grown primarily a crop
   (C) a crop grown primarily
   (D) a grown crop primarily

8. The Franklin stove, which became common in the 1790s, burned wood _____ an open fireplace.

   (A) efficiently much more than
   (B) much more efficiently than
   (C) much more than efficiently
   (D) more efficiently much than

9. Mutualism is a relationship between
   A
   animal species which in both benefit.
   B   C   D

10. Reinforced concrete is concrete that is strengthened by metal bars _____.

    (A) in it that are embedded
    (B) embedded that are in it
    (C) are that it embedded in
    (D) that are embedded in it

11. Most southern states had set up primary school systems by the late eighteenth century, but only in New England _____ and open to all students.

    (A) primary schools were free
    (B) were primary schools free
    (C) free were primary schools
    (D) were free primary schools

12. Sloths are moving slow, shaggy mammals
    A
    that are often seen hanging upside down
    B   C
    from tree limbs.
    D

13. Geometry is useful _____ carpentry and navigation.

    (A) as in such diverse occupations
    (B) such as in diverse occupations
    (C) in such diverse occupations as
    (D) diverse occupations such as in

14. To grow well, a tree must be well-suited to
    A   B   C
    the area where is it planted.
    D

15. The <u>minerals grains</u> in basalt are <u>much too</u>
          A   B
    small <u>to be seen</u> with the <u>unaided eye</u>.
          C   D

16. Frank Lloyd Wright is <u>known for</u> his
                    A
    <u>original highly</u> methods of
        B
    <u>harmonizing buildings</u> with
          C
    their <u>surroundings</u>.
        D

17. _____ of the early years of space exploration was the discovery of the Van Allen radiation belt in 1958.

    (A) Perhaps the greatest triumph
    (B) The triumph perhaps greatest
    (C) The greatest perhaps triumph
    (D) The triumph greatest perhaps

18. Some algae are <u>microscopic</u> and consist of
                A
    <u>one only cell</u>, but others are large plants <u>con-</u>
        B   C
    <u>taining</u> many cells.
      D

19. A <u>fully grown</u> <u>male mountain lion</u> may <u>be</u>
       A   B   C
    <u>eight long feet</u>.
      D

20. Today _____ major new products without conducting elaborate market research.

    (A) corporations hardly introduce ever
    (B) hardly ever corporations introduce
    (C) hardly ever introduce corporations
    (D) corporations hardly ever introduce

21. Across the Chesapeake Bay from the rest of the state _____, whose farms produce beans, tomatoes, and other garden vegetables.

    (A) there lies Maryland's Eastern Shore
    (B) lies Maryland's Eastern Shore
    (C) Maryland's Eastern Shore lies there
    (D) Maryland's Eastern Shore lies

22. Stone fruits are fruits <u>such as</u> peaches and
                      A
    plums <u>in which</u> a hard pit <u>surrounded is</u> by
         B   C
    <u>soft pulp</u>.
      D

23. Acidophilus bacteria are _____ in an acid medium.

    (A) those that grow best
    (B) those grow best that
    (C) that those grow best
    (D) grow best those that

24. Job enrichment is a <u>technique used</u> to
                        A
    increase <u>satisfaction workers'</u> by
              B
    <u>giving them</u> <u>more responsibilities</u>.
       C   D

REVIEW TEST F: STRUCTURE

Directions: For Sentence Completion items, mark the answer choice that correctly completes the sentence. For Error Identification items, circle the underlined portion of the sentence that would not be considered correct.

1. Commercial bakeries can make
   thousands of <u>loaves</u> of bread <u>on one time</u>
         A   B   C
   by <u>using</u> automated equipment.
      D

2. _____ book *Jubilee*, which was based on the life of her great-grandmother, Margaret Walker was awarded the Pulitzer Prize.

    (A) For her
    (B) Her
    (C) It was her
    (D) That her

3. North America is a <u>third largest</u> <u>of</u> the seven
               A   B   C
   <u>continents</u>.
     D

4. Rarely _____ more than fifty miles from the coast.

    (A) redwood trees grow
    (B) redwood trees do grow
    (C) grow redwood trees
    (D) do redwood trees grow

5. Until 1960, the state of Maine was unique
   —
   A
   in that it held Presidential and Congres-
                   —————————————
                   B
   sional elections on September, two months
   ————————————   —
                          C
   earlier than the rest of the nation.
   ——————
       D

6. Fuel injection engines employ injectors
                            ——————————
                            A
   instead a carburetor to spray fuel into the
   ——————   —————   ————
   B   C   D
   cylinders.

7. Nerve cells, or neurons, _____ in the
   human body.

   (A) the most complex cells are
   (B) are the most complex cells
   (C) most complex the cells are
   (D) most are the complex cells

8. Ocean currents have a enormous effect
        ————   —————————
        A   B
   on life on Earth.
   ————— ————
     C   D

9. About 8,000 years ago, people began using
            —————————   —————
                A   B
   animals to carry themselves and
                  ——————————
                     C
   their belongings.
   ——————
      D

10. A successful salesperson must have an
    ——————————   —————————
         A   B
    intuitive understanding of
              ——————————
                  C
    psychology human.
    ——————————
         D

11. A lodestone is _____.

    (A) an occurring naturally magnet
    (B) a magnet naturally occurring
    (C) naturally a magnet occurring
    (D) a naturally occurring magnet

12. Many folk songs have been written about
        ————   ——————   ————
         A   B   C
    railroads and railroads workers.
    ———————   ———————
                     D

13. The black walnut tree is grown principally
                        ——————————
                            A
    for its lumber, which is used for cabinets
    —————   ————————
      B   C
    and furnitures.
    ——————————
         D

14. Nashville, Tennessee, has _____ the
    capital of country music.

    (A) as long been known
    (B) been known long as
    (C) long been known as
    (D) long as been known

15. Flying squirrels can launch itself from
                      —————— ————
                         A   B
    the top of one tree and glide to another.
    ——————————   ———————————
        C   D

16. Frequently, the combination of several
                   ———————————
                        A
    spices will result of a more pleasing flavor
           ——————————   ——————————
                B   C
    than the use of just one.
    ————
      D

17. Hydraulic elevators are still used in some
                        ——————————
                             A
    old buildings, but all almost new buildings
    ————————   ——————————
         B   C
    are equipped with electrical elevators.
    ——————————
         D

18. Most birds that do not migrate eat seeds,
                   —————————— ——————
                        A   B
    and therefore do not depend insects for
    ————————   ——————————
        C   D
    food.

19. Some underground water is enough safe to
        ——————————   ——————————
            A   B
    drink, but all surface water must be treated.
    —————   ——————————
      C   D

20. _____ charming shops and restaurants,
    Old Town is the most picturesque section
    of Albuquerque.

    (A) With its
    (B) Its
    (C) Because its
    (D) For its

Lesson 28

CONJUNCTIONS

You may encounter errors with either **correlative conjunctions** or **coordinate conjunctions**.

ERRORS WITH CORRELATIVE CONJUNCTIONS

Correlative conjunctions are two-part adjectives. Errors usually involve an incorrect combination of the two parts, such as *neither . . . or* or *not only . . . and*. Anytime you see a sentence containing correlative conjunctions you should be on the lookout for this type of error. This is an easy error to spot!

Correlative Conjunctions

either . . . or
neither . . . nor
both . . . and
not only . . . but also
whether . . . or

Another error is the use of *both . . . and* to join three elements.

Sample Items

X rays have important applications, not only in medicine and in industry.
     A   B   C   D

The correct answer is (C). The correct pattern is *not only . . . but also*.

The air that surrounds our planet is both odorless, colorless, and invisible.
  A   B   C   D

The correct answer is (D). Because *both . . . and* can only be used to join two elements, the word *both* must be eliminated to correct the sentence.

ERRORS WITH COORDINATE CONJUNCTIONS

The conjunction *and* is correctly used to show addition; *or* is used to show choice between alternatives; *but* is used to show contrast or opposition.

Sample Item

Brakes and clutches <u>serve</u> very different <u>functions</u> in an automobile, <u>and</u> their principles of
          A   B   C

operation are <u>nearly the same.</u>
         D

The correct answer is (C). The first clause discusses how brakes and clutches are different; the second clause discusses how they are the same. Therefore, the conjunction joining them must show contrast. Choice (C) should read *but*.

EXERCISE 28

Focus: Identifying errors involving conjunctions
Directions: For Sentence Completion items, mark the answer choice that correctly completes the sentence. For Error Identification items, circle the underlined portion of the sentence that would not be considered correct.

1. Model airplanes <u>can be</u> guided <u>both</u> by
               A   B
<u>control wires</u> <u>or</u> by radio transmitters.
    C   D

2. Specialty stores, unlike department stores, handle only one line of merchandise _____ a limited number of closely related lines.

   (A) either
   (B) but
   (C) instead
   (D) or

3. Thomas Eakins studied not only painting _____ anatomy when he was training to become an artist.

   (A) moreover
   (B) but also
   (C) as well
   (D) and

4. Information in a computer <u>can be lost</u>
               A
<u>because</u> it is <u>not longer</u> stored <u>or</u> because it
   B   C   D
is stored but cannot be retrieved.

5. A mosaic is a <u>picture</u> <u>done</u> from small bits
            A   B
of <u>either</u> colored <u>glass or tile.</u>
   C   D

6. Although topology is the youngest branch of geometry, _____ is considered the most sophisticated.

   (A) but it
   (B) so it
   (C) it
   (D) however it

7. John Lancaster Spaulding <u>was</u> not only a
                     A
<u>religious leader</u> <u>and</u> also a social <u>reformer.</u>
   B   C   D

8. In 1923, Jean Toomer wrote a book titled *Cane* which combined fiction _____ poetry to describe the experience of being black in the United States.

   (A) and
   (B) to
   (C) also
   (D) or

9. Although <u>fish can hear, they</u> have neither
        A   B
<u>external ears or eardrums.</u>
   C   D

10. In all animals, whether simple <u>and complex,</u>
    A   B
enzymes aid in the <u>digestion</u> <u>of food.</u>
           C   D

11. Endive can be used as a salad green or as a cooking vegetable.

    (A) such
    (B) both
    (C) either
    (D) neither

12. The two most common methods florists
    _____
       A
    are used to tint flowers are the spray
    _____
       B
    method and the absorption method.
    _____   _____
        C   D

13. Beekeepers can sell both the honey and the
    _____   ____   ___
        A   B
    beeswax that their bees produces.
            _____   _____
              C   D

14. Glucose does not have to be digested,
    _____ it can be put directly into the
    bloodstream.

    (A) so
    (B) while
    (C) and since
    (D) such

15. The human brain is often compared to a
                     _____
                            A
    computer, and such an analogy can be
              _____ _____
                B   C
    misleading.
    _____
        D

16. Not only rust corrodes the surface of metal,
    _____ ____   _____
        A   B
    but it also weakens its internal structure.
    _____   _____
        C   D

17. Natural fiber comes from either animal
    _____ plant sources.

    (A) or
    (B) otherwise
    (C) and
    (D) nor

18. A work of science fiction generally uses
                              _____ ____
                                           A
    scientific discoveries and advanced technol-
               _____
                    B
    ogy, either real or imaginary, as part of their
           ____ ____   _____
                 C   D
    plot.

19. Community theater not only provides
    _____ _____

    entertainment for local audiences as well as
    _____   _____
          A   B
    furnishes a creative outlet for amateurs
    _____   _____
       C   D
    interested in drama.

20. Paint is _____ used to protect wood.

    (A) not only the substance
    (B) the substance which is not only
    (C) not only a substance which is
    (D) not the only substance

Lesson 29

COMPARISONS

You may see sentences involving comparisons in both types of Structure items. Many of these involve the comparative or superlative forms of adjectives.

Most adjectives have three forms: the absolute (the basic adjective form), the comparative, and the superlative. Comparatives are used to show that one item has more of some quality that another does.

George is *taller* than his brother.

Superlatives are used to show that one item in a group of three or more has the greatest amount of some quality.

He was the *tallest* man in the room.

The chart explains how comparatives and superlatives are formed:

	Absolute	**Comparative**	**Superlative**
One-syllable adjectives	warm	warmer	the warmest
Two-syllable adjectives ending with *-y*	funny	funnier	the funniest
Other two-syllable adjectives	common	more common	the most common
Adjectives with three or more syllables	important	more important	the most important

Some two-syllable adjectives have two correct forms of both the comparative and the superlative:

narrower	clever	polite
more narrow	more clever	more polite
narrowest	cleverest	politest
most narrow	most clever	most polite

A "negative" comparison can be expressed with the words *less* and *least*. *Less* and *least* are used no matter how many syllables an adjective has.

less bright	less expensive
the least bright	the least expensive

The absolute form of a few adjectives ends in *-er* (*tender, bitter, slender, clever,* and so on.) Don't confuse these with the comparative forms (*more bitter* or *bitterer,* for example).

Many adverbs also have comparative and superlative forms. The comparative and superlative forms of all *-ly* adverbs are formed with *more* and *most*.

more brightly	more importantly
most brightly	most importantly

A few adjectives and adverbs have irregular comparative and superlative forms:

Irregular Comparatives and Superlatives

good/well	better	the best
bad/badly	worse	the worst
far	farther	the farthest
	further	the furthest

(*Far* has two comparative and superlative forms, depending on how the word is used, but the distinction between these two forms will not be tested.)

There are two main types of errors involving comparatives and superlatives:

INCORRECT CHOICE OF THE THREE FORMS

Any of the three forms—absolute, comparative, or superlative—may be incorrectly used in place of one of the other forms.

Sample Items

> Basketball is played at a much fast pace than baseball.
>   A   B   C   D

The correct answer is (C). The comparative form *faster* is needed because two concepts—the pace of *basketball* and the pace of *baseball*—are being compared.

> The deep oceans contain some of the stranger of all living creatures.
>   A   B   C   D

The correct answer is (C). This sentence does not compare two groups; a superlative form (*strangest*) is required.

INCORRECT FORMS OF COMPARATIVES AND SUPERLATIVES

Incorrect forms such as *more bigger*, *most hot*, and so on, may appear.

Sample Item

> The most small vessels in the circulatory system are capillaries.
>   A   B   C D

The correct answer is (A). The correct form is *smallest* because *small* is a one-syllable adjective.

EXERCISE 29

Focus: Identifying and correcting errors and correct forms of comparatives and superlatives.

Directions: For Sentence Completion items, mark the answer choice that correctly completes the sentence. For Error Identification items, circle the underlined portion of the sentence that would not be considered correct.

1. The American and Canadian political systems
   <u> </u>
   A
   are like in that both are dominated by two
   <u> </u> <u> </u> <u> </u>
   B   C   D
   major parties.

2. Wild strawberries are _____ cultivated strawberries.

   (A) not sweeter
   (B) not as sweet as
   (C) less sweeter than
   (D) not sweet as

3. The period is probably the most easiest
   <u> </u> <u> </u> <u> </u>
   A   B   C
   punctuation mark to use.
   <u> </u>
   D

4. When metal replaced wood
   <u> </u>
   A
   in the construction of ships' hulls,
   <u> </u>
   B
   more strong ships could be built.
   <u> </u>   <u> </u>
   C   D

5. Sea bass _____ freshwater bass.

   (A) are larger than
   (B) the larger the
   (C) are as large
   (D) than are larger

6. Charcoal is the more commonly used
   <u> </u> <u> </u>
   A   B
   cooking fuel in the world.
   <u> </u>   <u> </u>
   C   D

7. Automobiles, airplanes, and buses use more
   energy per passenger _____.

   (A) as do trains
   (B) than trains do
   (C) trains do
   (D) like trains

8. Few American politicians have spoken more
   <u> </u>   <u> </u>
   A   B
   eloquently as William Jennings Bryan.
   <u> </u>   <u> </u>
   C   D

9. The larger a drop of water, _____
   freezing temperature.

   (A) the higher its
   (B) its higher
   (C) higher than its
   (D) the highest

10. _____ San Diego and San Francisco,
    Los Angeles has no natural harbor.

    (A) Dissimilar
    (B) Unlike
    (C) Dislike
    (D) Different

11. During a depression, economic conditions
    <u> </u>   <u> </u>
    A   B
    are far worst than they are during a
    <u> </u>   <u> </u>
    C   D
    recession.

12. The spinal column is alike the brain in that
    <u> </u>
    A
    its main functions can be classified as either
    <u> </u>
    B
    sensory or motor functions.
    <u> </u>   <u> </u>
    C   D

13. The water of the Great Salt Lake is
    _____ seawater.

    (A) saltier than that of
    (B) as salty as that of
    (C) saltier than
    (D) so salty as

14. Fungi are the most important decomposers
    <u> </u>
    A
    of forest soil, just like bacteria are the most
    <u> </u>   <u> </u>
    B   C
    important decomposers of grassland soil.
    <u> </u>
    D

15. A psychosis is a severe mental disorder,
    _____ a neurosis.

    (A) the most serious
    (B) as serious
    (C) more serious than
    (D) as though serious

16. The surfboards used thirty-five years ago
            A   B
    were more heavy than the ones used by
         C   D
    surfers today.

17. The horse chestnut has a stronger, bitter
       A   B   C
    taste than other chestnuts.
             D

18. The social system of bumblebees is not as
    complex _____.

    (A) than honeybees
    (B) as honeybees
    (C) that honeybees are
    (D) as that of honeybees

19. Chicago's Field Museum is one of
                               A
    the largest and better known natural history
         B   C
    museums in the United States.
          D

20. The administration of private colleges is
    nearly _____ that of public colleges.

    (A) same
    (B) just as
    (C) the same as
    (D) similar

Lesson 30

APPOSITIVES

An **appositive** is a noun phrase that explains or rephrases another noun phrase. It usually comes after the noun that it rephrases. It may also come before the subject of a sentence.

Buffalo Bill, *a famous frontiersman*, operated his own Wild West Show. (appositive following a noun)

A famous frontiersman, Buffalo Bill operated his own Wild West Show. (appositive before the subject)

Appositives are actually reduced adjective clauses that contain the verb *to be*. However, unlike adjective clauses, they do not contain a marker or a verb.

Oak, *which is one of the most durable hard woods*, is often used to make furniture. (adjective clause)

Oak, *one of the most durable hard woods*, is often used to make furniture. (appositive)

Appositives are usually separated from the rest of the sentence by commas, but short appositives (usually names) are not.

Economist *Paul Samuelson* won a Nobel Prize in 1970.

In Structure items, all or part of an appositive phrase may be missing. In addition, the noun that the appositive refers to or other parts of the main clause may be missing.

Sample Item

The National Road, _____ of the first highways in North America, connected the East Coast to the Ohio Valley.

(A) which one
(B) it was one
(C) one
(D) was one

The correct answer is (C). Choice (A) is incorrect; there is no verb in the relative clause. Choice (B) has no connecting word to join the clause to the rest of the sentence. Choice (D) is incorrect because a verb cannot be used in an appositive phrase. Note: *which was one* would also be a correct answer for this problem.

EXERCISE 30

Focus: Completing structure problems involving appositives. (Note: The focus for one or two items in this exercise is NOT appositives; these sentences are marked in the answer key with asterisks.)

Directions: Mark the answer choice that correctly completes the sentence.

1. The Democratic party is older than the other major American political party, _____.

   (A) which the Republican party
   (B) the Republican party
   (C) it is the Republican party
   (D) the Republican party is

2. _____ relations with friends and acquaintances, play a major role in the social development of adolescents.

   (A) What are called peer group relations are
   (B) Peer group relations are
   (C) Peer group relations, the
   (D) By peer group relations, we mean

3. Joseph Henry, _____ director of the Smithsonian Institution, was President Lincoln's adviser on scientific matters.

   (A) the first
   (B) to be the first
   (C) was the first
   (D) as the first

4. The Wassatch Range, _____ extends from southeastern Idaho into northern Utah.

   (A) which is a part of the Rocky Mountains,
   (B) a part of the Rocky Mountains that
   (C) is a part of the Rocky Mountains
   (D) a part of the Rocky Mountains, it

5. _____ Ruth St. Dennis turned to Asian dances to find inspiration for her choreography.

   (A) It was the dancer
   (B) The dancer
   (C) That the dancer
   (D) The dancer was

6. _____ a vast network of computers that connects many of the world's businesses, institutions, and individuals, primarily through modems and phone lines.

   (A) The Internet,
   (B) That the Internet, as
   (C) The Internet is
   (D) The Internet, which

7. In 1878, Frederick W. Taylor invented a concept called scientific management, _____ of obtaining as much efficiency from workers and machines as possible.

   (A) it is a method
   (B) a method which
   (C) a method
   (D) called a method

8. A group of Shakers, _____ settled around Pleasant Hill, Kentucky, in 1805.

   (A) members of a strict religious sect which
   (B) whose members of a strict religious sect
   (C) members of a strict religious sect,
   (D) were members of a strict religious sect

9. In physics, _____ "plasma" refers to a gas that has a nearly equal number of positively and negatively charged particles.

   (A) the term
   (B) by the term
   (C) is termed
   (D) terming

Lesson 31

MISPLACED MODIFIERS

A **misplaced modifier** is a participial phrase or other modifier that comes before the subject, but does NOT refer to the subject.
Look at this sentence:

*Driving down the road, a herd of sheep suddenly crossed the road in front of Liza's car.
(INCORRECT)

This sentence is incorrect because it seems to say that a herd of sheep—rather than Liza—was driving down the road. The participial phrase is misplaced. The sentence could be corrected as shown:

As Liza was driving down the road, a herd of sheep suddenly crossed the road in front of her.
(CORRECT)

This sentence now correctly has Liza in the driver's seat instead of the sheep.
The following sentence structures are often misplaced:

Misplaced Structure	Example	Correction
present participle	Walking along the beach, the ship was spotted by the men.	Walking along the beach, the men spotted the ship.
past participle	Based on this study, the scientist could make several conclusions.	Based on this study, several conclusions could be made by the scientist.
appositive	A resort city in Arkansas, the population of Hot Springs is about 35,000.	A resort city in Arkansas, Hot Springs has a population of about 35,000.
reduced adjective clause	While peeling onions, his eyes began to water.	While he was peeling onions, his eyes began to water.
adjective phrases	Warm and mild, everyone enjoys the climate of the Virgin Islands.	Everyone enjoys the warm, mild climate of the Virgin Islands.
expressions with like or unlike	Like most cities, parking is a problem in San Francisco.	Like most cities, San Francisco has a parking problem.

Structure items with misplaced modifiers are usually easy to spot. They generally consist of a modifying element at the beginning of the sentence followed by a comma, with the rest or most of the rest of the sentence missing. The answer choices tend to be long. To find the answer, you must decide what subject the modifier correctly refers to.

Sample Item

Using a device called a cloud chamber, _____ .

(A) experimental proof for the atomic theory was found by Robert Millikin
(B) Robert Millikin's experimental proof for the atomic theory was found
(C) Robert Millikin found experimental proof for the atomic theory
(D) there was experimental proof found for the atomic theory by Robert Millikin

The correct answer is (C). Choices (A) and (B) are incorrect because the modifier (*Using a device called a cloud chamber...*) could not logically refer to the subjects (*experimental proof* and *Robert Millikin's experimental proof*). Choice (D) is incorrect because a modifier can never properly refer to the introductory words *there* or *it*.

EXERCISE 31

Focus: Completing structure problems involving misplaced modifiers. (Note: ALL the items in this exercise focus on misplaced modifiers.)

Directions: Mark the answer choice that correctly completes the sentence.

1. Fearing economic hardship, _____ .

   (A) many New Englanders emigrated to the Midwest in the 1820s
   (B) emigration from New England to the Midwest took place in the 1820s
   (C) it was in the 1820s that many New Englanders emigrated to the Midwest
   (D) an emigration took place in the 1820s from New England to the Midwest

2. Rich and distinctive in flavor, _____ .

   (A) there is in the United States a very important nut crop, the pecan
   (B) the most important nut crop in the United States, the pecan
   (C) farmers in the United States raise pecans, a very important nut crop
   (D) pecans are the most important nut crop in the United States

3. Orbiting from 2.7 to 3.6 billion miles from the sun, _____ .

   (A) the astronomer Clyde Tombaugh discovered Pluto in 1930
   (B) Pluto was discovered by the astronomer Clyde Tombaugh in 1930
   (C) it was in 1930 that the astronomer Clyde Tombaugh discovered Pluto
   (D) the discovery of Pluto was made by Clyde Tombaugh in 1930

4. A popular instrument, _____ .

   (A) only a limited role has been available to the accordion in classical music
   (B) there is only a limited role for the accordion in popular music
   (C) classical music provides only a limited role for the accordion
   (D) the accordion has played only a limited role in classical music

5. Unlike most birds, _____ .

   (A) the heads and necks of vultures lack feathers
   (B) feathers are not found on the heads and necks of vultures
   (C) vultures do not have feathers on their heads and necks
   (D) there are no feathers on vultures' heads and necks

6. Widely reproduced in magazines and books, _____ .

   (A) Ansel Adams depicted the Western wilderness in his photographs
   (B) the Western wilderness was depicted in the photographs of Ansel Adams
   (C) Ansel Adams' photographs depicted the Western wilderness
   (D) it was through his photographs that Ansel Adams depicted the Western wilderness

7. Smaller and flatter than an orange, _____A_____.

 (A) a tangerine is easy to peel and its sections separate readily
 (B) the peel of a tangerine is easily removed and its sections are readily separated
 (C) it's easy to peel a tangerine and to separate its sections
 (D) to peel a tangerine is easy, and its sections can be readily separated

8. Like the federal government, _____B_____.

 (A) taxation provides most of the funds for state and local governments as well
 (B) state and local governments obtain most of their funds through taxation
 (C) through taxation is how state and local governments obtain most of their funds
 (D) funds are provided from taxation for state and local governments

9. Originally settled by Polynesians around 700 AD, _____A_____.

 (A) Hawaii received its first European visitor in 1778, when Captain James Cook landed there
 (B) Hawaii's first European visitor, Captain James Cook, landed there in 1778
 (C) in 1778 the first European, Captain James Cook, visited Hawaii
 (D) the first European to visit Hawaii was Captain James Cook, landing there in 1778

Lesson 32

The answer choices for this type of item are four negative expressions, such as the ones listed below:

Negative Word	Use	Meaning	Example
no	adjective	not any	There was *no* milk in the refrigerator.
none	pronoun	not one	They took a lot of pictures, but almost *none* of them turned out.
nothing	pronoun	not anything	There was *nothing* in his briefcase.
no one	pronoun	not anyone	*No one* arrived at the meeting on time.
nor	conjunction	and . . . not	He's never been fishing, *nor* does he plan to go.
without	preposition	not having	She likes her coffee *without* milk or sugar.
never	adverb	at no time	I've *never* been to Alaska.

The negative word *not* is used to make almost any kind of word or phrase negative: verbs, prepositional phrases, infinitives, adjectives, and so on.

Both *no* and *not* can be used before nouns, depending on meaning:

There is *no* coffee in the pot. (It's empty.)
This is *not* coffee. (It's tea.)

The adjective *no* is also used before the word *longer* to mean "not anymore":

I no longer read the afternoon paper.

Sample Item

There is almost _____ vegetation in the Badlands, a barren region of South Dakota.

(A) not
(B) nor
(C) none
(D) no

The correct answer is (D). Choices (A), (B), and (C) cannot be used before nouns as adjectives.

By the way, probably the most common correct answer for this type of problem is the adjective *no*.

EXERCISE 32

Focus: Completing structure problems involving negative words. (Note: ALL the items in this exercise focus on negative words.)

Directions: For Sentence Completion items, mark the answer choice—(A), (B), (C), or (D)—that correctly completes the sentence. For Error Identification items, circle the underlined portion of the sentence that would not be considered correct.

1. Early carpenters, having ___*not*___ nails, had to use wooden pegs to secure their constructions.

    (A) no
    (B) not
    (C) without
    (D) neither

2. Old Faithful is the most famous but _____ the most powerful geyser in Yellowstone National Park.

    (A) none of
    (B) no
    (C) nothing
    (D) not

3. Joseph Priestly, the <u>discoverer</u> of oxygen,
                              A
   had little or <u>not</u> interest in <u>science</u> until he
                  B   C
   <u>met</u> Benjamin Franklin in Paris.
    D

4. Mobile homes were ___*nor*___ counted as permanent houses until the 1960 census.

    (A) not
    (B) nor
    (C) no
    (D) none

5. Most solo musicians play ___*without*___ sheet music in front of them.

    (A) without
    (B) not having
    (C) lacking
    (D) and no

6. Desertification is the creation of deserts where _____ had existed before.

    (A) never
    (B) no one
    (C) none
    (D) not one

7. A peanut is <u>not</u> actually a nut <u>but</u> a legume
      C   A   B
   <u>alike</u> peas <u>and</u> beans.
      C   D

8. Glass snakes are actually legless lizards, ___*not*___ snakes.

    (A) no
    (B) not
    (C) nor
    (D) none

9. Twenty-four carat gold is <u>no</u> one hundred
                               A
   <u>percent gold</u> because <u>pure gold</u> is <u>too soft</u>
       B   C   D
   to be used in jewelry.

10. There is ___*no*___ truth to the old expression "Lightning never strikes the same place twice."

    (A) without
    (B) none
    (C) no
    (D) not

11. ___*Not one of*___ single person can be said to have invented the automobile.

    (A) There was not a
    (B) Nor a
    (C) Not one of
    (D) No

12. A serious study of physics is impossible ___*without*___ some knowledge of mathematics.

    (A) not with
    (B) no
    (C) not having
    (D) without

REVIEW TEST G: STRUCTURE

Directions: For Sentence Completion items, select the answer choice—(A), (B), (C), (D)—that correctly completes the sentence. For Error Identification items, select the answer choice—(A), (B), (C), (D)—that corresponds to the underlined portion of the sentence that would not be considered correct.

1. _____ one of Canada's greatest engineering projects, is a twenty-seven mile long waterway between Lake Erie and Lake Ontario.

   (A) Because the Welland Ship Canal is
   (B) The Welland Ship Canal is
   (C) That the Welland Ship Canal is
   (D) The Welland Ship Canal,

2. Pikes Peak, named for explorer Zebulon Pike, is Colorado's most famous but not its
   A   B   C
   most highest mountain.
   D

3. Oceanography is not a single science and
                        A   B
   rather a group of disciplines with a com-
                                   C
   mon focus.
   D

4. The art of landscape architecture is _____ that of architecture itself.

   (A) almost as old as
   (B) as almost old
   (C) almost as old than
   (D) old as almost

5. The term *forgetting* refers to the loss,
                        A
   whether temporary and long-term, of
                        B
   material that has previously been learned.
              C   D

6. Early astronomers believed that the fainter a star, _____.

   (A) it was farther away
   (B) the farther away was it
   (C) that it was farther away
   (D) the farther away it was

7. Released in 1915, _____.

   (A) D. W. Griffith made an epic film about the Civil War, *Birth of a Nation*
   (B) the Civil War was the subject of D. W. Griffith's epic film, *Birth of a Nation*
   (C) D. W. Griffith's epic film *Birth of a Nation* was about the Civil War
   (D) the subject of D. W. Griffith's epic film *Birth of a Nation* was the Civil War

8. One way pumpkins and watermelons are like is that both grow on vines
   A   B
   trailing along the surface of the ground.
   C   D

9. _____ the reptiles alive today is capable of flight.

   (A) No
   (B) None of
   (C) Not one
   (D) Not

10. When the female oriole is absent from the
    A   B
    nest, the male oriole serves like a sentinel.
    C   D

11. Elfego Baca, _____ legendary Mexican-American folk hero, was a lawman in New Mexico in the late 1880s.

    (A) a
    (B) who, as a
    (C) was a
    (D) and he was a

12. Until the 1940s, a historian's own era was
    A
    no regarded as a proper field of study.
    B   C   D

13. An operetta has some of the same musical elements as an opera and is much lighter in
                    A   B   C
    both subject and style.
    D

14. Properly administered, _____.

(A) the symptoms of many mental illnesses can be treated with drugs
(B) drugs can be used to treat the symptoms of many mental illnesses
(C) doctors can use drugs to treat symptoms of many mental illnesses
(D) many of the symptoms of mental illness can be treated with drugs

15. Early explorers in Utah named the cliffs
            A
they encountered "reefs" because they
                      B
thought these cliffs looked alike coral
       C   D
formations.

16. Neither humans or dogs can hear as well as
          A   B   C
cats.
D

17. _____ popular child's toy since 1905, the teddy bear was named after President Theodore Roosevelt.

(A) It has been a
(B) A
(C) Once a
(D) First it became a

18. Just like microscopes have provided access
    A   B
to the world of small objects, high-speed
           C
cameras have provided access to the world
of short-duration events.
      D

19. _____ plant has a nervous system, and most respond very slowly to stimuli in their environments.

(A) Not a
(B) Never a
(C) No
(D) None

20. Gold topaz is much rare than either white
        A   B   C
or blue topaz.
D

21. Vermont is the only state in New England _____ an Atlantic coastline.

(A) without
(B) not with
(C) which not having
(D) doesn't have

22. The Colorado beetle is a beautiful insect, _____ it causes a great deal of damage to food crops.

(A) but
(B) what
(C) or
(D) which

23. Jupiter's moons can be easily seen through _____ binoculars or a small telescope.

(A) either
(B) if
(C) whether
(D) or

24. The Kennedy-Nixon race of 1960 was the
                  A
most closest U.S. presidential election of the
   B   C   D
twentieth century.

25. _____ a river on land, an ocean current does not flow in a straight line.

(A) Alike
(B) Likewise
(C) Like
(D) Likely

Section 3

READING

RED ALERT

INTRODUCTION

This part of the exam tests your ability to read and answer items about passages in formal written English. It contains four or five passages. After each passage there are 10 to 14 items about that passage for a total of 50 to 60 questions in this part. The passages vary in length from about 250 to 350 words.

This section tests your ability to find main ideas, supporting ideas, and details; use context clues to understand the meaning of vocabulary; draw inferences; recognize coherence; figure out the organization of the passage; and perform other basic reading skills. This part of the test is **linear**—it is NOT computer adaptive. You can skip items and come back to them later or change answers at a later time. The items you are given are not chosen according to your previous answers. Because this section is linear, the tactics you use will be somewhat different from those in the first two parts of the test.

Some item types are "computer unique"— they did not appear on the paper-based test. There are also item types that have changed somewhat to take advantage of the computer's capabilities.

THE PASSAGES

The passages cover a wide range of topics, but in general can be classified as follows:

1. **Science and Technology**
   Includes astronomy, geology, chemistry, physics, mathematics, zoology, botany, medicine, engineering, mechanics, and so on.

2. **North American History, Government, Geography, and Culture**

3. **Art**
   Includes literature, painting, architecture, dance, drama, and so on.

4. **Social Science**
   Includes anthropology, economics, psychology, urban studies, sociology, and so on.

5. **Biography**

Some passages may be classified in more than one way. For example, a biography might be about the life of a historical figure, an artist, or a scientist.

If there is a national context for any of the passages, it is American or occasionally Canadian. Therefore, if a passage is about history, it will be about the history of the United States or Canada.

Although the passages deal with various topics, the style in which they are written is similar, and they usually follow fairly simple patterns of organization.

The vocabulary used in the Reading portion is fairly sophisticated. There will almost certainly be words that you do not recognize. Sometimes you can guess the meaning of these words by context. However, it is not necessary to understand all the vocabulary in the passages in order to answer the questions.

THE ITEMS

According to the way they are answered, there are three types of items on the test.

Standard Multiple-Choice Items

These are very similar to the items found on the paper-based test. Most multiple-choice items can be categorized as one of the following seven types of items:

Type of Item	Explanation	Example
1. Overview Items	These ask you to identify an answer choice that correctly summarizes the author's main idea, the subject of the whole passage, or the author's reason for writing the passage.	"What is the main idea of the passage?" "What is the passage primarily about?" "Why did the author write the passage?"
2. Detail Items	These ask you to locate and identify answers to questions about specific information and details in the passage.	"According to the passage, where did . . . ?" "According to the author, why did . . . ?" "Which of the following is true, according to the passage?"
3. Negative Items	These ask which of the answer choices is NOT discussed in the passage.	"Which of the following is NOT true about . . ." "All of the following are true EXCEPT . . ."
4. Purpose Items	These ask you to explain why the author of the passage uses a certain word, sentence, or example or what the purpose of a sentence or example is.	"Why does the author mention . . . in paragraph 2"? "What is the purpose of the following sentence in paragraph 2"?
5. Inference Items	These ask you to draw conclusions based on information in the passage.	"The author implies that which of the following is true?" "Which of the following can be inferred from the passage?"
6. Vocabulary-in-Context Items	These ask you identify the meaning of a word or phrase as used in the passage.	"The word ▨▨▨ in line 5 is closest in meaning to . . ."
7. Reference Items*	These ask you to identify the noun to which a pronoun or other expression refers.	"The word 'it' in line 15 refers to . . ." "In line 20, the word 'there' refers to which of the following?"

* Most reference items are "click on" items, but a few are multiple choice.

About half the multiple-choice items have **closed stems**; they begin with direct questions. The others have **open stems**; they begin with incomplete sentences.

CLOSED STEM
Which of the following is the main topic of the passage?

OPEN STEM
The main topic of the passage is

Click on the Passage Items

These types of items are NOT followed by a list of four possible answers with ovals by them. Instead, you must click on some part of the passage. For most of these items, you can only click on the part of the passage that is in **bold** or in a paragraph that is marked with an arrow. For a few items, you can click anywhere in the passage.

Type of Item	Explanation	Example
Scanning Items	These ask you to find a word, phrase, or paragraph in the passage that plays a specific logical or organizational role in the passage.	Click on the paragraph in the passage that outlines . . . Click on the sentence in paragraph 2 that explains . . .
Synonym/Antonym Items	These ask you to find a word or phrase in a marked part of the passage that has the same meaning (synonym) or the opposite meaning (antonym) as a highlighted word.	Look at the word _____ in the passage. Click on the word or phrase in the **bold** text that is closest in meaning to _____. Look at the word _____ in the passage. Click on the word or phrase in the **bold** text that is most nearly opposite _____ in meaning.
Reference Items	These ask you to find in a marked portion of a passage the noun to which a highlighted pronoun or other word refers.	Look at the word them in the passage. Click on the word or phrase in the **bold** text to which it refers.

Sentence Addition Items

This type of item provides you with a sentence that can be inserted into a passage. You must decide where this sentence belongs. When you see a sentence addition item, small black squares will appear between the sentences in part of the passage—usually one or two paragraphs long. You have to click on the squares between the two sentences where you think the sentence should be inserted.

WHAT IS THE BEST WAY TO ATTACK THE PASSAGES?

First, read the article at a comfortable speed. After you have read the first screen, scroll through the rest of the passage at a steady pace.

Word-by-word reading slows you down and interferes with your comprehension. Try to read in units of thought, grouping words into related phrases.

During your first reading, don't worry about understanding or remembering details. You can come back and look for that information later. Try to get a general idea of what each of the paragraphs is about and what the passage as a whole is about.

WHAT IS THE BEST WAY TO ANSWER THE ITEMS?

It's important to remember that your goal is not to understand the passages perfectly but to answer as many items correctly as you can. You need to focus on the items, not the passage. Although you CAN skip items in this section, this is not a good idea. You should answer each item as it comes up, even if you have to guess. However, if you have any doubts, you should write down the number of that item on your notepaper. (You will be given six sheets of notepaper after the break between Section 2 and 3; it is actually for the Writing section, but you can use it during the Reading section as well to keep track of difficult items).

ARE THERE ANY "SECRETS" FOR FINDING ANSWERS IN THE PASSAGE QUICKLY?

Yes! When you are answering some types of items—mainly detail items and inference items—the most important factor is simply to locate the information quickly. Here are some pointers that will help:

1. The items—except for the first and maybe the last item in each set—strictly follow the order of the passage. In other words, the answers for the first few items will be near the top of the passage. To find information for the last few items, you will have to scroll down to the last part of the passage.

2. Reference items and vocabulary items can help you pinpoint the information you need to answer other types of items. Let's say that Item 2 is a synonym item. The computer will highlight a word. Let's say Item 3 is a detail item and Item 4 is an inference item. Then let's say Item 5 is a reference item. Again the computer will highlight a word. This tells us that the information needed to answer Items 3 and 4 is somewhere between the two words that are highlighted.

WHAT ARE SOME IMPORTANT FACTORS IN SCORING HIGH IN THIS SECTION?

Timing

Timing is an important factor. Most test takers find this the hardest to complete because reading the passages takes up so much time. You will have 70 to 90 minutes to complete this section—an average of about fifteen minutes to read each passage and answer the items about it. Use the clock on the screen to pace yourself.

What should you do if, near the end of the test, you realize that you don't have enough time to finish? Don't panic! Let's say that you have one more passage to complete and there are only about four or five minutes remaining. You should skim over the passage to get the main idea. Answer the first item about the passage (which will probably be a main idea item). Then answer all of the vocabulary items and reference items because these require less time. (You'll need to click on the Next icon to locate these). Then go back and answer any remaining items (clicking on the Prev icon). Refer to the passage as little as possible. If you can't find the information needed to answer the item in about 10 seconds, just pick the choice that seems most logical. Then, in the last few seconds, answer any remaining items by clicking on your "guess answer."

On the other hand, if you *do* finish the test before time is called, go back and work on items

that you had trouble with the first time. Don't exit this section until all the time is up.

Concentration

Concentration is another important factor. This is the longest section of the test. For some people, it's the most difficult. You may find it hard to concentrate on a computer screen for so long. Your eyes may get tired. You may find it more difficult to maneuver through passages on a screen than in a book.

Practice can help. If you purchased the CD-ROM version of this book, you can access Peterson's online TOEFL practice test. Otherwise, visit www.petersons.com and register to take the online practice test. Also visit sites on the Internet that interest you or work with CD-ROM encyclopedias.

Strategies for Section 3

- As with the other sections, be familiar with the directions and examples for Section 3 so that you can begin work immediately.

- For each passage, begin by briefly looking over the questions (but not the answer choices). Try to keep these questions in mind during your reading.

- Read each passage at a comfortable speed.

- Answer the questions, referring to the passage when necessary.

- Eliminate answers that are clearly wrong or do not answer the questions. If more than one option remains, guess.

- Mark difficult or time-consuming answers so that you can come back to them later if you have time. Erase all these marks before the end of the test.

- Don't spend more than about 10 minutes on any one reading and the questions about it.

- When only a few minutes remain, **don't** start guessing blindly. Skim the remaining passage or passages quickly, then answer the first question in each set. Then answer any questions with line numbers. After that, read the remaining questions, and if you can't find the question quickly, choose the one that seems most logical to you.

- When there are only a few seconds left, fill in all remaining blanks with your guess letter.

This section of the test measures your ability to understand the meaning of words and to comprehend written materials.

Directions: The remainder of this section contains several passages, each followed by 10–14 questions. Read the passages and, for each question, choose the *one* best answer—(A), (B), (C), or (D)—based on what is stated in or on what can be inferred from the passage.

Passage 1

The technology of the North American Colonies did not differ strikingly from that of Europe, but in one respect, the colonists enjoyed a great advantage. Especially by comparison with Britain, Americans had a wonderfully plentiful supply of wood.

The first colonists did not, as many people imagine, find an entire continent covered by a climax forest. Even along the Atlantic seaboard, the forest was broken at many points. Nevertheless, all sorts of fine trees abounded, and through the early colonial period, those who pushed westward encountered new forests. By the end of the Colonial era, the price of wood had risen slightly in eastern cities, but wood was still extremely abundant.

The availability of wood brought advantages that have seldom been appreciated. Wood was a foundation of the economy. Houses and all manner of buildings were made of wood to a degree unknown in Britain. Secondly, wood was used as a fuel for heating and cooking. Thirdly, it was used as the source of important industrial compounds, such as potash, an industrial alkali; charcoal, a component of gunpowder; and tannic acid, used for tanning leather.

The supply of wood conferred advantages, but had some negative aspects as well. Iron at that time was produced by heating iron ore with charcoal. Because Britain was so stripped of trees, she was unable to exploit her rich iron mines. But the American Colonies had both iron ore and wood; iron production was encouraged and became successful. However, when Britain developed coke smelting, the Colonies did not follow suit because they had plenty of wood and besides, charcoal iron was stronger than coke iron. Coke smelting led to technological innovations and was linked to the emergence of the Industrial Revolution. In the early nineteenth century, the former Colonies lagged behind Britain in industrial development because their supply of wood led them to cling to charcoal iron.

1. What does the passage mainly discuss?

   (A) The advantages of using wood in the colonies
   (B) The effects of an abundance of wood on the colonies
   (C) The roots of the Industrial Revolution
   (D) The difference between charcoal iron and coke iron

2. The word strikingly in the first paragraph is closest in meaning to

   (A) realistically.
   (B) dramatically.
   (C) completely.
   (D) immediately.

3. Which of the following is a common assumption about the forests of North America during the Colonial period?

   (A) They contained only a few types of trees.
   (B) They existed only along the Atlantic seaboard.
   (C) They had little or no economic value.
   (D) They covered the entire continent.

4. Look at the word plentiful in the **bold** text below.

Especially by comparison with Britain, Americans had a wonderfully plentiful supply of wood.

The first colonists did not, as many people imagine, find an entire continent covered by a climax forest. Even along the Atlantic seaboard, the forest was broken at many points. Nevertheless, there was an abundant supply of fine trees of all types, and through the early colonial period, those who pushed westward encountered new forests.

Underline the word or phrase in the **bold** text that has the same meaning as plentiful.

5. According to the passage, by the end of the Colonial period, the price of wood in eastern cities

    (A) rose quickly because wood was becoming so scarce.
    (B) was much higher than it was in Britain.
    (C) was slightly higher than in previous years.
    (D) decreased rapidly because of lower demand for wood.

6. What can be inferred about houses in Britain during the period written about in the passage?

    (A) They were more expensive than American houses.
    (B) They were generally built with imported materials.
    (C) They were typically smaller than homes in North America.
    (D) They were usually built from materials other than wood.

7. Why does the author mention gunpowder in paragraph 3?

    (A) To illustrate the negative aspects of some industrial processes
    (B) To give an example of a product made with wood compounds
    (C) To remind readers that the Colonial era ended in warfare
    (D) To suggest that wood was not the only important product of the Colonies

8. The phrase follow suit in paragraph 4 means

    (A) do the same thing.
    (B) make an attempt.
    (C) have the opportunity.
    (D) take a risk.

9. According to the passage, why was the use of coke smelting advantageous?

    (A) It led to advances in technology.
    (B) It was less expensive than wood smelting.
    (C) It produced a stronger type of iron than wood smelting.
    (D) It stimulated the demand for wood.

10. Look at the phrase cling to in the bold text below.

Britain abandoned the charcoal method and went on to develop coke smelting. The colonies did not follow suit because they had plenty of wood, and besides, charcoal iron was stronger than coke iron. Coke smelting led to technological innovations and was linked to the emergence of the Industrial Revolution. The former colonies lagged behind Britain in industrial development because their supply of wood led them to cling to charcoal iron.

Underline the word or phrase in the **bold** text that is most nearly OPPOSITE in meaning to the phrase cling to.

11. Put an X next to the paragraph that outlines the main disadvantage of an abundance of wood.

Passage 2

The Peales were a distinguished family of American artists. Charles Willson Peale is best remembered for his portraits of leading figures of the American Revolution. He painted portraits of Franklin and Jefferson and over a dozen of George Washington. His life-size portrait of his sons Raphaelle and Titian was so realistic that George Washington reportedly once tipped his hat to the figures in the picture.

Charles Willson Peale gave up painting in his middle age and devoted his life to the Peale Museum, which he founded in Philadelphia. The world's first popular museum of art and natural science, it featured paintings by Peale and his family as well as displays of animals in their natural settings. Peale found the animals himself and devised a method of taxidermy to make the exhibits more lifelike. The museum's most popular display was the skeleton of a mastodon—a huge, extinct elephant—which Peale unearthed on a New York farm in 1801.

Three of Peale's seventeen children were also famous artists. Raphaelle Peale often painted still lifes of flowers, fruit, and cheese. His works show the same luminosity and attention to detail that the works of the Dutch masters show. In the late eighteenth century, however, portraiture was the rage, and so Raphaelle Peale found few buyers for his still lifes at the time. His brother Rembrandt studied under his father and painted portraits of many noted people, including one of George Washington. Another brother, Rubens Peale, painted mostly landscapes and portraits.

James Peale, the brother of Charles Willson Peale, specialized in miniatures. His daughter Sarah Miriam Peale was probably the first professional female portrait painter in America.

12. What is the main topic of the passage?

    (A) The life of Charles Willson Peale
    (B) Portraiture in the 18th century
    (C) The Peale Museum
    (D) A family of artists

13. Look at the word **He** in the **bold** text below.

    The Peales were a distinguished family of American artists. Charles Willson Peale is best remembered for his portraits of leading figures of the American Revolution. He painted portraits of Franklin and Jefferson and over a dozen of George Washington.

    Underline the word or phrase in the **bold** text that the word He refers to.

14. The author probably mentions that Washington tipped his hat to the figures in the painting (paragraph 1) to indicate that

    (A) Charles Willson Peale's painting was very lifelike.
    (B) Washington respected Charles Willson Peale's work.
    (C) Washington was friendly with Raphaelle and Titian Peale.
    (D) The painting of the two brothers was extremely large.

15. Look at the word displays in the **bold** text below.

    The world's first popular museum of art and natural science it featured paintings by Peale and his family as well as displays of animals in their natural settings. Peale found the animals himself and devised a method of taxidermy to make the exhibits more lifelike.

    Underline the word or phrase in the **bold** text that has the same meaning as displays.

16. For which of the following terms does the author give a definition in the second paragraph?

    (A) natural science
    (B) skeleton
    (C) taxidermy
    (D) mastodon

17. Which of the following questions about the Peale Museum does the passage NOT supply enough information to answer?

    (A) Who found and prepared its animal exhibits?
    (B) In what city was it located?
    (C) Where did its most popular exhibit come from?
    (D) In what year was it founded?

18. The word unearthed in the second paragraph is closest in meaning to

    (A) displayed.
    (B) dug up.
    (C) located.
    (D) looked over.

19. Look at the word rage in the bold text below.

    His works show the same luminosity and attention to detail that the works of the Dutch masters show. In the late eighteenth century, however, still lifes were not the fashion. Portraiture was the rage, and so Raphaelle Peale found few buyers at that time.

    Underline the word or phrase in the **bold** text that has the same meaning as rage.

20. According to the passage, Rembrandt Peale and his father both painted

    (A) miniatures.
    (B) portraits of George Washington.
    (C) paintings of flowers, fruit, and cheese.
    (D) pictures of animals.

21. Underline the sentence in paragraph 3 in which the author compares the paintings of one of the Peale family with those of other artists.

22. Which of the following is NOT one of the children of Charles Willson Peale?

    (A) Titian Peale
    (B) Rubens Peale
    (C) Raphaelle Peale
    (D) Sarah Miriam Peale

23. The author's attitude toward the Peales is generally

    (A) envious.
    (B) puzzled.
    (C) admiring.
    (D) disappointed.

Passage 3

According to the best evidence gathered by space probes and astronomers, Mars is an inhospitable planet, more similar to Earth's Moon than to Earth itself—a dry, stark, seemingly lifeless world. Mars' air pressure is equal to Earth's at an altitude of 100,000 feet. The air there is 95 percent carbon dioxide. Mars has no ozone layer to screen out the sun's lethal radiation. Daytime temperatures may reach above freezing, but because the planet is blanketed by the mere wisp of an atmosphere, the heat radiates back into space. Even at the equator, the temperature drops to −50°C (−60°F) at night. Today there is no liquid water, although valleys and channels on the surface show evidence of having been carved by running water. The polar ice caps are made of frozen water and carbon dioxide, and water may be frozen in the ground as permafrost.

Despite these difficult conditions, certain scientists believe that there is a possibility of transforming Mars into a more Earth-like planet. Nuclear reactors might be used to melt frozen gases and eventually build up the atmosphere. This in turn could create a greenhouse effect that would stop heat from radiating back into space. Liquid water could be thawed to form a polar ocean. Once enough ice has melted, suitable plants could be introduced to build up the level of oxygen in the atmosphere so that, in time, the planet would support animal life from Earth and even permanent human colonies. "This was once thought to be so far in the future as to be irrelevant," said Christopher McKay, a research scientist at the National Aeronautics and Space Administration. "But now it's starting to look practical. We could begin work in four or five decades."

The idea of "terra-forming" Mars, as enthusiasts call it, has its roots in science fiction. But as researchers develop a more profound understanding of how Earth's ecology supports life, they have begun to see how it may be possible to create similar conditions on Mars. Don't plan on homesteading on Mars any time soon, though. The process could take hundreds or even thousands of years to complete, and the cost would be staggering.

24. With which of the following is the passage primarily concerned?

(A) The possibility of changing the Martian environment
(B) The challenge of interplanetary travel
(C) The advantages of establishing colonies on Mars
(D) The need to study the Martian ecology

25. The word stark in the first paragraph is closest in meaning to

(A) harsh.
(B) unknown.
(C) dark.
(D) distant.

26. The word there in the first paragraph refers to

(A) a point 100 miles above the Earth.
(B) the Earth's Moon.
(C) Mars.
(D) outer space.

27. According to the passage, the Martian atmosphere today consists mainly of

(A) carbon dioxide.
(B) oxygen.
(C) ozone.
(D) water vapor.

28. Underline the sentence in the first paragraph that explains why Mars is so cold at night.

29. Which of the following does the author NOT list as a characteristic of the planet Mars that would make colonization difficult?

(A) There is little liquid water.
(B) Daytime temperatures are dangerously high.
(C) The sun's rays are deadly.
(D) Nighttime temperatures are extremely low.

30. It can be inferred from the passage that the greenhouse effect mentioned in the second paragraph is

(A) the direct result of nuclear reactions.
(B) the cause of low temperatures on Mars.
(C) caused by the introduction of green plants.
(D) a possible means of warming Mars.

31. Look at the word thawed in the **bold** text below.

Frozen water could be thawed to form a polar ocean. Once enough ice has melted, suitable plants could be introduced to build up the level of oxygen in the atmosphere so that, in time, the planet would support animal life from Earth and even permanent human colonies.

Underline the word or phrase in the **bold** text that has the same meaning as thawed.

32. Look at the word feasible in the **bold** text below.

"Not many years ago, no one would have considered this a viable plan," said Christopher McKay, a research scientist at the National Aeronautics and Space Administration. "But now it's starting to look feasible. We could begin work in four or five decades."

Underline the word or phrase in the **bold** text that has the same meaning as feasible.

33. According to Christopher McKay, the possibility of transforming Mars

(A) could only occur in science fiction stories.
(B) will not begin for hundreds, even thousands of years.
(C) is completely impractical.
(D) could be started in forty to fifty years.

34. According to the article, the basic knowledge needed to transform Mars comes from

(A) the science of astronomy.
(B) a knowledge of Earth's ecology.
(C) data from space probes.
(D) science fiction stories.

35. Look at the word they in the **bold** text below.

The idea of "terra-forming" Mars, as enthusiasts call it, has its roots in science fiction. But as researchers develop a more profound understanding of how Earth's ecology supports life, they have begun to see how it may be possible to create similar conditions on Mars.

Underline the word or phrase in the **bold** text that the word they refers to.

36. The word staggering in the third paragraph is closest in meaning to

(A) astonishing.
(B) restrictive.
(C) increasing.
(D) unpredictable.

Passage 4

Another critical factor that plays a part in susceptibility to colds is age. A study done by the University of Michigan School of Public Health revealed particulars that seem to hold true for the general population. Infants are the most cold-ridden group, averaging more than six colds in their first year. Boys have more colds than girls up to age three. After the age of three, girls are more susceptible than boys, and teenage girls average three colds a year to boys' two.

The general incidence of colds continues to decline into maturity. Elderly people who are in good health have as few as one or two colds annually. One exception is found among people in their twenties, especially women, who show a rise in cold infections, because people in this age group are most likely to have young children. Adults who delay having children until their thirties and forties experience the same sudden increase in cold infections.

The study also found that economics plays an important role. As income increases, the frequency at which colds are reported in the family decreases. Families with the lowest income suffer about a third more colds than families at the highest end. Lower income generally forces people to live in more cramped quarters than those typically occupied by wealthier people, and crowding increases the opportunities for the cold virus to travel from person to person. Low income may also adversely influence diet. The degree to which poor nutrition affects susceptibility to colds is not yet clearly established, but an inadequate diet is suspected of lowering resistance generally.

37. The paragraph that precedes this passage most probably deals with

   (A) minor diseases other than colds.
   (B) the recommended treatment of colds.
   (C) a factor that affects susceptibility to colds.
   (D) methods of preventing colds among elderly people.

38. Which of the following is closest in meaning to the word particulars in the first paragraph?

   (A) minor errors
   (B) specific facts
   (C) small distinctions
   (D) individual people

39. What does the author claim about the study discussed in the passage?

   (A) It contains many inconsistencies.
   (B) It specializes in children.
   (C) It contradicts the results of earlier studies in the field.
   (D) Its results apparently are relevant for the population as a whole.

40. According to the passage, which of the following groups of people is most likely to catch colds?

   (A) Infant boys
   (B) Young girls
   (C) Teenage boys
   (D) Elderly women

41. Look at the word incidence in the **bold** text below.

The general incidence of colds continues to decline into maturity. Elderly people who are in good health have as few as one or two colds annually. One exception is found among people in their twenties, especially women. The rate at which they are infected with colds rises because people in this age group are most likely to have young children.

Underline the word or phrase in the **bold** text that has the same meaning as incidence.

42. There is information in the second paragraph of the passage to support which of the following conclusions?

(A) Men are more susceptible to colds than women.
(B) Children infect their parents with colds.
(C) People who live in a cold climate have more colds than those who live in a warm one.
(D) People who don't have children are more susceptible to colds than those who do.

43. Look at the phrase people in this age group in the **bold** text below.

Elderly people who are in good health have as few as one or two colds annually. One exception is found among people in their twenties, especially women. The rate at which they are infected with colds rises because people in this age group are most likely to have young children. Adults who delay having children until their thirties and forties experience the same sudden increase in cold infections.

Underline the word or phrase in the **bold** text that has the same meaning as the phrase people in this age group.

44. The author's main purpose in writing the last paragraph of the passage is to

(A) explain how cold viruses are transmitted.
(B) prove that a poor diet causes colds.
(C) discuss the relationship between income and frequency of colds.
(D) discuss the distribution of income among the people in the study.

45. Look at the word cramped in the **bold** text below.

Families with the lowest income suffer a third more colds than families at the highest end. Lower income generally forces people to live in more cramped quarters than those typically occupied by wealthier people, and crowded conditions increase the opportunities for the cold virus to travel from person to person.

Underline the word or phrase in the **bold** text that has the same meaning as cramped.

46. The following sentence can be added to paragraph three.

Low income may also have an adverse effect on diet.

Where would it best fit in the paragraph?

The study also found that economics plays an important role. **(A)** As income increases, the frequency at which colds are reported in the family decreases. **(B)** Families with the lowest income suffer a third more colds than families at the highest end. **(C)** Lower income generally forces people to live in more cramped quarters than those typically occupied by wealthier people, and crowded conditions increase the opportunities for the cold virus to travel from person to person. **(D)** The degree to which deficient nutrition affects susceptibility to colds is not yet clearly established. **(E)** However, an inadequate diet is suspected of lowering resistance generally.

Circle the letter in parentheses that indicates the best position for the sentence.

47. Look at the word deficient in the **bold** text below.

Lower income generally forces people to live in more cramped quarters than those typically occupied by wealthier people, and crowded conditions increase the opportunities for the cold virus to travel from person to person. The degree to which deficient nutrition affects susceptibility to colds is not yet clearly established. However, an inadequate diet is suspected of lowering resistance generally.

Underline the word or phrase in the **bold** text that has the same meaning as deficient.

48. The author's tone in this passage could best be described as

(A) neutral and objective.
(B) humorous.
(C) tentative but interested.
(D) highly critical.

Passage 5

About fifty years ago, plant physiologists set out to grow roots by themselves in solutions in laboratory flasks. The scientists found that the nutrition of isolated roots was quite simple. They required sugar and the usual minerals and vitamins. However, they did not require organic nitrogen compounds. These roots got along fine on mineral inorganic nitrogen. Roots are capable of making their own proteins and other organic compounds. These activities by roots require energy, of course. The process of respiration uses sugar to make the high energy compound ATP, which drives the biochemical reactions. Respiration also requires oxygen. Highly active roots require a good deal of oxygen.

The study of isolated roots has provided an understanding of the relationship between shoots and roots in intact plants. The leaves of the shoots provide the roots with sugar and vitamins, and the roots provide the shoots with water and minerals. In addition, roots can provide the shoots with organic nitrogen compounds. This comes in handy for the growth of buds in the early spring when leaves are not yet functioning. Once leaves begin photosynthesizing, they produce protein, but only mature leaves can "export" protein to the rest of the plant in the form of amino acids.

49. What is the main topic of the passage?

(A) The relationship between a plant's roots and its shoots
(B) What can be learned by growing roots in isolation
(C) How plants can be grown without roots
(D) What elements are necessary for the growth of plants

50. The word themselves in the first paragraph refers to

(A) plant physiologists.
(B) solutions.
(C) laboratory flasks.
(D) roots.

51. According to the passage, what is ATP?

(A) A biochemical process
(B) The tip of a root
(C) A chemical compound
(D) A type of plant cell

52. The word intact in the second paragraph is closest in meaning to

(A) mature.
(B) wild.
(C) whole.
(D) tiny.

53. The use of the phrase comes in handy in the second paragraph indicates that the process is

(A) useful.
(B) predictable.
(C) necessary.
(D) successful.

54. It can be inferred from the passage that, in the early spring, the buds of plants

(A) "export" protein in the form of amino acids.
(B) do not require water.
(C) have begun photosynthesizing.
(D) obtain organic compounds from the roots.

55. Which of the following best describes the organization of the passage?

(A) The results of two experiments are compared.
(B) A generalization is made and several examples of it are given.
(C) The findings of an experiment are explained.
(D) A hypothesis is presented, and several means of proving it are suggested.

Lesson 33

MAIN IDEA, MAIN TOPIC, AND MAIN PURPOSE QUESTIONS

After almost every passage, the first question is an **overview question** about the main idea, main topic, or main purpose of a passage. **Main idea questions** ask you to identify the most important thought in the passage.

Sample Questions

- What is the main idea of the passage?

- The primary idea of the passage is. . . .

- Which of the following best summarizes the author's main idea?

When there is not a single, readily identified main idea, **main topic questions** may be asked. These ask you what the passage is generally "about."

Sample Questions

- The main topic of the passage is. . . .

- What does the passage mainly discuss?

- The passage is primarily concerned with. . . .

Main purpose questions ask *why* an author wrote a passage. The answer choices for these questions usually begin with infinitives.

Sample Questions

- The author's purpose in writing is to. . . .

- What is the author's main purpose in the passage?

- The main point of this passage is to. . . .

- Why did the author write the passage?

Sample Answer Choices

- To define . . .

- To relate . . .

- To discuss . . .

- To propose . . .

- To illustrate . . .

- To support the idea that . . .

- To distinguish between . . . and . . .

- To compare . . . and . . .

Don't answer the initial overview question about a passage until you have answered the other questions. The process of answering the detail questions may give you a clearer idea of the main idea, topic, or purpose of the passage.

The correct answers for main idea, main topic, and main purpose questions correctly summarize the main points of the passage; they must be more general than any of the supporting ideas or details, but not so general that they include ideas outside the scope of the passages.

Distractors for this type of question have one of these characteristics:

1. They are too specific.

2. They are too general.

3. The are incorrect according to the passage.

4. They are irrelevant (unrelated) to the main idea of the passage.

If you're not sure of the answer for one of these questions, go back and quickly scan the passage. You can usually infer the main idea, main topic, or main purpose of the entire passage from an understanding of the main ideas of the paragraphs that make up the passage and the relationship between them.

OTHER OVERVIEW ITEMS

A number of other items test your overall understanding of the passage. These are often the last question in a set of questions.

Tone items ask you to determine the author's feelings about the topic by the language that he or she uses in writing the passage. Look for vocabulary that indicates if the author's feelings are positive, negative, or neutral.

Sample Questions

- What tone does the author take in writing this passage?

- The tone of this passage could best be described as. . . .

Sample Answer Choices

• Positive	• Humorous	• Worried
• Favorable	• Negative	• Outraged
• Optimistic	• Critical	• Neutral
• Amused	• Unfavorable	• Objective
• Pleased	• Angry	• Impersonal
• Respectful	• Defiant	

If you read the following sentences in passages, would the tone of those passages most likely be positive or negative?

1. That was just the beginning of a *remarkable* series of performances by this *brilliant* actress.

2. Despite some minor problems, this device has a number of *admirable* features.

3. This practice is *a waste of time and money*.

4. At the time his poems were first published, they were very popular, but today most critics find them *simplistic and rather uninteresting*.

The italicized words in sentences 1 and 2 show a positive tone; in 3 and 4, the italicized words indicate a negative attitude. Notice that sentence 2 contains negative words ("minor problems") but the overall meaning of the sentence is positive. Sentence 4 contains positive language ("very popular") but overall, the tone is negative. (Words like *despite, but, although, however*, and similar words can "reverse" the tone of the passage.)

Most TOEFL reading passages have a neutral tone, but sometimes an author may take a position for or against some point. However, answer choices that indicate strong emotion—*angry*, *outraged*, *sad*, and so forth—will seldom be correct.

Attitude questions are very similar to tone questions. Again, you must understand the author's opinion. The language that the author uses will tell you what his or her position is.

What is the author's attitude toward smoking on airplanes as expressed in the sentence below?

Although some passengers may experience a slight discomfort from not smoking on long flights, their smoking endangers the health of all the passengers and crew.

The author opposes smoking during flights. He admits that there is some argument in favor of smoking—some passengers may feel discomfort—but this is not as important as the fact that smoking can be dangerous to everyone on the flight. The use of the word *although* shows this.

Sample Questions

- What is the author's attitude toward. . . . ?

- The author's opinion of _____ is best described as. . . .

- The author's attitude toward _____ could best be described as one of. . . .

- How would the author probably feel about. . . . ?

Another type of attitude question presents four statements and asks how the author would feel about them.

- Which of the following recommendations would the author most likely support?

- The author would be LEAST likely to agree with which of the following statements?

- The author of the passage would most likely be in favor of which of the following policies?

Organization items ask about the overall structure of a passage or about the organization of a particular paragraph.

Sample Question

- Which of the following best describes the organization of the passage?

Sample Answer Choices

- A general concept is defined and examples are given.

- Several generalizations are presented, from which a conclusion is drawn.

- The author presents the advantages and disadvantages of _____.

- The author presents a system of classification for _____.

- Persuasive language is used to argue against _____.

- The author describes _____.

- The author presents a brief account of _____.

- The author compares _____ and _____.

Items about previous or following paragraphs ask you to assume that the passage is part of a longer work: what would be the topic of the hypothetical paragraph that precedes or follows the passage? To find the topic of the previous paragraph, look for clues in the first line or two of the passage; for the topic of the following passage, look in the last few lines. Sometimes incorrect answer choices mention topics that have already been discussed in the passage.

Sample Questions

- With what topic would the following/preceding paragraph most likely deal?

- The paragraph prior to/after the passage most probably discusses. . . .

- It can be inferred from the passage that the previous/next paragraph concerns. . . .

- What most likely precedes/follows the passage?

EXERCISE 33.1

Focus: Identifying correct answers and recognizing distractors in main idea/main topic/main purpose questions

Directions: Read the passages. Then mark each answer choice according to the following system:

    S   Too specific
    G   Too general
    X   Incorrect
    I   Irrelevant
    C   Correct

The first one is done as an example.

Passage 1

There are two main types of cell division. Most cells are produced by a process called mitosis. In mitosis, a cell divides and forms two identical daughter cells, each with an identical number of chromosomes. Most one-celled creatures reproduce by this method, as do most of the cells in multicelled plants and animals. Sex cells, however, are formed in a special type of cell division called meiosis. This process reduces the number of chromosomes in a sex cell to half the number found in other kinds of cells. Then, when sex cells unite, they produce a single cell with the original number of chromosomes.

1. What is the main topic of this passage?

    ___S___   (A)   The method by which one-celled organisms reproduce

    ___C___   (B)   A comparison between mitosis and meiosis

    ___X___   (C)   Meiosis, the process by which identical cells are produced

Passage 2

The last gold rush belongs as much to Canadian history as it does to American. The discovery of gold along the Klondike River, which flows from Canada's Yukon Territory into Alaska, drew some 30,000 fortune hunters to the north. The Yukon became a territory, and its capital at the time, Dawson, would not have existed without the gold rush. The gold strike furnished material for a dozen of Jack London's novels; it inspired Robert Service to write "The Shooting of Dan McGrew" and other poems; and it provided the background for the wonderful Charlie Chaplin movie, *The Gold Rush*. It also marked the beginnings of modern Alaska.

2. This author's main purpose in writing is to

    _____   (A)   discuss the significance of mining in Canada and the United States.
    _____   (B)   show the influence of the Klondike gold strike on the creative arts.
    _____   (C)   point out the significance of the Klondike gold strike.

Passage 3

Until the nineteenth century, when steamships and transcontinental trains made long-distance travel possible for large numbers of people, only a few adventurers, mainly sailors and traders, ever traveled out of their own countries. "Abroad" was a truly foreign place about which the vast majority of people knew very little indeed. Early map makers, therefore, had little fear of being accused of mistakes, even though they were often wildly inaccurate. When they compiled maps, imagination was as important as geographic reality. Nowhere is this more evident than in old maps illustrated with mythical creatures and strange humans.

3. Which of the following best expresses the main idea of the passage?

   _____ (A) Despite their unusual illustrations, maps made before the nineteenth century were remarkably accurate.
   _____ (B) Old maps often included pictures of imaginary animals.
   _____ (C) Map makers could draw imaginative maps before the nineteenth century because so few people had traveled.

Passage 4

Circumstantial evidence is evidence not drawn from the direct observation of a fact. If, for example, there is evidence that a piece of rock embedded in a wrapped chocolate bar is the same type of rock found in the vicinity of the candy factory, and that rock of this type is found in few other places, then there is circumstantial evidence that the stone found its way into the candy during manufacture and suggests that the candy maker was negligent. Despite a popular notion to look down on the quality of circumstantial evidence, it is of great usefulness if there is enough of it and if it is properly interpreted. Each circumstance, taken singly, may mean little, but a whole chain of circumstances can be as conclusive as direct evidence.

4. What is the main idea of the passage?

   _____ (A) A manufacturer's negligence can be shown by direct evidence only.
   _____ (B) Enough circumstantial evidence is as persuasive as direct evidence.
   _____ (C) Circumstantial evidence can be very useful in science.

Passage 5

The Northwest Ordinance was passed by Congress in 1787. It set up the government structure of the region north of the Ohio River and west of Pennsylvania, then called the Northwest Territory. It set the conditions under which parts of the Territory could become states having equality with the older states. But the ordinance was more than just a plan for government. The law also guaranteed freedom of religion and trial by jury in the Territory. It organized the Territory into townships of 36 square miles and ordered a school to be built for each township. It also abolished slavery in the Territory. The terms were so attractive that thousands of pioneers poured into the Territory. Eventually, the Territory became the states of Ohio, Indiana, Illinois, Michigan, and Wisconsin.

5. What is the main topic of this passage?

   _____ (A) The structure of government
   _____ (B) The provisions of an important law
   _____ (C) The establishment of schools in the Northwest Territory

Passage 6

The story of the motel business from 1920 to the start of World War II in 1941 is one of uninterrupted growth. Motels (the term comes from a combination of the words *motor* and *hotels*) spread from the West and the Midwest all the way to Maine and Florida. They clustered along transcontinental highways, such as U.S. Routes 40 and 66, and along the north-south routes running up and down both the East and West Coasts. There were 16,000 motels by 1930 and 24,000 by 1940. The motel industry was one of the few industries that was not hurt by the Depression of the 1930s. Their cheap rates attracted travelers who had very little money.

6. What does the passage mainly discuss?

_____ (A) How the Depression hurt U.S. motels
_____ (B) The origin of the word *motels*
_____ (C) Two decades of growth for the motel industry

Passage 7

An old but still useful proverb states, "Beware of oak, it draws the stroke." This saying is handy during thunderstorm season. In general, trees with deep roots that tap into groundwater attract more lightning than do trees with shallow, drier roots. Oaks are around 50 times more likely to be struck than beeches. Spruces are nearly as safe as beeches. Pines are not as safe as these two but are still much safer than oaks.

7. What is the author's main point?

_____ (A) Old proverbs often contain important truths.
_____ (B) Trees with shallow roots are more likely to avoid lightning than those with deep roots.
_____ (C) The deeper a tree's roots, the safer it is during a thunderstorm.

Passage 8

Alternative history is generally classified as a type of science fiction, but it also bears some relation to historical fiction. This type of writing describes an imaginary world that is identical to ours up to a certain point in history, but at that point, the two worlds diverge; some important historical event takes place in one world but not in the other, and they go in different directions. Alternative histories might describe worlds in which the Roman Empire had never fallen, in which the Spanish Armada had been victorious, or in which the South had won the Civil War. Or they may suppose that some technology had been introduced earlier in the world's history than actually happened. For example: What if computers had been invented in Victorian times? Many readers find these stories interesting because of the way they stimulate the imagination and get them thinking about the phenomenon of cause and effect in history.

8. What is the main idea of this passage?

_____ (A) Alternative histories describe worlds in which history has taken another course.
_____ (B) Alternative histories are a type of historical novel.
_____ (C) Science fiction writers have accurately predicted certain actual scientific developments.

EXERCISE 33.2

Focus: Answering a variety of overview questions about short passages
Directions: Read the passages and mark the best answer choice—(A), (B), (C), or (D).

Passage 1

American folk music originated with ordinary people at a time when the rural population was isolated and music was not yet spread by radio, tapes, CDs, or music videos. It was transmitted by oral tradition and is noted for its energy, humor, and emotional impact. The major source of early American folk songs was music from the British Isles, but songs from Africa as well as songs of the American Indians have a significant part in its heritage. Later settlers from other countries also contributed songs. In the nineteenth century, composer Steven Foster wrote some of the most enduringly popular of all American songs, which soon became part of the folk tradition. Beginning in the 1930s, Woody Guthrie gained great popularity by adapting traditional melodies and lyrics and supplying new ones as well. In the 1950s and 1960s, signer-composers such as Pete Seeger, Bob Dylan, and Joan Baez continued this tradition by creating "urban" folk music. Many of these songs dealt with important social issues, such as racial integration and the war in Vietnam. Later in the 1960s, musical groups such as the Byrds and the Turtles combined folk music and rock and roll to create a hybrid form known as *folk-rock*.

1. The primary purpose of this passage is to

   (A) trace the development of American folk music.
   (B) explain the oral tradition.
   (C) contrast the styles of folk-rock musicians.
   (D) point out the influence of social issues on "urban" folk music.

Passage 2

Every scientific discipline tends to develop its own special language because it finds ordinary words inadequate, and psychology is no different. The purpose of this special jargon is not to mystify non-psychologists; rather, it allows psychologists to accurately describe the phenomena they are discussing and to communicate with each other effectively. Of course, psychological terminology consists in part of everyday words such as *emotion*, *intelligence*, and *motivation*, but psychologists use these words some-what differently. For example, a non-psychologist may use the term *anxiety* to mean nervousness or fear, but most psychologists reserve the term to describe a condition produced when one fears events over which one has no control.

2. The main topic of this passage is

   (A) effective communication.
   (B) the special language of psychology.
   (C) two definitions of the word "anxiety."
   (D) the jargon of science.

Passage 3

Gifford Pinchot was the first professionally trained forester in the United States. After he graduated from Yale in 1889, he studied forestry in Europe. In the 1890s he managed the forest on the Biltmore estate in North Carolina (now Pisgah National Forest) and became the first to practice scientific forestry. Perhaps his most important contribution to conservation was persuading President Theodore Roosevelt to set aside millions of acres in the West as forest reserves. These lands now make up much of the national parks and national forests of the United States. Pinchot became the chief forester of the U.S. Forest Service in 1905. Although he held that post for only five years, he established guidelines that set forest policy for decades to come.

3. The passage primarily deals with

   (A) Gifford Pinchot's work on the Biltmore Estate.
   (B) the practice and theory of scientific forestry.
   (C) the origin of national parks and national forests in the United States.
   (D) the contributions Gifford Pinchot made to American forestry.

Passaage 4

Off-Broadway theater developed in New York City in about 1950 as a result of dissatisfaction with conditions on Broadway. Its founders believed that Broadway was overly concerned with producing safe, commercially successful hit plays rather than drama with artistic quality. Off-Broadway producers tried to assist playwrights, directors, and performers who could not find work on Broadway. Off-Broadway theaters were poorly equipped, had limited seating, and provided few conveniences for audiences. But the originality of the scripts, the creativity of the performers, and the low cost of tickets made up for these disadvantages, and off-Broadway theater prospered. However, by the 1960s, costs began to rise, and by the 1970s, off-Broadway theater was encountering many of the difficulties of Broadway and had lost much of its vitality. With its decline, an experimental movement called *off-off-Broadway* theater developed.

4. What is the main idea of this passage?

   (A) After initial success, off-Broadway theater began to decline.
   (B) Off-Broadway theaters produced many hit commercial plays.
   (C) Theaters on Broadway were not well equipped.
   (D) Off-Broadway plays were highly creative.

5. The paragraph that follows this passage most likely deals with

   (A) the help off-Broadway producers provided directors, playwrights, and performers.
   (B) methods off-broadway theaters used to cope with rising prices.
   (C) the development of off-off-Broadway theater.
   (D) the decline of Broadway theater.

Passage 5

At the time of the first European contact, there were from 500 to 700 languages spoken by North American Indians. These were divided into some sixty language families, with no demonstrable genetic relationship among them. Some of these families spread across several of the seven cultural areas. The Algonquin family, for instance, contained dozens of languages and occupied a vast territory. Speakers of Algonquin languages included the Algonquins of the Eastern Woodland, the Blackfoots of the Plains, and the Wiyots and Yuroks of California. Other language families, like the Zuni family of the Southwest, occupied only a few square miles of area and contained only a single tribal language.

6. What is the main idea of this passage?

    (A) Each of the cultural areas was dominated by one of the language families.

    (B) The Zuni language is closely related to the Algonquin language.

    (C) There is considerable diversity in the size and the number of languages in language families of the North American Indians.

    (D) Contact with Europeans had an extraordinary effect on the languages of the Indian tribes of North America.

Passage 6

Further changes in journalism occurred around this time. In 1846, Richard Hoe invented the steam cylinder rotary press, making it possible to print newspapers faster and cheaper. The development of the telegraph made possible much speedier collection and distribution of news. Also in 1846, the first wire service was organized. A new type of newspaper appeared around this time, one that was more attuned to the spirit and needs of the new America. Although newspapers continued to cover politics, they came to report more human interest stories and to record the most recent news, which they could not have done before the telegraph. New York papers, and those of other northern cities, maintained corps of correspondents to go into all parts of the country to cover newsworthy events.

7. The main purpose of the passage is to

    (A) present a brief history of American journalism.

    (B) outline certain developments in mid-nineteenth-century journalism.

    (C) explain the importance of the steam cylinder rotary press.

    (D) present some biographical information about Richard Hoe.

8. What is the most probable topic of the paragraph preceding this one?

    (A) Other types of rotary presses

    (B) Alternatives to using wire services

    (C) Newspapers that concentrated on politics

    (D) Other developments in journalism

9. The tone of the passage could best be described as

    (A) objective.

    (B) optimistic.

    (C) angry.

    (D) humorous.

Passage 7

In the western third of North America, the convoluted folds of the Earth's surface and its fractured geologic structure tend to absorb the seismic energy of an earthquake. Even if an earthquake measuring 8.5 on the Richter scale struck Los Angeles, its force would fade by the time it reached San Francisco, some 400 miles away. But in the eastern two thirds of the continent, the same energy travels more easily. The earthquake that struck New Madrid, Missouri, in 1811, estimated at 8 on the Richter scale, shook Washington, D.C., about 800 miles away, and was felt as far as Boston and Toronto.

10. Which of the following best expresses the main idea of this passage?

(A) If a major earthquake strikes Los Angeles, it will probably damage San Francisco as well.
(B) The New Madrid earthquake of 1811 was felt in Boston and Toronto.
(C) The geology of the western United States is much more complex than that of the eastern United States.
(D) Earthquakes travel farther in the East than in the West.

Passage 8

There has never been an adult scientist who has been half as curious as any child between the ages of four months and four years. Adults sometimes mistake this superb curiosity about everything as a lack of ability to concentrate. The truth is that children begin to learn at birth, and by the time they begin formal schooling at the age of 5 or 6, they have already absorbed a fantastic amount of information, perhaps more, fact for fact, than they will learn for the rest of their lives. Adults can multiply by many times the knowledge children absorb if they appreciate this curiosity while simultaneously encouraging the children to learn.

11. What is the main idea of this passage?

(A) Children lack the ability to concentrate.
(B) Young children have a much greater curiosity than adult scientists do.
(C) The first few years of school are the most important ones for most children.
(D) Adults can utilize children's intense curiosity to help children learn more.

EXERCISE 33.3

Focus: Understanding the meaning of multi-paragraph passages by identifying the main point of each of the paragraphs

Directions: Read the following passages and the questions about them. Decide which of the choices best answers the question, and mark the answer.

Passage 1

In most of Europe, farmers' homes and outbuildings are generally located within a village. Every morning, the farmers and farm laborers leave their village to work their land or tend their animals in distant fields and return to the village at the end of the day. Social life is thus centripetal; that is, it is focused around the community center, the village. Only in certain parts of Quebec has this pattern been preserved in North America.

Throughout most of North America, a different pattern was established. It was borrowed from northern Europe, but was pushed even further in the New World where land was cheap or even free. It is a centrifugal system of social life, with large isolated farms whose residents go to the village only to buy goods and procure services. The independence associated with American farmers stems from this pattern of farm settlement. The American farmer is as free of the intimacy of the village as is the urbanite.

1. The main topic of the first paragraph is

   (A) European farm products.
   (B) social life in Quebec.
   (C) the European pattern of rural settlement.

2. The main topic of the second paragraph is

   (A) the relative isolation of North American farm families.
   (B) the relationship between farmers and urbanites in North America.
   (C) the low cost of farmland in North America.

3. The main topic of the entire passage is

   (A) a comparison of farming in northern and southern Europe.
   (B) the difference between farming in Quebec and the rest of North America.
   (C) European influence on American agriculture.
   (D) a contrast between a centripetal system of rural life and a centrifugal system.

Passage 2

While fats have lately acquired a bad image, one should not forget how essential they are. Fats provide the body's best means of storing energy, a far more efficient energy sources than either carbohydrates or proteins. They act as insulation against cold, as cushioning for the internal organs, and as lubricants. Without fats, energy would be no way to utilize fat soluble vitamins. Furthermore, some fats contain fatty acids that contain necessary growth factors and help with the digestion of other foods.

An important consideration of fat intake is the ratio of saturated fats to unsaturated fats. Saturated fats, which are derived from dairy products, animal fats, and tropical oils, increase the amount of cholesterol in the blood. Cholesterol may lead to coronary heart disease by building up in the arteries of the heart. However, unsaturated fats, derived from vegetable oils, tend to lower serum cholesterol if taken in a proportion twice that of saturated fats.

The consumption of a variety of fats is necessary, but the intake of too much fat may lead to a variety of health problems. Excessive intake of fats, like all nutritional excesses, is to be avoided.

4. The main idea of the first paragraph is that

   (A) fats deserve their bad image.
   (B) fats serve important functions in the body.
   (C) fats store food more efficiently than proteins or carbohydrates.

5. What is the main idea of the second paragraph?

   (A) Unsaturated fats may reduce cholesterol levels.
   (B) The consumption of any type of fat leads to heart disease.
   (C) Fats taken in the proper proportion may reduce serum cholesterol.

6. The main idea of the third paragraph is that

   (A) people are eating less and less fat today.
   (B) fats should be gradually eliminated from the diet.
   (C) excessive consumption of fats may be dangerous to one's health.

7. With which of the following is the whole passage primarily concerned?

   (A) The role of fats in human health
   (B) The dangers of cholesterol
   (C) The benefits of fats in the diet
   (D) The importance of good nutrition

Passage 3

The term *weathering* refers to all the ways in which rock can be broken down. It takes place because minerals formed in a particular way (say at high temperatures, in the case of igneous rocks) are often unstable when exposed to various conditions. Weathering involves the interaction of the lithosphere (the Earth's crust) with the atmosphere and hydrosphere (air and water). It occurs at different rates and in different ways, depending on the climactic and environmental conditions. But all kinds of weathering ultimately produce broken minerals and rock fragments and other products of the decomposition of stone.

Soil is the most obvious and, from the human point of view, the most important result of the weathering process. Soil is the weathered part of the Earth's crust that is capable of sustaining plant life. The character of soil depends on the nature of rock from which it is formed. It also depends on the climate and on the relative "age" of the soil. Immature soils are little more than broken rock fragments. Over time, immature soil develops into mature soil, which contains quantities of humus, formed from decayed plant matter. Mature soil is darker, richer in microscopic life, and more conducive to plant growth.

8. The first paragraph primarily describes

   (A) the process by which rocks are broken down.
   (B) the weathering of igneous rocks.
   (C) gradual changes in the Earth's weather patterns.

9. The main topic of the second paragraph is

   (A) a description of immature soil.
   (B) the growth of plants.
   (C) the evolution of soil.

10. The main topic of the entire passage is that

    (A) weathering breaks down rocks and leads to the development of soil.
    (B) soils may be classified as mature or immature.
    (C) the process of soil development is more important to humans than that of weathering.
    (D) the Earth's crust is constantly changing.

Lesson 34

DETAIL, NEGATIVE, AND SCANNING ITEMS

DETAIL ITEMS

Detail items ask about explicit facts and details given in the passage. They often contain one of the *wh-* question words: *who, what, when, where, why, how much,* and so on.

Detail items often begin with the phrases "According to the passage . . ." or "According to the author. . . ." When you see these phrases, you know that the information needed to answer the question is directly stated somewhere in the passage (unlike answers for inference questions).

To answer detail items, you have to locate and identify the information that the question asks about. If you are not sure from your first reading where to look for specific answers, use the following techniques.

- Focus on one or two key words as you read the stem of each item. These are usually names, dates, or other nouns—something that will be easy to find as you scan. Lock these words in your mind.

- Scan the passage as you scroll down looking for these words or their synonyms. Look only for these words. Do NOT try to read every word of the passage. Do NOT try to read every word of the passage.

- It may help to use the eraser end of your pencil as a pointer to focus your attention. Don't reread the passage completely—just look for these words.

- Sometimes you can use reference items and vocabulary items to help you pinpoint the location of the information you need.

- When you find the key words in the passage, carefully read the sentence in which they occur. You may have to read the sentence preceding or following that sentence as well.

- Compare the information you read with the four answer choices.

The order of detail questions in a passage almost always follows the order in which the ideas are presented in the passage. In other words, the information you need to answer the first detail question will usually come near the beginning of the passage; the information for the second will follow that, and so on. Knowing this should help you locate the information you need.

Correct answers for detail questions are seldom the same, word for word, as information in the passage; they often contain synonyms and use different grammatical structures.

There are generally more factual questions—twelve to eighteen per reading section—than any other type except (on some tests) vocabulary-in-context questions.

NEGATIVE ITEMS

These items ask you to determine which of the four choices is not given in the passage. These questions contain the words NOT, EXCEPT, or LEAST (which are always capitalized).

- According to the passage, all of the following are true EXCEPT

- Which of the following is NOT mentioned in the passage?

- Which of the following is the LEAST likely . . .

Scan the passage to find the answers that ARE correct or ARE mentioned in the passage. Sometimes the three distractors are clustered in one or two sentences; sometimes they are scattered throughout the passage. The correct answer, of course, is the one that does not appear.

Negative questions often take more time than other questions. Therefore, you may want to guess and come back to these questions if you have time.

There are generally from three to six negative questions per reading section.

SCANNING ITEMS

These items ask you to find a sentence (or sometimes a paragraph) in the passage that plays a certain role in the organization of a paragraph or passage. When you find the sentence or paragraph, you click anywhere on it and it will be highlighted. Use the same techniques for scanning that are given in Part A for detail items.

Sample Questions

- Click on the sentence in Paragraph 1 that explains . . .

- Click on the sentence in Paragraph 3 that discusses . . .

- Click on the sentence in Paragraph 4 that stresses . . .

- Click on the paragraph in the passage that outlines . . .

EXERCISE 34.1

Focus: Reading passages to locate answers for scanning items
Directions: For each question, locate the sentences in the paragraphs that the questions ask about and underline them.

Passage 1

Antlers grow from permanent knoblike bones on a deer's skull. Deer use their antlers chiefly to fight for mates or for leadership of a herd. Among most species of deer, only the males have antlers, but both male and female reindeer and caribou have antlers. Musk deer and Chinese water deer do not have antlers at all.

Deer that live in mild or cold climates lose their antlers each winter. New ones begin to grow the next spring. Deer that live in tropical climates may lose their antlers and grow new ones at other times of year. New antlers are soft and tender. Thin skin grows over the antlers as they develop. Short, fine hair on the skin makes it look like velvet. Full-grown antlers are hard and strong. The velvety skin dries up and the deer rubs the skin off by scraping its antlers against trees. The antlers fall off several months later.

The size and shape of a deer's antlers depend on the animal's age and health. The first set grows when the deer is from 1 to 2 years old. On most deer, the first antlers are short and straight. As deer get older, their antlers grow larger and form intricate branches.

1. Find the sentence in paragraph 1 that explains how deer primarily use their antlers.

2. Find the sentence in paragraph 2 that explains how deer remove the skin from their antlers.

3. Find the sentence in paragraph 3 that describes the antlers of young deer.

Passage 2

Not until the 1830s was there any serious attempt to record the songs and stories of the Native Americans. Henry Schoolcraft collected a great deal of authentic folklore from the Ojibwa tribe and from several other groups. But Schoolcraft lived in a romantic age. There seems to be little doubt that he not only changed but also invented some of the material, and that he mixed the traditions of several tribes. In spite of his failings, he did succeed in bringing the traditions of Native Americans to the attention of the American public.

Schoolcraft's work contrasted sharply with that of the ethnographers who worked in the last decade of the nineteenth century and the first decade of the twentieth. Their aim was to achieve complete accuracy in creating a record of Native American life. They tended to take notes in the original language. With the development of the phonograph, it became possible to preserve not just words but also the tone and emphasis of oral delivery.

4. Find the sentence in paragraph 1 that indicates how Schoolcraft's work had a positive influence.

5. Find the sentence in paragraph 2 that explains what the primary goal of the ethnographers was.

www.petersons.com   214   *Peterson's* ■ *TOEFL CBT Success*

Passage 3

Because of exposure to salt spray and fog, coastal and ocean structures such as bridges, pipelines, ships, and oil rigs require more corrosion protection than structures located inland. One study found that anti-corrosion coatings with a 25-year lifespan inland were good for only five years in coastal areas. Seeking to reduce maintenance coasts for gantries and other structures at the Kennedy Space Center on Florida's Atlantic Coast, NASA (the National Aeronautic and Space Administration) conducted research aimed at developing a superior coating. This coating had to resist salt corrosion as well as protect launch structures from hot rocket exhaust. The successful research resulted in a new type of inorganic coating that has many commercial applications.

6. Find the sentence in the passage that outlines the qualities for the coating that were required by NASA.

Passage 4

In 1903 the Wright brothers made the first powered flight in history at Kitty Hawk, North Carolina. This site was chosen because of its winds, which would lift the plane like a kite. The first attempt lasted only twelve seconds and covered a distance of less than the wing span of the largest airplanes of modern aircraft. Soon the Wrights and other inventors and pilots were busy improving the airplane. They made much longer flights and even put it to some practical uses. In 1909 the Wrights delivered the first military plane to the United States Army. As early as 1914, a plane had begun to carry passengers on daily flights, and in 1918 regular air-mail service was started between Washington and New York.

7. Find a sentence that offers a description of the first airplane flight.

Passage 5

Today's supermarket is a large departmentalized retail store. It sells mostly food items, but also health and beauty aids, housewares, magazines, and much more. The dominant features of supermarkets are large in-store inventories on self-service aisles and centralized checkout lines.

The inclusion of non-food items on supermarket shelves was once considered novel. This practice is sometimes called "scrambled marketing." It permits the supermarket, as well as other types of retail stores, to sell items that carry a higher margin than most food items. In general, however, supermarket profits are slim—only about one to three percent. Owners rely on high levels of inventory turnover to reach their profit goals.

Supermarkets were among the first retailers to stress discount strategies. Using these strategies, supermarkets sell a variety of high-turnover goods at low prices. To keep prices down, of course, super-markets must keep their costs down. Other than the cost of the goods they sell, supermarkets' primary costs involve personnel. By not offering delivery and by hiring cashiers and stockers rather than true sales personnel, supermarkets are able to keep prices at a relatively low level.

8. Find the sentence in paragraph 1 that gives the most important characteristics of supermarkets.

9. Find the sentence in paragraph 2 that explains the advantage of "scrambled marketing."

10. Find the sentence in paragraph 3 that explains how supermarkets are able to sell goods cheaply.

Passage 6

There have been many significant innovations in the energy efficiency of windows. One of the most recent is filling the gap between two panes of glass with argon instead of air. Argon is a naturally occurring inert gas that is as transparent as air. Since argon is extremely dense, there is less movement of the gas between the glass panes, and therefore less heat is lost. Adding argon instead of air can improve the insulation value of windows by 30 percent. Argon also deadens outdoor noise.

11. Find the sentence that explains how the use of argon improves insulation.

EXERCISE 34.2

Focus: Answering factual, negative, and scanning questions about reading passages

Directions: Read the following passages and the questions about them. Decide which of the choices—(A), (B), (C), or (D)—best answers the question, and mark the answer.

Passage 1

Mesa Verde is the center of the prehistoric Anasazi culture. It is located in the high plateau lands near Four Corners, where Colorado, Utah, New Mexico, and Arizona come together. This high ground is majestic but not forbidding. The climate is dry but tiny streams trickle at the bottom of deeply cut canyons, where seeps and springs provided water for the Anasazi to irrigate their crops. Rich red soil provided fertile ground for their crops of corn, beans, squash, tobacco, and cotton. The Anasazi domesticated the wild turkey and hunted deer, rabbits, and mountain sheep.

For a thousand years the Anasazi lived around Mesa Verde. Although the Anasazi are not related to the Navajos, no one knows what these Indians called themselves, and so they are commonly referred to by their Navajo name, Anasazi, which means "ancient ones" in the Navajo language.

Around 550 A.D., early Anasazi—then a nomadic people archaeologists call the Basketmakers—began constructing permanent homes on mesa tops. In the next 300 years, the Anasazi made rapid technological advancements, including the refinement of not only basket-making but also pottery-making and weaving. This phase of development is referred to as the Early Pueblo Culture.

By the Great Pueblo Period (1100–1300 A.D.), the Anasazi population swelled to more than 5,000 and the architecturally ambitious cliff dwellings came into being. The Anasazi moved from the mesa tops onto ledges on the steep canyon walls, creating two- and three-story dwellings. They used sandstone blocks and mud mortar. There were no doors on the first floor and people used ladders to reach the first roof. All the villages had underground chambers called *kivas*. Men held tribal councils there and also used them for secret religious ceremonies and clan meetings. Winding paths, ladders, and steps cut into the stone led from the valleys below to the ledges on which the villages stood. The largest settlement contained 217 rooms. One might surmise that these dwellings were built for protection, but the Anasazi had no known enemies and there is no sign of conflict.

But a bigger mystery is why the Anasazi occupied these structures such a short time. By 1300, Mesa Verde was deserted. It is conjectured that the Anasazi abandoned their settlements because of drought, overpopulation, crop failure, or some combination of these. They probably moved southward and were incorporated into the pueblo villages that the Spanish explorers encountered 200 years later. Their descendants still live in the Southwest.

1. The passage does NOT mention that the Anasazi hunted

   (A) sheep.
   (B) turkeys.
   (C) deer.
   (D) rabbits.

2. The name that the Anasazi used for themselves

(A) means "Basketmakers" in the Navajo language.
(B) is unknown today.
(C) was given to them by archaeologists.
(D) means "ancient ones" in the Anasazi language.

3. How long did the Early Pueblo Culture last?

(A) 200 years
(B) 300 years
(C) 550 years
(D) 1,000 years

4. Where did the Anasazi move during the Great Pueblo Period?

(A) To settlements on ledges of canyon walls
(B) To pueblos in the South
(C) Onto the tops of the mesas
(D) Onto the floors of the canyons

5. According to the passage, the Anasazi buildings were made primarily of

(A) mud.
(B) blocks of wood.
(C) sandstone.
(D) the skins of animals.

6. According to the passage, the Anasazi entered their buildings on the ledges

(A) by means of ladders.
(B) from underground chambers.
(C) by means of stone stairways.
(D) through doors on the first floor.

7. According to the passage, *kivas* were used for all the following purposes EXCEPT

(A) clan meetings.
(B) food preparation.
(C) religious ceremonies.
(D) tribal councils.

8. According to the passage, the LEAST likely reason that the Anasazi abandoned Mesa Verde was

(A) drought.
(B) overpopulation.
(C) war.
(D) crop failure.

9. Put an X next to the paragraph that presents theories about why the Anasazi left.

Passage 2

Dulcimers are musical instruments that basically consist of wooden boxes with strings stretched over them. In one form or another, they have been around since ancient times, probably originating with the Persian santir. Today there are two varieties: the hammered dulcimer and the Appalachian, or mountain dulcimer. The former is shaped like a trapezoid, has two or more strings, and is played with wooden mallets. It is the same instrument played in a number of Old World countries. The Appalachian dulcimer is classified by musicologists as a box zither. It is a descendant of the Pennsylvania Dutch scheitholt and the French epinette. Appalachian dulcimers are painstakingly fashioned by artisans in the mountains of West Virginia, Kentucky, Tennessee, and Virginia. These instruments have three or four strings and are plucked with quills or the fingers. They are shaped like teardrops or hourglasses. Heart-shaped holes in the sounding board are traditional. Most performers play the instruments while seated with the instruments in their laps, but others wear them around their necks like guitars or place them on tables in front of them. Originally used to play dance music, Appalachian dulcimers were popularized by performers such as John Jacob Niles and Jean Ritchie during the folk music revival of the 1960s.

10. According to the passage, which of the following is NOT an ancestor of the Appalachian dulcimer?

   (A) The box zither
   (B) The santir
   (C) The scheitholt
   (D) The epinette

11. According to the passage, how many strings does the Appalachian dulcimer have?

   (A) One or two
   (B) Three or four
   (C) Four or five
   (D) Six or more

12. According to the passage, a hammered dulcimer is made in the shape of

   (A) an hourglass.
   (B) a heart.
   (C) a trapezoid.
   (D) a teardrop.

13. According to the author, most performers play the Appalachian dulcimer

   (A) while sitting down.
   (B) with the instrument strapped around their neck.
   (C) while standing at a table.
   (D) with wooden hammers.

14. According to the author, what are John Jacob Niles and Jean Ritchie known for?

   (A) Playing dance music on Appalachian dulcimers
   (B) Are artisans who design Appalachian dulcimers
   (C) Helped bring Appalachian dulcimers to the public's attention
   (D) Began the folk music revival of the 1960s

15. Underline the sentence in the passage that tells where Appalachian Dulcimers are made.

Passage 3

Humanitarian Dorothea Dix was born in Hampden, Maine, in 1802. At the age of 19, she established a school for girls, the Dix Mansion School, in Boston, but had to close it in 1835 due to her poor health. She wrote and published the first of many books for children in 1824. In 1841, Dix accepted an invitation to teach classes at a prison in East Cambridge, Massachusetts. She was deeply disturbed by the sight of mentally-ill persons thrown in the jail and treated like criminals. For the next eighteen months, she toured Massachusetts institutions where other mental patients were confined and reported the shocking conditions she found to the state legislature. When improvements followed in Massachusetts, she turned her attention to the neighboring states and then to the West and South.

Dix's work was interrupted by the Civil War; she served as superintendent of women hospital nurses for the federal government. Dix saw special hospitals for the mentally ill built in some fifteen states. Although her plan to obtain public land for her cause failed, she aroused concern for the problem of mental illness all over the United States as well as in Canada and Europe. Dix's success was due to her independent and thorough research, her gentle but persistent manner, and her ability to secure the help of powerful and wealthy supporters.

16. In what year was the Dix Mansion School closed?

    (A) 1821
    (B) 1824
    (C) 1835
    (D) 1841

17. Underline the sentence in the first paragraph that explains why Dorothea Dix first went to a prison.

18. Where was Dorothea Dix first able to bring about reforms in the treatment of the mentally ill?

    (A) Canada
    (B) Massachusetts
    (C) The West and South
    (D) Europe

19. Dorothea Dix was NOT successful in her attempt to

    (A) become superintendent of nurses.
    (B) publish books for children.
    (C) arouse concern for the mentally ill.
    (D) obtain public lands.

20. Underline the sentence in paragraph 2 in which the author gives specific reasons why Dix was successful.

Passage 4

Ambient divers are, unlike divers who go underwater in submersible vehicles or pressure resistant suits, exposed to the pressure and temperature of the surrounding (*ambient*) water. Of all types of diving, the oldest and simplest is free diving. Free divers may use no equipment at all, but most use a face mask, foot fins, and a snorkel. Under the surface, free divers must hold their breath. Most free divers can only descend 30 to 40 feet, but some skilled divers can go as deep as 100 feet.

Scuba diving provides greater range than free diving. The word *scuba* stands for *s*elf-contained *u*nderwater *b*reathing *a*pparatus. Scuba divers wear metal tanks with compressed air or other breathing gases. When using open-circuit equipment, a scuba diver simply breathes air from the tank through a hose and releases the exhaled air into the water. A closed-circuit breathing device, also called a rebreather, filters out carbon dioxide and other harmful gases and automatically adds oxygen. This enables the diver to breathe the same air over and over.

In surface-supplied diving, divers wear helmets and waterproof canvas suits. Today, sophisticated plastic helmets have replaced the heavy copper helmets used in the past. These divers get their air from a hose connected to compressors on a boat. Surface-supplied divers can go deeper than any other type of ambient diver.

21. Ambient divers are ones who

   (A) can descend to extreme depths.
   (B) use submersible vehicles.
   (C) use no equipment.
   (D) are exposed to the surrounding water.

22. According to the passage, a free diver may use any of the following EXCEPT

   (A) a rebreather.
   (B) a snorkel.
   (C) foot fins.
   (D) a mask.

23. According to the passage, the maximum depth for free divers is around

   (A) 40 feet.
   (B) 100 feet.
   (C) 200 feet.
   (D) 1,000 feet.

24. When using closed-circuit devices, divers

   (A) exhale air into the water.
   (B) hold their breath.
   (C) breathe the same air over and over.
   (D) receive air from the surface.

25. According to the passage, surface-supplied divers today use helmets made from

   (A) glass.
   (B) copper.
   (C) plastic.
   (D) canvas.

26. Underline the sentence in paragraph 3 that explains how surface-supplied divers are able to breath.

Lesson 35

INFERENCE AND PURPOSE ITEMS

INFERENCE ITEMS

As in the Listening section, there are questions in the Reading section that require you to make **inferences.** The answers to these questions are not directly provided in the passage—you must "read between the lines." In other words, you must make conclusions based indirectly on information in the passage. Many test-takers find these questions the most difficult type of reading question.

Inference questions may be phrased in a number of ways. Many of these questions contain some form of the words *infer* or *imply*.

- Which of the following can be inferred from the passage?

- It can be inferred from the passage that . . .

- The author implies that . . .

- Which of the following does the passage imply?

- Which of the following would be the most reasonable guess about _____?

- The author suggests that . . .

- It is probable that . . .

There will probably be from five to eight of these questions per reading section.

Sample Item

A star very similar to the Sun is one of the nearest stars to Earth. That star is Alpha Centauri, just 4.3 light-years away. Other than our own Sun, the nearest star to the Earth is a tiny red star, not visible without a telescope, called Proxima Centauri.

It can be inferred from this passage that

(A) Proxima Centauri is similar to the Earth's Sun.
(B) Proxima Centauri is the closest star to the Earth.
(C) Alpha Centauri is invisible from the Earth.
(D) Proxima Centauri is less than 4.3 light-years from the Earth.

The correct answer is (D). Choice (A) is not a valid inference; Alpha Centauri is similar to the Earth, but Proxima Centauri is "a tiny red star." Choice (B) also cannot be inferred; the closest star to the Earth is our own Sun. Nor can choice (C) be inferred; Proxima Centauri is invisible, but there is no information as to whether Alpha Centauri is. Since Alpha Centauri is 4.3 light-years away, it can be inferred that Alpha Centauri, the closest star, is less than that.

PURPOSE ITEMS

These items ask why the author of a passage mentions some piece of information, or includes a quote from a person or a study, or uses some particular word or phrase.

Sample Items

- Why does the author mention _____?

- The author refers to _____ to indicate that . . .

- The author quotes _____ in order to show . . .

- The phrase _____ in line _____ is mentioned to illustrate the effect of . . .

Sample Answer Choices

- To strengthen the argument that _____

- To provide an example of _____

- To challenge the idea that _____

- To contradict _____

- To support the proposal to _____

There are usually from one to four purpose questions per reading section.

EXERCISE 35.1

Focus: Identifying valid inferences based on sentences
Directions: Read each sentence, then mark the one answer choice—(A), (B), or (C)—that is a valid inference based on that sentence.

1. A metal-worker of 3,000 years ago would recognize virtually every step of the lost-wax process used to cast titanium for jet engines.

    (A) Titanium has been forged for thousands of years.
    (B) The lost-wax method of casting is very old.
    (C) Metal working has changed very little in 3,000 years.

2. When apple growers talk about new varieties of apples, they don't mean something developed last month, last year, or even in the last decade.

    (A) Apple growers haven't developed any new varieties in recent decades.
    (B) Some varieties of apples can be developed in a short time, but others take a long time.
    (C) New varieties of apples take many years to develop.

3. High cholesterol used to be thought of as a problem only for adults.

    (A) High cholesterol is no longer a problem for adults.
    (B) Only children have a problem with high cholesterol.
    (C) High cholesterol affects both adults and children.

4. Alpha Centauri, one of the closest stars to Earth, is just 4.3 light years away. It can be seen only from the Southern Hemisphere. However, the closest star, other than our own Sun of course, is a tiny red star, Proxima Centauri, that is not visible without a telescope.

    (A) Proxima Centauri is the closest star to the Earth.
    (B) Alpha Centauri is invisible from Earth without a telescope.
    (C) Proxima Centauri is closer than 4.3 light years from the Earth.

222

5. Compared with the rest of its brain, the visual area of a turtle's brain is comparatively small since turtles, like all other reptiles, depend on senses other than sight.

   (A) No reptile uses sight as its primary sense.
   (B) Animals that depend on sight all have larger visual areas in their brains than turtles do.
   (C) The visual areas of other reptile brains are comparatively smaller than those of turtles.

6. Contrary to popular belief, there is no validity to the stories one hears of initials carved in a tree by a young boy becoming elevated high above his head when he visits the tree as an old man.

   (A) Trees don't grow the way many people think they do.
   (B) If a child carves initials in a tree, it won't grow.
   (C) Over time, initials that are carved into a tree will be elevated.

7. Illegible handwriting does not indicate weakness of character, as even a quick glance at the penmanship of George Washington, Franklin D. Roosevelt, or John Kennedy reveals.

   (A) Washington, Roosevelt, and Kennedy all had handwriting that was difficult to read.
   (B) A person's handwriting reveals a lot about that person.
   (C) The author believes that Washington, Roosevelt, and Kennedy all had weak characters.

8. William Faulkner set many of his novels in and around an imaginary town, Jefferson, Mississippi, which he closely patterned after his hometown of Oxford, Mississippi.

   (A) William Faulkner wrote many of his novels while living in Jefferson, Mississippi.
   (B) The town of Oxford, Mississippi, exists only in Faulkner's novels.
   (C) Faulkner actually wrote about his hometown but did not use its real name.

9. Most fish take on, to a certain degree, the coloration of their natural surroundings, so it is not surprising that the fish inhabiting warm, shallow waters around tropical reefs are colored all the brilliant tints of the rainbow.

   (A) Tropical fish are unlike other fish because they take on the coloration of their environment.
   (B) Tropical fish are brightly colored because they inhabit warm waters.
   (C) Tropical reefs are brightly colored environments.

10. Although sheepherding is an older and more beloved occupation, shepherds never caught the attention of American filmmakers the way cowboys did.

    (A) There have been more American films about cowboys than about shepherds.
    (B) Films about shepherds were popular before films about cowboys.
    (C) Cowboys are generally younger than shepherds.

11. The Okefenokee Swamp is a fascinating realm that both confirms and contradicts popular notions of a swamp, because along with huge cypresses, dangerous quagmires, and dim waterways, the Okefenokee has sandy pine islands, sunlit prairies, and clear lakes.

    (A) People generally feel that swamps are fascinating places.
    (B) The Okefenokee has features that most people do not associate with swamps.
    (C) Most swamps do not have huge cypresses, dangerous quagmires, and dim waterways.

12. As an architect, Thomas Jefferson preferred the Roman style, as seen in the University of Virginia, to the English style favored by Charles Bullfinch.

    (A) The University of Virginia was influenced by the Roman style.
    (B) Bullfinch was an English architect.
    (C) Jefferson preferred to build in the English style of architecture.

EXERCISE 35.2

Focus: Answering inference and purpose questions

Directions: Read the following passages and the questions about them. Decide which of the choices—(A), (B), (C), or (D)—best answers the question, and mark the answer.

Passage 1

Pigeons have been taught to recognize human facial expressions, upsetting long-held beliefs that only humans had evolved the sophisticated nervous systems to perform such a feat. In recent experiments at the University of Iowa, eight trained pigeons were shown photographs of people displaying emotions of happiness, anger, surprise, and disgust. The birds learned to distinguish between these expressions. Not only that, but they were also able to correctly identify the same expressions on photographs of unfamiliar faces. Their achievement does not suggest, of course, that the pigeons had any idea what the human expressions meant.

Some psychologists have theorized that because of the importance of facial expression to human communication, humans developed special nervous systems capable of recognizing subtle expressions. The pigeons cast doubt on that idea, however.

In fact, the ability to recognize facial expressions of emotion is not necessarily innate even in human babies, but may have to be learned in much the same way pigeons learn. In experiments conducted several years ago at the University of Iowa, it was found that pigeons organize images of things into the same logical categories that humans do.

None of this work would come as any surprise to Charles Darwin, who long ago wrote about the continuity of mental development from animals to humans.

1. From the passage, which of the following can be inferred about pigeons?

   (A) They can show the same emotions humans can.
   (B) They can understand human emotions.
   (C) They can only identify the expressions of people they are familiar with.
   (D) They have more sophisticated nervous systems than was once thought.

2. The passage implies that, at birth, human babies

   (A) have nervous systems capable of recognizing subtle expressions.
   (B) can learn from pigeons.
   (C) are not able to recognize familiar faces.
   (D) may not be able to identify basic emotions through facial expressions.

3. Why does the author mention the experiments conducted several years ago at the University of Iowa?

   (A) They proved that pigeons were not the only kind of animal with the ability to recognize facial expressions.
   (B) They were contradicted by more recent experiments.
   (C) They proved that the ability to recognize human expressions was not innate in human babies.
   (D) They showed the similarities between the mental organization of pigeons and that of humans.

4. If Charles Darwin could have seen the results of this experiment, his most probable response would have been one of

   (A) rejection.
   (B) surprise.
   (C) agreement.
   (D) amusement.

Passage 2

The spectacular and famous eruptions of Old Faithful geyser in Yellowstone National Park do not occur like clockwork. Before the earthquake of 1959, eruptions came every 60 to 65 minutes; today they are as little as 30 minutes or as much as 90 minutes apart. Changes in weather and in atmospheric pressure can influence the regularity of the eruptions and the height of the column. The geyser usually gives a warning: a short burst of steam. Then a graceful jet of water and steam rises up to 150 feet in the air, unfurling in the sunlight with the colors of the rainbow playing across it.

The eruption is only the visible part of the spectacle. In order for a geyser to erupt, there are three necessary ingredients: a heat source, a water supply, and a plumbing system. In the geyser fields of Yellowstone, a steady supply of heat is provided by hot spots of molten rock as little as two miles below the surface. The water supply of Old Faithful comes from groundwater and rainfall, but other geysers in Yellowstone are located on river banks. Geysers have various types of plumbing systems. Geologists studying Old Faithful theorized that it had a relatively simple one consisting of an underground reservoir connected to the surface by a long, narrow tube. In 1992 a probe equipped with a video camera and heat sensors was lowered into the geyser and confirmed the existence of a deep, narrow shaft and of a cavern, about the size of a large automobile, about 45 feet beneath the surface.

As water seeps into Old Faithful's underground system, it is heated at the bottom like water in a tea-kettle. But while water in a kettle rises because of convection, the narrow tube of the plumbing system prevents free circulation. Thus, the water in the upper tube is far cooler than the water at the bottom. The weight of the water puts pressure on the column, and this raises the boiling point of the water near the bottom. Finally, the confined, superheated water rises, and the water in the upper part of the column warms and expands, some of it welling out of the mouth of the geyser. This abruptly decreases the pressure on the superheated water, and sudden, violent boiling occurs throughout much of the length of the tube, producing a tremendous amount of steam and forcing the water out of the vent in a superheated mass. This is the eruption, and it continues until the water reservoir is emptied or the steam runs out.

There are two main types of geysers. A fountain geyser shoots water out in various directions through a pool. A columnar geyser such as Old Faithful shoots water in a fairly narrow jet from a conical formation at the mouth of the geyser that looks like a miniature volcano.

5. It can be inferred from the passage that the earthquake of 1959 made Old Faithful geyser erupt

   (A) more frequently.
   (B) less regularly.
   (C) more suddenly.
   (D) less spectacularly.

6. Why does the author mention a rainbow in paragraph 1?

   (A) The column of water forms an arc in the shape of a rainbow.
   (B) In the sunlight, the column of water may produce the colors of the rainbow.
   (C) Rainbows can be seen quite frequently in Yellowstone National Park.
   (D) The rainbow, like the geyser, is an example of the beauty of nature.

7. It can be inferred from the passage that which of the following would be LEAST likely to cause any change in Old Faithful's eruptions?

   (A) A drop in atmospheric pressure
   (B) An earthquake
   (C) A rise in the water level of a nearby river
   (D) A period of unusually heavy rainfall

8. The passage implies that Old Faithful would probably not erupt at all if

   (A) the tubes of the geyser system were very wide.
   (B) the climate suddenly changed.
   (C) there had not been an earthquake in 1959.
   (D) the underground tubes were longer.

9. The author implies that, compared to Old Faithful, many other geysers

    (A) are more famous.
    (B) have a more complex plumbing system.
    (C) shoot water much higher into the air.
    (D) have far larger reservoirs.

10. The author mentions the probe that was lowered into Old Faithful in 1992 to indicate that

    (A) it is very difficult to investigate geysers.
    (B) the geologists' original theory about Old Faithful was correct.
    (C) Old Faithful's structure was more intricate than had been believed.
    (D) some very surprising discoveries were made.

11. The author probably compares the formation at the mouth of Old Faithful with a volcano because of the formation's

    (A) age.
    (B) power.
    (C) size.
    (D) shape.

Passage 3

In 1881, a new type of weed began spreading across the northern Great Plains. Unlike other weeds, the tumbleweed did not spend its life rooted to the soil; instead, it tumbled and rolled across fields in the wind. The weed had sharp, spiny leaves that could lacerate the flesh of ranchers and horses alike. It exploited the vast area of the plains, thriving in regions too barren to support other plants. With its ability to generate and disseminate numerous seeds quickly, it soon became the scourge of the prairies.

To present-day Americans, the tumbleweed symbolizes the Old West. They read the Zane Grey novels in which tumbleweeds drift across stark western landscapes and see classic western movies in which tumbleweeds share scenes with cowboys and covered wagons. Yet just over a century ago, the tumbleweed was a newcomer. The first sign of the invasion occurred in North and South Dakota in the late 1870s.

Farmers had noticed the sudden appearance of the new, unusual weed. One group of immigrants, however, did not find the weed at all unfamiliar. The tumbleweed, it turns out, was a native of southern Russia, where it was known as Tartar thistle. It was imported to the United States by unknown means.

Frontier settlers gave the plants various names: saltwort, Russian cactus, and wind witch. But botanists at the Department of Agriculture preferred the designation *Russian thistle* as the plant's common name. However, these botanists had a much harder time agreeing on the plant's scientific name. Generally, botanists compare a plant to published accounts of similar plants, or to samples kept as specimens. Unfortunately, no book described the weed and no samples existed in herbaria in the United States.

12. Which of the following can be inferred about tumbleweeds?

    (A) They have strong, deep roots.
    (B) They require a lot of care.
    (C) They reproduce efficiently.
    (D) They provided food for ranchers and animals.

13. The passage suggests that most present-day Americans

    (A) consider the tumbleweed beneficial.
    (B) don't know when tumbleweeds came to North America.
    (C) have never heard of tumbleweeds.
    (D) believe tumbleweeds are newcomers to the United States.

14. The author mentions the novels of Zane Grey and classic western movies (paragraph 2) because they

(A) tell the story of the invasion of tumbleweeds.
(B) are sources of popular information about tumbleweeds.
(C) present very inaccurate pictures of tumbleweeds.
(D) were written long before tumbleweeds were present in the United States.

15. It is probable that the "group of immigrants" mentioned in paragraph 3

(A) was from southern Russia.
(B) had lived in North and South Dakota for many years.
(C) imported tumbleweeds into the United States.
(D) wrote a number of accounts about tumbleweeds.

16. From the passage it can be inferred that the botanists at the Department of Agriculture

(A) could not find any tumbleweeds on the plains.
(B) gave the names saltwort, Russian cactus, and wind witch to the tumbleweed.
(C) could not decide on a common designation for the tumbleweed.
(D) found it difficult to classify the plant scientifically.

Passage 4

For most modern airports, the major design problem is scale—how to allow adequate space on the ground for maneuvering wide-body jets while permitting convenient and rapid movement of passengers departing, arriving, or transferring from one flight to another.

Most designs for airport terminals take one of four approaches. In the linear plan, the building may be straight or curved. The passengers board aircraft parked next to the terminal. This plan works well for small airports that need to provide boarding areas for only a few aircraft at a time.

In the pier plan, narrow corridors or piers extend from a central building. This plan allows many aircraft to park next to the building. However, it creates long walking distances for passengers.

In the satellite plan, passengers board aircraft from small terminals that are separated from the main terminals. Passengers reach the satellites by way of shuttle trains or underground passageways that have shuttle trains or moving sidewalks.

The transporter plan employs some system of transport to move passengers from the terminal building to the aircraft. If buses are used, the passengers must climb a flight of stairs to board the aircraft. If mobile lounges are used, they can link up directly with the aircraft and protect passengers from the weather.

17. It can be inferred that scale would not pose a major design problem at airports if

(A) airports were larger.
(B) aircraft did not need so much space to maneuver on the ground.
(C) other forms of transportation were more efficient.
(D) airplanes could fly faster.

18. The linear plan would probably be best at

(A) a busy airport.
(B) an airport used by many small aircraft.
(C) an airport with only a few arrivals or departures.
(D) an airport that serves a large city.

19. The passage implies that the term "satellite plan" is used because

(A) satellites are launched and tracked from these sites.
(B) small terminals encircle the main terminal like satellites around a planet.
(C) the plan makes use of the most modern, high-technology equipment.
(D) airports that make use of this plan utilize data from weather satellites.

20. The passage suggests that shuttle trains transfer passengers to satellite terminals from

    (A) the main terminal.
    (B) airplanes.
    (C) downtown.
    (D) other satellite terminals.

21. It can be inferred that mobile lounges would be more desirable than buses when

    (A) passengers are in a hurry.
    (B) flights have been delayed.
    (C) the weather is bad.
    (D) passengers need to save money.

Lesson 36

When ETS eliminated the first section of Section 3, which consisted of 30 discrete vocabulary items, it replaced them with an increased number of questions (from 12 to 18) about the vocabulary in the reading passages. Most test takers find that, in general, it is easier to answer vocabulary questions based on the context of a passage than it is to answer questions about vocabulary in single, isolated sentences.

In vocabulary items, you must determine which of four words or phrases can best substitute for a word or words in the passage.

Most of the questions ask about single words (usually nouns, verbs, adjectives, and adverbs). Some ask about two- or three-word phrases.

Sometimes two of the answer choices for these items might be "correct" definitions of the word that is asked about. In those cases, you must decide which of the two is correct in the context of the passage.

In ordinary reading, there are a number of clues that can help you determine the meaning of an unknown word:

- **Synonyms**
  The first state to institute *compulsory* education was Massachusetts, which made it mandatory for students to attend school twelve weeks a year.
  The word *mandatory* is a synonym for the word *compulsory*.

- **Examples**
  Many gardeners use some kind of *mulch*, such as chopped leaves, peat moss, grass clippings, pine needles, or wood chips, in order to stop the growth of weeds and hold in moisture.
  From the examples given, it is clear that *mulch* is plant matter.

- **Contrast**
  In the 1820s, the Southern states supported improvements in the national transportation system, but the Northern states *balked*.
  Since the Southern states supported improvements, and since a word signaling contrast (*but*) is used, it is clear that the Northern states disagreed with this idea, and that the word *balked* must mean *objected or refused*.

- **General context**
  In a desert, vegetation is so *scanty* as to be incapable of supporting any large human population.
  As is generally known, deserts contain little vegetation, so clearly the word *scanty* must mean *scarce* or *barely sufficient*.

When answering vocabulary items, you must most often depend on the general context of the sentence to help you choose the correct answer.

You should follow these steps to answer vocabulary items.

1. Look at the word being asked about and the four answer choices. If you are familiar with the word, guess which answer is correct. Do NOT mark your answer sheet yet.

2. Read the sentence in which the word appears. If you were familiar with the word and guessed at the answer, make sure that the word that you chose fits with the word as it is used in the sentence. If you were unfamiliar with the word, see if context clues in the sentence or in the sentences before or after help you guess the meaning.

3. If you are not sure which answer is correct, read the sentence with each of the four answer choices in place. Does one seem more logical, given the context of the sentence, than the other three? If not, do any seem illogical? (You can eliminate those.)

4. If you're still not sure, make the best guess you can and go on.

Sample Items

In Britain's North American colonies, university-trained physicians were at a premium. At the time of the Revolution, there were probably only around 400 physicians and some 3,000 practitioners who had on-the-job training as barber-surgeons or physicians' apprentices. Whether university trained or not, none had much knowledge of the causes of disease, and the "cures" they often recommended— bleeding, blistering, and the use of violent purgatives—were at best ineffective and at worst lethal.

1. The phrase at a premium in the first sentence is closest in meaning to

   (A) well-paid.
   (B) not very numerous.
   (C) very experienced.
   (D) not well-respected.

The correct answer is (B). The phrase "only around 400" indicates that there was a shortage of university-trained physicians.

2. Which of the following words could best be substituted for the word lethal in the last sentence?

   (A) Impractical
   (B) Brutal
   (C) Impossible
   (D) Deadly

The correct answer is (D). The phrase "at best ineffective and at worst lethal" indicates that the correct answer must describe a situation much worse than ineffective. Choices (A) and (C) don't create logical sentences when substituted for *lethal*. Choice (B), *brutal* (which means savage or violent), is more logical, but only choice (D) is synonymous with the word that is asked about.

EXERCISE 36.1

Focus: Using context clues to answer "click-on" items

Directions: Write the word from the passage that is the closest in meaning (or most nearly opposite in meaning) in the blanks.

Passage 1

Everyday life in the British colonies of North America may now seem glamorous, especially as reflected in antique shops. But judged by modern standards, it was quite a drab existence. For most people, the labor was heavy and constant from daybreak to nightfall.

Basic comforts now taken for granted were lacking. Public buildings were often not heated at all. Drafty homes were heated only by inefficient fireplaces. There was no running water or indoor plumbing. The flickering light of candles and whale oil lamps provided inadequate illumination. There was no sanitation service to dispose of garbage; instead, long-snouted hogs were allowed to roam the streets, consuming refuse.

1. Find the word or phrase in paragraph 1 that is most nearly OPPOSITE in meaning to the word glamorous. _____

2. Find the word or phrase in paragraph 2 that is closest in meaning to the word refuse. _____

Passage 2

Blood is a complex fluid composed of several types of cells suspended in plasma, the liquid portion of the blood. Red blood cells make up the vast majority of blood cells. Hemoglobin in the red blood cells picks up oxygen in the blood and delivers it to the tissues of the body. Then these cells carry carbon dioxide from the body's cells to the lungs.

Think of it as a railroad that hauls freight. The cargo (oxygen) is loaded into a railroad car (hemoglobin). Then the locomotive (a red blood cell) carries the cars where they are needed. After unloading, the train returns with a different cargo (carbon dioxide) and the process starts over.

Hemoglobin is the part of the cell that traps oxygen and carbon dioxide. It contains a compound called porphyrin that consists of a carbon-based ring with four nitrogen atoms facing a central hole. The nitrogen bonds to an iron atom, and the iron then captures one molecule of oxygen or carbon dioxide.

3. Find the word or phrase in paragraph 2 that is closest in meaning to the word hauls. _____

4. Find the word or phrase in paragraph 2 that is closest in meaning to the word cargo. _____

5. Find the word or phrase in paragraph 3 that is closest in meaning to the word traps. _____

Passage 3

Taking over as president of Harvard in 1869, Charles W. Eliot pioneered a break with the traditional curriculum. The usual course of studies at U.S. universities at the time emphasized classical languages, mathematics, rhetoric, and ethics. Eliot initiated a system under which most required courses were dropped in favor of elective courses. The university increased its offerings and stressed physical and social sciences, the fine arts, and modern languages. Soon other universities all over the United States were following Harvard's lead.

6. Find the word or phrase in the passage that is closest in meaning to the word pioneered. _____

7. Find the word or phrase in the passage that is closest in meaning to the word curriculum. _____

8. Find the word or phrase in the passage that is closest in meaning to the word emphasized. _____

9. Find the word or phrase in the passage that is most nearly OPPOSITE in meaning to the word required. _____

Passage 4

The Pleiades, named after the seven sisters of Greek mythology, is a star cluster that can be seen with the naked eye. It appears as a dipper-shaped group of stars high overhead on autumn evenings. It is so young (only a few million years old) that many of its stars appear to be surrounded by a luminous blue mist. This haze is actually starlight reflecting off debris left behind after the stars were formed. Our own Sun's stellar neighborhood probably looked much like this just after its formation.

10. Find the word or phrase in the passage that is closest in meaning to the word cluster. _____

11. Find the word or phrase in the passage that is closest in meaning to the word mist. _____

Passage 5

Interior designers may claim that a solitary goldfish displayed in a glass bowl makes a striking minimalist fashion statement, but according to a team of British researchers, goldfish learn from each other and are better off in groups than alone. In one experiment, two groups of goldfish were released into a large aquarium separated by a transparent plastic panel. On one side, food was hidden in various locations. The fish on that side foraged for the food while the fish on the other side of the clear panel watched. When released into the feeding area, these observant fish hunted for the food exactly in the proper locations. Other experiments showed that fish raised in a group are less fearful of attack than fish raised alone. And not only are they less skittish, they are also better at avoiding enemies in the event of actual danger.

12. Find the word or phrase in the passage that is closest in meaning to the word solitary. _____

13. Find the word or phrase in the passage that is closest in meaning to the word transparent. _____

14. Find the word or phrase in the passage that is closest in meaning to the word foraged. _____

15. Find the word or phrase in the passage that is closest in meaning to the word skittish. _____

Passage 6

Although business partnerships enjoy certain advantages over sole proprietorships, there are drawbacks as well. One problem that may afflict partnerships is the fact that each general partner is liable for the debts incurred by any other partner. Moreover, he or she is responsible for lawsuits resulting from any partner's malpractice. Interpersonal conflicts may also plague partnerships. All partnerships, from law firms to rock groups, face the problem of personal disagreements. Another problem is the difficulty of dissolving partnerships. It is much easier to dissolve a sole proprietorship than it is to terminate a partnership. Generally, a partner who wants to leave must find someone—either an existing partner or an outsider acceptable to the remaining partners—to buy his or her interest in the firm.

16. Find the word or phrase in the passage that is most nearly OPPOSITE in meaning to the word drawbacks. _____

17. Find the word or phrase in the passage that is closest in meaning to the word liable. _____

18. Find the word or phrase in the passage that is closest in meaning to the word conflicts. _____

19. Find the word or phrase in the passage that is closest in meaning to the word plague. _____

20. Find the word or phrase in the passage that is closest in meaning to the word dissolve. _____

EXERCISE 36.2

Focus: Answering both types of vocabulary items about words or phrases in reading passages.

Directions: Answer the items about the vocabulary in the passages. Mark the proper oval for multiple-choice items and underline the appropriate word or phrase in the bold text to answer "click on" items.

Passage 1

The Civil War created feverish manufacturing activity to supply critical material, especially in the North. When the fighting stopped, the stage was set for dramatic economic growth. Wartime taxes on production had vanished, and the few taxes that remained leaned heavily on real estate, not on business. The population flow from farm to city increased, and the labor force it provided was buttressed by millions of newly arrived immigrants willing to work for low wages in the mills of the North and on the railroad crews of the Midwest and West.

The federal government's position toward economic expansion was nothing if not accommodating. The government established tariff barriers, provided loans and grants to build a transcontinental railroad, and assumed a studied stance of nonintervention in private enterprise. The Social Darwinism of British philosopher Herbert Spencer and American economist William Graham Summer prevailed. The theory was that business, if left to its own devices, would eliminate the weak and nurture the strong. But as business expanded, the rivalry heated up. In the 1880s, five railroads operating between New York and Chicago vied for traffic, and two more were under construction. As a result of the battle, the fare between the cities decreased to one dollar. Petroleum companies likewise competed savagely and, in the 1880s, many of them failed.

1. The word feverish in paragraph 1 is closest in meaning to

   (A) extremely rapid.
   (B) sickly and slow.
   (C) very dangerous.
   (D) understandable.

2. Which of the following is closest in meaning to the word critical in paragraph 1?

   (A) industrial
   (B) serious
   (C) crucial
   (D) insulting

3. The phrase the stage was set in paragraph 1 is closest in meaning to which of the following?

   (A) The play was over.
   (B) The progress continued.
   (C) The foundation was laid.
   (D) The direction was clear.

4. Look at the word newcomers in the **bold** text below.

   The population flow from farm to city increased, and the labor force it provided was buttressed by millions of recent immigrants. These newcomers were willing to work for low wages in the mills of the North and on the railroad crews of the Midwest and West.

   Underline the word or phrase in the bold text that is closest in meaning to the word newcomers.

5. The phrase real estate in paragraph 1 refers to

   (A) tools and machines.
   (B) actual income.
   (C) new enterprises.
   (D) land and buildings.

6. The word buttressed in paragraph 1 is closest in meaning to

   (A) concerned.
   (B) supplemented.
   (C) restructured.
   (D) enriched.

7. The word accommodating in paragraph 2 is closest in meaning to

   (A) persistent.
   (B) indifferent.
   (C) balanced.
   (D) helpful.

8. Look at the word stance in the **bold** text below.

   The federal government's position toward economic expansion was nothing if not accommodating. It established tariff barriers, provided loans and grants to build a transcontinental railroad, and assumed a studied stance of nonintervention in private enterprise.

   Underline the word or phrase in the **bold** text that is closest in meaning to the word stance.

9. The word prevailed in paragraph 2 is closest in meaning to

   (A) influenced.
   (B) triumphed.
   (C) premiered.
   (D) evolved.

10. The phrase left to its own devices in paragraph 2, means

    (A) forced to do additional work.
    (B) allowed to do as it pleased.
    (C) made to change its plans.
    (D) encouraged to produce more goods.

11. Look at the word vied in the **bold** text below.

    In the 1880s, five railroads operating between New York and Chicago vied for traffic, and two more were under construction. As a result of the battle, the fare between the cities decreased to one dollar. Petroleum companies likewise competed savagely and, in the 1880s, many of them failed.

    Underline the word or phrase in the **bold** text that is closest in meaning to the word vied.

12. The word savagely in paragraph 2 is closest in meaning to

    (A) fiercely.
    (B) suddenly.
    (C) surprisingly.
    (D) genuinely.

Passage 3

All birds have feathers, and feathers are unique to birds. No other major group of animals is so easy to categorize. All birds have wings, too, but wings are not peculiar to birds.

Many adaptations are found in both feathers and wings. Feathers form the soft down of geese and ducks, the long showy plumes of ostriches and egrets, and the strong flight feathers of eagles and condors. Wings vary from the short, broad ones of chickens, who seldom fly, to the long, slim ones of albatrosses, who spend almost all their lives soaring on air currents. In penguins, wings have been modified into flippers and feathers into a waterproof covering. In kiwis, the wings are almost impossible to detect.

Yet diversity among birds is not so striking as it is among mammals. The difference between a hummingbird and a penguin is immense, but hardly as startling as that between a bat and a whale. It is variations in details rather than in fundamental patterns that have been important in the adaptation of birds to many kinds of ecosystems.

13. Look at the words peculiar to in the **bold** text below.

    All birds have feathers, and feathers are unique to birds. No other major group of animals is so easy to categorize. All birds have wings, too, but wings are not peculiar to birds.

    Underline the word or phrase in the **bold** text closest in meaning to the words peculiar to.

14. The word categorize in paragraph 1 is closest in meaning to

    (A) appreciate.
    (B) comprehend.
    (C) classify.
    (D) visualize.

15. The word showy in paragraph 2 is closest in meaning to which of the following?

    (A) Ornamental
    (B) Graceful
    (C) Colorless
    (D) Powerful

16. Look at the word slim in the **bold** text below.

    Feathers form the soft down of geese and ducks, the long showy plumes of ostriches and egrets, and the strong flight feathers of eagles and condors. Wings vary from the short, broad ones of chickens, who seldom fly, to the long slim ones of albatrosses, who spend almost all their lives soaring on air currents.

    Underline the word or phrase in the **bold** text most nearly OPPOSITE in meaning to the word slim.

17. The word detect in paragraph 2 is closest in meaning to

    (A) utilize.
    (B) extend.
    (C) observe.
    (D) describe.

18. Which of the following is closest in meaning to the word diversity in paragraph 3?

    (A) function
    (B) heredity
    (C) specialty
    (D) variety

19. Look at the word striking in the **bold** text below.

> **Yet diversity among birds is not so striking as it is among mammals. The difference between a hummingbird and a penguin is immense, but hardly as startling as that between a bat and a whale.**

Underline the word or phrase in the **bold** text closest in meaning to the word striking.

20. The word hardly in paragraph 3 is closest in meaning to

(A) definitely.
(B) not nearly.
(C) possibly.
(D) not always.

21. The word fundamental in paragraph 3 is closest in meaning to

(A) basic.
(B) shifting.
(C) predictable.
(D) complicated.

Passage 4

Manufactured in the tranquil New England town of Concord, New Hampshire, the famous Concord Coach came to symbolize the Wild West. Its rugged body and a suspension system of leather straps could handle the hard jolts from rough roads. A journalist in 1868, describing a railroad shipment of 30 coaches bound for Wells, Fargo and Company, wrote, "They are splendidly decorated . . . the bodies red and the running parts yellow. Each door has a handsome picture, mostly landscapes, and no two coaches are exactly alike."

Wells, Fargo and Company was founded in 1852 to provide mail and banking services for the gold camps of California and later won a monopoly on express services west of the Mississippi. A Wells, Fargo Concord Coach carried nine to fourteen passengers plus baggage and mail. The accommodations were by no means plush. However, while conditions may have been primitive and service not always prompt, the stagecoach was the swiftest method of travel through much of the Far West.

22. The word tranquil in paragraph 1 is closest in meaning to

(A) peaceful.
(B) bustling.
(C) industrial.
(D) tiny.

23. The word symbolize in paragraph 1 is closest in meaning to

(A) recollect.
(B) fulfill.
(C) deny.
(D) represent.

24. Which of the following could best substitute for the word rugged in paragraph 1?

(A) streamlined
(B) roomy
(C) sturdy
(D) primitive

25. Which of the following is closest in meaning to the word jolts in paragraph 1?

    (A) signs
    (B) shocks
    (C) sights
    (D) shots

26. The phrase bound for in paragraph 1 is closest in meaning to

    (A) belonged to.
    (B) destined for.
    (C) built by.
    (D) paid for.

27. Look at the word splendidly in the **bold** text below.

"They are decorated splendidly . . . the bodies red and the running parts yellow. Each door is superbly painted, mostly with landscapes, and no two coaches are exactly alike."

Underline the word or phrase in the **bold** text closest in meaning to the word splendidly.

28. Look at the word plush in the **bold** text below.

The accommodations were by no means plush. However, while conditions may have been primitive and service not always prompt, the stagecoach was still the swiftest method of travel through much of the Far West.

Underline the word or phrase in the bold text most nearly OPPOSITE in meaning to the word plush.

29. Which of the following is closest in meaning to the word swiftest in paragraph 2?

    (A) most comfortable
    (B) cheapest
    (C) most direct
    (D) fastest

Lesson 37

REFERENCE ITEMS

Reference items ask you to find the noun (called the **referent**) that a pronoun or other word refers to. Two things to remember:

1. The referent almost always comes before the reference word in the passage.

2. The referent is NOT always the noun that is closest to the reference word in the sentence.

On the computer-based test, most reference items are Click on the Passage items but a few are Multiple-Choice items.

Click on Reference Items

When you see this type of item, a section of the passage—usually one or two sentences—appears in **bold** text, just as in Vocabulary items. A pronoun or other reference word will be highlighted. You have to find the referent in the bold text that the highlighted word or phrase refers to.

You can identify "possible answers" in the bold text according to the type of reference word that is highlighted. For example, if the pronoun he is being asked about, you would only look for nouns that name a singular male person. Here's a list of common reference words and the kinds of nouns they refer to:

Reference Words				Possible Referents
she	her	hers	herself	A singular female
he	his	him	himself	A singular male
it	its	itself		A singular thing, place, animal, action, idea
they	their	them	themselves	Plural persons, things, animals, places, actions, ideas
who	whose			Person(s)
which				Things(s), place(s), animal(s), action(s), idea(s)
that (relative pronoun)				Person(s), thing(s), place(s), animal(s), action(s), idea(s)
then				Time
there				Place
this	that	(demonstrative)		Singular thing, action, idea
these	those			Plural things, actions, ideas

This, *that*, *these*, and *those* can also be used with nouns: *this person*, *that time*, *those animals*, *these places*.

After you have identified possible answers, you should read the sentence with the answers in place of the reference. Which one is the most logical substitute? If you are not sure, you can at least eliminate unlikely choices and guess.

Multiple-Choice Reference Items

A few reference items will ask you to choose which one of four nouns a pronoun or other word refers to. Again, you should read the sentence with each of the four choices in place of the highlighted word to decide which of the four answers is the most logical.

EXERCISE 37.1

Focus: Identifying the referents for pronouns and other expressions in sentences and very short passages

Directions: Read the items. Decide which word or phrase in the items is the correct referent for the highlighted word or phrase and underline it or (for Multiple-Choice items) mark the correct answer. If there are two highlighted words or phrases, circle the first reference and underline the second.

1. X-rays allow art historians to examine paintings internally without damaging them.

2. The poisonous, plantlike anemone lives in a coral reef. When a small fish ventures near this creature, it is stung and eaten. For some reason, the anemone makes an exception of the clown fish. When the clown fish is endangered by another fish, it dashes among the anemone's tentacles. It even builds its nest where the anemone can protect it.

3. Florists often refrigerate cut flowers to protect their fresh appearance.

   (A) florists'
   (B) flowers'

4. Unlike a box kite, a flat kite needs a tail to supply drag and to keep it pointed toward the sky. A simple one consists of cloth strips tied end to end.

5. Water is an exception to many of nature's rules because of its unusual properties.

6. Ropes are cords at least .15 inches in diameter and are made of three or more strands which are themselves formed of twisted yarns.

   (A) yarns
   (B) ropes
   (C) strands
   (D) cords

7. Grocers slice sides, quarters, and what are called primal cuts of beef into smaller pieces. These pieces are then packaged and sold.

8. Leaves are found on all deciduous trees, but they differ greatly in size and shape.

9. Yasuo Kuniyashi was born in Japan in 1883 and studied art at the Los Angeles School of Art and Design. He also studied art in New York City, where he gave his first one-man show. In 1925 he moved from there to Paris where he was influenced by the works of Chagall and other artists.

   (A) Japan
   (B) Paris
   (C) Los Angeles
   (D) New York City

10. In the past, biologists considered mushrooms and other fungi a type of non-green plant. Today, however, they are most commonly regarded as a separate kingdom of living things.

11. William Dean Howells, a contemporary and friend of Mark Twain, wrote a number of books that realistically portrayed life on farms in Midwestern America. One of his followers, Hamlin Garland, was even more bitter in his criticism of rural America than his mentor.

12. The Wisconsin Dells is a region where the Wisconsin River cuts through soft sandstone. The strange formations that have been carved out of the rocks there are a delight to tourists. They have names such as Devil's Elbow, Grand Piano, and Fat Man's Misery.

EXERCISE 37.2

Focus: Answering reference questions based on longer passages

Directions: Read the following passages and the questions about them. For Multiple-Choice items, decide which of the choices—(A), (B), (C), or (D)—best answers the question, and mark the answer. Underline the correct referents for "click-on" items.

Passage 1

In addition to these various types of deep mining, several types of surface mining may be used when minerals lie relatively close to the surface of the Earth. One type is open-pit mining. The first step is to remove the overburden, the layers of rock and earth lying above the ore, with giant scrapers. The ore is broken up in a series of blasting operations. Power shovels pick up the pieces and load them into trucks or, in some cases, ore trains. These carry it up ramps to ground level. Soft ores are removed by drilling screws, called augers.

Another type is called "placer" mining. Sometimes heavy metals, such as gold, are found in soil deposited by streams and rivers. The soil is picked up by a power shovel and transferred to a long trough. Water is run through the soil in the trough. This carries soil particles away with it. The metal particles are heavier than the soil and sink to the bottom where they can be recovered.

The finishing-off process of mining is called mineral concentration. In this process, the desired substances are removed from the waste in various ways. One technique is to bubble air through a liquid in which ore particles are suspended. Chemicals are added that make the minerals cling to the air bubbles. The bubbles rise to the surface with the mineral particles attached, and they can be skimmed off and saved.

1. Look at the word them in the **bold** text below.

    The ore is broken up in a series of blasting operations. Power shovels pick up the pieces and load them into trucks.

    Underline the word or phrase in the **bold** text that refers to them.

2. Look at the word These in the **bold** text below.

    Power shovels pick up the pieces and load them into trucks. These carry it up ramps to ground level. Soft ores are removed by drilling screws, called augers.

    Underline the word or phrase in the **bold** text that refers to These.

3. The phrase Another type in paragraph 2 is a reference to another type of

    (A) deep mining.
    (B) ore.
    (C) metal.
    (D) surface mining.

4. Look at the word it in the **bold** text below.

    The soil is picked up by a power shovel and transferred to a long trough. Water is run through the soil in the trough. This carries soil particles away with it.

    Underline the word or phrase in the **bold** text that refers to it.

5. Look at the word they in the **bold** text below.

    This carries soil particles away with it. The metal particles are heavier than the soil and sink to the bottom where they can be recovered.

    Underline the word or phrase in the **bold** text that refers to they.

6. In paragraph 3, the phrase this process refers to

    (A) surface mining.
    (B) the depositing of soil.
    (C) mineral concentration.
    (D) placer mining.

7. Look at the word they in the **bold** text below.

Chemicals are added that make them cling to the air bubbles. The bubbles rise to the surface with the ore particles attached, and they can be skimmed off and saved.

Underline the word or phrase in the **bold** text that refers to they.

Passage 2

Mount Rainier, the heart of Mt. Rainier National Park, is the highest mountain in the state of Washington and in the Cascade Range. The mountain's summit is broad and rounded. It is 14,410 feet above sea level and has an area of about one square mile. Numerous steam and gas jets occur around the crater, but the volcano has been sleeping for many centuries.

    Mount Rainier has a permanent ice cap and extensive snow fields, which give rise to more than forty glaciers. These feed swift streams and tumbling waterfalls that race through the glacial valleys. Forests extend to 4,500 feet. There are alpine meadows between the glaciers and the forests, which contain beautiful wild flowers. The Nisqually Glacier is probably the ice region that is most often explored by visitors. Paradise Valley, where hotel accommodations are available, perches on the mountain's slope at 5,400 feet. The Wonderland Trail encircles the mountain. Its 90-mile length can be covered in about a week's time.

8. Look at the word It in the **bold** text below.

Mount Rainier, the heart of Mt. Rainier National Park, is the highest mountain in the state of Washington and in the Cascade Range. The mountain's summit is broad and rounded. It is 14,410 feet above sea level and has an area of about one square mile.

Underline the word or phrase in the **bold** text that refers to It.

9. Look at the word These in the **bold** text below.

Mount Rainier has a permanent ice cap and extensive snowfields, which give rise to over forty glaciers. These feed swift streams and tumbling waterfalls that race through the glacial valleys.

Underline the word or phrase in the **bold** text that refers to These.

10. The word which in paragraph 2 refers to

    (A) forests.
    (B) wild flowers.
    (C) alpine meadows.
    (D) glacial valleys.

11. Look at the word Its in the **bold** text below.

Paradise Valley, where hotel accommodations are available, perches on the mountain's slope at 2,700 feet. The Wonderland Trail encircles the mountain. Its 90-mile length can be covered in about a week's time.

Underline the word or phrase in the **bold** text that refers to Its.

Passage 3

Some people associate migration mainly with birds. Birds do travel vast distances, but mammals also migrate. Caribou graze on the grassy slopes of northern Canada. When the weather turns cold, these animals travel south until spring. Their tracks are so well-worn that they are clearly visible from the air. Another example is the Alaskan fur seal. These seals breed only in the Pribilof Islands in the Bering Sea. The young are born in June and by September are strong enough to go with their mothers on a journey of over 3,000 miles. Together they swim down the Pacific Coast of North America. The females and young travel as far as southern California. The males do not journey so far. They swim only to the Gulf of Alaska. In the spring, males and females all return to the islands, and there the cycle begins again. Whales are among the greatest migrators of all. The humpback, fin, and blue whales migrate thousands of miles each year from the polar seas to the tropics. Whales eat huge quantities of tiny plants and animals. These are most abundant in cold polar waters. In winter, the whales move to warm waters to breed and give birth to their young.

12. Look at the word they in the **bold** text below.

    Caribou graze on the grassy slopes of northern Canada. When the weather turns cold, these animals travel south until spring. Their tracks are so well worn that they are clearly visible from the air.

    Underline the word or phrase in the **bold** text that refers to they.

13. The phrase Another example in the passage refers to an example of

    (A) a migratory mammal.
    (B) a place where animals migrate.
    (C) a bird.
    (D) a person who associates migration with birds.

14. Look at the word They in the **bold** text below.

    The females and young travel as far as southern California. The males do not journey so far. They swim only to the Gulf of Alaska. In the spring, males and females all return to the islands, and there the cycle begins again.

    Underline the word or phrase in the **bold** text that refers to They.

15. In the passage, the word there refers to

    (A) the Gulf of Alaska.
    (B) the Pribilof Islands.
    (C) southern California.
    (D) the Pacific Coast of North America.

16. Look at the word These in the **bold** text below.

    Whales eat huge quantities of tiny plants and animals. These are most abundant in cold polar waters. In winter, the whales move to warm waters to breed and give birth to their young.

    Underline the word or phrase in the **bold** text that refers to These.

Passage 4

Design is the arrangement of materials to produce certain effects. Design plays a role in visual arts and in the creation of commercial products as well. Designers are concerned with the direction of lines, the size of shapes, and the shading of colors. They arrange these patterns in ways that are satisfying to viewers. There are various elements involved in creating a pleasing design.

Harmony, or *balance*, can be obtained in a number of ways. It may be either symmetrical (in balance) or asymmetrical (out of balance, but still pleasing to the eye). Or a small area may balance a large area if it has an importance to the eye (because of color or treatment) equaling that of the larger area.

Contrast is the opposite of harmony. The colors red and orange harmonize, since orange contains red. A circle and an oval harmonize, as they are both made up of curved lines. But a triangle does not harmonize with a circle. Because of its straight lines and angles, it is in contrast.

Unity occurs when all the elements in a design combine to form a consistent whole. Unity resembles balance. A design has balance if its masses are balanced or if its tones and colors harmonize. But unity differs from balance because it implies that balanced elements work together to form harmony in the design as a whole.

17. Look at the word They in the **bold** text below.

    Designers are concerned with the direction of lines, the size of shapes, and the shading of colors. They arrange these patterns in ways that are satisfying to viewers.

    Underline the word or phrase in the **bold** text that refers to They.

18. Look at the word that in the **bold** text below.

    Or a small area may balance a large area if it has an importance to the eye (because of color or treatment) equaling that of the larger area.

    Underline the word or phrase in the **bold** text that refers to that.

19. Look at the word they in the **bold** text below.

    The colors red and orange harmonize, since orange contains red. A circle and an oval harmonize, as they are both made up of curved lines.

    Underline the word or phrase in the **bold** text that refers to they.

20. Look at the word it in the **bold** text below.

    A circle and an oval harmonize, as they are both made up of curved lines. But a triangle does not harmonize with a circle. Because of its straight lines and angles, it is in contrast.

    Underline the word or phrase in the **bold** text that refers to it.

21. In the last sentence, the word it refers to

    (A) unity.
    (B) balance.
    (C) a design.
    (D) a consistent whole.

Lesson 38

SENTENCE ADDITION ITEMS

This type of item provides you with a sentence that can be added to a passage. You have to decide where to place this sentence. Black squares will appear between the sentences of one of the paragraphs of the passage. You have to click on the square where you think the sentence belongs. There will probably be from four to ten possible sites where you can insert the sentence.

You will generally see two to five Sentence Addition items per test.

Sentence Addition problems test your knowledge of paragraph organization and **coherence**. You can think of coherence as the "glue" that holds the sentences of a paragraph together.

There are some devices that writers use to achieve cohesion. You can use these as clues to help you find the best place to put the missing sentences. These devices may occur in either the missing sentence or the passage.

1. **Signal Words**
   Scientists have many theories about why the Ice Ages took place. *However*, none of these theories can fully explain why ice sheets form at certain periods and not at others.

   Stone tools are more durable than bones. *Therefore*, the tools of early humans are found more frequently than the bones of their makers.

   If we watch a cell divide under a microscope, what do we see? *First*, the nucleus of the cell begins to look different. The dense material thins out in the middle, forming two parts. *Then* these two parts separate, and there are two nuclei instead of one. *Finally*, a new cell wall forms between the new nuclei. The cell has divided.

2. **Personal Pronouns**
   Blood travels first through the great arteries. *It* then passes into smaller arteries until reaching the capillaries. *They* join to form veins, which carry the blood back to the heart.

3. **Demonstratives**
   There were a number of methods of improving worker motivation and performance introduced in the 1970s. One of *these* was called Management by Objectives (M.O.). *This technique* was designed to improve morale by having workers set their own goals.

4. **Synonyms**
   The earliest remains of ancient animals are those of soft-bodied jellyfish-like animals, worms, and proto-insects. *The fossils* of these creatures show us that, while some animals remained simple, others were becoming increasingly complex.

5. **Repetition of Words**
   Hydrilla is an invasive plant imported to Florida from Sri Lanka forty years ago for use in aquariums. *Hydrilla* has overgrown more than 40 percent of the state's rivers and lakes, making life miserable for boaters and often impossible for native wildlife.

In addition to these language clues, you can also use content clues. The missing sentence might be in contrast to one of the sentences in the passage, or one of the sentences in the paragraph might be in contrast to the missing sentence. The missing sentence might give an example of something mentioned in the passage or might represent a missing step from a process or a chronology described in the passage.

In order for anyone to answer this type of item correctly, there must be some clues in either the missing sentence or the passage. There must be something—an idea or a word or a phrase—that links the missing sentence either to the sentence that comes before it or to the one that comes after it. It's up to you to find the clues!

You should follow these steps when you answer a sentence addition problem:

1. Read the missing sentence carefully and read over the sentences marked with squares (in our exercises, we have used numbers in parentheses instead of boxes to make it easier to discuss the answers).

2. Look for signal words, personal pronouns, demonstratives, synonyms, and repetition of words, first in the sentence and then in the passage. Do any of these devices link the missing sentence to any other sentence in the passage?

3. Look for places in the passage where the focus seems to shift from one topic to another abruptly, with no transition.

4. If the answer is not clear, look for content clues that tie the sentence either to the sentence that comes before it or to the sentence that comes after it.

5. You may be able to eliminate certain squares between two sentences because those sentences are closely joined and could not logically be separated.

6. If you still cannot find the answer, guess and go on.

Sentence Addition items are generally quite difficult and take up a lot of your time—and you don't get any extra credit for answering these questions correctly! Don't spend too much time on these items on your first time through the test. If possible, come back to them later if you have extra time.

EXERCISE 38

Focus: Understanding paragraph organization and cohesion and answering sentence addition questions

Directions: Circle the proper number in parentheses to mark the place where the sentence best fits into the passage.

Passage 1

When a mammal is young, it looks much like a smaller form of an adult. **(1)** However, animals that undergo metamorphosis develop quite differently from mammals. **(2)** The young of these animals, which are called larvae, look very little like the mature forms and have a very different way of life. **(3)** Take the example of butterflies and caterpillars, which are the larval form of butterflies. **(4)** Caterpillars, on the other hand, are wingless and have more than six legs. They move by crawling and feed on leaves. **(5)** To become adults, the larvae must radically change their forms. **(6)**

To accomplish this change, a larva must go through the process of metamorphosis. **(7)** It does this in the second stage of life, called the pupa stage. **(8)** When they are ready to pupate, caterpillars settle in sheltered positions. **(9)** Some spin a cocoon around themselves. **(10)** The caterpillar then sheds its old skin and grows a protective pupal skin. **(11)** Inside this skin, the body of the caterpillar gradually transforms itself. **(12)** The wingbuds, which were under the caterpillar's skin, grow into wings. **(13)** When the change is complete the pupal skin splits open and the butterfly emerges. **(14)** But soon it dries out, its wings unfurl, and it flies off. **(15)** Now it is ready to mate and to lay eggs that will develop into larvae. **(16)**

1. The following sentence can be added to paragraph 1.

   Butterflies have two pairs of wings and six legs and feed on the nectar of flowers.

   Circle the correct number to show where it would best fit into the paragraph.

2. The following sentence can be added to paragraph 2.

   At first it is damp and its wings are curled up.

   Circle the correct number to show where it would best fit into the paragraph.

Passage 2

The process of miniaturization began in earnest with the transistor, which was invented in 1947. **(1)** It was much smaller than the smallest vacuum tube it was meant to replace and, not needing a filament, it consumed far less power and generated virtually no waste heat. **(2)** There was almost no limit to how small the transistor could be once engineers had learned how to etch electronic circuits onto a substrate of silicon. **(3)** In the 1950s, the standard radio had five vacuum tubes and dozens of resistors and capacitors, all handwired and soldered onto a chassis about the size of a hardbound book. **(4)** In fact, the limiting factor in making appliances smaller is not the size of the electronic components but the human inter-face. **(5)** There is no point in reducing the size of a palm-held computer much further unless humans can evolve smaller fingers. **(6)**

3. The following sentence can be added to the passage.

   Today all that circuitry and much more can fit into a microprocessor smaller than a postage stamp.

   Circle the correct number to show where it would best fit into the passage.

Passage 3

It is believed that the first Americans were hunters who arrived by way of the only link between the hemispheres, the Siberian-Alaskan land bridge. **(1)** This strip of land remained above water until about 10,000 years ago. **(2)** These migrants unquestionably brought with them the skills to make weapons, fur clothing, and shelters against the bitter cold. **(3)** It seems safe to assume that they also brought myths and folktales from the Old World. **(4)** But which myths and which folktales? **(5)**

Among myths, the most impressive candidate for Old World origin is the story of the Earth Diver. **(6)** This is the story of a group of water creatures who take turns diving for a piece of solid land. **(7)** The duck, the muskrat, the turtle, the crawfish, or some other animal succeeds but has to dive so deep that by the time it returns to the surface, it is half-drowned or dead. **(8)** The animals magically enlarge this tiny piece of solid land until it becomes the Earth. **(9)** Not every Native American tribe has a myth about the creation of the world, but of those that do, the Earth Diver myth is the most common. **(10)** It is found in all regions of North America except the Southwestern United States and the Arctic regions, and is also found in many locations in Asia and the Pacific Islands. **(11)**

Another common myth is that of the Theft of Fire. **(12)** In this story, a creature sets out to steal fire from a distant source, obtains it, often through trickery, and carries it home. **(13)** The best known version of this story is the Greek myth of Prometheus. **(14)** Other Old World versions of this story are told in Central Asia, India, and Africa. **(15)** In some New World locations, it is replaced by Theft of the Sun, Theft of Daylight, or Theft of Heat stories. **(16)**

4. The following sentence can be added to paragraph 1.

   More recent arrivals no doubt took the same route, crossing on winter ice.

   Circle the correct number to show where it would best fit into the paragraph.

5. The following sentence can be added to paragraph 2.

   But in its claws, the other animals find a bit of mud.

   Circle the correct number to show where it would best fit into the paragraph.

6. The following sentence can be added to paragraph 3.

   In the New World, it appears among many Native American tribes west of the Rocky Mountains and in the American Southeast.

   Circle the correct number to show where it would best fit into the paragraph.

Passage 4

When drawing human figures, children often make the head too large for the rest of the body. **(1)** A recent study offers some insight into this common disproportion in children's illustrations. **(2)** As part of the study, researchers asked children between four and seven years old to make several drawings of adults. **(3)** When they drew frontal views of these subjects, the size of the heads was markedly enlarged. **(4)** The researchers suggest that children draw bigger when they know they must leave room for facial details. **(5)** Therefore, the distorted head size in children's illustrations is a form of planning ahead and not an indication of a poor sense of scale. **(6)**

7. The following sentence can be added to the passage.

However, when the children drew rear views of the adults, the size of the heads was not nearly so exaggerated.

Circle the correct number to show where it would best fit into the passage.

Passage 5

It has been observed that periods of maximum rainfall occur in both the northern and southern hemispheres at about the same time. **(1)** This phenomenon cannot be adequately explained on a climatological basis, but meteors may offer a plausible explanation. **(2)** When the Earth encounters a swarm of meteors, each meteor striking the upper reaches of the atmosphere is vaporized by frictional heat. **(3)** The resulting debris is a fine smoke or powder. **(4)** This "stardust" then floats down into the lower atmosphere, where such dust might readily serve as nuclei upon which ice crystals or raindrops could form. **(5)** The delay of a month allows time for the dust to fall through the upper atmosphere. **(6)** Occasionally, large meteors leave visible traces of dust. **(7)** In a few witnessed cases, dust has remained visible for over an hour. **(8)** In one extreme instance—the great meteor that broke up in the sky over Siberia in 1908—the dust cloud traveled all over the world before disappearing. **(9)**

8. The following sentence can be added to the passage.

Confirmation that this phenomenon actually happens is found in the observed fact that increases in world rainfall come about a month after meteor systems are encountered in space.

Circle the correct number to show where it would best fit into the passage.

Passage 6

Lawn tennis is a comparatively modern modification of the ancient game of court tennis. **(1)** Major Walter C. Wingfield thought that something like court tennis might be played outdoors on the grass and in 1873 he introduced his new game under the name *Sphairistikè* at a lawn party in Wales. **(2)** Players and spectators soon began to call the new game "lawn tennis." **(3)** In 1874 a woman named Mary Outerbridge returned to New York with the basic equipment of the game, which she had obtained from a British Army store in Bermuda. **(4)** The first game of lawn tennis in the United States was played on the grounds of the Staten Island Cricket and Baseball Club in 1874. **(5)**

The game went on in a haphazard fashion for a number of years. **(6)** A year later, the U.S. Lawn Tennis Association was formed. **(7)** International matches for the Davis Cup began in 1900. **(8)** They were played at Chestnut Hill, Massachusetts, between British and American players. **(9)** The home team won this first championship match. **(10)**

9. The following sentence can be added to paragraph 1.

It was an immediate success and spread rapidly, but the original name quickly disappeared.

Circle the correct number to show where it would best fit into the paragraph.

10. The following sentence can be added to paragraph 2.

Then in 1879, standard equipment, rules, and measurements for the court were instituted.

Circle the correct number to show where it would best fit into the paragraph.

Passage 7

Photosynthesis is the process by which plants capture the Sun's energy to convert water and carbon dioxide into sugars to fuel their growth. **(1)** In fact, chlorophyll is so essential to the life of plants that it forms almost instantly in seedlings as they come in contact with sunlight. **(2)** A green pigment, chlorophyll is responsible for the green coloring of plants. **(3)** But what turns the leaves of deciduous plants brilliant red and orange and gold in the autumn? **(4)**

Trees do not manufacture new pigments for fall. **(5)** Orange, red, yellow, and other colored pigments are present in the leaves throughout the spring and summer. **(6)** However, these are masked by the far greater quantity of chlorophyll. **(7)** When the days grow shorter and temperatures fall, leaves sense the onset of fall. **(8)** They form an "abscission layer." **(9)** This layer is a barrier of tissue at the base of each leaf stalk. **(10)** Thus, sugar builds up in the leaf, causing the chlorophyll to break down. **(11)** The greens of summer then begin to fade. **(12)** The orange, red, yellow, and brown pigments now predominate, giving the leaves their vibrant autumn colors. **(13)**

11. The following sentence can be added to paragraph 1.

    This process cannot take place without chlorophyll.

    Circle the correct square number to show where it would best fit into the paragraph.

12. The following sentence can be added to paragraph 2.

    It prevents nourishment from reaching the leaf and, conversely, prevents sugar created in the leaf from reaching the rest of the tree.

    Circle the correct number to show where it would best fit into the paragraph.

REVIEW TEST H: READING

Directions: This test consists of several passages, each followed by 10–15 questions. Read the passages and, for each question, choose the one best answer based on what is stated in the passage or can be inferred from the passage.

As soon as you understand the directions, begin work.

Passage 1

Humans have struggled against weeds since the beginnings of agriculture. Marring our gardens is among the milder effects of weeds—any plants that thrive where they are unwanted. They destroy wildlife habitats and impede farming. Their spread eliminates grazing areas and accounts for one-third of all crop loss. They compete for sunlight, nutrients, and water with useful plants. They may also hamper harvesting.

The global need for weed control has been answered mainly by the chemical industry. Its herbicides are effective and sometimes necessary, but some pose serious problems, particularly if they are misused. Toxic compounds may injure animals, especially birds and fish. They threaten the public health when they accumulate in food plants, ground water, and drinking water. They also directly harm workers who apply them.

In recent years, the chemical industry has introduced several herbicides that are more ecologically sound than those of the past. Yet new chemicals alone cannot solve the world's weed problems. Hence, an increasing number of scientists are exploring biological alternatives that harness the innate weed-killing powers of living organisms, primarily insects and microorganisms.

The biological agents now used to control weeds are environmentally benign and offer the benefit of specificity. They can be chosen for their ability to attack selected targets and leave crops and other plants untouched, including plants that might be related to the target weeds. They spare only those that are naturally resistant or those that have been genetically modified for resistance. Furthermore, a number of biological agents can be administered only once, after which no added applications are needed. Chemicals typically must be used several times per growing season.

Biological approaches may never supplant standard herbicides altogether, but they should sharply limit the use of dangerous chemicals and reduce the associated risks. They might also make it possible to conquer weeds that defy management by conventional means.

1. With what topic does this passage primarily deal?

   (A) The importance of the chemical industry
   (B) The dangers of toxic chemicals
   (C) Advantages of biological agents over chemical ones
   (D) A proposal to ban the use of all herbicides

2. The word marring in paragraph 1 is closest in meaning to

   (A) spoiling.
   (B) dividing.
   (C) replacing.
   (D) planting.

3. Look at the word hamper in the **bold** text below.

   They destroy wildlife habitats and impede farming. Their spread eliminates grazing areas and accounts for one-third of all crop loss. They compete for sunlight, nutrients, and water with useful plants. They may also hamper harvesting.

   Click on the word or phrase in the **bold** text that is closest in meaning to the word hamper.

4. Which of the following terms does the author define in paragraph 1?

   (A) Nutrients
   (B) Grazing areas
   (C) Weeds
   (D) Wildlife habitats

5. Look at the word harm in the **bold** text below.

   Its herbicides are effective and sometimes necessary, but some pose serious problems, particularly if they are misused. Toxic compounds may injure animals, especially birds and fish. They threaten the public health when they accumulate in food plants, ground water, and drinking water. They also harm directly workers who apply them.

   Click on the word or phrase in the **bold** text that is closest in meaning to the word harm.

6. With which of the following statements about the use of chemical agents as herbicides would the author most likely agree?

   (A) It should be increased.
   (B) It has become more dangerous recently.
   (C) It is safe but inefficient.
   (D) It is occasionally required.

7. Which of the following is NOT given as an advantage of using biological agents over chemical herbicides?

   (A) They are less likely to destroy desirable plants.
   (B) They are safer for workers.
   (C) They are more easily available.
   (D) They do not have to be used as often.

8. According to the passage, biological agents consist of

   (A) insects and microorganisms.
   (B) useful plants.
   (C) weeds.
   (D) herbicides.

9. The following sentence can be added to the paragraph below:

In contrast, some of the most effective chemicals kill virtually all the plants they come in contact with.

Where would it best fit in the paragraph?

The biological agents now used to control weeds are environmentally benign and offer the benefit of specificity. **(1)** They can be chosen for their ability to attack selected targets and leave crops and other plants untouched, including plants that might be related to the target weeds. **(2)** They spare only those that are naturally resistant or those that have been genetically modified for resistance. **(3)** Furthermore, a number of biological agents can be administered only once, after which no added applications are needed. **(4)** Chemicals typically must be used several times per growing season. **(5)**

Circle the number that indicates the best position for the sentence.

10. The word applications in paragraph 4 could best be replaced by which of the following?

(A) Requests
(B) Special purposes
(C) Treatments
(D) Qualifications

11. Look at the word they in the **bold** text below.

Biological approaches may never supplant standard herbicides altogether, but they should sharply limit the use of dangerous chemicals and reduce the associated risks.

Underline the word or phrase in the **bold** text that the word refers to they.

12. Look at the word standard in the **bold** text below.

Biological approaches may never supplant standard herbicides altogether, but they should sharply limit the use of dangerous chemicals and reduce the associated risks. They might also make it possible to conquer weeds that defy management by conventional means.

Underline the word or phrase in the **bold** text that is closest in meaning to the word standard.

13. Which of the following best describes the organization of the passage?

(A) A general idea is introduced and several specific examples are given.
(B) A recommendation is analyzed and rejected.
(C) A problem is described and possible solutions are compared.
(D) Two possible causes for a phenomenon are compared.

Passage 2

West Side Story is a musical tragedy based on William Shakespeare's timeless love story, *Romeo and Juliet*. It is set in the early 1950s, when gang warfare in big cities led to injuries and even death. *West Side Story* transformed the Montagues and Capulets of Shakespeare's play into rival street gangs, the Jets and the Sharks. The Sharks were newly arrived Puerto Ricans, the Jets nativeborn New Yorkers. The plot tells the story of Maria, a Puerto Rican whose brother Bernardo is the leader of the Sharks, and of Tony, a member of the Jets. As the opposing gangs battle in the streets of New York, these two fall in love. While attempting to stop a street fight, Tony inadvertently kills Maria's brother Bernardo and is ultimately killed himself.

West Side Story featured the talents of a trio of theatrical legends. Leonard Bernstein, who composed the brilliant score, was a classical composer and the conductor of the New York Philharmonic. Stephen Sondheim, making his Broadway debut, revealed a remarkable talent for writing lyrics. Among the hit songs of the play are "Tonight," "Maria," "America," "Gee Officer Krupke," and "I Feel Pretty." Jerome Robbins' electrifying choreography broke new ground for musical theater in the 1950s. Before *West Side Story,* no one thought that dance could be as integral to a narrative as the music and the lyrics. But the dances in *West Side Story* are among the most thrilling elements of the play.

The play opened on September 26, 1957. It ran for 734 performances, toured for 10 months, and then returned to New York for an additional 246 performances. The classic motion picture staring Natalie Wood was released in 1961. It garnered ten Academy Awards, including ones for Best Picture and Best Director. The play was successfully revived in New York in 1980 and then again in 1995, almost forty years after its premier performance.

14. The author's attitude toward the play is generally

(A) favorable.

(B) critical.

(C) emotional.

(D) regretful.

15. According to the passage, when does the action of the play *West Side Story* take place?

(A) In Shakespeare's time

(B) In the early 1950s

(C) In 1957

(D) In 1980

16. It can be inferred from the passage that the Capulets and Montagues

(A) were families in Shakespeare's play.

(B) were 1950s street gangs.

(C) fought against the Jets and Sharks.

(D) were groups of actors, dancers, and singers.

17. Look at the word rival in the **bold** text below.

> *West Side Story* **transformed the Montagues and Capulets of Shakespeare's play into rival street gangs, the Jets and the Sharks. The Sharks were newly arrived Puerto Ricans, the Jets native-born New Yorkers. The plot tells the story of Maria, a Puerto Rican whose brother Bernardo is the leader of the Sharks, and of Tony, a member of the Jets. As the opposing gangs battle in the streets of New York, these two fall in love.**

Underline the word or phrase in the **bold** text that is closest in meaning to the word rival.

18. Underline the sentence in paragraph 1 that introduces the main characters in *West Side Story.*

19. According to the article, the words to the songs of *West Side Story* were written by

    (A) Jerome Robbins.
    (B) Leonard Bernstein.
    (C) William Shakespeare.
    (D) Stephen Sondheim.

20. The word score in paragraph 2 could best be replaced by which of the following?

    (A) Talent
    (B) Music
    (C) Performance
    (D) Dialogue

21. Look at the word electrifying in the **bold** text below.

Jerome Robbins' electrifying choreography broke new ground for musical theater in the 1950s. Before *West Side Story*, no one thought that dance could be as integral to a narrative as the music and the lyrics. But the dances in *West Side Story* are among the most thrilling elements of the play.

Underline the word or phrase in the **bold** text that is closest in meaning to the word electrifying.

22. Look at the word ones in the **bold** text below.

The play opened on September 26, 1957. It ran for 734 performances, toured for 10 months, and then returned to New York for an additional 246 performances. The classic motion picture starring Natalie Wood was released in 1961. It garnered ten Academy Awards, including ones for Best Picture and Best Director.

Underline the word or phrase in the **bold** text that the word refers to ones.

23. What can be inferred from the passage about musical plays produced before *West Side Story*?

    (A) They involved fewer songs.
    (B) Dance was not such an important feature in them.
    (C) They depended on dance and song more than on plot.
    (D) Legendary talents did not help create them.

24. During its initial appearance in New York, how many times was *West Side Story* performed?

    (A) 10
    (B) 26
    (C) 246
    (D) 734

Passage 3

The National Automobile Show in New York has been one of the top auto shows in the United States since 1900. On November 3 of that year about 8,000 people looked over the "horseless carriages." It was opening day and the first opportunity for the automobile industry to show off its wares to a large crowd; however, the black-tie audience treated the occasion more as a social affair than as a sales extravaganza. It was also on the first day of this show that William McKinley became the first U.S. president to ride in a car.

The automobile was not invented in the United States. That distinction belongs to Germany. Nikolaus Otto built the first practical internal-combustion engine there in 1876. Then German engineer Karl Benz built what are regarded as the first modern automobiles in the mid-1880s. But the United States pioneered the merchandising of the automobile. The auto show proved to be an effective means of getting the public excited about automotive products.

By happenstance, the number of people at the first New York show equaled the entire car population of the United States at that time. In 1900 ten million bicycles and an unknown number of horse-drawn carriages provided the prime means of personal transportation. Only about 4,000 cars were assembled in the United States in 1900, and only a quarter of those were gasoline powered. The rest ran on steam or electricity.

After viewing the cars made by 40 car makers, the show's audience favored electric cars because they were quiet. The risk of a boiler explosion turned people away from steamers, and the gasoline-powered cars produced smelly fumes. The Duryea Motor Wagon Company, which launched the American auto industry in 1895, offered a fragrant additive designed to mask the smells of the naphtha that it burned. Many of the 1900 models were cumbersome—the Gasmobile, the Franklin, and the Orient, for example, steered with a tiller like a boat instead of with a steering wheel. None of them was equipped with an automatic starter.

These early model cars were practically handmade and were not very dependable. They were basically toys of the well-to-do. In fact, Woodrow Wilson, then a professor at Princeton University and later President of the United States, predicted that automobiles would cause conflict between the wealthy and the poor. However, among the exhibitors at the 1900 show was a young engineer named Henry Ford. But before the end of the decade, he would revolutionize the automobile industry with his Model T Ford. The Model T, first produced in 1909, featured a standardized design and a streamlined method of production—the assembly line. Its lower costs made it available to the mass market.

Cars at the 1900 show ranged in price from $1,000 to $1,500, or roughly $14,000 to $21,000 in today's prices. By 1913, the Model T was selling for less than $300, and soon the price would drop even further. "I will build cars for the multitudes," Ford said, and he kept his promise.

25. The passage implies that the audience viewed the 1900 National Automobile Show primarily as

   (A) a formal social occasion.
   (B) a chance to buy automobiles at low prices.
   (C) an opportunity to learn how to drive.
   (D) a chance to invest in one of thirty-two automobile manufacturers.

26. According to the passage, who developed the first modern car?

   (A) Karl Benz
   (B) Nikolaus Otto
   (C) William McKinley
   (D) Henry Ford

27. Underline the sentence in paragraph 2 that explains the U.S. contribution to the early development of automobiles.

28. Approximately how many cars were there in the United States in 1900?

(A) 4,000
(B) 8,000
(C) 10 million
(D) An unknown number

29. Which of the following is closest in meaning to the phrase by happenstance as used in paragraph 3?

(A) Generally
(B) For example
(C) Coincidentally
(D) By design

30. Approximately how many of the cars assembled in the year 1900 were gasoline powered?

(A) 32
(B) 1,000
(C) 2,000
(D) 4,000

31. According to the passage, people at the 1900 National Automobile Show favored cars powered by

(A) electricity.
(B) naphtha.
(C) gasoline.
(D) steam.

32. Look at the word fragrant in the **bold** text below.

The risk of a boiler explosion turned people away from steamers, and the gasoline powered cars produced smelly fumes. The Duryea Motor Wagon Company, which launched the American auto industry in 1895, offered a fragrant additive designed to mask the smells of the naphtha that it burned. Many of the 1900 models were cumbersome—the Gasmobile, the Franklin, and the Orient, for example, steered with a tiller like a boat instead of with a steering wheel.

Underline the word or phrase in the **bold** text that is most nearly OPPOSITE in meaning to the word fragrant.

33. The purpose of the additive mentioned in paragraph 4 was to

(A) increase the speed of cars.
(B) make engines run more efficiently.
(C) hide strong smells.
(D) make cars look better.

34. The word cumbersome in paragraph 4 is closest in meaning to

(A) clumsy.
(B) unshapely.
(C) fragile.
(D) inconvenient.

35. Which of the following is NOT mentioned in the passage as steering with a tiller rather than with a steering wheel?

(A) A Franklin
(B) A Duryea
(C) An Orient
(D) A Gasmobile

36. Look at the phrase well-to-do in the **bold** text below.

These early model cars were practically handmade and were not very dependable. They were basically toys of the well-to-do. In fact, Woodrow Wilson, then a professor at Princeton University and later President of the United States, predicted that automobiles would cause conflict between the wealthy and the poor.

Underline the word or words in the **bold** text that is closest in meaning to the phrase well-to-do.

37. The following sentence can be added to paragraph 3.

The cars he exhibited at the 1900 show apparently attracted no special notice.

Where would it best fit in the paragraph?

These early model cars were practically handmade and were not very dependable. **(1)** They were basically toys of the well-to-do. **(2)** In fact, Woodrow Wilson, then a professor at Princeton University and later President of the United States, predicted that automobiles would cause conflict between the wealthy and the poor. **(3)** However, among the exhibitors at the 1900 show was a young engineer named Henry Ford. **(4)** But before the end of the decade, he would revolutionize the automobile industry with his Model T Ford. **(5)** The Model T, first produced in 1909, featured a standardized design and a streamlined method of production—the assembly line. **(6)** Its lower costs made it available to the mass market.

Circle the number that indicates the best position for the sentence.

38. What was the highest price asked for a car at the 1900 National Automobile Show in the dollars of that time?

    (A) $300
    (B) $1,500
    (C) $14,000
    (D) $21,000

Section 4

ESSAY WRITING

On the computer-based test, the Essay Writing section is a MANDATORY (required) section of every test. This section (previously called the Test of Written English, or the TWE) is given after the three multiple-choice sections of the test. The Writing section differs from the rest of the TOEFL® test in that it is **productive.** Instead of choosing one of four answer choices, you have thirty minutes in which to write your own short essay. You may either write your answer with pencil and paper or word-process (type) it on the computer. If you choose to write the essay by hand, someone at the center will give you a special test form on which to write it.

THE PROMPTS

The Essay Writing section consists of a single essay topic, called a **prompt.** There is no choice of topic; you must write on the prompt that is given. All of the prompts are very general. They do not require any special knowledge, and they are not about any controversial issues.

Some common contexts for essay writing prompts are: education, business, the future, technology, travel, family, friendship, sports and games, entertainment, communication, and transportation.

There are three common types of prompts:

1. Defend an Opinion

This type of prompt presents two points of view and asks you to choose one side to support. These prompts usually follow this pattern: "Some people believe A, but other people believe B. Which do you believe?"

Sample Item
Some people believe that money spent on space research benefits all of humanity. Other people take the opposite view and say that money spent on this type of research is wasted. Tell which point of view you agree with and explain why, using specific details and reasons.

2. Agree or Disagree with a Statement

This type of prompt presents a general statement and asks whether you agree or disagree with it.

Sample Item
Do you agree or disagree with this statement? It is much easier to learn in a small class than in a large one. Use specific examples and reasons to support your answer.

3. Explain the Importance of a Development, Invention, or Phenomenon

This type of prompt essentially says, "There have been many important X's in the world, such as _____. Choose another example of X, and explain why it is important."

Sample Item
Developments in transportation such as the automobile have had an enormous impact on modern society. Choose another development in transportation that you think is of great importance. Use specific examples and reasons for your choice.

ETS now publishes a list of all the prompts that will appear on the test in any given year. You can find this list in the *Bulletin* and on the TOEFL® Web site. Of the 110 topics listed, you will see one on the day that you test. (If only you knew which one!) It's a good idea to look over this list and think about how you would respond to each topic.

THE WRITING PROCESS

You have only thirty minutes to write the essay, so you will be under a certain amount of time pressure. You should divide your time more or less like this:

Pre-Writing (About 5 Minutes)

- Reading the prompt
- Thinking about the prompt
- Brainstorming and note taking
- Making an informal outline

Writing the Essay (About 20 Minutes)

Checking the Essay (About 5 Minutes)

Looking for and correcting structural, mechanical, and grammatical problems

THE ESSAY

To get a top score in this section, your essay should be around 200–300 words in length. Typically, this type of essay is organized into four or five paragraphs.

- Introductory Paragraph
- Body Paragraph 1
- Body Paragraph 2
- Concluding Paragraph

Some essays may have a third or even fourth body paragraph.

Specific hints for organizing each paragraph are provided in Lesson 40, "Writing the Essay."

Computer or Handwritten?

You have the choice of writing the essay by hand or word-processing it. Which method should you choose? You should probably handwrite the essay if you . . .

- have little or no experience typing
- cannot type more than about 10–15 words a minute in English
- have seldom or never used a keyboard with English characters

Otherwise, you should definitely write the essay on the computer. In fact, word processing is such an important skill to have—especially if you plan to attend a university in an English-speaking country—that you may want to consider learning how to type before you take the test. There are computer programs that can teach you the basics or you can practice on your own.

Here are some advantages of writing the essay on computer:

- The finished product is much neater and will be easier for the readers to read.
- There are certain functions—especially cut and paste—that you can do only on a computer.
- If you are somewhat experienced at word-processing, you can work much more quickly on the computer than with a pencil.
- You can make corrections more quickly and more neatly.
- Finally—and this may be the most important advantage—if you word-process your essay, you will get your final grade in about two weeks, but if you handwrite your essay, it will take about five weeks.

SCORING THE ESSAY

At ETS, your essay is read by two readers who score it **holistically.** In other words, the essay is not judged according to individual mistakes you might make but by the overall effectiveness of your writing. These are some of the points that scorers look for:

- **Topic**

  Does the writer write on the topic that is given in the prompt? Does the essay respond to the entire prompt or just to part of it?

- **Organization**

  Is the essay clearly divided into an introduction, a body, and a conclusion? Does the writer seem to follow an overall plan or does he or she move from point to point for no particular reason?

- **Development**

  Does the writer use specific reasons, examples, and details to support his or her ideas?

- **Clarity**

  Are the writer's ideas expressed clearly? Can a reader move from the beginning of the essay to the end without being confused?

- **Unity**

  Are all the paragraphs directly related to the main idea of the essay? Are all the sentences in each paragraph clearly related?

- **Coherence**

  Do the paragraphs and the sentences follow each other in an orderly way? Are transitions used to connect paragraphs and sentences?

- **Sentence Variety**

  Does the writer use sentences involving different structures and of different lengths?

- **Vocabulary**

  Does the writer use sophisticated language?

- **Grammar**

  Are there frequent grammatical mistakes? Do the mistakes make it difficult to understand the writer's thoughts?

- **Spelling**

  Are there many misspelled words? Is it sometimes difficult to understand which word the writer intended?

- **Mechanics**

  Are there frequent mistakes in capitalization and punctuation? Are the paragraphs indented?

The score is based on a scale of 1 to 6; half-point scores (5.5, 4.5, and so on) are also given. The scoring system ETS uses is similar to the following one:

Score	Explanation of Score
6	Strongly indicates the ability to write a well-organized, well-developed, and logical essay. Specific examples and details support the main ideas. All the elements of the essay are unified and cohesive. A variety of sentence structures are used successfully, and sophisticated vocabulary is employed. Grammatical and mechanical errors are infrequent, but a few minor mistakes may occur.
5	Indicates the ability to write an organized, developed, and logical essay. The main ideas are adequately supported by examples and details. Sentence structure may be less varied than that of a level 6 essay and vocabulary less sophisticated. Some grammatical and mechanical errors will appear.
4	Indicates some ability in writing an acceptable essay, but involves weaknesses in organization and development. Sentence structure and vocabulary may lack sophistication, and there may be frequent grammatical and mechanical errors.
3	Indicates a moderate ability to write an acceptable essay. Although main ideas may be adequately supported, serious weaknesses in organization and development are apparent. Sentence structure and vocabulary problems occur frequently. Grammatical errors are frequent and may make the writer's ideas difficult to comprehend.
2	Indicates the inability to write an acceptable essay. Organization and development are very weak or nonexistent. May lack unity and cohesion. Few specific details are given in support of the writer's ideas. If details are given, they may seem inappropriate. Significant and frequent errors in grammar occur throughout the essay, making it difficult to understand the writer's ideas. Writer may not have fully understood the essay prompt.
1	Strongly indicates the inability to write an acceptable essay. No apparent development or organization. Sentences may be brief, fragmentary, and unrelated to each other. Very significant grammatical and mechanical errors occur throughout the essay and make it very difficult to understand any of the author's ideas. Writer may have completely misunderstood the essay prompt.
0	Did not write an essay, did not write on the topic, or wrote in a language other than English.

Following are six essays, each illustrating one of the six scores. They are written on the following topic:

Some people believe that money spent on space research benefits all of humanity. Other people take the opposite view and say that money spent on this type of research is wasted. Tell which point of view you agree with and explain why, using specific details and reasons.

ESSAY 1
Score 6

It has become quite a common proverb that "there is no free lunch." Another way to say this is that spending money always has it's "opportunity cost." In other words, money spent on some venture could have been used for financing some other alternative venture. Some people believe that money spent on space research has a benefit for all people. Other people believe that there are better opportunities for spending this fund.

The first group of people say that space research has helped all peoples' lives very much. They point out that research on space has informed us about many environmental damages which we have caused to our planet. Similarly, they say that today's modern satelite system is due to the research done in the past on space. There are also many new materials and inventions that can be traced directly to space research. These people want to spend more money on research, visit all the planets, and build space colonies.

In the other hand, there are people who think that money spent on space is a complete wastage because it does not have enough direct benefit to all of the humanity. For example, billions of US$ were spent on the Project Apollo and they only brought back a bag of rocks. In the meanwhile, there is a sizeable portion of the humanity that does not have any access to food, education, sanitation, health care, and especially peace.

Personally, I find that I cannot allign myself completely with either group. I have some reservation about both positions. No one can deny that weather satelites and communication satelites are a good investment. But I think that "unrealistic" research like exploring Mars or Venus does not have any good bearing on most of humans' development at the present time. Some scientists may be interested in the composition of those planets, but the opportunity cost is too much. In my opinion, it is like the poor man who wants to buy diamond jewlry when his family does not have enough food to eat or clothes to wear.

ESSAY 2
Score 5

Some people do really believe that space reseaches benefit all of humanity. And it's quite understandable because all the history of humanity development is connected with the space discovers. From the beginning people have been looking the sky and observing the star's movement and its influence. For example, everyone knows about astrology and how ancient people try to predict the future using knowledge of the stars.

The present space discovery started in 1957, when the sputnik was launched. The first person flew in the space in 1961, and after several years first Americans landed on moon.

Nowdays space researches can solve a lot of problems, For example, reseaches with new materials and technologies. Such materials can be used in medicine, chemistry, and etc. With the help of space satellites we can observe the atmosphere around the Earth and that's why we can try to predict storms and so on. Through such observation we can save people's lifes and decrease destructions, also we can solve problems with the different kinds of pollutions of ocean and atmosphere.

However, it is quite understandable the position of those who say that space researches are wasted. There are to many places where the main problem of life is to survive. My native country once was part of Soviet Union, where the big first steps in space were taken. I see people there who works hard and doesn't receive enough or any salary. I wonder if they approve the space reseaches?

But I'm sure that if we concentrate only on the question of how to survive, the humanity will lose the reason for development. If we refuse from space researches,or any kind of the scientific researches, we will stop moving forward. And the absence of moving forward means the death of the humanity's spirit. That's why I agree with the statement.

Essay 3

Score 4

One of history's greatest event caught us here in the 21st century. An international space station members have decoded some of the mysterious sounds recorded lately. It seems human being from other planet are going to meet us as their lost brothers. Psychologists say, that the emotions and style of thinking of these message senders as compared with Earth population is very close to twins! These messages are spread out throughout the space only once in hundred year. These message senders can teach us things that will take thousand of years to learn by ourselves.

Almost this is as great as the discovery ten years ago, when the big meteor going to hit the Earth was seen by a satellite and could be exploded before it could make any damage.

Could you imagine the perspective if we were stopped space research as some scientists and other peoples had requested at the beginning of the 21st century.

(Article of the World Tribune, 28 December 2049)

Essay 4

Score 3

Well, about the topic, I think that there others subjects much more importants to be researching. One of them, and to me the most important, is the health. The cancer cure is not totally developed yet. The AIDs' victims increasing at an incredibly way. So, although I find in "space" a very fascinating and misterious subject, I should agree with the opposite view that the money spend on it wasted when are so many of people dying around the world as a result of unknowns diseases or not having answers or cures for the ones we already known, or because is not enough money for purification of the water or vaccines for the diseases. More money for the education is also very important.

I believe cientifics should focus "health" in the first place and then to extend the researches in other field.

Essay 5

Score 2

At the first the research in any thing is very useful for people because without research we will not development our life, so that I believe that the money spent in space research benefit the humanity.

Maybe the other side people thing that the money which paid for these research is so much and if we paid it for poor people it well be help him in they life and help him for many thing like food or healthy or any way of they life.

But the people which agrees with have a lot of point for example: one of this is the life must be development. Other point, the rule materials become less and we must find a new one and must find new resource of power, so that they agree with a research in space.

Essay 6

Score 1

The peoples take the opposive view because we don't buy something one time and we don't see another things. That is a save way.

the money is important things. for this reason to spent money the peoples need to be very cerfully I have two opinion for spent money. The money important to spent all humanity, because this point is very important. I'm not agree money wested. in the futurre very important

Tactics for Essay Writing

- Decide before the test whether you are going to word process the essay or write it in longhand.

- As with all parts of the TOEFL® Test, be familiar with the directions for Essay Writing so that you don't have to waste time reading them.

- Use the clock on the screen to pace yourself. You have only a half hour in which to complete your work. Give yourself 5 minutes to read the prompt and plan the essay, 20 minutes to write it, and 5 minutes to check it.

- Don't exit the essay early. Keep working until time is up.

- Read the prompt carefully. You must write on the topic exactly as it is given.

- Before you begin to write, spend a minute or two "brainstorming." Think about the topic and the best way to approach it.

- Take notes and plan your essay before you begin.

- Follow a clear, logical organization. Most essays consist of three basic parts: an introduction, a body of two or three paragraphs, and a conclusion.

- Use concrete examples and specific reasons. Whenever you make a general statement, support it with specific examples. If you state an opinion, give reasons.

- Use signal words to indicate transitions. Signal words can be used to join paragraph to paragraph and sentence to sentence.

- If you choose to handwrite your essay, be sure your handwriting is as clear and legible as possible. Your handwriting should not be too big or too small.

If you intend to word process the essay, you should practice taking this preview test on the computer by using any word processing program. You can use the cut, paste, and undo functions, but don't use the spell-check, grammar-check, or thesaurus functions.

PREVIEW TEST 4: ESSAY WRITING

- Before you begin, think about the prompt. You may want to make some notes to organize your thoughts. Use the space for notes that has been provided.

- Write only on the topic that is presented.

- If you finish in less than 30 minutes, check your essay for errors.

- Stop writing after 30 minutes.

ESSAY PROMPT

Good, affordable housing is one of the factors that makes a community a desirable place to live. Choose one other factor that you think is important. Give specific details and reasons for your choice.

NOTES
Use this space for essay notes only. Write the final version of your essay on the next two pages.

_____

_____

_____

_____

_____

_____

_____

_____

_____

_____

_____

_____

_____

_____

_____

_____

_____

_____

_____

_____

_____

_____

_____

Name: _____

Write your essay here.

_____

_____

_____

_____

_____

_____

_____

_____

_____

_____

_____

_____

_____

_____

_____

_____

_____

_____

_____

_____

_____

_____

_____

_____

_____

_____

268

Lesson 39

PRE-WRITING

You should spend about five minutes "pre-writing" the essay. What should you do during this time? You will have three main tasks:

1. Read the essay prompt (topic) carefully.

2. Brainstorm (think about) the topic.

3. Plan your essay.

During the second and third tasks, you should take notes to use as an outline when you write the essay.

You should spend only five minutes on pre-writing—but it's a very important time!

READING THE PROMPT

In some ways, this is the most important step of the entire process. If you don't understand the prompt, you can't properly respond to it. If you write an essay that does not fully respond to the prompt, you will receive a lower score, no matter how well you have written the essay.

The essay prompts tend to be written in very simple English. If any of the vocabulary is "difficult," it is usually explained.

Not only do you need to read the prompt carefully, you also need to understand what it is asking you to do. You need to analyze the prompt—to **paraphrase** it (put it into your own words) and to explain to yourself what it asks you to do. (You don't need to do this analysis in writing, only mentally.)

Read these analyses of the sample prompts given in the introduction:

Prompt A

Some people believe that money spent on space research benefits all of humanity. Other people take the opposite view and say that money spent on this type of research is wasted. Tell which point of view you agree with and explain why, using specific details and reasons.

Analysis

This prompt says that there are two opinions about space research. Some people think that money spent on space research (for satellites, space shuttles, probes to other planets, and so on) is generally a good thing, helping all people. Other people think it is a waste of money. They think this money could be used for better things. To respond to this prompt, I have to decide which of these positions I want to support. I could give some good reasons why I think space research benefits everyone. On the other hand, if I choose to defend the opposite side of this argument, I have to explain why I think money for space research should be spent on something else.

Prompt B

Do you agree or disagree with this statement?

It is much easier to learn in a small class than in a large one.

Use specific examples and reasons to support your answer.

Analysis

This prompt asks about my opinion of class size and whether I think it has an effect on learning. I can choose one of two positions. One position is that small class size DOES make it easier to learn, and I'll need to give examples of ways in which it does. If I choose the other side, I have to say that size is NOT an important factor. I could say that a good teacher can make sure students learn in even a large class and give examples of ways in which he or she could do that.

Prompt C

Developments in transportation such as the automobile have had an enormous impact on modern society. Choose another development in transportation that you think is of great importance. Use specific examples and reasons for your choice.

Analysis

For this prompt, I have to choose some development in transportation that I think is important or almost as important as the development of the automobile. I can't choose the automobile because the prompt says to choose *another* development. I could, for example, choose the development of the railroad and talk about how this had an impact on the world in general or on one country in particular.

BRAINSTORMING

The process of brainstorming involves generating ideas on the topic. Just sit back for a moment think about the topic, and write down any ideas that come to you. These may be things you have read in newspapers and magazines, things you've heard in classes or on television, or personal experiences. These ideas may turn out to be useful or not—just write them all down.

Let's say that you are assigned the first prompt. You would try to think about anything—positive or negative—that you have read about or heard about in connection with space exploration, and quickly write these ideas down. For the second topic, you would probably use your own experiences. Can you remember any positive experience with either a large class or a small one? Any negative ones? Write them down.

Someone brainstorming the first topic might jot down these ideas:

many benefits for people on Earth—weather satellites, etc.

consumer products—PCs, freeze-dried foods, etc.

people think astronauts are heroes

people need a challenge like space

but very expensive—money could be used in many other ways—schools, housing, etc.

PLANNING THE ESSAY

This stage of pre-writing actually blurs with Step B; while you are brainstorming, you are beginning to plan your essay.

The first step in planning is to choose your basic **thesis.** A thesis is the central or controlling idea of an essay. For the first two types of prompts—defending an opinion and agreeing/disagreeing with a statement—choosing a thesis simply means choosing which side of the argument you are going to support. For example, for the first prompt your thesis might be, "In my opinion, research in space benefits humanity." For the second, your thesis might be, "With the right teacher, large class size has little effect on learning." For the third prompt, you have to choose what development you are going to discuss. "I believe that the development of jet airliners was extremely important."

Remember, when you choose a thesis, there is no right or wrong answer. The readers at ETS don't care whether you are in favor of space research or against it, whether you like small classes or big ones, or whether you think the development of rockets, railroads, or roller skates was most important. In fact, you should choose whatever side of the argument is easiest to support. It's possible, for example, that you have had generally good experience in large classes, but that you can think of more reasons why small classes are better.

It is not necessary to fully support either point of view. Sample essay 1 is an example of an essay that partially supports both points of view.

Once you have chosen a thesis, you need to think of ways to support it. Look at the notes you took while brainstorming. Are there any concrete details or compelling reasons that support the thesis you have chosen? If not, think of some now.

Next, you need to write a simple outline. You don't have to write a formal outline with Roman numerals and letters, just a basic plan for your four or five paragraphs.

You may be tempted to skip this step to save time, but writing an outline is very important. Following a simple outline is the best way to keep an essay organized, and good organization is one of the most important things readers look for in scoring your essay.

For the "opinion" prompts (types 1 and 2), there are two basic ways to organize your essay. One is to write two or more paragraphs, each providing a reason why your opinion is the "correct" one.

- **Introduction**
  Here is my opinion.
- **Body Paragraph 1**
  My opinion is right because . . .
- **Body Paragraph 2**
  My opinion is also right because . . .
- **Conclusion**
  As you can see, my opinion IS right.

Another approach is to restate both sides of the argument—A and B—in your introduction. The introduction does not say which side of the argument is "correct." Then, in one paragraph of the body, you provide several reasons to support the side that you do NOT agree with—opinion A. This tactic is sometimes called **admitting the opposition.** Then, in the next paragraph of the body, you give even stronger reasons why the other point of view, opinion B, is the better or more logical one. The conclusion restates the idea that opinion B is the right one.

- **Introduction**
  There are two possible opinions on this topic, opinions A and B.
- **Body Paragraph 1**
  Here are some reasons to believe opinion A is right.
- **Body Paragraph 2**
  Here are some even better reasons to believe opinion B is right.
- **Conclusion**
  As you can see, opinion B IS right.

Simple outlines for the three prompts given in this lesson may look like this:

Prompt A

Notes

Introduction

Space research for +50 years: expensive—$ well spent or wasted?

– ideas	+ ideas
costs billions; also human resources; no real benefits	consumer products; e.g., PCs, freeze-dried foods, pacemakers
e.g., trip to Moon only brought back rocks	weather & communication satellites
many important uses for this $ on Earth: e.g., education, environment, housing	scientific knowledge about planets, Moon, even Earth

Conclusion

As shown, many benefits—also, human race needs challenge just as individuals do— therefore, space research is worth all the money spent

Prompt B

Notes

Introduction

Sometimes it's necessary to have big classes. Good teacher can make big classes as good a learning environment as small ones

Introductory classes, lecture the same no matter what size
Sometimes lecturers more dynamic in large classes

Some people think not as much interaction in big classes
But . . . teacher can break class into small groups for discussion, projects, etc.
teacher can use teaching assistant to lead discussion groups

Conclusion

Many people think small is best, but big classes can be good places to learn too

Prompt C

Notes

Introduction

One of most important developments is international jet transport—since '60s—because of speed & low costs, has changed way people think about travel

Speed

100 years ago, took weeks to cross ocean: today, few hours—this has changed people's concept of space

Low Costs

In past, only wealthy could travel comfortably; poor people had to save for years—today, more and more people can travel

    businesspeople
    students
    tourists

Conclusion

Countries no longer so isolated; people think of world as own hometowns

EXERCISE 39.1

Focus: Reading and analyzing Essay Writing prompts
Directions: Read the six prompts given below. Then choose three prompts—one of each type—and write an analysis for each one similar to the analyses found earlier in the lesson.

TYPE A

Prompt 1

Some people believe that schools should primarily teach students how to best compete with others. Other people believe that schools should primarily teach students how to cooperate with others. Which of these approaches do you favor? Use specific reasons and examples to support your answer.

Prompt 2

Some university students prefer living in campus housing such as dormitories. Other students prefer living in off-campus housing, such as apartments. If you were faced with this decision, which of these two options would you choose? Use specific reasons and details to explain your choice.

TYPE B

Prompt 3

Do you agree or disagree with the following statement?

> Professional athletes (such as football stars) and entertainers (such as singers and actors) are paid too much money for the work that they do.

Use specific details and examples to support your answer.

Prompt 4

Do you agree or disagree with the following statement?

> It is better for university students to first get a general education, taking classes in many fields, than it is for them to take classes only in their own field of study.

Use specific details and examples to support your answer.

TYPE C

Prompt 5

Imagine that you can talk for one hour with any person who has lived at any time in history. Which person would you choose to meet? Use specific details and examples to explain your choice.

Prompt 6

Your hometown has just received a grant from an international organization to fund one single improvement project. Which of the following would you recommend to receive the funding?

the city airport	the police department
the local schools	the city parks
the fire department	the streets and roads
the public transportation system	the local hospitals
the art museum	

Give specific examples and reasons to support your recommendation.

ANALYSIS 1

_____

_____

_____

_____

_____

_____

_____

ANALYSIS 2

_____

_____

_____

_____

_____

_____

_____

ANALYSIS 3

_____

_____

_____

_____

_____

_____

_____

EXERCISE 39.2

Focus: Brainstorming and taking notes on Essay Writing prompts

Directions: Brainstorm the three prompts that you chose in Exercise 39.1 and take notes on any ideas that occur to you. Don't spend more than 1 or 2 minutes per prompt.

NOTES 1

_____

_____

_____

_____

_____

_____

NOTES 2

_____

_____

_____

_____

_____

_____

NOTES 3

_____

_____

_____

_____

_____

_____

_____

EXERCISE 39.3

Focus: Writing informal outlines for essays

Directions: Using the three prompts you chose in Exercise 39.1, write short, informal outlines for essays. Do not spend more than 3 or 4 minutes per outline.

Outline 1

_____

_____

_____

_____

_____

_____

_____

_____

_____

Outline 2

_____

_____

_____

_____

_____

_____

_____

_____

_____

OUTLINE 3

_____

_____

_____

_____

_____

_____

_____

_____

_____

_____

Lesson 40

WRITING THE ESSAY

After spending about five minutes on pre-writing, you are now ready to get down to the real task: writing the essay.

You have only about 20 minutes in which to write it, and you need to produce a 200–300 word essay. That's about 10–15 words a minute. You can do this if you concentrate and keep working.

ETS says that quality is more important than quantity in the essay, but typically only longer essays get top scores. A long essay does not guarantee a good score on this section, but a short essay almost guarantees a low one.

This lesson will discuss writing all three parts of the typical essay.

WRITING THE INTRODUCTION

There are a number of functions that a good introduction can serve (but no introduction will serve all these functions):

- To get the readers' attention

- To restate the ideas of the prompt

- To present some general background information about the topic

- To preview the main points that will appear in the essay

- To present a clear statement of the main idea of the essay. (This is called the **thesis statement**; it typically is the last sentence of the introduction, but sometimes it appears in the conclusion.)

Here are three introductory paragraphs, written in response to the three prompts presented in Lesson 39.

Introduction 1

For around fifty years, a number of nations have been involved in the exploration of outer space. This research has been very costly, of course. Has this money been well-spent or wasted?

This introduction makes a couple of very general statements about space research to provide background, and then asks if research is worth the cost. Notice that this question is NOT answered in the introduction. The answer to that question—which is really the thesis statement of the essay—will appear in the conclusion.

Introduction 2

Many students believe that small classes offer much better educational opportunities than large ones. However, in my experience, that is not necessarily true. I believe that, with a good teacher, a large class can provide as good a learning opportunity as a small one.

In the introduction, the writer paraphrases the prompt in the first sentence. However, in the second sentence the writer disagrees with the idea stated in the prompt. In the last sentence of the introduction, the writer gives the thesis statement: that learning depends on good teaching, not class size.

Introduction 3

I believe that one of the most important developments in transportation has been the development of international jet transport. Jet airliners first appeared in the early 1960s. Since then, planes have gotten bigger and faster and capable of flying longer distances. Jet transport has had some revolutionary effects. Because of the high speeds and the relatively low costs of this type of travel, it has changed the way people look at the world.

In the first sentence of the paragraph, the writer answers the question brought up in the prompt. The writer then goes on to provide a little background information about this development, and then the writer provides a preview of the main points that the body of the essay will discuss: speed and low costs and how these have changed people's view of the world.

WRITING THE BODY OF THE ESSAY

It is in the body of the essay that the writer develops the thesis (main idea).

A typical paragraph in the body begins with a **topic sentence,** which contains the main idea of that paragraph (just as the thesis statement contains the main idea of the essay). It also contains several sentences that support this main idea. The writer should provide specific details, reasons, examples, and/or personal experiences to support these sentences.

Topic Sentence

Supporting Sentence
    Detail
    Detail

Supporting Sentence
    Detail
    Detail

Remember that the supporting sentences and the details must be directly relevant to the main idea of the paragraph; do not include irrelevant material.

Look at these paragraphs from the body of essays written in response to the prompts in Lesson 39.

Body 1

Some people believe that all or most space research should be eliminated because of its incredible expense, not only in terms of money, but also in terms of scientific and human resources. These people point out the fact that it cost billions of dollars to send astronauts to the Moon, but all they brought back were some worthless rocks. These people say that the money and effort now being wasted in outer space could be spent on more important projects right here on Earth, such as providing housing for homeless people, improving the educational system, saving the environment, and finding cures for diseases.

However, other people believe that space research has provided many benefits to humankind. They point out that hundreds of useful products, from personal computers to heart pacemakers to freeze-dried foods, are the direct or indirect results of space research. They say that weather and communication satellites, which are also products of space research, have benefited people all over the globe. In addition to these practical benefits, supporters of the space program point to the scientific knowledge that has been acquired about the Sun, the Moon, the planets, and even our own Earth as a result of space research.

In the first paragraph, the writer "admits the opposition," giving reasons why opinion A (money spent on space is wasted) is correct. This is clearly stated in the topic sentence of the first paragraph. The writer then provides reasons to support this idea: there have been no great rewards for spending all this money (just "worthless rocks") and lists more important ways to spend this money, such as on housing and education.

In the second paragraph, the writer presents the opposite point of view, that money spent on space has benefited everyone. Specific benefits are listed: useful products, weather and communications satellites, and scientific knowledge.

Body 2

When I was an undergraduate student, most of the large classes I took were introductory classes for first- and second-year students. For example, I took classes in world history and economics that had over 100 students and met in large lecture halls. I think these classes were as good as some of the small classes I took later. At the basic level, the lectures that a professor gives are basically the same no matter what size the class is. Moreover, the professors who taught these classes seemed more enthusiastic and energetic than the teachers I had in smaller classes. Personally, I think they enjoyed having a large audience!

One supposed advantage of small classes is that there is usually a lot more interaction among students and between the teacher and the students than in large ones. However, in the large classes I took, there were discussion sessions held every week with a graduate teaching assistant in which there was a lot of interaction. Besides, the teachers for these classes had long office hours, and they were always willing to answer questions and talk over problems.

The writer uses personal experiences with large and small classes in both paragraphs to support the thesis statement. In the first paragraph, the writer says that in introductory classes the teachers' lectures are basically the same no matter how many students there are. In fact, in the writer's experience, teachers were more dynamic in larger classes.

The second paragraph says that people think there is more interaction in small classes than in large ones, but that, in fact, the writer found there was a lot of interaction in the weekly discussion sessions held in conjunction with the large classes. The writer also says that the teachers held long office hours in which to answer questions.

Body 3

The most obviously important characteristic of jet travel is the high speed involved. A hundred years ago, it took weeks to cross the Atlantic or Pacific oceans by ship. However, today, those same trips can be completed in a matter of hours. One can attend a meeting in Paris and have dinner in New York on the same day. These amazing speeds have changed people's concepts of space. Today the world is much smaller than it was in the past.

Another important aspect of jet travel is its relatively low cost. An international journey one hundred years ago was extremely expensive. Only wealthy people could afford to travel comfortably, in first class. Poor people had to save for years to purchase a ticket, and the conditions in which they traveled were often miserable. Today it is possible for more and more people in every country to travel in comfort. Thus it is possible for business people to do business all over the world, for students to attend universities in other countries, and for tourists to take vacations anywhere in the world.

In its topic sentence, the first paragraph gives the first reason why jet transport is an important development: its speed. It goes on to compare the speed of jets with those of ships one hundred years ago, gives an example of the speed of jets (meeting in Paris, dinner in New York), and shows the effect of this speed on the way people view the world.

The second paragraph begins by stating another important aspect of jet travel, its relatively low cost. The writer again compares travel today with travel in the past and shows how more and more people travel comfortably. The writer gives examples of specific types of people who have been affected by this: businesspeople, students, and tourists.

WRITING THE CONCLUSION

The final paragraph of an essay should give the reader the feeling of completion, NOT a feeling that the writer has simply run out of ideas or out of time.

Here are some of the functions a conclusion can serve:

- To present the thesis statement (if this is NOT presented in the introduction)
- To restate the thesis statement (if this IS given in the introduction)
- To summarize the main points presented in the body
- To show the significance of the points made in the body
- To present one last compelling reason why the writer's opinion is the correct one

Look at these examples of concluding paragraphs:

Conclusion 1

I agree with those people who support space research and want it to continue. Space research, as shown, has already brought many benefits to humanity. Perhaps it will bring more benefits in the future, ones that we can't even imagine now. Moreover, just as individual people need challenges to make their lives more interesting, I believe the human race itself needs a challenge, and I think that the peaceful exploration of outer space provides just such a challenge.

This conclusion begins with the thesis statement for the essay—that the writer agrees with those who support space research. The writer also presents two more reasons why the reader should agree with this idea: because there may be more benefits in the future, and because space exploration provides a challenge for the human race.

Conclusion 2

In conclusion, I don't think that the size of a class is very important. I think that learning depends more on the quality of the teaching than on the number of students in the class.

This is a very simple conclusion that restates the thesis statement from the introduction and summarizes the main point of the body paragraphs.

Conclusion 3

To summarize, the speed and low cost of international jet travel have changed the world. Individual nations are not as isolated as they were in the past, and people now think of the whole planet as they once thought of their own hometowns.

This conclusion summarizes points made in the body paragraphs and shows the significance of these points.

EXERCISE 40.1

Focus: Writing introductions for essays

Directions: Write introductory paragraphs for the three prompts you wrote notes for in Lesson 39. If possible, write your introduction on a computer.

EXERCISE 40.2

Focus: Writing body paragraphs for essays

Directions: Write body paragraphs for the three introductions you wrote in Exercise 40.1. If possible, write your paragraphs on a computer.

EXERCISE 40.3

Focus: Writing conclusions for essays

Directions: Write conclusions for the three essays you wrote in Exercises 40.1 and 40.2. If possible, write your conclusions on a computer.

Lesson 41

IMPROVING YOUR ESSAY

There are several techniques you can use to write more interesting, more sophisticated, and clearer essays.

VARYING SENTENCE LENGTH

Good writing in English consists of a more or less equal balance between short, simple sentences having only one clause and longer sentences containing two or more clauses. Make an effort to use sentences of various lengths.

Here are some of the most common ways to combine simple (one-clause) sentences:

1. With adjective clause markers (relative pronouns)

    There are many reasons to agree with this statement. I will discuss three of them in this essay.

    There are many reasons to agree with this statement, three of which I will discuss in this essay.

2. With adverb clause markers (subordinate conjunctions)

    The invention of the automobile is undoubtedly one of humankind's greatest inventions. Not everybody can enjoy the benefits of owning a car.

    Although the invention of the automobile is undoubtedly one of humankind's greatest inventions, not everybody can enjoy the benefits of owning a car.

3. With coordinate conjunctions (*but, and, or, so,* and so on)

    The invention of the automobile is undoubtedly one of humankind's greatest inventions. Not everybody can enjoy the benefits of owning a car.

    The invention of the automobile is undoubtedly one of humankind's greatest inventions, but not everybody can enjoy the benefits of owning a car.

Look back at the paragraphs you wrote for Exercises 40.1, 40.2, and 40.3. If most of the sentences you wrote were simple one-clause sentences, you should be combining some of these sentences using these and other techniques. On the other hand, if all of the sentences you wrote are complicated and contain two or more clauses, you should write some of these as shorter, simpler sentences.

VARYING THE ORDER OF SENTENCE PARTS

You should also vary the order of parts of a sentence. Begin some sentences with prepositional phrases or subordinate clauses.

Instead of
    I disagree with this idea for several reasons.

Try
    For several reasons, I disagree with this idea.

Instead of
    I support Idea A even though Idea B has some positive attributes.

Try
    Even though Idea B has some positive attributes, I support Idea A.

USING SIGNAL WORDS

Signal words can be used to join paragraph to paragraph and sentence to sentence. These words make your essay clearer and easier to follow. Some of these expressions and their meanings are given below.

1. **Expressions used to list points, examples, or reasons**

    First Example or Reason
    First,
    For example,
    The first reason for this is that . . .

    Additional Examples or Reasons
    Second, (Third, Fourth,)
    A second (third, fourth) example is . . .
    Another example is . . .
    Another reason is that . . .
    In addition,
    Furthermore,
    Moreover,

    Final Example or Reason
    Finally,

    To Give Individual Examples
    For example,
    For instance,
    To give a specific example, X is an example of Y.

    To Show Contrast
    However,
    On the other hand,
    Nevertheless,

    To Show a Conclusion
    Therefore,
    Consequently,
    Thus,

    To Show Similarity
    Likewise,
    Similarly,

    To Begin a Concluding Paragraph
    In conclusion,
    In summary,

    To Express an Opinion
    In my opinion,
    Personally,

2. Examples of the Use of Signal Words

I agree with the idea of stricter gun control for a number of reasons. *First,* statistics show that guns are not very effective in preventing crime. *Second,* accidents involving guns frequently occur. *Finally,* guns can be stolen and later used in crimes.

I believe that a good salary is an important consideration when looking for a career. *However,* the nature of the work is more important to me. *Thus,* I would not accept a job that I did not find rewarding.

For me, the reasons for living in an urban area are stronger than the reasons for living in a rural community. *Therefore,* I agree with those people who believe it is an advantage to live in a big city.

Don't overuse signal words. Generally, don't use more than one or two per paragraph.

EXERCISE 41.1

Focus: Joining simple, one-clause sentences into more complicated sentences

Directions: Using the words listed below, join the sentences into a single sentence. Don't change the order in which the clauses are given. In some cases, there may be more than one way to join the sentences.

so	who	even though	although	since
but	or	which	and	because

1. One of the most important holidays in my country is Independence Day. It is celebrated on September 16th.

   _____

   _____

2. Young children have a special talent for language learning. Children should be taught other languages at an early age.

   _____

   _____

3. My brother began studying at the university. He has taken several large classes.

   _____

   _____

4. Some forms of advertising serve a useful purpose. Many forms of advertising do not.

   _____

   _____

5. A friend is an acquaintance. He or she will help you whenever possible.

_____

_____

6. I believe corporations should do more to recycle materials. I believe they should do more to reduce air pollution.

_____

_____

7. Small classes are the best environment for learning. Sometimes universities must have large classes.

_____

_____

EXERCISE 41.2

Focus: Varying the order of adverb clauses and prepositional phrases

Directions: You wrote four sentences in the previous exercise using adverb clause markers (_because, since, although,_ and _even though_). Rewrite these four sentences in the first four spaces below, changing the order of the main clause and the adverb clause.

Then rewrite the next two sentences, changing the position of prepositional phrases or other sentence parts.

1. _____

_____

2. _____

_____

3. _____

_____

4. _____

_____

5. Students get more personal attention in small classes.

_____

_____

6. I would use e-mail if I needed to get in touch with a business associate.

_____

_____

EXERCISE 41.3

Focus: Recognizing signal words and understanding their use

Directions: A number of signal words are used in the sample introductions, bodies, and conclusions presented in Lesson 40. Look back at these samples and underline all the signal words that you can find. In each case, try to understand why the writer used those words.

EXERCISE 41.4

Focus: Using signal words to link sentences

Directions: Use the signal words listed to link the sentences below. In some cases, there may be more than one correct answer. Not all the signal words will be used.

likewise	furthermore	therefore	for example
however	in conclusion	on the other hand	personally

1. I believe that women should have the right to serve in the military. _____, I don't believe that they should be assigned to combat roles.

2. Many actors, rock musicians, and sports stars receive huge amounts of money for the work that they do. _____, a baseball player was recently offered a contract worth over twelve million dollars. _____, I feel that this is far too much to pay a person who simply provides entertainment.

3. The development of the automobile has had a great impact on people everywhere. _____, the development of high-speed trains has had an impact on people in many countries, including my home country of France.

4. I used to work in a restaurant when I was in college. I realize what a difficult job restaurant work is. _____, whenever I go out to eat, I try to leave a good tip for my waiter or waitress.

5. Many people would agree with the idea that the best use for the open space in our community is to build a shopping center in this community. _____, there are other people who feel we should turn this open space into a park.

EXERCISE 41.5

Focus: Using sentence variety to improve the quality of writing in an essay

Directions: The following essay contains short, simple sentences consisting of only one clause. Rewrite the essay. Combine sentences, vary the order of sentence parts, use signal words, and make whatever other changes you think are necessary to create a more interesting essay.

Remember, don't eliminate all single-clause sentences. Good writing consists of a mixture of short, simple sentences and longer, more complicated ones.

This essay was written in response to the following prompt:

Some people like to go to the same place for their vacations. Other people like to take their vacations in different places. Which of these two choices do you prefer? Give specific reasons for your choice.

There are certain people. They always like to take their vacations in the same place. They return from a vacation. They ask themselves, "When can I go back there again?" There are other people. They like to go many places. They like to do many different things on their vacations. They return from a vacation. They ask themselves, "Where can I go next?"

My parents are perfect examples of the first kind of people. They always like to go to a lake in the mountains. They went there on their honeymoon. They bought a vacation cabin there. They bought it several years after they were married. They have gone there two or three times a year for over twenty-five years. My parents have made friends. They have made friends with the people who also own cabins there. They enjoy getting together with them. Both my parents enjoy sailing and swimming. My father likes to go fishing. My parents enjoy variety. They say they can get variety by going to their cabin at different times of the year. They particularly like to go there in the autumn. The leaves are beautiful then.

I am an example of a person. I like to go to different places for her vacation. I was a child. I went to my parents' cabin. I got older. I wanted to travel to many different places. I spent a lot of time and money learning how to ski. I wanted to travel to places where I could ski. I could ski in Switzerland. I was interested in visiting historic places. I went to Angkor Wat in Cambodia. It was difficult to get there. I would like to go to Egypt. I want to see the pyramids there. I would like to go to Rome. I want to see the Coliseum there.

I enjoy going to familiar places. I find that going to strange places is more exciting. The world is so huge and exciting. I don't want to go to the same place twice. I also understand my parents' point of view. They believe that you can never get to know a place too well.

EXERCISE 41.6

Focus: Using sentence variety to improve the quality of your own writing

Directions: Look back at the three introductions, bodies, and conclusions you wrote for Exercises 40.1, 40.2, and 40.3. Can these essays be improved by varying the length of the sentences (either combining short sentences or breaking longer ones into two sentences), by varying the order of sentence parts, or by using signal words appropriately? Make any changes in these paragraphs that you think will make them clearer and more interesting.

Lesson 42

CHECKING AND EDITING YOUR ESSAY

You should spend the last five minutes of the thirty-minute period **checking** your essay (looking for errors) and **editing** it (correcting the errors). There are three types of checking and editing you should do. Of course, you can do any editing more easily and more neatly if you write the essay on computer.

CHECKING FOR AND EDITING ORGANIZATIONAL PROBLEMS

You will not have time to make any major changes in the organization of the essay. However, you should ask yourself these questions:

- Is there a thesis statement that summarizes the main idea of the essay? (If not, add it.)

- Do all the sentences in the essay support this main idea? (If not, delete them.)

CHECKING FOR AND EDITING GRAMMATICAL ERRORS

There are many types of grammatical errors that you can check for. Some of the more common ones are listed here:

1. Verb Errors

Verb errors are so common that you should carefully check all the verbs in the essay. Be sure that the verb agrees with the subject, that the verb is in the right tense, and that you are using active forms and passive forms appropriately.

>   is
> Each of these theories ~~are~~ very important.

>   moved
> I ~~have moved~~ to my present apartment three months ago.

>   agree
> I ~~am agree~~ with this statement.

2. Pronoun Error

The most common pronoun error involves pronoun agreement (using a singular pronoun to refer to a plural noun or using a plural pronoun to refer to a singular noun).

>   It
> The only way this problem can be solved is with the help of the government. ~~They~~ must spend more money on schools and teachers' salaries in order to improve the educational system.

3. Sentence Fragments and Run-on Sentences

A **sentence fragment** is an incomplete sentence; the sentence is missing an essential element, such as the subject or verb. A **run-on sentence** is a sentence that goes on "too long." It usually consists of two or more clauses that are not properly connected.

>   such as
> My country imports several agricultural products. ~~For example~~, wheat and beef.

>   . Psychology
> I believe the most important subject I have ever studied is economics~~, psychology~~ is another important subject.

4. Singular and Plural Words

Check nouns to make sure a singular form is used when needed and a plural form is used when needed. Also remember that there is no plural adjective form in English as there is in some languages.

> research
> In my opinion, medical ~~researches~~ should receive more funding.

> scientific
> Many ~~scientifics~~ experiments still need to be performed.

5. Word Forms

Be sure you are using the correct form (adjective, adverb, noun, or verb) of the word.

> institution
> To me, the most important ~~institutional~~ in any country is the legal system.

There are, of course, many other types of grammatical errors. If you have ever taken a writing class, look at the corrections the teacher made on your papers to see what kinds of mistakes you commonly made, and look for those mistakes when you check your essay.

CHECKING AND EDITING MECHANICAL ERRORS

1. Spelling Errors

Look for words that you may have misspelled. Look especially for words that are similar in your language and English but have different spellings. However, don't spend too much time looking for spelling mistakes—the scorers will not subtract much for misspellings unless they are especially frequent and make it difficult to understand your essay.

2. Punctuation Errors

The most important thing to check is that each sentence ends with a period or, in the case of questions, with a question mark. Also check for commas after initial adverb clauses, between cities and states or cities and countries, and between dates and years.

> I come from the West African country of Togo. My country became an independent republic on April 27, 1960.

> When I first came to the United States, I lived in Cambridge, Massachusetts.

3. Capitalization Errors

Be sure that you have capitalized the first word of every sentence, the names of people and places, and the word *I*.

EXERCISE 42.1

Focus: Correcting grammatical and mechanical errors in essay paragraphs
Directions: Each of the following paragraphs contain a number of mistakes. Find the mistakes, cross them out, and when necessary, write the correction above the error.

Paragraph 1

There is many species of animals in the world threatened with extinction. One threatened animal is tiger. I believe that is very important that governments protect tiger. In Indonesia tigers protected by the government. Many of them is killed every year.

Paragraph 2

The technology has had major impact in many field. Nowadays we can't even suppose business, communication, or traveling without computers. I want to discuss about the impact of computers on the education. The modern technology has made live easy for students and professors. If a student want to contact with a professor, you haven't problem. It is enough only to send professor's an e-mail and you haven't to go to office. More over, many university created special network for students in order to make the studying process easy for its students. For such kind net you could enter only by using your pass word and identification number. There are many categories you can chose to enter, such as "student tools" or "assignment box" where you can know about your homeworks. Also is possible to access to the university library to make researches. Computers also give students opportunity to gather informations about various topic from the internet. It is one of most easiest ways of making research for student. One other way that computers can help students, especially those from another countries, to stay touch with their freinds and family at their home, personally I could not study in usa if not contact with my family, because I am both student as well as work as a manager in my families business so I must stay in touch with my assistents.

Paragraph 3

One of the most interesting book I am reading recently was a biography of winston churchill. he was prime minister of the great britain during the world war II. of course many peopel know what a great leadership he was during the war. but I found his life before and after the war were also very interesting.

Paragraph 4

Some people are believing that is impossible falling in love with someone "at first sight." In the other hand, there are others people who are believing that you recognition a person that you love immediately. I know its possible falling in love at first sight. Because this happened to my wife and I.

Paragraph 5

If you are ever in thailand in month of may I suggest you to go to the Rocket Festival. It held every year in a small town called yasothon about 300 mile from bangkok. bangkok has many beautiful temples, including the temple of the dawn. This festival is well known and famous in thailand. People from all over the country join the local people in celebrate. The local farmers launch hundred of colorful rockets for gaining the favor of spirits who they believe will bring rain to their rice crops. However, if you go, you need being careful. Both farmers or tourists sometime injure or even kill by rockets that goes out of control.

Paragraph 6

When I was child I live in the town of Sendai, the biggest city in the north part of japan. My grandmother live in Tokyo. Which is in the center part of Japan. While I was live in Sendai, I often went to see my grandmother, but it takes five hours to get to tokyo by local train. Since 1983, the high speed express train called the "Shinkansen" built, and connected between Sendai and Tokyo. For me personally, this was most importent development in transportation. It now take only a hour and half to travel to Tokyo from Sendai. The trip become very easy. It also was a great impact on sendai. Economics development there increased. In the negative side, prices for housing and other things went up. In the whole, however, this development was very big benefit for the city.

EXERCISE 42.2

Focus: Checking and editing your own writing

Directions: Look back at the three introductions, bodies, and conclusions you wrote for Exercises 40.1, 40.2, and 40.3. Look for organizational, grammatical, and mechanical errors and make corrections. Don't spend more than five minutes per essay.

If you intend to word-process the essay, you should practice taking this Review Test on the computer by using any word processing program. You can use the cut, paste, and undo functions, but don't use the spell-check, grammar-check, or thesaurus functions.

REVIEW TEST I: ESSAY WRITING

- Before you begin, think about the prompt. You may want to make some notes to organize your thoughts. Use the space for notes that has been provided.

- Write only on the topic that is presented.

- If you finish in less than 30 minutes, check your essay for errors.

- Stop writing after 30 minutes.

ESSAY PROMPT

Do you agree or disagree with this statement?

The most important knowledge does not come from books.

Use specific reasons and examples to explain your choice.

NOTES
Use this space for essay notes only. Write the final version of your essay on the next two pages.

_____

_____

_____

_____

_____

_____

_____

_____

_____

_____

_____

_____

_____

_____

_____

_____

_____

_____

_____

_____

_____

Name: _____

Write your essay here.

_____

_____

_____

_____

_____

_____

_____

_____

_____

_____

_____

_____

_____

_____

_____

_____

_____

_____

_____

_____

_____

_____

_____

_____

Practice Test

ABOUT TAKING THE PRACTICE TEST

One of the best ways to prepare for the TOEFL® test is to take a realistic practice test. The test included with this program is an up-to-date version of the latest computer-based tests and includes all the new item-types found on the computer-based test. As closely as possible, it duplicates the actual test in terms of format, content, and level of difficulty. Of course, it is not possible to completely duplicate the computer-testing environment in a book, but if you can do well on this version of the test, you should do well on the computer-based test when you actually take it.

There are certain guidelines you should follow for each section when you take these tests in the book:

- **Listening**
  To take the Listening Section, you will have to use the audio tapes or CDs. The items in this part are timed as the items were on the paper-and-pencil version of the TOEFL® test—in other words, they are 12 seconds apart. However, if you are taking this test alone, you can stop the tape or use the fast forward to give yourself more time or less time. If possible, listen to the taped material through headphones. If your book does not include audio tapes or CDs, ask a friend or teacher who speaks English to read out loud from the script at the end of this book.

  While the questions are being read, look only at the questions. Don't look at the four answer choices until you have heard the questions. Don't skip items and don't go back to any items after you have finished.

- **Structure**
  Use a watch to time yourself for this section. Do not skip any items and don't go back to any items after you have answered them.

- **Reading**
  Use a watch to time yourself. When working on this section, you CAN skip items and go back to them after you have marked the answers.

- **Essay Writing**
  Time yourself carefully. If possible, write your essay on a computer.

SCORING THE PRACTICE TESTS

You can use the charts on the next pages to calculate a range of scores for the test in this book. After completing the test, obtain a raw score by counting the number of correct answers in the three sections. Then look at the conversion chart to determine the range of scaled scores for each section. Add the three low scores from the range of scores for each section, then the three high scores. Your "actual" score on the TOEFL® test will lie somewhere in that range of numbers. You will then have to estimate your score for the Essay Writing section and add that number to your Structure score before you arrive at a final score. You can use the chart on the next page to estimate your Essay Writing score.

Suppose that, on the Practice Test, you had 28 correct answers in Listening, 21 in Structure, and 40 in Reading. And suppose that your estimated score on Essay Writing is 4. Your adjusted structure scores are now 24–25. Your score on the practice test would lie between 230 and 240.

	Raw Score (number correct)	Range of Scaled Scores (from conversion chart)
Section 1	28	21–22
Section 2	21	13–14
Section 3	40	24–26
Estimated score on Section 4	4	Add 11 to both Section 2 scores

Score Conversion Chart

Section 1		Section 2		Section 3	
Raw Scores	Range of Scaled Scores	Raw Scores	Range of Scaled Scores	Raw Scores	Range of Scaled Scores
36–38	28–30	24–25	14–15	48–50	28–30
33–35	25–26	21–23	13–14	45–47	27–29
30–32	23–24	18–20	12–13	43–44	26–28
27–29	21–22	15–17	11–12	41–42	25–27
24–26	19–20	12–14	10–11	39–40	24–26
21–23	17–18	9–11	8–10	37–38	23–25
18–20	15–16	6–8	7–9	35–36	22–24
15–17	13–14	3–5	6–8	33–34	21–23
12–14	11–12	0–2	4–6	31–32	20–22
9–11	9–10			29–30	19–21
6–8	7–9			27–28	18–20
3–5	5–6			25–26	17–19
0–2	3–4			23–24	16–18
				21–22	15–17
				19–20	14–16
				17–18	13–15
				15–16	12–14
				13–14	11–13
				11–12	9–12
				9–10	8–10
				7–8	7–9
				5–6	6–8
				3–4	5–7
				0–2	4–6

If your estimated score on the Essay Writing Section is 6, add 15 points to your Structure Score.

5.5, add 14	4.5, add 12	3.5, add 10	2.5, add 7	1.5, add 5
5, add 13	4, add 11	3, add 9	2, add 6	1, add 3

Use the blanks below to chart your progress as you take the Practice Test.

PERSONAL SCORE RECORD

Practice Test				
Section 1	Section 2	Section 3	Section 4 (Estimated)	Total Scores

Section 1

This section tests your ability to comprehend spoken English. It is divided into two parts, each with its own directions. There are 38 questions. The material that you hear and the questions about the material are presented only once.

PART A

Directions: Each item in this part consists of a brief dialogue involving two speakers. Following each conversation, a third voice asks a question. When you have heard each dialogue and question, read the four answer choices and select the one that best answers the question based on what is directly stated or on what can be inferred.

1. What does the woman imply about Sally Hill?

   (A) She doesn't have an appointment.
   (B) Her problem is complicated.
   (C) She must live somewhere else.
   (D) Her apartment isn't far away.

2. What does Mary tell the other woman?

   (A) She can use the phone if she wants.
   (B) There is no charge for phone calls.
   (C) Her phone is out of order, too.
   (D) She can call her later if she wants.

3. What did Lillian's parents do?

   (A) Disapproved of Lillian's plan
   (B) Watered Lillian's plants
   (C) Traveled overseas
   (D) Caught colds

4. What does the woman say her roommate did last night?

   (A) She cleaned up after cooking.
   (B) She forgot to put the pots and pans away.
   (C) She went out in a terrible storm.
   (D) She put some plants in the kitchen.

5. How did the woman mainly learn about trees?

   (A) She studied forestry in college.
   (B) She once worked in a forest.
   (C) She read a lot of books about them.
   (D) Her father taught her.

6. What does Tom ask Brenda?

   (A) How many pages he must write
   (B) What Professor Barclay discussed
   (C) How long the class lasted
   (D) When the paper is due

7. What does the woman imply about Julie?

   (A) She doesn't like any music except classical.
   (B) There is some classical music she doesn't like.
   (C) She likes classical music but she can't play it.
   (D) Classical music doesn't interest her at all.

8. What does the man say about the history test?

   (A) He was too busy to study for it.
   (B) He did quite well on it.
   (C) He left some questions unanswered on it.
   (D) He took it two times.

9. What does the woman say about the desk?

   (A) It was too expensive.
   (B) She bought it at the shop next door.
   (C) It was given to her as a gift.
   (D) She paid very little for it.

10. What can be inferred from the conversation?

    (A) The weather is going to change soon.
    (B) Emma's last two classes have been canceled.
    (C) The weather hasn't been pleasant until today.
    (D) Emma's classes will be held outside today.

11. What does the woman mean?

    (A) Gary thanked her for the tape player.
    (B) She wants her tape player back.
    (C) She's glad Gary is finally here.
    (D) Gary can keep her tape player.

12. What does the woman mean?

    (A) She originally supported Margaret Ling.
    (B) She can no longer support Ed Miller.
    (C) Ed Miller is no longer running in the race.
    (D) Margaret Ling is no longer a student.

13. What does the man suggest the woman do?

    (A) Borrow Stephanie's computer
    (B) Get her own computer
    (C) Save some money
    (D) Stay home and complete her assignment

14. What does the man say about Shelly?

    (A) She seems to be feeling better.
    (B) She has quite an imagination.
    (C) She takes beautiful pictures.
    (D) She's too sick to go out.

15. What had the man originally assumed about the woman?

    (A) She needed to prepare for an exam.
    (B) She had already passed the physics test.
    (C) She was going camping this weekend.
    (D) She wasn't studying physics anymore.

PART B

Directions: Part B involves longer talks. After each of these talks, there are a number of questions. You will hear each talk only once. When you have read and heard the questions, read the answer choices and select the best answer or answers based on what is directly stated or on what can be inferred. Don't forget: During actual exams, taking notes during the Listening Section is not permitted.

16. What do the two speakers have in common?

    (A) They are both studying social anthropology.
    (B) They are both going to the museum on Saturday.
    (C) They both have the same teacher.
    (D) They are both attending the same class.

17. When does the *woman's* class meet?

    (A) In the morning
    (B) In the afternoon
    (C) In the evening
    (D) Only on Saturdays

18. Which of the following topics would most likely be discussed in the *man's* class?

    (A) The relationships between parents and children
    (B) The tools used by ancient people
    (C) Leadership in contemporary society
    (D) Marriage customs

19. What is the main subject of the lecture?

    (A) An outcome of a football game
    (B) The development of jet engines
    (C) The results of the *Hindenburg* disaster
    (D) Airships of the past, present, and future

20. Match the type of airship with the category in which it belongs

(A) The Italian airship *Norge.*

```
[                              ]
```

(B) The blimp *Columbia.*

```
[                              ]
```

(C) The German zeppelin *Hindenburg.*

```
[                              ]
```

1. Rigid airship
2. Semi-rigid airship
3. Non-rigid airship

21. What does the speaker say about the Italian airship *Norge?*

(A) It flew over the North Pole.
(B) It was involved in military operations in World War I.
(C) It had a very unusual design.
(D) It carried many paying passengers across the Atlantic.

22. What event in the history of airships took place in Lakehurst, New Jersey, in 1937?

(A) The age of large airships ended in disaster there.
(B) It was there that the first blimp was designed.
(C) The first zeppelin to cross the Atlantic landed there.
(D) It was there that the last zeppelin was built.

23. What can be inferred about airships of the future?

Choose two.

(A) They would be safer than the rigid airships of the past.
(B) They would be much larger than the airships of the past.
(C) They would fly faster than modern jet airliners.
(D) They would use less fuel than modern jet airliners.

24. What will Ted be doing on Friday?

(A) Attending a class
(B) Going to a dance
(C) Reading his work aloud
(D) Going fishing

25. What has Ted been writing most recently?

(A) A novel
(B) A poem
(C) A newspaper article
(D) A biography

26. What is the subject of Ted's most recent writing?

(A) Childhood memories
(B) The lives of his college classmates
(C) The experiences of commercial fishers
(D) A trip to Alaska

27. The speaker mentions three types of materials that make up glaciers. Give the order in which these materials appear.

(A) Firn
(B) Glacial ice
(C) Rock ice
(D) Ordinary snow

```
1. [                              ]
2. [                              ]
3. [                              ]
```

28. Where can continental glaciers be found today?

Choose two.

(A) Greenland
(B) West Virginia
(C) Iceland
(D) Antarctica

29. Match the type of glacier with its description.

   Place the letter of the choice in the proper box. Use each choice only once.

   (A) Valley glacier

   [ ]

   (B) Continental glacier

   [ ]

   (C) Piedmont glacier

   [ ]

   1. Largest glacier; gigantic sheets of ice

   2. Formed from two or more glaciers

   3. Confined by mountains

30. What does the speaker say about receding glaciers?

   (A) They actually move uphill.
   (B) They are melting faster than they add new ice.
   (C) They tend to disappear very rapidly.
   (D) They appear completely stationary.

31. Which part of the picture represents a *cirque*?

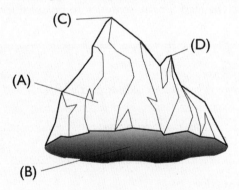

32. Which part of the picture represents a *horn*?

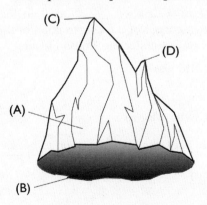

33. What is the main topic of this discussion?

   (A) The Uniform Time Act
   (B) The role of daylight saving time in wartime
   (C) Ways to save energy
   (D) The history of daylight saving time

34. When are clocks in the United States set *back*?

   (A) In the spring
   (B) In the summer
   (C) In the fall
   (D) In the winter

35. According to the professor, how would most people probably have characterized Benjamin Franklin's plan for daylight saving time when it was first proposed?

   (A) As confusing
   (B) As innovative
   (C) As ridiculous
   (D) As wasteful

36. When was daylight saving time first actually put into effect?

   (A) In the 1790s
   (B) During the Civil War
   (C) During World War I
   (D) During World War II

37. Which of these groups opposed daylight saving time?

   Choose two.

   (A) Military leaders
   (B) Farmers
   (C) Writers
   (D) Parents of small children

38. What was the effect of the Uniform Time Act of 1966?

   (A) To help standardize daylight saving time
   (B) To establish year round daylight savings time
   (C) To abolish daylight saving time
   (D) To shorten daylight saving time

This is the end of Section 1. Go on to Section 2.

Section 2

This section tests your ability to recognize both correct and incorrect English structures.

Directions: There are two types of items in this section. One type involves a sentence that is missing a word or phrase. Four words or phrases appear below the sentence.

You must choose the one that best completes the sentence.

Example

_____ large natural lakes are found in the state of South Carolina.

(A) There are no
(B) Not the
(C) It is not
(D) No

The correct answer is (D). This sentence should properly read, "No large natural lakes are found in the state of South Carolina."

The other type of item involves a sentence in which four words or phrases have been underlined. You must identify the one underlined word or phrase that must be changed for the sentence to be considered correct.

Example

When painting a fresco, an artist is applied paint directly to the damp plaster of a wall.
A   B   C   D

The correct answer is (B). This sentence should read, "When painting a fresco, an artist applies paint directly to the damp plaster of a wall."

As soon as you understand the directions, begin work on this section.

There are 25 questions.

1. _____ team sports require cooperation.

(A) Of all
(B) They are all
(C) All
(D) Why are all

2. Ceramics can be harder, light, and more
                    A

resistant to heat than metals.
   B   C   D

3. Not everyone realizes that the most largest
          A   B

organ of the human body is the skin.
      C   D

4. Clifford Holland, _____ civil engineer, was in charge of the construction of the first tunnel under the Hudson River.

(A) He was a
(B) a
(C) being a
(D) who was, as a

5. Mold is extremely destruction to books in a
                 A   B   C

library.
  D

6. A tapestry consists of a foundation weave,
   $\underline{\hphantom{consists}}$
   A
   called the warp, which across are passed
   $\underline{\hphantom{which across are passed}}$
   B
   different colored threads, called the weft,
   $\underline{\hphantom{colored threads}}$
   C
   forming decorative patterns.
   $\underline{\hphantom{patterns}}$
   D

7. Perhaps humans' first important musical
   $\underline{\hphantom{first}}$ $\underline{\hphantom{musical}}$
   A B
   influence were the songs of birds.
   $\underline{\hphantom{influence were}}$ $\underline{\hphantom{birds}}$
   C D

8. Frontier surgeon Ephraim MacDonald had
   to perform operations _____ anesthesia

   (A) no
   (B) not having
   (C) without
   (D) there wasn't

9. _____, her teaching, and her writing,
   Maria Cadrilla de Martinez helped preserve
   the traditions and customs of her native
   Puerto Rico.

   (A) Through her research
   (B) Her research
   (C) By researching
   (D) Her doing research

10. The techniques of science and magic are
    $\underline{\hphantom{magic}}$
    A
    quite different, but their basic aims—
    $\underline{\hphantom{different}}$
    B
    to understand and control nature—they are
    $\underline{\hphantom{to understand and control}}$ $\underline{\hphantom{they are}}$
    C D
    very similar.

11. It was in a cave near Magdalena, New

    Mexico when the oldest known ears of
    $\underline{\hphantom{when}}$ $\underline{\hphantom{oldest}}$ $\underline{\hphantom{known}}$
    A B C
    cultivated corn were discovered.
    $\underline{\hphantom{discovered}}$
    D

12. Most modern barns are both insulated,
    $\underline{\hphantom{Most modern}}$ $\underline{\hphantom{both}}$
    A B
    ventilated, and equipped with electricty.
    $\underline{\hphantom{equipped with}}$ $\underline{\hphantom{electricty}}$
    C D

13. Sharks can detect minute electrical dis-
    $\underline{\hphantom{can detect}}$ $\underline{\hphantom{electrical}}$
    A B
    charges coming from its prey.
    $\underline{\hphantom{coming}}$ $\underline{\hphantom{its}}$
    C D

14. A dark nebula consists of a cloud of
    $\underline{\hphantom{consists of a cloud}}$
    A
    interstellar dust enough dense to obscure
    $\underline{\hphantom{enough dense}}$ $\underline{\hphantom{to obscure}}$
    B C
    the stars beyond it.
    $\underline{\hphantom{beyond}}$
    E

15. The various parts of the body require so
    $\underline{\hphantom{various parts}}$ $\underline{\hphantom{so}}$
    A B
    different surgical skills that many surgical
    $\underline{\hphantom{surgical skills}}$ $\underline{\hphantom{many}}$
    C D
    specialties have developed.

16. One reason birds have been so successful is
    $\underline{\hphantom{have been}}$
    A
    because of their able to escape from danger
    $\underline{\hphantom{because of their}}$ $\underline{\hphantom{able}}$
    B C
    quickly.
    $\underline{\hphantom{quickly}}$
    D

17. A major concern among archaeologists
    today is the preservation of archaeological
    sites, _____ are threatened by develop-
    ment.

    (A) of which many
    (B) many of them
    (C) many of which
    (D) which many

18. _____ parrots are native to tropical
    regions is untrue.

    (A) That all
    (B) All
    (C) Why all
    (D) Since all

19. Chemical engineering is based on the
    $\underline{\hphantom{engineering}}$
    A
    principles of physics, chemists, and
    $\underline{\hphantom{principles}}$ $\underline{\hphantom{chemists}}$
    B C
    mathematics.
    $\underline{\hphantom{mathematics}}$
    D

20. Ballet performers must be believable actors
    $\underline{\hphantom{must be believable}}$ $\underline{\hphantom{actors}}$
    A B
    and actresses as well as experts dancers.
    $\underline{\hphantom{as well as}}$ $\underline{\hphantom{experts}}$
    C D

21. _____ young, chimpanzees are easily
    trained.

    (A) When are
    (B) When
    (C) They are
    (D) When are they

22. Chemical compounds with barium, cobalt,
              —————
                 A
and strontium are responsible to many of
              ————— —————
                 B   C
the vivid colors in fireworks.
    —————
       D

23. Rarely _____ seen far from water.

(A) spotted turtles
(B) spotted turtles are
(C) have spotted turtles
(D) are spotted turtles

24. The higher the temperature of a molecule,

_____

(A) the more energy it has
(B) than it has more energy
(C) more energy has it
(D) it has more energy

25. The work of the early American woodcarv-
        —————
           A
ers had many artistic qualities, but these
        —————
           B
craftsmen probably did not think of them as
                       ——————— —————————
                            C   D
artists.

This is the end of Section 2. Go on to Section 3.

Section 3

This section of the test measures your ability to understand the meaning of words and to comprehend written materials.

Directions: This section consists of several passages, each followed by 10-14 questions. Read the passages and, for each question, choose the one best answer based on what is stated in or can be inferred from the passage.

As soon as you understand the directions, begin work on this part.

Passage 1

The Sun today is a yellow dwarf star. It has existed in its present state for about 4 billion, 600 million years and is thousands of times larger than the Earth. The Sun is fueled by thermonuclear reactions near its center that convert hydrogen to helium. They release so much energy that the Sun can shine for about 10 billion years with little change in its size or brightness. This balance of forces keeps the gases of the Sun from pulling any closer together.

By studying other stars, astronomers can predict what the rest of the Sun's life will be like. About 5 billion years from now, the core of the Sun will shrink and become hotter. The temperature at the surface will fall. The higher temperature of the interior will increase the rate of thermonuclear reactions. The outer regions of the Sun will expand approximately 35 million miles, about the distance to Mercury, which is the closest planet to the Sun. The Sun will then be a red giant star. Temperatures on the Earth will become too hot for life to exist.

Once the Sun has used up its thermonuclear energy as a red giant, it will begin to shrink. After it shrinks to about the size of the Earth, it will become a white dwarf star. The Sun may throw off huge amounts of gases in violent eruptions called nova explosions as it changes from a red giant to a white dwarf.

After billions of years as a white dwarf, the Sun will have used up all its fuel and will have lost its heat. Such a star is called a black dwarf. After the Sun has become a black dwarf, the Earth will be dark and cold. If any atmosphere remains there, it will have frozen onto the Earth's surface.

1. What is the primary purpose of this passage?

   (A) To alert people to the dangers posed by the Sun
   (B) To discuss conditions on Earth in the far future
   (C) To present a theory about red giant stars
   (D) To describe changes that the Sun will go through

2. The word fueled in paragraph 1 is closest in meaning to

   (A) powered.
   (B) bombarded.
   (C) created.
   (D) propelled.

3. Look at the word They in the **bold** text below.

   It has existed in its present state for about 4 billion, 600 million years and is thousands of times larger than the Earth. The Sun is fueled by thermonuclear reactions near its center that convert hydrogen to helium. They release so much energy that the Sun can shine for about 10 billion years with little change in its size or brightness.

   Underline the word or phrase in the **bold** text that the word They refers to.

4. The following sentence can be added to paragraph 1.

   It maintains its size because the heat deep inside the Sun produces pressure that offsets the force of gravity.

   Where would it best fit in the paragraph?

   The Sun today is a yellow dwarf star. **(1)** It has existed in its present state for about 4 billion, 600 million years and is thousands of times larger than the Earth. **(2)** The Sun is fueled by thermonuclear reactions near its center that convert hydrogen to helium. **(3)** They release so much energy that the Sun can shine for about 10 billion years with little change in its size or brightness. **(4)** This balance of forces keeps the gases of the Sun from pulling any closer together.

   Circle the number in parentheses that indicates the best position for the sentence.

5. It can be inferred from the passage that the Sun

   (A) is approximately halfway through its life as a yellow dwarf.
   (B) has been in existence for 10 billion years.
   (C) is rapidly changing in size and brightness.
   (D) will continue as a yellow dwarf for another 10 billion years.

6. Look at the word core in the **bold** text below.

   About 5 billion years from now, the core of the Sun will shrink and become hotter. The temperature at the surface will fall. The higher temperature of the interior will increase the rate of thermonuclear reactions.

   Underline the word or phrase in the **bold** text that is most nearly OPPOSITE in meaning to the word core.

7. What will probably be the first stage of change as the Sun becomes a red giant?

   (A) The core will cool off and use less fuel.
   (B) The surface will become hotter and shrink.
   (C) The Sun will throw off huge amounts of gases.
   (D) The core will grow smaller and hotter.

8. When the Sun becomes a red giant, what will conditions be like on Earth?

   (A) Its atmosphere will freeze and become solid.
   (B) It will be enveloped in the expanding surface of the Sun.
   (C) It will become too hot for life to exist.
   (D) It will be destroyed in nova explosions.

9. As a white dwarf, the Sun will be.

   (A) the same size as the planet Mercury.
   (B) thousands of times smaller than it is today.
   (C) around 35 million miles in diameter.
   (D) cold and dark.

10. According to the passage, which of the following best describes the sequence of stages that the Sun will probably pass through?

    (A) Yellow dwarf, white dwarf, red giant, black giant
    (B) Red giant, white dwarf, black dwarf, nova explosion
    (C) Yellow dwarf, red giant, white dwarf, black dwarf
    (D) White giant, red giant, black dwarf, yellow dwarf

11. The phrase throw off in paragraph 3 is closest in meaning to

    (A) eject.
    (B) burn up.
    (C) convert.
    (D) let in.

12. Look at the word there in the **bold** text below.

After billions of years as a white dwarf, the Sun will have used up all its fuel and will have lost its heat. Such a star is called a black dwarf. After the Sun has become a black dwarf, the Earth will be dark and cold. If any atmosphere remains there, it will have frozen onto the Earth's surface.

Underline the word or phrase in the **bold** text that the word there refers to.

13. Which of the following best describes the tone of the passage?

    (A) Alarmed
    (B) Pessimistic
    (C) Comic
    (D) Objective

Passage 2

It is said that George Washington was one of the first to realize how important the building of canals would be to the nation's development. In fact, before he became President, he headed the first company in the United States to build a canal, which was to connect the Ohio and Potomac rivers. It was never completed, but it showed the nation the feasibility of canals. As the country expanded westward, settlers in western New York, Pennsylvania, and Ohio needed a means to ship goods. Canals linking natural waterways seemed to supply an effective method.

In 1791 engineers commissioned by the state of New York investigated the possibility of a canal between Albany on the Hudson River and Buffalo on Lake Erie to link the Great Lakes area with the Atlantic seacoast. It would avoid the mountains that served as a barrier to canals from the Delaware and Potomac rivers.

The first attempt to dig the canal, to be called the Erie Canal, was made by private companies but only a comparatively small portion was built before the project was halted for lack of funds. The cost of the project was an estimated five million dollars, an enormous amount for those days. There was some on-again-off-again federal funding, but this time the War of 1812 put an end to construction. In 1817 DeWitt Clinton was elected Governor of New York and persuaded the state to finance and build the canal. It was completed in 1825, costing two million dollars more than expected.

The canal rapidly lived up to its sponsors' faith, quickly paying for itself through tolls. It was far more economical than any other form of transportation at the time. It permitted trade between the Great Lake region and the East coast, robbing the Mississippi River of much of its traffic. It allowed New York to supplant Boston, Philadelphia, and other eastern cities as the chief center of both domestic and foreign commerce. Cities sprang up along the canal. It also contributed in a number of ways to the North's victory over the South in the Civil War.

An expansion of the canal was planned in 1849. Increased traffic would undoubtedly have warranted its construction had it not been for the development of the railroads.

14. Why does the author most likely mention George Washington in the first paragraph?

    (A) He was President at the time the Erie Canal was built.
    (B) He was involved in pioneering efforts to build canals.
    (C) He successfully opened the first canal in the United States.
    (D) He commissioned engineers to study the possibility of building the Erie Canal.

15. The word feasibility in paragraph 1 is closest in meaning to

    (A) profitability.
    (B) difficulty.
    (C) possibility.
    (D) capability.

16. Look at the word means in the **bold** text below.

It was never completed, but it showed the nation the feasibility of canals. As the country expanded westward, settlers in western New York, Pennsylvania, and Ohio needed a means to ship goods. Canals linking natural waterways seemed to supply an effective method.

Underline the word or phrase in the **bold** text that is closest in meaning to the word means.

17. According to the passage, the Erie Canal connected the

    (A) Potomac and Ohio rivers.
    (B) Hudson River and Lake Erie.
    (C) Delaware and Potomac rivers.
    (D) Atlantic Ocean and the Hudson River.

18. Look at the word halted in the **bold** text below.

The first attempt to dig the canal, to be called the Erie Canal, was made by private companies but only a comparatively small portion was built before the project was halted for lack of funds. The cost of the project was an estimated five million dollars, an enormous amount for those days. There was some on-again-off-again federal funding, but this time the War of 1812 put an end to construction.

Underline the word or phrase in the **bold** text that is closest in meaning to the word halted.

19. The phrase on-again-off-again in paragraph 3 could be replaced by which of the following with the least change in meaning?

    (A) Intermittent
    (B) Unsolicited
    (C) Ineffectual
    (D) Gradual

20. The completion of the Erie Canal was financed by

    (A) the state of New York.
    (B) private companies.
    (C) the federal government.
    (D) DeWitt Clinton.

21. The actual cost of building the Erie Canal was

    (A) five million dollars.
    (B) less than had been estimated.
    (C) seven million dollars.
    (D) more than could be repaid.

22. The word tolls in paragraph 4 is closest in meaning to which of the following?

    (A) Jobs
    (B) Grants
    (C) Links
    (D) Fees

23. Which of the following is NOT given as an effect of the building of the Erie Canal in paragraph 4?

    (A) It allowed the East coast to trade with the Great Lakes area.
    (B) It took water traffic away from the Mississippi River.
    (C) It helped determine the outcome of the Civil War.
    (D) It established Boston and Philadelphia as the most important centers of trade.

24. What can be inferred about railroads in 1849 from the information in the last paragraph?

    (A) They were being planned but had not yet been built.
    (B) They were seriously underdeveloped.
    (C) They had begun to compete with the Erie Canal for traffic.
    (D) They were weakened by the expansion of the canal.

25. The word warranted in paragraph 5 is closest in meaning to

    (A) guaranteed
    (B) justified
    (C) hastened
    (D) prevented

Passage 3

It's a sound you will probably never hear, a sickened tree sending out a distress signal. However, a team of scientists at the U.S. Department of Agriculture's Forest Service has recently heard the cries, and they think some insects also hear the trees and are drawn to them like vultures attracted to a dying animal.

Researchers hypothesized that these sounds—actually vibrations produced by the surface of plants—were caused by a severe lack of moisture. They fastened electronic sensors to the bark of drought-stricken trees and clearly heard distress calls. According to one of the scientists, most parched trees transmit their plight in the 50- to 500-kilohertz range. (The unaided human ear can detect no more than 20 kilohertz.) They experimented on red oak, maple, white pine, aspen, and birch and found that all make slightly different sounds. With practice, scientists could identify the species of tree by its characteristic sound signature.

The scientists surmise that the vibrations are created when the water columns inside tubes that run the length of the trees are cracked as a result of too little water flowing through them. These fractured columns send out distinctive vibration patterns. Because some insects communicate at ultrasonic frequencies, they may pick up the trees' vibrations and attack the weakened trees. Researchers are now running tests with potted trees that have been deprived of water to see if the sound is what attracts the insects. "Water-stressed trees also have a different smell from other trees, and they experience thermal changes, so insects could be responding to something other than sound," one scientist said.

26. Which of the following is the main topic of the passage?

    (A) The vibrations produced by insects
    (B) The mission of the U.S. Forest Service
    (C) The effect of insects on trees
    (D) The sounds made by trees

27. The word them in paragraph 1 refers to

    (A) trees.
    (B) scientists.
    (C) insects.
    (D) vultures.

28. Look at the word drawn in the **bold** text below.

It's a sound you will probably never hear, a sickened tree sending out a distress signal. However, a team of scientists with the U.S. Department of Agriculture's Forest Service has recently heard the cries, and they think some insects also hear the trees and are drawn to them like vultures attracted to a dying animal.

Underline the word or phrase in the **bold** text that is closest in meaning to the word drawn.

29. Look at the word parched in the **bold** text below.

Researchers hypothesized that these sounds—actually vibrations produced by the surface of plants—were caused by a severe lack of moisture. They fastened electronic sensors to the bark of drought-stricken trees and clearly heard distress calls. According to one of the scientists, most parched trees transmit their plight in the 50- to 500-kilohertz range. (The unaided human ear can detect no more than 20 kilohertz.)

Underline the word or phrase in the **bold** text that is closest in meaning to the word parched.

30. The word plight in paragraph 2 is closest in meaning to

(A) cry.
(B) condition.
(C) need.
(D) presence.

31. Underline the sentence in the second paragraph that explains how the researchers conducted their experiment.

32. It can be inferred from the passage that the sounds produced by the trees

(A) serve as a form of communication among trees.
(B) are the same no matter what type of tree produces them.
(C) cannot be heard by the unaided human ear.
(D) fall into the 1–20 kilohertz range plight parched.

33. Look at the word fractured in the **bold** text below.

The scientists surmise that the vibrations are created when the water columns inside tubes that run the length of the trees are cracked as a result of too little water flowing through them. These fractured columns send out distinctive vibration patterns.

Underline the word or phrase in the **bold** text that is closest in meaning to the word fractured.

34. Which of the following is believed to be a cause of the trees' distress signals?

(A) Torn roots
(B) Attacks by insects
(C) Experiments by scientists
(D) Lack of water

35. Look at the word they in the **bold** text below.

These fractured columns send out distinctive vibration patterns. Because some insects communicate at ultrasonic frequencies, they may pick up the trees' vibrations and attack the weakened trees.

Underline the word or phrase in the **bold** text that the word they refers to.

36. In paragraph 3, the phrase pick up could best be replaced by which of the following?

(A) Perceive
(B) Lift
(C) Transmit
(D) Attack

37. All of the following are mentioned as possible factors in drawing insects to weakened trees EXCEPT

    (A) thermal changes.
    (B) smells.
    (C) sounds.
    (D) changes in color.

38. It can be inferred from the passage that, at the time the passage was written, research concerning the distress signals of trees

    (A) had been conducted many years previously.
    (B) had been unproductive up until then.
    (C) was continuing.
    (D) was no longer sponsored by the government.

Passage 4

Probably the most famous film commenting on twentieth century technology is *Modern Times,* made in 1936. Charlie Chaplin was motivated to make the film by a reporter who, while interviewing him, happened to describe working conditions in industrial Detroit. Chaplin was told that healthy young farm boys were lured to the city to work on automotive assembly lines. Within four or five years, these young men's health was destroyed by the stress of work in the factories.

The film opens with a shot of a mass of sheep jammed into pens. Abruptly the scene shifts to a scene of factory workers packed into a narrow entranceway, jostling one another on their way to a factory. This biting tone of criticism, however, is not sustained throughout the film. It is replaced by a gentle note of satire. Chaplin preferred to entertain rather than lecture to the audience.

Scenes of factory interiors account for only about one-third of the footage of *Modern Times,* but they contain some of the most pointed social commentary as well as the funniest comic situations. No one who has seen the film can ever forget Chaplin vainly trying to keep pace with the fast-moving conveyor belt, almost losing his mind in the process. Another popular scene features an automatic feeding machine brought to the assembly line so that workers need not interrupt their labor to eat. It hurls food at Chaplin, who is strapped into his position on the assembly line and cannot escape. This serves to illustrate people's utter helplessness in the face of machines that are meant to serve their basic needs.

Clearly, *Modern Times* has its faults, but despite its flaws, it remains the best film treating technology within a social context. It does not offer a radical social message, but it does accurately reflect the sentiments of many who feel they are victims of an over-mechanized world.

39. The author's main purpose in writing this passage is to

    (A) criticize the factory system of the 1930s.
    (B) analyze an important film.
    (C) explain Chaplin's style of acting.
    (D) discuss how film reveals the benefits of technology.

40. According to the passage, Chaplin got the idea for the film *Modern Times* from

    (A) a newspaper article.
    (B) a scene in a movie.
    (C) a job he had once held.
    (D) a conversation with a reporter.

41. Look at the word jammed in the **bold** text below.

Within four or five years, these young men's health was destroyed by the stress of work in the factories.

The film opens with a shot of a mass of sheep jammed into pens. Abruptly the scene shifts to a scene of factory workers packed into a narrow entranceway, jostling one another on their way to a factory.

Underline the word or phrase in the **bold** text that is closest in meaning to the word jammed.

42. It can be inferred from the passage that two-thirds of the film *Modern Times*

(A) is extremely unforgettable.
(B) takes place outside a factory.
(C) is more critical than the other third.
(D) entertains the audience more than the other third.

43. Look at the word biting in the **bold** text below.

This biting tone of criticism, however, is not sustained throughout the film. It is replaced by a gentle note of satire. Chaplin preferred to entertain rather than lecture to the audience.

Underline the word or phrase in the **bold** text that is most nearly OPPOSITE in meaning to the word biting.

44. Which of the following could best replace the phrase losing his mind in paragraph 3?

(A) Getting fired
(B) Doing his job
(C) Going insane
(D) Falling behind

45. The following sentence can be added to paragraph 3.

All at once, this feeding device begins to malfunction.

Where would it best fit in the paragraph below?

Scenes of factory interiors account for only about one-third of the footage of *Modern Times*, but they contain some of the most pointed social commentary as well as the funniest comic situations. **(1)** No one who has seen the film can ever forget Chaplin vainly trying to keep pace with the fast-moving conveyor belt, almost losing his mind in the process. **(2)** Another popular scene features an automatic feeding machine brought to the assembly line so that workers need not interrupt their labor to eat. **(3)** It hurls food at Chaplin, who is strapped into his position on the assembly line and cannot escape. **(4)** This serves to illustrate people's utter helplessness in the face of machines that are meant to serve their basic needs. **(5)**

Circle the number in parentheses that indicates the best position for the sentence.

46. Look at the word their in the **bold** text below.

It hurls food at Chaplin, who is strapped into his position on the assembly line and cannot escape. This serves to illustrate people's utter helplessness in the face of machines that are meant to serve their basic needs.

Underline the word or phrase in the **bold** text that the word their refers to.

47. According to the passage, the purpose of the scene involving the feeding machine is to show people's

(A) ingenuity.
(B) adaptability.
(C) helplessness.
(D) independence.

48. The word utter in paragraph 3 is closest in meaning to which of the following?

    (A) Notable
    (B) Complete
    (C) Regrettable
    (D) Necessary

49. Look at the word faults in the **bold** text below.

Clearly, *Modern Times* has its faults, but despite its flaws, it remains the best film treating technology within a social context. It does not offer a radical social message, but it does accurately reflect the sentiments of many who feel they are victims of an over-mechanized world.

Underline the word or phrase in the **bold** text that is closest in meaning to the word faults.

50. The author would probably use all of the following words to describe the film *Modern Times* EXCEPT

    (A) revolutionary.
    (B) entertaining.
    (C) memorable.
    (D) satirical.

This is the end of Section 3. You may go back and check your answers in Section 3 until time is up for this section. Then go on to Section 4.

Section 4

- Before you begin, think about the prompt. You may want to make some notes to organize your thoughts. Use the space for notes that has been provided.

- Write only on the topic that is presented.

- If you finish in less than 30 minutes, check your essay for errors.

- Stop writing after 30 minutes.

ESSAY PROMPT

There are many different types of movies, including action movies, science fiction movies, and comedies. Which type of movie do you enjoy most? Why is this type your favorite? Use specific details and examples in your response.

NOTES
Use this space for essay notes only. Write the final version of your essay on the next two pages.

_____

_____

_____

_____

_____

_____

_____

_____

_____

_____

_____

_____

_____

_____

_____

_____

_____

_____

_____

_____

_____

_____

Name: _____

Write your essay here.

_____

_____

_____

_____

_____

_____

_____

_____

_____

_____

_____

_____

_____

_____

_____

_____

_____

_____

_____

_____

_____

Answer Keys and
Audio Scripts

Section 1

PREVIEW TEST 1: LISTENING

Part A

1. C	10. D
2. B	11. B
3. B	12. A
4. C	13. D
5. D	14. A
6. B	15. A
7. C	16. D
8. B	17. C
9. D	

Part B

18. B	30. D
19. C	31. A, B
20. C	32. B
21. B, D	33. A
22. A	34. A, C, B
23. A, D	35. B
24. C	36. C
25. A, D, B, C	37. B, C
26. C	38. C
27. A	39. D, C, A, B
28. A	40. C
29. C	

AUDIO SCRIPT

Part A

1. F1: I like your new bicycle, Henry.
    M1: Thanks, but it isn't new. I had my old one repainted.
    M2: What can be said about Henry's bicycle?

2. F2: Will that be cash, check, or charge?
    M1: I'm going to write a check, but I just realized I left my checkbook in my car. I'll be right back.
    M2: What will the man probably do next?

3. M1: I'll never be able to get through all these books on Professor Bryant's reading list.
    F2: But Mark, not all of them are required.
    M2: What does the woman tell Mark?

4. M1: What do you think of the new software?
    F1: It's really easy to use.
    M1: Isn't it though!
    M2: What does the man mean?

5. M1: Anyone call while I was gone?

    F1: Your brother did. He wants you to meet him for dinner.

    M1: Oh, really? Did he say what time?

    M2: What does the man want to know?

6. F2: Have you heard from Howard lately?

    M1: Funny you should ask. Yesterday, from out of the blue, I got a letter from him.

    M2: What does the man say about Howard?

7. M1: I think I deserved a higher grade in chemistry class. Does Professor Welch ever change the grades he gives?

    F1: Sure—about once a century!

    M2: What can be inferred about Professor Welch from this conversation?

8. M1: I'm going to drop my political science class. It meets too early in the morning for me.

    F2: Allen, is that *really* a good reason to drop the class?

    M2: What is the woman really saying to Allen?

9. M1: How did you do on Professor Porter's test?

    F1: I have no idea—she hasn't returned them yet.

    M1: No, but she's posted the grades on her office door.

    M2: What does the man say about Professor Porter?

10. F1: William comes up with some weak excuse or another for just about every mistake he makes, doesn't he?

    F2: Wait till you hear his latest!

    M2: What do the speakers imply about William?

11. F1: Did your student ID card ever turn up?

    M1: Yeah, the manager of the campus bookstore called me yesterday and said it was there. I guess I took it out when I cashed a check and didn't put it back in my wallet.

    F1: Well, you're lucky you got it back.

    M1: I know. I'm going to have to take better care of it in the future.

    M2: What did the man think he had lost?

12. F2: We should be arriving at the airport in another ten minutes.

    M1: Wait a second—this bus is going to the *airport*?

    M2: What can be inferred about the man?

13. M1: I wonder when the board of regents will pick a new dean.

    F1: Who knows? They're not even scheduled to meet until next month.

    M2: What does the woman imply?

14. M1: We should never have listened to Harvey.

    F1: If only we'd asked someone else for advice!

    M2: What do they mean?

15. M2: How was your room last night?

    M1: I slept like a baby. And the rates were quite reasonable.

    M2: What are the men probably discussing?

16. M1: All right, let's begin by taking a quick look at the syllabus I just handed out.

    F1: Uh, Professor White? A few of us in the back of the room didn't get a copy of it.

    M1: Hmm . . . there are 23 names on my class list, so I only brought 23 copies.

    M2: What can be inferred from Professor White's remark?

17. F2: Peter is favored to win the tennis match Saturday.

    M1: Oh, then that match wasn't canceled after all?

    M2: What had the man *originally* assumed?

Part B
Questions 18–20

    M1: (*knock, knock*) Hi, Professor Lamont. May I come in?

    F1: Oh, hi, Scott, sure. What's on your mind?

    M1: Well, I've decided I should drop my advanced math course.

    F1: Hmm, you're majoring in biochemistry, right? Well, that's a required course for your major.

    M1: I know. But maybe I could take it next semester.

    F1: Besides, to do well in biochemistry, you need to know math. Math is the language of science.

    M1: I know—my father always says trying to study science without knowing math is like trying to study music without knowing how to read notes.

    F1: Well, your father is absolutely right.

    M1: But I've gotten really low grades on the first two quizzes. Maybe I should just change majors.

    F1: I wouldn't do that if I were you, Scott. Why don't you try to get a graduate student to tutor you, and see if you can pull your grades up? I think you can do it.

18. What course does Scott want to drop?

19. What does Professor Lamont suggest that Scott do?

20. Which of the following best describes Professor Lamont's attitude towards Scott?

Questions 21–26

    M2: Listen to a student's presentation in an astronomy class. Students in the class are giving presentations on our Solar System. This presentation focuses on the planet Venus.

    M1: Well, uh, hi, everyone . . . Monday we heard Don tell us about the Sun and Lisa talk about Mercury, the planet closest to the Sun. My report today is about the next planet, Venus. Okay, now you may already know that, except for the Moon and Sun, Venus is the brightest object in the sky. You can see it in the morning and in the evening. In fact, a long time ago, people thought that Venus was two distinct objects: Phosphorus, the morning star, and Hesperus, the evening star. Oh, and when you look at Venus with a telescope, you can actually see the "phases" of Venus—just like the phases of the Moon. That's because different parts of Venus' sunlit area face Earth at different times.

        One of the articles I read about Venus said that sometimes it's called "Earth's twin." That's because Venus and Earth are just about the same size and also because they are so close together. Only Earth's moon gets closer to Earth than Venus does. But, from what I learned, Earth and Venus are not really that much alike. For a long time people didn't know much of anything about Venus because it's covered with clouds, which are mainly made of carbon dioxide and sulfur dioxide—and uh—some other gases, too. People used to think that under the clouds, there might be strange jungles full of alien monsters. But nowadays, we know Venus is way too hot for that—hotter than an oven! It's too hot even to have liquid water, so—no jungles! No monsters!

        Here's a strange fact about Venus. It takes Venus only 225 Earth days to go around the sun, as opposed to Earth, which takes 365 days, of course—that's what we call a year. But Venus spins around on its axis really slowly. It takes about 243 Earth days to spin around completely. The Earth takes—you guessed it . . . 24 hours. That means that a day on Venus is longer than a year on Venus! And here's something else weird—Venus doesn't rotate in the same direction as any of the other planets. It has what they call a, uh—let's see, a "retrograde" spin.

        Now, there have been a lot of space probes that have gone to Venus, so I'll only mention some of the most important ones. There's one there now called Magellan that is making incredibly detailed maps of the surface by using radar. It's been there since 1990. The first probe to go there was Mariner 2. That was back in 1962. Another important one was the Venera 4, which was a Soviet space probe. It arrived there in— let's see—1967 and dropped instruments onto the surface with a parachute. Then there was the Venus Pioneer 2, in 1978. It entered the atmosphere and found out the atmosphere was made mainly of carbon dioxide. As I said, there were a lot of other ones, too.

        Well, uh, that's about all I have to say about Venus, unless you have some questions. Caroline will be giving the next report, which is about the third planet from the Sun. Since we all live there, that one should be pretty interesting!

21. According to the speaker, in what ways are Earth and Venus twins?

22. Which of the following can be seen through a telescope aimed at Venus?

23. According to the speaker, which of the following were once common beliefs about the planet Venus?

24. Which of the following does the speaker say about the length of a day on Venus?

25. In what order were these space probes sent to Venus?

26. It can be inferred that the topic of the next student's presentation will be which of the following?

Questions 27–29

M2: Listen to a telephone conversation:
(Ring, ring. . . .)

F2: Hello, Financial Aid Office. Connie Wilson speaking.

F1: Hello, Ms. Wilson. My name is Dana Hart. I was calling to get some information about the work-study program.

F2: I'll be happy to tell you about it. What would you like to know?

F1: Well, I've got a bank loan to pay for my tuition, and my parents are helping me out with my room-and-board expenses, but I just don't have much for spending money.

F2: It sounds like work-study might be perfect for you, then.

F1: What sort of jobs are available right now? I don't want to work in a cafeteria. Are there any openings at the art gallery in the Student Union?

F2: Let me check. *(Sound of keystrokes on computer. . . .)* No, no openings there. But there is a position at the university museum, working in the gift shop.

F1: Hmm, I think I might enjoy doing that. What do I have to do to apply for this job?

F2: Well, the first step is to come down to the Financial Aid Office to fill out a couple of forms. You can get them from the receptionist at the front desk. Then I'll call and set up an interview for you with Dr. Ferrarra. He's the personnel director at the museum.
Dr. Ferrarra has to approve you for the position.

F1: OK, well, thanks a lot for all the information. I'll try to stop by either this afternoon or tomorrow.

27. Why does Dana want to find a job?

28. What job is Dana probably going to apply for?

29. What must Dana do first to apply for the job she is interested in?

Questions 30–35

M2: Listen to a lecture in a music class.

M1: Does anyone know what the first book to be published in the British colonies in North America was? *(Pause . . .)* No? Well, it was a book of religious music, called the *Bay Psalm Book*. It contained 13 tunes, some of which, such as "Old Hundred," are still sung today. Then, after about 1750, native-born musicians in New England began to write their own songs, and they were pretty strange songs, too, by the standards of the day. With their angular melodies and open-fifth chords, they were considered quite unusual by Europeans.

Now, after a while, traditional New England religious music migrated South and evolved into what we call Southern revival hymns. These songs include some standards, such as "Amazing Grace" and "Wayfaring Stranger." Most of them were livelier than the New England songs. Southern revival hymns were typically printed in "shape notes," an easy-to-read system of notation. In this system, the notes appear in the form of geometric shapes to represent the notes of the scale.

Another popular form of music in the nineteenth century, especially in the South, was the minstrel song. It was usually performed by a four-man troupe who performed on the banjo, tambourine, castanets, and fiddle. Decatur Emmet was the most famous composer of minstrel songs. His best-known work today is probably the song "Dixie."

Then there were parlor songs. Parlor songs were very sentimental songs, usually about ordinary aspects of domestic life. One example is "The Old Arm Chair," written in 1840 by Henry Russell, an English singer who toured the United States in the 1830s and 40s.

The greatest songwriter of the early nineteenth century, in my opinion, was Stephen Foster, who composed songs for the famous Christy Minstrels, such as "Oh, Susanna" and "Camptown Races" and parlor songs such as "Beautiful Dreamer." His songs are still popular today. His melodies were simple, much like traditional folk melodies, and he combined elements of English, Irish, and African-American music with Italian operatic tunes to create some immortal songs.

Well, I'm going to stop talking and give you all a chance to hear some of the music from the late eighteenth and early nineteenth centuries. First, there will be a couple of traditional religious tunes from New England, then some Southern revival hymns. After that, we'll hear some minstrel songs and some parlor songs and a medley of songs by Stephen Foster.

30. What is the main topic of this lecture?

31. What does the speaker indicate about the song "Old Hundred"?

32. Which of these is the best representation of the notational system used for Southern revival hymns?

33. Which of these instruments was typically used to play minstrel songs?

34. Match the song with the correct musical category.

35. What does the speaker say about Stephen Foster?

Questions 36–40

F1: Listen to a discussion involving an assignment in a psychology class:

M1: Class, today I'm going to talk about the final project for this class, which is to design and conduct your own psychological experiment.

M2: Is this in place of the final exam?

M1: No, it's in addition to it. However, you won't have to do a research paper in this class— just the final exam and this experiment. It's not due until the last day of the semester.

M3: Professor Hunter, could you tell us a little more about how to go about this?

M1: Yes, of course. As you'll learn from reading Chapter 2, a psychological experiment, like any experiment, begins with . . . anyone know? Tom?

M3: With a hypothesis?

M1: And what is a hypothesis, Tom?

M3: Well, it's a theory . . . an assumption that you try to prove in your experiment.

M1: Good definition. Now, the most basic psychological experiment consists of a number of subjects divided into a control group and an experimental group. What's the difference between these two groups? Raymond, do you know?

M2: Well, I think that, during the experiment, the conditions for the two groups have to be exactly the same except for one factor, right? So the experimental group is exposed to this factor, and the control group isn't.

M1: Uh huh, and we call that factor, whatever it is, the independent variable. If there is some measurable change in the behavior of the experimental group, then the experiment indicates that the independent variable may have been the cause of the change. And that change in behavior is called the dependent variable. Yes, Tom, you have a question?

M3: Yeah, okay, suppose I want to do an experiment to prove that students who exercise every day get better grades . . .

M1: Okay, that would be your hypothesis then—that daily exercise affects grade performance . . .

M3: So I divide up my subjects into two groups . . .

M1: Well, you'll want to figure out a way to randomly divide the subjects into two groups.

M2: Why is that?

M1: To avoid bias and keep the experiment as objective as possible. If you let the subjects divide themselves into a group, then people with the same interests and inclinations tend to form groups. If you do it yourself, then you may put certain people into certain groups to influence the outcome of the experiment.

M2: So, I get one group to agree to exercise every day for an hour or more, say, and I get the other group to agree not to do any special exercise.

M1: Good. Let's draw a simplified diagram of this experiment on the board . . . what would be the independent variable?

M3: Exercise, I suppose.

M1: Yes, and the dependent variable would be . . . what?

M3: Better grades, right?

M1: Precisely. This has the potential to be a very interesting experiment. You have a question?

M2: Professor, when did you say this project is due?

M1: Well, by sometime next week, I'd like you to submit a basic hypothesis and a summary of how you intend to test it. I'll need to approve that before you go on. Then, by October, you should complete a detailed design for your experiment and recruit subjects if you are going to be working with human subjects. By November, you should complete the experiment itself and start working on an analysis of the data and write up a conclusion. You'll need to submit a complete report on your experiment by the end of the term.

M3: You mean on the final exam day?

M1: No, on the last day of actual classes. I'll read over your reports and give you a grade and return them to you by the day of the final exam. Any other questions?

36. What is the main topic of this discussion?

37. It can be inferred that Professor Hunter would approve of which of these methods of selecting subjects for groups?

38. In the experiment proposed by the student, what can be inferred about the people in the control group?

39. In what order should the students complete these tasks?

40. When is the completed project due?

LISTENING PART A: DIALOGUES

EXERCISE 1.1

1.	B	7.	A
2.	B	8.	A
3.	A	9.	B
4.	A	10.	A
5.	A	11.	B
6.	B	12.	A

AUDIO SCRIPT

1. M1: I've never had to wait so long just to pay for a few groceries!
   F1: I think you should get in another line.
   M2: What does the woman suggest the man do?

2. M1: How did your baby-sitting job go?
   F2: Oh, fine—the children spent most of the day going down the hill on their new sled.
   M2: What did the children do?

3. M1: Where should I put these letters for you?
   F1: Just toss them in that file.
   M2: What does the woman tell the man to do with the letters?

4. F2: Did you get your suitcase packed?
   M1: Yeah—but now I can't close it!
   M2: What is the man's problem?

5. F1: What kind of bread did Annie bake?
   F2: My favorite—whole wheat bread!
   M2: What is learned about Annie's bread?

6. F1: Has Brenda finished writing her story for the radio news?
   M1: Oh, sure—she's just taping it now.
   M2: What does the man say about the story?

7. M1: Did you know Emily has a new address?
   F1: No, I didn't realize that. Do you have it?
   M1: Yeah, hang on—I wrote it down somewhere.
   M2: What is learned about Emily?

8. F2: How's the coffee here, Dennis?
   M1: I think it's a little better these days.
   M2: What does Dennis say about the coffee?

9. F1: I bought a ticket for the lottery. I hope I win.
   M1: What's the prize, Ellen?
   M2: What does the man ask Ellen?

10. M1: I wonder if this old bottle I found is worth any money. It's a beautiful color.
    F2: Yes, but look—there's a chip in it.
    M2: What does the woman say about the bottle?

11. F1: I saw Jerry is walking on crutches.

M1: Yeah, he had an accident last week.

F1: Really? What happened?

M1: His feet slipped in some oil, and he twisted his knee.

M2: What happened to Jerry?

12. M2: This is a beautiful part of the state.

M1: Yes, it certainly is. What's it most famous for?

M2: Well, you'll see some remarkable race horses here.

M2: Why is this area well known?

EXERCISE 1.2

1. B
2. C
3. D
4. A

5. A
6. D
7. C

AUDIO SCRIPT

1. F1: Steven, did you ever write a letter to your friend Gloria?

M1: I sent her an e-mail.

M2: What is learned about Steven and Gloria?

2. M1: I understand that Stuart is going to resign as vice president.

F1: As a matter of fact, he's so disappointed that he wasn't elected president, he's quitting the club.

M2: What does the woman say about Stuart?

3. F1: I'm planning to take a class in ecology next term.

M1: What will you be studying?

F1: Well, according to the course catalogue, it's the systematic study of life on this planet.

M1: That sounds interesting.

M2: What does the woman say about the class she is going to take?

4. M1: Are you ready to go now, Janet?

F1: As soon as the rain stops.

M2: What does Janet tell the man?

5. M1: I heard Darlene was having a hard time with her physics homework.

F2: Yes, but Sam has kindly offered to assist her.

M2: What does the woman say about Sam?

6. F1: I need to get a quick bite before we go to the workshop.

M1: There's a coffee shop here in the hotel.

M2: What does the man suggest the woman do?

7. M1: How can I take notes if I don't have anything to write with?

F2: You can probably borrow a pen from Gus—he always has one behind his ear.

M2: What does the woman say about Gus?

EXERCISE 2.1

1. A
2. B
3. B
4. A
5. B

6. A
7. B
8. B
9. B

AUDIO SCRIPT

1. **M1:** What did you get Suzie for her birthday?
   F2: Didn't you read the invitation to her party? She said she didn't want anyone to bring any presents.
2. **M2:** I've got to go back to the library again after dinner.
   F1: I know you've got a lot of research to do, but don't overdo it. You're spending half your life in the library.
3. **M2:** Did you hear that there was an explosion in the chemistry lab this morning?
   F2: No, was it bad?
   M2: Fortunately, no one was hurt, but it blew out a few panes of glass.
4. **F1:** I can't find my gloves.
   M1: Well, I certainly don't know where they are.
5. **M1:** I looked and looked for a parking place, but there just wasn't one anywhere.
   F2: So what did you do?
   M1: I parked in a loading zone.
   F2: You could have been fined for that!
6. **M1:** You need to fill out a change of address form.
   M2: Oh—is this the right form for that?
7. **M1:** You went to the meeting last night?
   M2: Yes, but I wish I hadn't. Was I ever bored!
8. **M1:** What kind of car are you looking for?
   F1: I don't care, as long as it's dependable. I can't stand a car that breaks down all the time.
9. **M2:** Don't you just love Andrew's boat?
   F2: It's terrific. And it's for sale, you know.

EXERCISE 2.2

1. A   5. A
2. B   6. A
3. A   7. A
4. B

AUDIO SCRIPT

1. **F1:** Where have you been keeping yourself, Ben? I haven't seen you since January at least.
   M2: I've had this terrible cold, and I haven't gotten out much.
2. **F2:** What a kind person Glen is.
   M1: Isn't he though!
3. **M1:** Will it be cold in the mountains?
   F1: I'd bring a light sweater if I were you—it may get a little chilly at night.
4. **M2:** Is this where the aeronautics exhibit is going to be?
   F2: No, it'll be in the north wing of the museum.
5. **F1:** Where did you get these statistics?
   M1: In the tables at the back of this book.
6. **M1:** I'm going to paint these old wooden chairs white. They'll look good as new.
   M2: You'd better take off that old coat of red first.
7. **M1:** How do you like your geology class?
   F2: It's an interesting subject—and tomorrow, we're going out into the field to look for fossils.
   M1: Well, good luck—hope you find some!

EXERCISE 2.3

1. A   **5.** A
2. B   **6.** D
3. B   **7.** A
4. B

AUDIO SCRIPT

1. M1: I'm ready to hand in my research paper.
   F1: Better check your writing first, Tom.
   M2: What does the woman suggest Tom do?

2. F2: How did you do on Dr. Johnson's history exam?
   M1: Well, I passed anyway. But I wish I'd studied more.
   M2: What are they discussing?

3. M1: I went to the national park this weekend.
   F2: Did you see the buffaloes?
   M1: Yeah, and you know what? It was the first herd of buffaloes I'd ever seen.
   M2: What does the man mean?

4. M1: Which line do I get in if I've already pre-registered?
   F2: Read the sign, why don't you?
   M2: What does the woman tell the man to do?

5. M2: Can I leave my luggage here for a couple of hours?
   F2: Sure, you can store it in that room up on the second floor.
   M2: Okay. But I don't think I can handle all these suitcases by myself.
   M2: What does the man mean?

6. F1: You're soaked, John. You look like you fell into a swimming pool. What happened?
   M1: I was caught out in a sudden shower.
   F1: Well, you should change your clothes.
   M2: What does the woman think John should do?

7. F2: Patrick, what did your classmates think when you won the award?
   M1: Well, it certainly didn't hurt my standing with them.
   M2: What does Patrick mean?

EXERCISE 3.1

1. A   **5.** B
2. A   **6.** B
3. B   **7.** A
4. A

AUDIO SCRIPT

1. M2: I had an interesting conversation with Caroline today.
   F1: Really? Where did you see her?
   M2: I bumped into her in the cafeteria.
   F2: What does the man mean?

2. M2: So, Rita, you left work early yesterday?
   F1: Yeah, and did I ever get in hot water for that!
   F2: What does Rita mean?

3. M1: I talked to Chuck at the party.
   F1: What did you think of Chuck?
   M1: Oh, we hit it off right away.
   F2: What does the man mean?

4. M2: How was the test?
    F1: Piece of cake!
    F2: What does the woman mean?
5. F1: Robert, are you ready to leave?
    M1: At the drop of a hat!
    F2: What does Robert imply?
6. F1: Julie wasn't at band practice today.
    M2: She's been under the weather lately.
    F2: What does the man imply about Julie?
7. F1: There's Albert and his grandfather.
    M1: Wow, Albert really takes after him, doesn't he?
    F2: What does the man say about Albert?

EXERCISE 3.2

Set A
  1. A
  2. B
  3. A
  4. A
  5. A

Set B

6.	B	12.	B
7.	B	13.	A
8.	A	14.	B
9.	B	15.	A
10.	B	16.	B
11.	B		

AUDIO SCRIPT

Set A

1. F1: Did you know Max is planning to open his own business? He could make a lot of money.
    M2: Yeah, I suppose—if it ever gets off the ground.
    F2: What does the man mean?
2. F1: How long have you had these old tires on your car?
    M2: For over five years. I wonder how much longer they'll last.
    F1: I wouldn't push my luck much further if I were you, Gary.
    F2: What does the woman imply?
3. F1: Well, that was a good program. Want to watch something else?
    M1: Not me—I'm ready to turn in.
    F2: What will the man do next?
4. M1: Alice, what did you think of that comedian's jokes?
    F1: To tell you the truth, a lot of them went over my head.
    F2: What does Alice mean?
5. M2: You look hot and tired. How about some ice water?
    F1: Just what the doctor ordered!
    F2: What does the woman mean?
6. F1: Your sister's name is Liz?
    M1: Well, everyone calls her that—it's short for Elizabeth.
    F2: What is learned from this conversation?

7. M2: I had lunch at that new restaurant over on College Avenue the other day.
    F1: Oh, I've heard some good things about that place. What did you think of it?
    M2: I'd call it run of the mill.
    F2: What does the man say about the restaurant?

8. M1: Just listen to the sound of the creek and the wind in the trees.
    F1: It's like music to my ears!
    F2: What does the woman mean?

9. M2: Whew, I'm tired. These boxes of books are heavy.
    F2: Want me to lend a hand?
    F2: What does the woman offer to do?

10. M2: Did you see that it was snowing earlier this morning?
    F1: I could hardly believe my eyes! Who ever saw snow here at this time of year?
    F2: What does the woman mean?

Set B

11. M1: You've been skiing a lot lately, Karen.
    F1: It really gets in the blood.
    F2: What does Karen mean?

12. M2: Norman thinks we don't study enough.
    F1: Look who's talking!
    F2: What does the woman imply about Norman?

13. M1: Would you like to go to the West Coast with my friends and me over spring break? We're going to drive out there in my friend Mike's van.
    F1: I'm not sure if I can afford to. Gasoline alone will cost a fortune.
    M1: Not if we all chip in.
    F2: What does the man mean?

14. M2: Donna, did you talk to Professor Holmes about that teaching assistantship?
    F1: Yeah, and I didn't even make an appointment. I just marched right into his office and told him why he should choose me!
    M2: Boy, that took a lot of nerve!
    F2: What does the man say about Donna?

15. F1: Dan, we still need to paint the kitchen.
    M1: I know, but let's call it a day for now.
    F2: What does Dan mean?

16. M2: Let's go over Scene 3 again. I'll get you a script to read from.
    F1: Oh, you don't have to—I've already learned my lines by heart.
    F2: What does the woman mean?

EXERCISE 3.3

1. C		8. A	
2. B		9. D	
3. C		10. A	
4. B		11. B	
5. A		12. B	
6. D		13. B	
7. C			

AUDIO SCRIPT

1. **F1:** Did you finish studying for your chemistry final?
   M1: No, but I'm ready to take a break. Want to go out for coffee?
   F1: Maybe later. Right now, I'm going to go work out at the gym.
   F2: What is the woman going to do next?

2. **F1:** The party is starting soon. Aren't you ready yet?
   M2: I just have to decide on a tie. Do you think this red one goes with my shirt?
   F2: What does the man want to know?

3. **M1:** Do you have notes from Professor Morrison's psychology class Friday? I missed class that day.
   F1: Guess we're in the same boat!
   F2: What does the woman imply?

4. **M2:** Is Ron still working as a cook?
   F1: Not anymore. He decided he's not cut out for restaurant work.
   F2: What can be concluded about Ron?

5. **F2:** Are you ready for the quiz in Dr. Davenport's class today?
   M1: A quiz? Today? Are you pulling my leg?
   F2: What does the man mean?

6. **F1:** Brian, did you watch the launch of the space shuttle on television this morning?
   M1: No, they had to put that off because of bad weather.
   F2: What does Brian mean?

7. **F1:** You're sure Jennifer was at the lecture?
   M2: Oh, she was definitely there. She really stood out in that bright red sweater of hers.
   F2: What does the man say about Jennifer?

8. **M1:** Phil just got another speeding ticket.
   F1: That serves him right.
   F2: What does the woman say about Phil?

9. **M1:** I think I'll ask George to help.
   F2: Save your breath!
   F2: What does the woman imply about George?

10. **F1:** Let me guess—you bought Jill a watch for a graduation present.
    M2: You're not even warm!
    F2: What is learned about Jill from this conversation?

11. **F1:** I heard Dora was having some trouble at work.
    M2: Yes, but as usual, she'll come out of it smelling like a rose.
    F2: What does the man say about Dora?

12. **F1:** Are you going to take a trip during spring break, Roy?
    M1: With all the studying I have to do, that's out of the question.
    F2: What does Roy tell the woman?

13. **F1:** I heard Mick is planning to go to medical school.
    M2: Yeah, I guess he's always wanted to follow in his father's footsteps.
    F2: What is learned about Mick from this conversation?

EXERCISE 4

1. C
2. B
3. C
4. D
5. A
6. C
7. C
8. B
9. B
10. A
11. B
12. B
13. A
14. D
15. B
16. D

AUDIO SCRIPT

1. F2: I understand Larry won another dance contest.
   M1: It's hard to believe we're from the same family, isn't it?
   M2: What can be inferred about the man?

2. M1: Take a look at this suit.
   F1: Nice. Are you going to buy it?
   M1: Do I look like a millionaire?
   M2: What can be inferred from this conversation?

3. F1: Do you think I've made enough food for the party?
   M1: I'd say you've made just the right amount—if a couple of hundred people show up!
   M2: What does the man imply?

4. M1: I'm exhausted. I've been in class all evening.
   F2: I didn't know you were taking any evening classes.
   M1: I'm not, actually—this was a special review session Professor Hennessy offered. It was for students who were worried about doing well on the test tomorrow.
   M2: What can be inferred about the man?

5. M1: Did you know Greg has changed his major?
   F2: Oh no, not again! How many times does this make?
   M2: What does the woman imply about Greg?

6. M1: Aren't Professor Sutton's lectures fascinating?
   F1: I can close my eyes when I'm listening to him, and I'm back in the Middle Ages.
   M1: I know what you mean!
   M2: What can be inferred from this conversation about Professor Sutton?

7. M1: Did you have to wait long to see the dentist yesterday?
   F1: It seemed like years!
   M2: What does the woman imply?

8. F2: Do the experts agree with this plan?
   M1: That depends on which expert you ask.
   M2: What does the man imply about the experts and the plan?

9. M1: Did you know that Louis has a new boss?
   F1: Let's hope he gets along better with this one.
   M2: What does the woman imply about Louis?

10. F1: Boy, this is some snowstorm. It's really coming down hard.
    M1: Sure is. I wonder if the university will cancel classes tomorrow.
    F1: Only if it keeps on snowing like this all night.
    M2: What does the woman imply?

11. M1: I joined the folk dancing club a couple of weeks ago.
    F2: You did? Since when are you interested in folk dancing?
    M1: Since I discovered it was a great way to meet people!
    M2: What does the man imply?

12. M1: Did you have a good seat for the concert?
    F1: A good seat! I practically needed a telescope just to see the stage!
    M2: What can be inferred from the woman's remark?

13. F1: Is it ever hot!
    M1: If you think *this* is hot, you should have been here last summer.
    M2: What does the man imply?

14. M1: Is the swimming pool on campus open to the public?
    F2: It is, but if you're not a student, you'll have to pay a fee to swim there.
    M2: What can be inferred from this conversation?

15. F1: Just look at those stars!
    M1: They certainly don't look so clear and bright from the city, do they?
    F1: No, never.
    M2: What can be inferred about the speakers?

16. M2: There's a phone call for you, Mike.
    M1: For me? But I almost never work on Saturdays. No one knows I'm here today.
    F2: What does Mike imply?

REVIEW TEST A: DIALOGUES

1.	D	9.	B
2.	C	10.	D
3.	B	11.	A
4.	B	12.	C
5.	C	13.	C
6.	A	14.	B
7.	B	15.	B
8.	C	16.	C

AUDIO SCRIPT

1. F1: What do you think about Wanda?
   M1: When I first met her, I didn't like her that much, but I really warmed up to her after a while.
   M2: What does the man imply about Wanda?

2. M1: Have you seen that old Humphrey Bogart movie *Casablanca*?
   F2: Seen it! Only about a million times!
   M2: What does the woman imply about the movie?

3. M1: Try a glass of this juice and see how you like it. It's a new brand.
   F1: Umm . . . I'd say it stacks up pretty well against the other kinds.
   M2: What does the woman mean?

4. F2: Adam, do you know the tools I lent you when you were building those bookshelves last month? I'd like to have them back.
   M1: Uh, well, I hate to tell you this . . . but I can't seem to lay my hands on them.
   M2: What does Adam imply?

5. F1: Excuse me . . . could I get another glass of iced tea?
   F2: Sure, I'll tell your waitress to bring you one.
   M2: What can be inferred from this conversation?

6. F2: Now, if there are no more questions, let's move on to the next chapter.
   M1: Excuse me, professor—could we go over that last point once more?
   M2: What does the man want to do?

7. M1: I'm almost out of money again this month.
   F2: Why don't you keep track of your expenses and payments? That might help you make ends meet.
   M1: Well . . . it wouldn't hurt to give it a try.
   M2: What does the woman think the man should do?

8. M1: I see you bought a new lamp.
   F1: Yeah, isn't it great? Where do you think I should put it, in my living room or in my bedroom?
   M1: If I were you, I'd put it in the closet.
   M2: What can be inferred from the man's comment?

9. F1: Look over there. Isn't that Ernie in the red car?
   M1: No, but it certainly looks like him.
   M2: What does the man mean?

10. F2: I didn't think John had ever been scuba diving before.
    M1: Oh, sure. John's an old hand at scuba diving.
    M2: What does the man say about John?
11. M2: Becky, are you going to be using your computer much longer? If so, I can go use one at the library.
    F1: I'm almost finished.
    M2: All right, I'll just wait then.
    M2: What can be inferred from this conversation?
12. F1: Wow, did you see that ring Laura bought?
    F2: Uh huh—must have cost her a pretty penny.
    M2: What do the speakers mean?
13. F1: What room is Professor Clayburn speaking in tonight?
    M1: Professor Clayburn is speaking tonight?
    M2: What does the man imply by his remark?
14. M2: I thought I heard barking coming from Joe's room.
    F1: Barking! Doesn't Joe know there's a rule against keeping pets in the dorm!
    M2: What can be concluded from this conversation?
15. F2: Bill, I thought you had so much work to do.
    M1: I'm just taking a little break.
    M2: What can be inferred from this conversation?
16. F1: Hey Paul, could you help me move this box upstairs?
    M1: Sure, I . . . say, what do you have in here? Your rock collection?
    M2: What can be inferred from this conversation?

EXERCISE 5.1

1. B
2. A
3. B
4. A
5. B
6. B
7. A
8. B
9. A

AUDIO SCRIPT

1. M1: The science building is so old, it ought to be torn down!
   M2: I couldn't agree with you less! It's a landmark!
2. F1: The wind is really bad today.
   M1: Is it ever! It took some paintings right out of my hands.
3. M1: I didn't think Professor Hall's lecture was very informative.
   M2: You didn't? I can't say I agree with you on that.
4. F1: Anthony is quite a singer.
   M2: You bet he is!
5. M1: I think the service at that new café is pretty good.
   F2: I wish I could say the same.
6. M1: Certainly Curtis won't run for student class president now!
   F2: Don't be so sure about that.
7. M2: It's been a long, hard day.
   F1: Hasn't it though!
8. F2: I think sky diving must be exciting.
   M2: You wouldn't catch *me* jumping out of an airplane!
9. M1: Good thing there was a fire extinguisher in the hallway.
   F1: I'll second that!

Exercise 5.2

1. A
2. D
3. C
4. D
5. B
6. B
7. D
8. B
9. C
10. A

Audio Script

1. F1: I'd rather have a final exam than write a research paper.
   M1: Me, too. Research papers take a lot more time.
   M2: What does the man mean?
2. M1: This first chapter in the statistics textbook seems pretty simple.
   F2: Of course, but I'm sure the other chapters are more difficult.
   M2: How does the woman feel about the first chapter?
3. F1: The university should make it easier for students to register for classes.
   M1: I couldn't agree with you more!
   M2: How does the man feel about the woman's idea?
4. M1: Jack's story was certainly well written.
   F2: Wasn't it though! And so full of interesting details.
   M2: What was the woman's opinion of Jack's story?
5. F1: What a perfect day to take a bike ride!
   M1: You can say that again!
   M2: What does the man mean?
6. M1: I can't understand why Arthur dropped his chemistry class. He was doing so well in it.
   F2: Well, me neither, but he must have a good reason.
   M2: What does the woman mean?
7. M1: Tom's plan is so impractical, it will never work.
   F1: That's not necessarily so.
   M2: What does the woman say about Tom's plan?
8. M1: Did you read this editorial in the morning paper?
   F2: I sure did, and did it ever make me angry!
   M1: I felt the same way when I first read it, but you know, the more I thought about it, the more I agreed with it.
   M2: What was the man's *initial* reaction to the editorial?
9. M1: The library sure is crowded this evening.
   F1: Is it ever! You can tell it's getting near final exam week.
   M2: What does the woman say about the library?
10. F2: Madeleine designed the costumes for the play. They're wonderful, don't you think?
    M1: Absolutely. Who wouldn't?
    M2: What does the man mean?

Exercise 6.1

1. A
2. A
3. B
4. B
5. B
6. A
7. A
8. B
9. B
10. A
11. A
12. B
13. A

AUDIO SCRIPT

1. **F1:** May I help you?
   M1: Thanks, but I'm just looking around.
2. **M2:** Can you come to the recital this evening?
   F2: I'm supposed to be working on my research this evening, but you know, I think a break would be nice.
3. **M1:** That author we both like is going to be signing books at Appleton's Bookstore this afternoon.
   F1: I'm not busy this afternoon. Why don't we go?
4. **F2:** Mark, would you mind taking care of my tropical fish next week? I'm going to be out of town.
   M2: Oh, no, I wouldn't mind at all.
5. **M1:** I need to get more exercise.
   F2: You could always try bicycling. That's great exercise.
6. **F1:** Can I see the photographs you took on the trip?
   M2: If you want to, why not?
7. **M1:** I can't seem to get my car started.
   M2: You know what *I'd* do, Ed?
8. **M1:** These math problems are hard.
   F2: Want me to give you a few hints?
9. **M2:** Cynthia, if you have a class, I could take your brother to the airport for you.
   F1: Could you? That would be great.
10. **M1:** Should I turn on the television?
    F2: Please don't.
11. **F2:** You could save a lot of time at the supermarket by making up a list before you go.
    M1: It's worth a try, I guess.
12. **M1:** Bob, get me a cup of coffee, will you?
    M2: Who do you think I am, your waiter?
13. **F1:** I'm going to go out and get something to eat. Want to come?
    M1: I've got a better idea. Let's have a pizza delivered.

EXERCISE 6.2

1. C
2. D
3. A
4. A
5. B
6. D
7. A
8. C
9. C
10. A
11. B
12. B

AUDIO SCRIPT

1. **F1:** Do you mind if I smoke?
   M1: As a matter of fact, I *do*.
   M2: What does the man mean?
2. **M1:** I don't know what to wear this evening. My blue suit hasn't come back from the cleaners yet.
   F2: Well, there's always your gray one. That looks nice on you.
   M2: What does the woman say about the gray suit?
3. **F1:** We need someone to plan the class trip.
   M1: How about Cathy?
   M2: What does the man say about Cathy?
4. **F2:** Shall I make some more coffee?
   M1: Not on my account.
   M2: What does the man mean?

5. M1: Should I open the window? It's getting a little warm in here.
 F1: Don't bother, I'll do it.
 M2: What does the woman mean?

6. M1: I don't know what to order for lunch. I'm tired of the sandwiches in the cafeteria.
 F2: What about some vegetable soup?
 M1: You know, that doesn't sound too bad.
 M2: What will the man probably do?

7. M1: I'm going to clean my living room this afternoon.
 F2: Shouldn't you clean your kitchen, too?
 M2: What does the woman imply?

8. M1: What office are you looking for?
 F1: The registrar's office. I need some information about signing up for classes next semester.
 M1: That's across campus from here. Would you like me to show you on this map?
 M2: What does the man offer to do for the woman?

9. M1: Well, that's it for our statistics homework. We should work on our math problems next.
 F1: What about taking a little break first?
 M2: What does the woman suggest they do?

10. F2: Do you think this toaster can be repaired?
 M1: If I were in your shoes, Lisa, I think I'd just buy another one.
 M2: What does the man suggest that Lisa do?

11. F2: Would you mind if I read your magazine? That looks like an interesting article.
 M1: No, go right ahead. I'm finished with it.
 M2: What does the man tell the woman?

12. M1: You know, I think I'm going to get a new computer desk. This one is just too small for me to work at.
 F2: What about buying a new computer instead? Yours is practically an antique!
 M2: What does the woman think the man should do?

EXERCISE 7

1. D
2. B
3. B
4. A
5. C
6. A
7. A
8. D
9. D
10. A
11. A
12. D
13. C
14. B
15. B

AUDIO SCRIPT

1. M2: Ginny may join us for dinner tomorrow night. Is that all right?
 F1: Sure, but if she does, I guess I'd better serve fish. She doesn't care for chicken.
 M2: Actually, I'm sure she *does*.
 F2: What does the man say about Ginny?

2. F2: Mona is moving into a new apartment on Sunday.
 M1: So she finally found a place, did she?
 F2: What had the man assumed about Mona?

3. M1: I was told to go to the dean's office.
 F1: By whom?
 F2: What does the woman want to know?

4. F1: I told everyone that of course you weren't interested in running for class president.
 M1: But as a matter of fact, I *am*.
 F2: What does the man mean?

5. F2: Carol's word-processing the final draft of her paper right now.
   M2: Oh, so she finally finished the research for it?
   F2: What had the man assumed about Carol?

6. M2: Bert says he loves to ride horses.
   F1: Sure, but you don't actually see him on horseback very often, do you?
   F2: What does the woman imply about Bert?

7. F1: Anyone call while I was out?
   M1: Yeah, your travel agent called. She said she'd made your flight reservation.
   F1: I see. How long ago was this?
   F2: What does the woman want to know?

8. M2: Did you know Cliff is working part-time in the cafeteria now?
   F1: Oh, he finally decided to get a job, then?
   F2: What had the woman assumed about Cliff?

9. M1: We spent the whole day hiking.
   F1: Really? How far did you go?
   F2: What does the woman want to know?

10. M1: I need some new clothes.
    F1: There are some nice clothes in that store on Collins Street, and it seems to me the prices there are pretty reasonable.
    M1: Reasonable! I wouldn't call them reasonable.
    F2: What does the man mean?

11. M1: There's going to be a meeting to discuss the proposed recreation center.
    F1: Really? Where?
    F2: What does the woman ask the man?

12. M2: Joy is going to study overseas in a special program next year.
    F1: That's not until next year?
    F2: What had the woman assumed?

13. M1: I went to a party at Ben's house this weekend.
    F1: Did you have a good time?
    F2: What does the woman ask the man?

14. F1: Ted didn't do a good job on these problems. He'll have to do them all over.
    M2: Well, a few of them, anyway.
    F2: What does the man mean?

15. F1: I stopped at the grocery store on the way home from class.
    M2: Yeah? How come?
    F2: What does the man ask the woman?

EXERCISE 8

1.	A	7.	C
2.	D	8.	B
3.	D	9.	B
4.	B	10.	C
5.	B	11.	B
6.	D	12.	D

AUDIO SCRIPT

1. F2: I can't believe how icy the highway is tonight.
    F1: Yeah, I've never seen it so bad. Maybe we should just stay at a motel and see if it's any better in the morning.
    M2: What are they talking about?

2. F1: *(Ring . . . ring)*
    F2: Hello.
    F1: Great party you threw last night, Beth.
    F2: Yeah, but you should see my apartment this morning. What a mess! I feel like moving somewhere else!
    F1: Don't worry. I'll come over this afternoon and help you out.
    M2: What are they probably going to do this afternoon?

3. F1: Joe and Nancy and I were hoping to get a ride to the party with you.
    M1: With me? But I drive a little two-seater.
    M2: What is the problem?

4. M2: You mean it's *still* closed?
    M1: Yes, sir, the repairs won't be done for another two weeks. You'll have to take Highway 17 to Springdale and cross the river on the one down there.
    M2: What are they probably talking about?

5. M2: Okay, so tomorrow, I'll bring the portable stove and the food.
    M1: And I'll bring the tent and we'll each bring a sleeping bag.
    M2: Hey, this is going to be fun!
    M2: What are the speakers probably planning to do tomorrow?

6. F1: I like your new glasses, Brian.
    M1: I like these new frames, too, but my vision is blurry and I've been having headaches. I've got to go back to Dr. Lamb and get some new lenses prescribed.
    M2: What does Brian intend to do?

7. F2: Do you think I'll need to put on two coats of this latex?
    M1: Will you be using brushes or a roller?
    M2: What are these people discussing?

8. F1: Want to watch that documentary about polar bears in Canada now?
    M1: Well, I am a little tired, but okay, sure—what channel?
    M2: What is the man going to do next?

9. M1: Uh, Denise, do you remember that art book I borrowed from you last month?
    F2: Oh, right. Do you have it for me? I'm going to need it back soon.
    M1: Ummm, well, actually, I'm going to have to replace it. See, Tuesday I was looking at it out in the yard, and forgot to bring it in with me—and you remember that rain we had Tuesday night?
    M2: What problem did the man have with the book?

10. M2: Take a look at this model. It's incredibly fast, and it has an extended keyboard.
    F1: Does it have much memory?
    M2: What are the speakers probably discussing?

11. F2: Shirley, are you going to go right on to business school when you finish your undergraduate program?
    F1: Actually, I hope to get some practical experience with a big international corporation first.
    F2: That's a good idea, I think.
    M2: What will Shirley probably do right after she finishes her undergraduate program?

12. F2: Dave, Phyllis is going to be upset with you if you don't send her a postcard while we're here on vacation
    M1: Yeah, well, I'd like to send her one, but I've been by the post office twice to buy stamps and for some reason it hasn't been open.
    M2: What is Dave's problem?

EXERCISE 9

1.	B	8.	A
2.	B	9.	A
3.	B	10.	A
4.	A	11.	B
5.	A	12.	A
6.	B	13.	B
7.	B		

AUDIO SCRIPT

1. F1: Doug and Rose are such good friends.
    M1: Well—they *used* to be.
    M2: What does the man say?

2. M1: I'm going to re-wire my house myself.
    F2: If I were you, Roger, I think I'd have a professional do it.
    M2: What does the woman tell Roger?

3. F1: I thought this was a classical music station.
    M1: It used to be, but now it's a twenty-four hour news station.
    M2: What does the man say about the radio station?

4. F1: Lynn, who did you get to change your oil?
    F2: Now why would I need anyone to do *that* for me?
    M2: What can be inferred from Lynn's remark?

5. F1: I'm having a hard time getting used to this early morning class.
    M1: Yeah, me too.
    M2: What does the man mean?

6. M2: Peggy, do you ever go skating anymore?
    F2: Sometimes, but not as much as I used to.
    M2: What does Peggy mean?

7. F1: You got some egg on your tie, Kenny.
    M1: I know. I'll have to get it cleaned.
    M2: What does Kenny mean?

8. F2: There's something different about your apartment, isn't there?
    M1: That poster over my desk used to be over the sofa.
    M2: What does the man mean?

9. M2: Will your boss let you take a vacation in August?
    F1: If he doesn't, I'll just look for another job when I get back.
    M2: What does the woman mean?

10. F2: Greg, that was an interesting point you made in class.
    M1: Thanks. But when the teacher made me explain what I meant, I didn't know exactly what to say to her.
    M2: What did Greg's teacher do?

11. F1: Carter just doesn't look the same these days.
    F2: I know. I'm not used to seeing him without glasses either.
    M2: What do the speakers say about Carter?

12. F1: You look nice today, Sally.
    F2: Thanks—our club is having our photo taken today for the yearbook.
    M2: What does Sally mean?

13. F2: Nick, how do you like this hot, humid weather?
    M1: Well, growing up in New Orleans, I'm pretty much used to it.
    M2: What does Nick tell the woman?

REVIEW TEST B: DIALOGUES

1.	A	**9.**	A
2.	D	**10.**	C
3.	D	**11.**	A
4.	B	**12.**	D
5.	A	**13.**	A
6.	D	**14.**	C
7.	D	**15.**	D
8.	B	**16.**	D

AUDIO SCRIPT

1. M1: So, what makes these so valuable?

    F2: Well, they're first editions, that adds value. And they're in mint condition.

    M1: And since they have the original dust jackets, I suppose that makes them worth more too, huh?

    M2: What are they discussing?

2. M1: I'm tired. My neighbor kept me up until two, playing his stereo at the highest volume. I'm thinking about looking for a new apartment.

    F1: Before you do, why don't you have a chat with your neighbor. Maybe he'd be willing to turn down his stereo at night.

    F2: What does the woman suggest?

3. M1: Sonya, are you planning to sign up for Professor Osborne's seminar next semester?

    F1: I think so, but I've got to get his permission first.

    M1: Actually, I don't think you do.

    F2: What does the man tell Sonya about the seminar?

4. F1: Adam, do you remember the tools I lent you when you were building those bookshelves? I'd like to have them back.

    M2: Uh, well, I hate to tell you this, but I can't seem to lay my hands on them..

    F2: What does Adam imply?

5. M1: My sister is looking for a roommate. Do you know anyone who might want to move in with her?

    F1: How about Grace? She'll need a place at the end of the month.

    M1: Hmmmm . . . can't you think of anyone else?

    M2: What does the man imply?

6. M1: We'd better leave right now.

    F2: What's the rush, Mark?

    M2: What does the woman ask Mark?

7. M1: It's freezing out here! I'm going to put on my scarf and gloves.

    F2: Shouldn't you put on a hat, too?

    M2: What does the woman mean?

8. M1: I didn't think the team was very well prepared for that game.

    M2: To tell you the truth, neither did I.

    F2: What does the second man mean?

9. F2: Why are you walking that way, Richard? Did you hurt yourself when you went skiing?

    M1: No, no—it's these shoes; they're not broken in yet.

    M2: What problem is Richard having?

10. M1: I didn't realize you were an art history major.

    F2: I'm not. I'm taking a class in art history, but I'm studying to be a commercial artist.

    M2: What are these people discussing?

11. M2: We should have a dinner party.

    F1: You took the words right out of my mouth.

    M2: What does the woman mean?

12. F2: Victor sure is outgoing.
    M1: Isn't he! It's hard to believe he used to be shy.
    M2: What do the speakers imply about Victor?
13. F1: Can I look at your painting for a second?
    M1: Be my guest.
    M2: What does the man mean?
14. M1: Great weather we're having, huh?
    F1: Yeah, but don't get too used to it. I heard on the radio that there's a big change in store tomorrow.
    M2: What does the woman tell the man?
15. F1: I stopped by Doctor Norton's office at the medical center.
    F2: Really? What for?
    M2: What does the woman want to know?
16. F1: Did you know Angela had finished all her required courses? She'll be graduating in May.
    M1: Oh, so she doesn't have to repeat that chemistry course after all.
    M2: What had the man assumed about Angela?

LISTENING PART B: LONGER TALKS

EXERCISE 10

1. B
2. B, C
3. C
4. A, D
5. B
6. B
7. A
8. D

AUDIO SCRIPT

F2: Listen to a conversation between a teacher and a student.
M1: Professor Mueller, I've almost finished preparing my presentation for your class, but I'm not really satisfied with it. Could you give me some advice?
F2: I'll be happy to. What topic did you choose?
M1: It's about methods of predicting earthquakes, but so far, it's just a lot of facts and figures. How can I make it more interesting?
F2: Maybe you could use some computer graphics to help the class make sense of your statistics.
1. What will the main topic of this conversation probably be?
F2: Listen to part of a discussion in an economics class. The class has been studying taxation.
M2: In last Friday's class, I asked you to read the first part of Chapter 22, about taxation. The text says there are two main types of taxation. Anyone remember what they are? Yes, Troy?
M1: I think the book said they were direct and indirect—right?
M2: Right, Troy. And can anyone define direct taxation? Cheryl?
F1: That's when the person or firm who is taxed pays the government directly. Like income tax.
M2: You got it. And so indirect taxation . . .
F1: If I understand the book, it's when the person or firm who is taxed passes the tax on to someone else. A good is imported into a country, the government taxes the company that owns it, and then that company charges customers—that's indirect taxation—right?
M2: Yes, exactly. Can anyone think of another example? Troy?
M1: Well, last year, the city raised property taxes, and my landlady raised my rent to help pay the higher taxes. Is that an example?
M2: It certainly is. Cheryl, you have a question?
F1: Yes, Professor, I was just wondering—what about sales taxes? Are they indirect or direct?
M2: Ummm, good question. I'll let you all think about that for a minute, and then you tell me. . . .

2. What are the main purposes of this discussion?

    F2: Listen to the following conversation in a university library.

    F1: I'm in Professor Quinn's political science class. She told us that she'd put some articles on reserve for her class.

    F2: Yes, those would be at the reserve desk.

    F1: Do I need a library card to look at those articles?

    F2: No, just a student ID card. If you've never checked out any reserve materials, I can tell you what you need to do.

3. What will the main subject of this conversation probably be?

    F2: Listen to part of a lecture about a dance program.

    F1: Since all of you have expressed interest in joining the university dance program, I probably don't have to say much about the physical and psychological rewards of being in a dance program such as this one. Instead, I want to concentrate on some of the drawbacks—the early mornings and late nights, the aches and pains and the physical exhaustion, and all the other sacrifices you'll be called on to make if you are chosen for the program. And if, despite what you hear, you still want to try out for the program, I'll let you know how to set up your preliminary dance audition.

4. What will the rest of this talk mainly be about?

    F2: Listen to a conversation between two students.

    M1: Well, I had a pretty relaxing vacation. How about you, Tina?

    F1: I wouldn't exactly call it relaxing, but it certainly was interesting.

    M1: I remember you said you were either going to Europe or you were going to work at your parents' company.

    F1: I changed my mind and didn't do either. My anthropology professor talked me into volunteering for an archaeological project in New Mexico.

5. What will the two speakers probably discuss?

    F2: Listen to part of a discussion in a psychology class.

    F1: Excuse me, Professor Norton, I'm a little confused...

    M1: Why is that, Deborah?

    F1: Well, when you were talking about ESP, you said that most scientists today don't believe it exists.

    M1: That's right. First, does everyone in class know what ESP is?

    M2: Sure—ESP means extra-sensory perception. Mind-reading and that kind of thing.

    M1: Good definition. It's sometimes called para-psychology.

    F1: Well, the reason I'm confused is that I read an article about ESP studies at some university. It said that the researchers concluded that a number of people did have ESP abilities.

    M1: You're probably thinking of the experiments at Duke University. A Professor named J. P. Rhine established a parapsychology lab there, about fifty years ago, and he developed experiments that seemed to show that some people had remarkable ESP talents.

    F1: Yes, that's it—I remember it was at Duke University.

    M2: So Professor, what happened to change everyone's minds about ESP?

    M1: Well, since then, a lot of researchers have decided that Rhine's evidence was questionable. Today, when experiments are more carefully controlled, similar performances are rare. And in science, the trend should be the opposite.

    M2: What do you mean, Professor?

    M1: Well, if the phenomenon you're investigating is real, and the experiments are improved, then the results you get should be more certain, not less certain.

    F1: So, you don't think ESP is possible?

    M1: Well, let's just say that I don't think there's any experimental proof for it.

6. What are the speakers mainly discussing?

    F2: Listen to part of a lecture in an American history class.

    M2: Good afternoon. I'm Robert Wolfe, president of the State Historical Society. Professor Lewis has asked me to give a guest lecture. I'm going to give you a short presentation on some famous shipwrecks, especially ones that took place in the waters off New England, and I'm going to spend most of my time explaining how a study of shipwrecks can contribute to an understanding of history.

7. What is this lecture primarily going to concern?

F2: Listen to part of a lecture given in an advertising class.

M2: Good morning, students. In our last class, we were talking about regulation in the advertising industry. In fact, as you may remember, I said advertising was one of the most heavily regulated industries in the United States, and I gave as an example the law that prohibits advertising tobacco products on television. Now, in today's class, I want to tell you about self-regulation in advertising, which the industry has adopted as a way to stop abuses before they can occur. As we'll see, these self-imposed codes of ethics are intended to control not only bad taste but also misrepresentation and deception—although, they don't always work. Any questions before we get started?

8. What will the rest of the lecture probably concern?

EXERCISE 11

1. A	14. B, C
2. B	15. D
3. B, C	16. C
4. C	17. B, C
5. D	18. C
6. D	19. A
7. A	20. D
8. D	21. C
9. C	22. A, B
10. A	23. B
11. B, C	24. B
12. A	25. B
13. B	

AUDIO SCRIPT

F2: Listen to a conversation between two students.

F2: You look exhausted this morning, Steve.

M1: I *am* pretty tired. I stayed up nearly all night getting ready for my chemistry mid-term exam this morning.

F2: Have you gotten the results of the test yet?

M1: Yes, and unfortunately, my grade could have been much better. But I'm not all that surprised. No matter how much time I spend studying, I never seem to do well on tests.

F2: You know, Steve, if I were you, I'd consider taking some of the seminars offered by the Study Skills Center.

M1: The Study Skills Center? Never heard of it.

F2: Well, it's run by a group of graduate students and professors who help undergraduate students improve their study techniques.

M1: What kind of seminars does the Center offer that could help me?

F2: Well, they have one on test-taking skills.

M1: That definitely sounds like something I need.

F2: There's also a seminar that teaches you to manage your time efficiently. You should find *that* useful, I should think.

M1: Yeah, maybe. So, where is the Center?

F2: They hold most of their seminars in the library, but the main office is in Staunton Hall, right across the quadrangle from the Physics Tower.

M1: You know, I think I'll go over there right now and talk to someone.

F2: Why don't you wait until tomorrow? Right now, you should go back to your dorm and catch up on your sleep.

1. Why is Steve tired?
2. How did Steve feel about the grade he received?
3. Who teaches the seminars at the Study Skills Center?
4. What seminar will Steve probably take?
5. Where is the main office of the Study Skills Center?
6. What does the woman think Steve should do next?

M2: Listen to part of a talk given in a space science class.

F2: The skies above Earth are turning into a junkyard. Ever since the Soviet Union launched *Sputnik*, the first satellite, way back in 1957, virtually every launch has contributed to the amount of debris in Earth orbit. Luckily, most of this junk burns up after it re-enters the Earth's atmosphere, but some will be up there in orbit for years to come. Today, there are about 8,000 bodies in orbit being monitored from Earth. Out of all those, only around 3 to 400 are active and useful. There are also probably half a million pieces of debris too tiny to be monitored.

Some orbital debris is as big as a bus, but most is in the form of tiny flecks of paint or pieces of metal. The debris includes food wrappers, an astronaut's glove, the lens cap from a camera, broken tools, and bags of unwashed uniforms. The largest pieces— mostly empty booster rockets—are not necessarily the most dangerous because they can be detected and spacecraft can avoid them. And the smallest particles generally cause only surface damage. However, a collision with a particle an eighth of an inch in diameter—say about the size of an aspirin—could puncture the hull of a spacecraft or space station and cause de-pressurization. Imagine what might happen if a spacecraft struck a screwdriver or a wrench that some astronaut had dropped during a space walk! These small objects are so dangerous, of course, because of their tremendous speed.

So what can be done about this problem? Well, two engineers recently proposed a novel solution to the problem of orbital junk: a collector that consists of an array of water-spraying cones lined with plastic fibers to collect the debris. The debris is then stored in a canister located behind the cones. I brought a model of this collector along with me so you can see what it looks like. Although this invention is still in its conceptual stage, two possible uses have been proposed. It could be launched with a free-flying unmanned satellite to actively seek out debris or it could be launched into orbit with a manned spacecraft to serve as a defensive shield.

7. When did orbital debris first appear?
8. What happens to most pieces of orbital debris?
9. How many orbital bodies are being monitored today?
10. Why is it impossible to monitor most pieces of orbital debris?
11. Which of the following types of orbital debris are probably most dangerous to astronauts on a spacecraft?
12. What makes orbital debris such a danger to spacecraft?
13. Assume that this is a representation of a satellite equipped with a collector. Where would the space debris be stored?
14. In which ways could the collector be used to solve the problem of orbital debris?
15. What can be inferred about the collector described in this portion of the talk?

M2: Listen to a discussion that takes place before a biology class.
F1: Hello, Rebecca, hello, John. Did you have a good spring break?
M1: Hi Professor—actually, I just stayed in town and worked. I didn't do anything too exciting.
F2: And I went home to see my parents. How about you, Professor—what did you do over the break?
F1: Well, one of my colleagues, Professor Nugent from the history department, is doing research on California mission churches, so I went to California to help by taking some photographs. Also, we were able to arrange our trip so that we were in the town of San Juan Capistrano when the swallows returned. That's something I always wanted to see. As you know, I'm interested in migration patterns, and this is one of the more remarkable migrations in all the animal kingdom.

M1: Where is San Juan Capistrano, Professor?

F1: It's on the Pacific Coast, between Los Angeles and San Diego.

F2: I've head about those swallows before—they always return on the same date, don't they?

F1: That's right—on March 19. And they always fly away on the same day, October 23rd. In the meantime, they migrate over 7,000 miles to get to their winter homes.

M1: Seven thousand miles—imagine! And always arriving on the same day.

F1: Yes, almost always. One year, a long time ago, they were delayed for several days by a storm at sea.

F2: So there's a mission church in San Juan Capistrano?

F1: Well, there's the ruins of one. The town grew up around a church that the Spanish built in the 1770s. But it was mostly destroyed by an earthquake in the early 1800s. Today, there are just a few walls and part of the tower of the old church still standing. In fact, the swallows like to build their nests in the ruins.

F2: So were there a lot of tourists there to see the swallows return?

F1: Oh yes, thousands of them. There's quite a celebration. The townspeople even have a parade to welcome the swallows back.

M1: Wow. They must really like those swallows!

F1: Sure—not only do the swallows bring lots of tourist money to town, but they also eat insects—including mosquitoes!

16. Where is the town of San Juan Capistrano located?
17. What were the professor's main reasons for going to San Juan Capistrano?
18. What can be inferred about the swallows?
19. When do the swallows return to San Juan Capistrano?
20. How far do the swallows migrate?
21. According to the professor, how was the mission church in San Juan Capistrano damaged?
22. According to the professor, why are the swallows popular with the people of San Juan Capistrano?

M2: Listen to a conversation that takes place on a college campus.

M1: I'm here for the campus tour.

F2: I'm sorry, we only offer guided tours during the first week of the semester.

M1: Oh really? That's too bad. I was really hoping to get a good orientation. Last week, I spent nearly an hour trying to find a classroom in the Fine Arts Building.

F2: You know what you *can* do—you can take the self-guided tour. This pamphlet tells you exactly what to do, where to go, and what to look for, and it has a complete map of the campus.

M1: Sounds easy enough—where do I start?

F2: The first stop is right here, in the Student Center Building. Then you go next door to the Science Building—there's a great planetarium there, by the way—and from there you go to the University Recreation Center. After that, just follow the directions in the pamphlet, and you can't go wrong.

23. When is the guided tour of the campus given?
24. What did the man have trouble locating the week before?
25. Where does the self-guided tour start?

EXERCISE 12

1. C, D, A, B
2. B, A, C
3. B, C, A
4. A, D, C, B
5. C, A, B
6. D, A, B, C
7. C, B, A
8. A, B, C

AUDIO SCRIPT

F2: You will hear part of a lecture in a chemistry class. The class has been focusing on hydrocarbon compounds.

F1: We've been considering various useful hydrocarbon compounds, and today, we're going to look at one of the most useful of all of these. That's right, I'm talking about coal. There probably wouldn't have been an Industrial Revolution in the eighteenth century without coal. Even today, life would be very different if we didn't have coal. So, where does coal come from? Well, imagine what the Earth was like say, 300 million years ago—during the Carboniferous period. Much of the land was covered with luxuriant vegetation, especially ferns—ferns big as trees. Eventually, these plants died and were submerged in the waters of swamps, where they gradually decomposed. And we've seen what happens when plants decompose—the vegetable matter loses oxygen and hydrogen atoms, leaving a deposit with a high percentage of carbon. In this way, peat bogs were formed. Then, as time went on, layers of sand and mud settled from the water over the peat bogs. These deposits grew thicker and thicker, and the pressure increased, and the deposits were compressed and hardened. And so you have—coal!

All grades of coal have uses. Lignite, the lowest grade of coal, is often burned in furnaces for heat. Most bituminous coal, which has a higher carbon content, is used by utility companies to produce electricity. Anthracite, which has the highest carbon content, is often distilled to produce coke. Coke is almost pure carbon and is used in the manufacture of steel. And coal tar, one of the by-products of producing coke, is used to make many different types of plastic.

1. The lecturer discusses the steps involved in the creation of coal. Summarize this process by putting the events in the proper order.

2. Match the form of coal with the type of industry which primarily uses it.

F2: Listen to part of a discussion in an accounting seminar. The seminar is talking about some of the basic principles of accounting.

M2: Hello, everyone. As you can see from our course syllabus, our topic today is something called "GAAP." Anyone have any idea what we mean by that acronym, GAAP? Yes, Susan?

F1: Um, I think it means "Generally Accepted Accounting Practices."

M2: Almost right. Anyone else? Michael?

M1: Generally Accepted Accounting *Principles*, I think.

M2: Bingo, you got it. Today we're going to talk about three of the most important of these principles. First, the business entity principle. Who can explain that principle— Elaine?

F2: Uh, it means that a business has to keep its accounts separate from its owner's account. Is that right?

M2: Indeed it is, Elaine. It means an owner's assets and liabilities are not the same as his or her business's assets and liabilities. Now, another principle we're going to consider today is the cost principle. Michael, what do you think that might be?

M1: I don't know, professor—does it mean that costs always have to be recorded in the books?

M2: Well, not just that they have to be recorded, but that they have to be recorded at the price at which they were originally purchased—*not* at today's market value. Let's say you bought 10 computers five years ago for $1,000 each, and that today they are worth half that. This principle says that you have to keep them on your books as being worth $1,000. We'll talk more about this later, but first I want to mention the last principle we'll consider today, which is the matching principle. Anyone know what that is? Susan?

F1: No idea, Professor.

M1: Anyone else? No? Well, this principle simply states that a firm has to record any expenses it incurs while selling goods or services in the period when the sale was made. If you own a used car lot and your books say you sold a car in December, you have to record the expense of the salesperson's December salary along with that sale. Okay, we're going to go back and talk about all these principles in more detail, but before we do that, does anyone have any questions?

3. Match the accounting principle with the appropriate description of it.

> F2: You will hear part of a guest lecture given in a class in agronomy. The lecture focuses on locally grown crops.
>
> M1: Hello, I'm Floyd Haney. I'm the U.S. Department of Agriculture's county agent here in Harrison County. Professor Mackenzie asked me to talk to you about the agricultural situation in Harrison County today. Now, you probably already know that our main crop is traditionally wheat, followed by corn. Wheat is still the most important, but did you realize that, in the last few years, soy beans have become considerably more important economically than corn? I'll bet that's a surprise for most of you. Then, of course, in the southern part of the county, there are a number of organic fruit farms, mostly growing apples and pears, but so far, these are not nearly as important to our county economically as any of the three crops I mentioned.
>
> So let's talk about our top crop, which is wheat, as I said. According to the U.S. Department of Agriculture, there are seven types of wheat, depending on their texture and color. You'll find three or four of those growing here in Harrison County. You get a lot of durum wheat here, which is mainly used for making pasta—spaghetti, macaroni, and so on. Then there's soft white wheat, which is generally purchased by companies that make breakfast cereals. And of course, you have hard red wheat, which makes wonderful bread flour.

4. The lecturer mentions four types of crops that are grown in Harrison County. Rank these four crops in their order of economic importance, beginning with the MOST important.

5. Match the type of wheat with the product that is most often made from it.

> F2: Listen to part of a discussion in a history class. The class has been focusing on the history of exploration.
>
> M1: Okay, we're going to go on with our discussion of explorers and exploration. Today we're talking about twentieth-century explorers. You know, usually, when we talk about explorers in the twentieth century, we think of space explorers walking on the Moon. But in the early part of the century, the most important sphere of discovery was Antarctica.
>
> Tell me, has anyone here ever read anything about the early exploration of Antarctica?
>
> F1: When I was in high school, I read a book by Admiral Byrd called *Alone*, about the winter he spent in a shelter in Antarctica by himself.
>
> M1: Yes, that's a fascinating book.
>
> F1: I was amazed at how he could survive in that terrible cold, dark shelter all winter by himself.
>
> M2: Professor Smith, was Byrd the first person to get to the South Pole?
>
> M1: No, he was the first person to fly over the South Pole, in 1929, but not the first person to go there on foot. In 1929, he also established the first large-scale camp in Antarctica. Since he was from the United States, he named it Little America.
>
> M2: So who was the first to the South Pole, then?
>
> M1: That's an interesting question. About twenty years before Byrd's flight, there was something of a race to get to the South Pole by foot. It was a little like the space race in the 50s and 60s. The first explorer to get *near* the South Pole was a British explorer, named Shackleton. That was in 1909. He was less than a hundred miles from the Pole when he had to turn around.
>
> M2: Why did he turn back when he was so close?
>
> M1: Well, he was running low on supplies, and, as so often happens in Antarctica, the weather turned bad. Then in 1911, two expeditions headed for the Pole. The first one to leave was under the Norwegian explorer Roald Amundson, the other was under another British explorer, Robert Scott.
>
> F1: Don't keep us in suspense—who won?
>
> M1: Amundson's party reached the Pole in December of 1911. Scott's party got there about a month later, in January of 1912.
>
> F1: Oh, the people in Scott's party must have been terribly disappointed.
>
> M2: Yes, apparently they were very discouraged, and the return trip to their base turned into a nightmare. They suffered setback after setback, then, of course, terrible storms came up, and none of them survived the trip.

6. The professor discusses some of the history of Antarctic exploration. Summarize this history by putting these expeditions in the order in which they began.

7. Match these Antarctic explorers with the countries from which they came.

F1: Listen to a lecture in a musical acoustics class about decibel levels.

F2: Sound levels below about 40 decibels are not very useful in music. They require that background noise, such as audience movement or ventilating systems, be even lower—and that often is not the case. Levels over about 100 are not only unpleasantly loud but also can be damaging to the ear. As a matter of fact, lately I've been doing a little research on my own on decibel levels that I want to share with you. Last week, I went to an amplified rock concert by a band called the Creatures—at least, I think that's what they were called—and I took a sound-level meter with me. I measured sound levels as high as 115 decibels from my seat. Oh, and I can vouch for the fact that this level of sound is painfully loud! A couple of nights later, I measured the sound levels at a concert by the Metropolitan Philharmonic Symphony. Although a full orchestra is theoretically capable of producing sounds at a much higher level, I didn't record any sounds from my seat above 90 decibels. Most of the sound levels were much lower. And when the first violinist performed a solo, the highest level I detected was around only 60 decibels.

8. Match the performance with its maximum decibel level.

REVIEW TEST C: LONGER TALKS

1. A
2. C
3. C
4. C, D
5. C
6. C
7. D, A, B, C
8. B
9. B
10. A, C, B
11. B
12. B
13. A
14. B
15. A
16. B
17. B
18. C
19. D
20. B, D

AUDIO SCRIPT

M2: Listen to a conversation at a university library.

M1: Hi, Martha. What brings you to the library?

F2: Oh, I just came to look up some terms in the *Encyclopedia of Art* for my art history class. What about you, Stanley?

M1: I've got two papers due at the end of this term, and I've been getting an early start on them by collecting some references and writing down some statistics. I've spent most of the day here.

F2: Really? Well, you ought to be ready for a break them. Want to go get a snack or something?

M1: You know, that sounds great—let me just get my things together and . . . hey, where are my notes?

F2: What notes?

M1: The notes I spent all day working on. I don't see them.

F2: You mean you lost your notebook?

M1: No, I don't use a notebook—I take notes on index cards.

F2: Well, just think about where you could have left them. Re-trace your steps since you came in the library.

M1: Let's see—when I first arrived, I came here, to the reference room.

F2: Maybe they're somewhere in this room, then.

M1: No, I had them after that. I went to the stacks next . . .

F2: Stacks? What do you mean, the stacks?

M1: You know, the book stacks. That's what they call the main part of the library, where most of the books are shelved.

F2: Well, that's where you should look.

M1: No, after that I went up to look at some journals in the periodicals room up on the third floor, and I remember having them up there. I'll bet that's where they are.

F2: Well, you go look up there, and I'll check with one of the librarians behind the main desk, just in case someone turned them in.

M1: Okay, and thanks for helping me out. Just as soon as I find my note cards, we'll go get a bite to eat.

1. Why did Martha come to the library?

2. What did Stanley lose?

3. According to Stanley, what does the term "stacks" refer to?

M2: Listen to a lecture in an anthropology class. The class has been discussing the domestication of animals.

F1: All right, class, last week we talked about the process of domesticating animals in general. Today, we're going to talk in some detail about the first animal to be domesticated—the dog.

No one knows when or where the dog was first domesticated. It's believed, however, that the process took place more than 10,000 years ago. The remains of what is thought to be an early example of a domesticated dog was found in a cave in Idaho. These remains are believed to be around 10,500 years old. So, domestication took place during humankind's earliest stage of development—the hunter-gatherer period.

All of the dogs you see today, from Chihuahuas to Great Danes, are descendants of wolves. Obviously, domestication of these wild creatures required that humans select the most useful and easily trained young animals as breeding stock. As such selection continued over countless generations, dogs became adapted to many tasks.

Dogs apparently first served as guards. With their keen sense of smell and hearing, dogs made it almost impossible for strangers to approach a sleeping village by surprise. And later, humans took advantage of dogs' hunting instincts. Dogs learned to help humans procure meat and skins from wild animals. Then, after humans domesticated herd animals such as goats, cattle, and sheep, dogs helped round these herd animals up and move them from place to place by barking and nipping at their heels.

Take a look at this fresco from the wall of a sandstone grotto in the Sahara. It's probably about 5,000 years old. The herders are driving their oxen home from the field, while their "best friend" is apparently helping them.

Of course, after that, at some unknown time, dogs began to take on a new role, the role that most of them have today. They began to be valued not so much for the work they did as for the company they provided.

4. What are the main purposes of the lecture?

5. According to the lecturer, how did early humans adapt dogs to different tasks?

6. Why does the lecturer mention Idaho?

7. The lecturer mentions a number of roles that dogs have played since they were first domesticated. List these roles in the correct chronological order.

8. Click on the part of the picture that represents the herders' "best friend."

M2: Listen to a discussion in a drama class. The class is trying to decide which play they will stage.

F2: In the next few days, we have to chose a play to put on in the spring.

F1: I have an idea, Professor Kemp. How about Thornton Wilder's play *Our Town*. My senior class put that on when I was in high school. I thought it was a really interesting play.

F2: That's a good idea, Lynn, but that play is usually performed without any costumes or any kind of elaborate scenery, and I would like the students interested in costume and scenery design to have a chance to show off their talents as well as the actors. Any other ideas? Yes, Larry?

M1: Suppose we did a musical, like *A Chorus Line*?

F2: That would be a lot of fun. But I'm afraid I wouldn't be able to direct a musical—I just don't have the experience or the musical background myself.

F1: I've always loved Shakespeare—we could put on one of his comedies, like *The Tempest*.

F2: I love Shakespeare myself, and that's tempting. The only problem is that, every summer, the university has a Shakespeare festival and puts on three Shakespearean plays at the amphitheater on campus. I don't really want it to seem like our spring production is in competition with the festival in any way.

M1: How about Arthur Miller's play *The Crucible*? I saw a version of that play on television a few months ago, and I was really impressed.

F2: Ummm. . . . *The Crucible*. I think you might be on to something there, Larry. That's an excellent choice. Anyone else have an opinion on that play?

F1: Tell you the truth, I've never seen it or read it. What's it about?

F2: Well, it takes place in the late seventeenth century, and it's about the Salem Witch Trials.

F1: Oh, I studied those in history class. A lot of innocent women were persecuted because people thought they were witches, right?

F2: Right, Lynn. In a broader sense, it's really about any group that persecutes a minority because they are afraid of them. Arthur Miller wrote this play in the 1950s, which was the early part of the Cold War. At the time, the Congress was investigating dissidents in the United States. In fact, Miller himself was investigated. So, the witch trials are a kind of metaphor for that investigation.

F1: Well, I think it sounds like a good choice . . . it's not only a period play, but it's also a play that has a contemporary message.

F2: I'll tell you what . . . I'd like everyone to get hold of a copy of *The Crucible*, either from the bookstore or the library, and take a look at it, and the next time class meets, we'll make a final decision.

9. Why does Professor Kemp NOT want to stage the play *Our Town* this spring?

10. Professor Kemp and her students discuss a number of plays. Match the characteristics of the play with the title of the play.

11. In what time period is the play *The Crucible* set?

12. Which of these plays does Professor Kemp show the most enthusiasm for staging?

13. What does Professor Kemp ask the students to do before their next class?

M2: Listen to a conversation between two students.

M1: Hi, Nicole, what are you reading?

F1: Just the campus paper. Hey, did you see the lead story?

M1: No, I didn't. What's going on?

F1: The Board of Regents voted to raise tuition again here at Babcock University next year. Can you believe it?

M1: Again? This is the third year in a row, isn't it? We must be attending the most expensive university in the state now.

F1: According to the article, only Hambleton College is more expensive.

M1: So, does the article say what the university is going to use this money for? I hope they plan to replace some of the computers in the computer labs. A lot of them are ancient.

F1: Well, here, I'll read what it says about that: "Student Council president Penny Chang asked the Board of Regents for a corresponding increase in student services, such as longer hours at the library and more contact time with faculty. But a spokesperson for the administration said that the money has already been earmarked for higher insurance premiums that the university is being charged and for the construction of a new addition to one of the dormitories, Nevin Hall."

M1: Well—I'm glad I have only one more semester to go. Otherwise, I just couldn't afford to go to school here.

14. What does the article that Nicole is reading say about Hambleton College?

15. Who is Penny Chang?

16. What can be inferred from the remark made by the spokesperson for the administration?

M2: Listen to a lecture in a linguistics class. The class has been discussing the differences between American English and British English.

M1: Today I'm going to talk a little about Noah Webster and the impact he had on American English. Webster was born in Connecticut in 1758 and graduated from Yale University in 1778, during the American Revolution. Right after graduation, Webster joined George Washington's army to fight against the British. The end of the war brought independence from Britain for the thirteen colonies, but political independence alone didn't satisfy Webster. He wanted the former colonies to be intellectually independent from Britain as well.

In 1783, Webster published a spelling book which would become known to generations of schoolchildren as the "blue-backed book" because of its blue cover. A couple of years later, he published his dictionary. It is for his dictionary that Webster is chiefly remembered today. The *Webster's Dictionary* popular today is a direct descendant of that book published in the 1780s.

In his dictionary, Webster made many changes in the way English was used in the United States. He suggested new ways of pronouncing words and added words used only in the former colonies to the language. Most of the changes, though, involved spelling. Today, most people in the United States spell certain words differently from people in Britain because of Webster's original dictionary. Let me just give you a couple of examples—in Britain, words like *center* end in *R-E*. In the United States, these words end in *E-R* because that's how they were spelled in Webster's dictionary. Webster also took out the letter *U* from words like *color*. In the British spelling, that word ends with the letters *O-U-R*, but in the American spelling, it ends with *O-R*.

Still, Webster did not go as far in revising spelling as his friend Benjamin Franklin wanted him to. Franklin wanted to drop all silent letters from words. The word *wrong* would have been spelled *R-O-N-G*, and the word *lamb* would have been L-A-M.

17. According to the speaker, when did Webster graduate from Yale University?
18. What is Noah Webster mainly remembered for today?
19. According to the speaker, what kind of book was the "blue-backed book"?
20. Which of the following are spellings that Benjamin Franklin would probably have approved of?

Section 2

STRUCTURE

PREVIEW TEST 2: STRUCTURE

1. one — The only choice that correctly completes this sentence is an appositive.

2. <u>thousand</u> — The plural verb *are* indicates that a plural subject, *thousands*, must be used.

3. or — The correct pattern is *neither . . . nor.*

4. have — A verb is required to complete the sentence.

5. <u>it was</u> — The use of the pronoun subject *it* is unnecessary; *it* should be omitted.

6. analysis of stars — For parallelism, a noun phrase is required.

7. <u>most old</u> — The superlative form of a one-syllable adjective (*old*) is formed with the suffix *-est*: *oldest.*

8. <u>which in</u> — The preposition must precede the relative pronoun: *in which.*

9. <u>are</u> — The subject of the clause (*one species*) is singular, so the singular verb *is* must be used.

10. as gold — The correct way to complete this comparison is by completing the *as* + adjective + *as* phrase (*as pliable as gold.*)

11. obtained — The only correct way to complete this sentence is with a participle (*obtained* really means *which is obtained*).

12. <u>engineer</u> — In order to be parallel with the other words in the series (*logic* and *probability*), the name of the field (*engineering*) must be used.

13. no — The adjective *no* is needed before the noun phrase *federal laws.*

14. <u>potential</u> — An adverb (*potentially*), not an adjective (*potential*), is needed.

15. Through — This sentence can be correctly completed only with an introductory prepositional phrase (*through experimental studies*).

16. <u>Despite</u> — *Despite* is only used before noun phrases. An adverb-clause marker (*although*) must be used with a clause.

17. <u>injure</u> — A noun (*injury*), not a verb (*injure*), is required.

18. the Statue of Liberty was given to the United States by the people of France — This is the only subject of the sentence that logically goes with the modifier, *Designed by . . .*

19. both of which — This choice correctly follows the pattern quantifier + *of* + relative pronoun.

20. Although — This sentence can be completed correctly only with an adverb clause introduced by the marker *Although.* (*Even though* would also be correct.)

21. That diamonds — This sentence can be completed correctly only with a noun clause introduced by the marker *That.*

22. <u>that</u> — The pronoun refers to a plural noun phrase (*public buildings*), so the plural pronoun *those* must be used.

23. are botanical gardens — A main verb such as *are* is required to complete the clause (*to be* is not a main verb), and the subject and verb must be inverted because the clause begins with the negative phrase *not only.*

24. <u>Since</u> — The verb in this sentence is in the past tense to indicate that something occurred at a specific time in the past. The preposition *In* should therefore replace *Since*. *Since* is used with the present perfect tense.

25. <u>believe</u> — The noun *belief* should be used in place of the verb *believe.*

STRUCTURE LESSONS AND REVIEW TESTS

Note: Items marked with an asterisk (∗) do not focus on the structures that are presented in that lesson. Corrections for error identification items appear in parentheses after the answer.

Exercise 13

1.	B	9.	A
2.	D	10.	B
3.	A	11.	A
4.	B	*12.	D
5.	A	13.	A
6.	D	14.	D
7.	C	15.	B
*8.	A	16.	C

Exercise 14

1.	D	*11.	A
*2.	C	12.	B
3.	C	13.	A
4.	B	14.	C
5.	C	15.	B
6.	A	16.	C
7.	A	17.	B
8.	A	*18.	B
9.	B	19.	D
*10.	C	20.	C

Exercise 15

1.	C	11.	C
2.	B	12.	C
3.	A	13.	C
4.	D	14.	A
5.	A	15.	A
*6.	B	*16.	C
7.	D	17.	C
8.	B	*18.	B
9.	D	19.	A
*10.	C	20.	D

Exercise 16

1.	D	7.	C
2.	B	8.	B
3.	A	9.	A
4.	D	10.	B
5.	D	11.	C
*6.	B	*12.	B

EXERCISE 17.1

1. C
2. X   the quality of the water (*or* the water quality)
3. C
4. X   warm
5. X   stories
6. C
7. X   grinding
8. X   religion
9. X   heat
10. X   a critic

EXERCISE 17.2

1. D	11. D
2. C	12. D
3. B	13. C
4. A	14. B
5. C	15. C
6. A	16. D
7. A	17. C
8. B	*18. C
9. C	19. C
10. A	20. A

REVIEW TEST D: STRUCTURE

1. The vacuum milking machine was invented — This choice correctly supplies a subject and a verb.

2. by which — The correct pattern is preposition + adjective clause marker.

3. that resemble — The adjective clause marker *that* is not needed and should be omitted.

4. when the work — The adverb clause marker, *when*, and the subject of the adverb clause, *the work*, are missing.

5. Despite — *Despite* is only used before noun phrases; before a clause an adverb clause marker such as *although* is needed.

6. colorful — The noun *color* is needed for parallelism.

7. That all deserts — Only a noun clause can correctly complete this sentence.

8. prevent — The verb *prevent* is needed for parallelism.

9. If two — An adverb clause is required to complete this sentence correctly.

10. There are many — This is the only choice that supplies the missing main verb.

11. safety — The adjective *safe* is needed for parallelism.

12. that — The adjective clause marker *that* cannot introduce an identifying (restrictive) adjective clause (one that is set off by commas); the marker *which* should be used instead.

13. a musician — A noun phrase is required for parallelism.

14. Although — This sentence can be correctly completed with a reduced adverb clause.

15. because their — The expression *because of* must be used in place of *because* before a noun phrase.

16. It takes — The only way to complete this sentence is with the pattern *It takes* + time expression + *for* someone /something + infinitive.

17. one of which, — This choice correctly follows the pattern quantifier + *of* + adjective clause marker.

18. uses it — The object pronoun *it* is used unnecessarily in this clause; the relative pronoun *which* is the object of the clause.

19. What psychologists   A noun clause is required to complete the call cognition sentence; the first choice incorrectly uses direct question word order.

20. <u>superstitious</u>   The noun *superstitions* is needed for parallelism.

EXERCISE 18.1

1. differ	difference		differently
2.	competition (*or* competitiveness)	competitive	competitively
3. deepen	depth	deep	
4. decide		decisive (*or* decided)	decisively (*or* decidedly)
5.	beauty (*or* beautification)	beautiful	beautifully
6.	prohibition	prohibitive (*or* prohibited)	prohibitively
7. emphasize	emphasis		emphatically
8. inconvenience	inconvenience		inconveniently
9. glorify (*or* glory)		glorious	gloriously
10.	mystery (*or* mystification)	mysterious	mysteriously
11. generalize	generality (*or* generalization)		generally
12. simplify	simplicity (*or* simplification)	simple	

EXERCISE 18.2

1.	musician	musical
2. surgery		surgical
3. poetry	poet	
4. technology		technological (*or* technical)
5.	administrator	administrative
6. finance	financier	
7. photography		photographic
8.	theoretician (*or* theorist)	theoretical (*or* theoretic)
9. athletics	athlete	
10.	grammarian	grammatical
11. philosophy		philosophical (*or* philosophic)
12. crime		criminal

EXERCISE 18.3

1. greatly	7. permanently
2. annually	8. widely
3. Regular	9. close
4. simple	10. easy
5. beautiful	11. incredible
6. Generally/simple	12. automatically

EXERCISE 18.4

1. fictional (Adj)
2. industry (N)/products (N)
3. fragrant (Adj))
4. mathematical (Adj)/equal (Adj)
5. severity (N)
6. development (N)
7. differ (V)/originate (V)
8. magician (PN)
9. depth (N)
10. distinction (N)/perfectly (Adv)
11. scholarly (Adj)/immigration (N)
12. food (N)/rainy (Adj)
13. symbolize (V)/occupation (N
14. relieve (V)
15. member (PN)/interpreter (PN)
16. outer (Adj)/constantly (Adv)

EXERCISE 18.5

1. intellectually (intellectual)
2. destruction (destructive)
3. important (importance)
4. analysis (analyzes)
5. dancers (dances)
6. strong (strength)
7. weigh (weight)
*8. purpose (purposes)
9. farms (farming)
10. good (well)
11. measuring (measurement)
12. literary (literature)
13. react (reaction)
14. sharp (sharpness)
15. live (life)
16. healthy (health)
17. neighbors (neighborhoods)
*18. exposed of (exposed to)
19. success (successful)
20. collect (collection)

EXERCISE 19.1

1. made
2. done
3. made
4. do
5. did
6. make
7. made
8. make

EXERCISE 19.2

1. so
2. too
3. So
4. such a
5. too
6. as
7. such a
8. so

EXERCISE 19.3

1. another
2. other
3. other
4. another
5. other
6. another
7. other
8. Other
9. other

EXERCISE 19.4

1. Many
2. little
3. much
4. few
5. number/amount
6. little
7. amounts
8. many

EXERCISE 19.5

1. before	9. tell
2. twice	10. never
3. afterwards	11. near
4. Most	12. live
5. age	13. percent
6. earliest	14. old
7. round	15. after
8. somewhat	16. most

EXERCISE 19.6

1. an alive (a live)	6. ever (never)
2. so much (as much)	*7. symbolize (symbol)
3. near (nearly)	8. making (doing)
4. age (of age, *or* old)	9. another (other)
5. few (little)	

EXERCISE 20.1

1. is	7. are
2. was	8. was
3. are	9. makes
4. was	10. are
5. is	11. is
6. are	12. varies

EXERCISE 20.2

1. X shipped	7. X are played
2. X was built	8. X was
3. X is known	9. X came
4. X worn	10. C
5. X has been growing	11. X ran
(*or* has grown)	12. C
6. X does	

EXERCISE 20.3

1. A	11. A
2. B	12. B
3. D	*13. B
4. D	14. D
5. C	*15. C
6. C	16. D
7. C	17. B
8. B	18. A
9. D	19. A
10. D	20. D

Exercise 21.1

1. known
2. astonishing
3. written
4. twisting
5. working
6. filled
7. named
8. appearing

Exercise 21.2

1. A
2. B
3. B
4. B
5. D
6. D
*7. D
8. A
9. A
10. C
*11. B
12. C
*13. D
*14. A
15. D
16. C

Exercise 22.1

1. to control
2. move
3. producing
4. to have
5. to grow
6. to catch
7. to communicate
8. bringing
9. to bend
10. miss
11. to snap
12. to rupture

Exercise 22.2

1. B
2. D
3. C
4. B
5. B
*6. B
7. C
*8. B
9. A
10. B
*11. D
12. D
13. A
14. D
15. A
16. B
17. C
18. C
19. D
20. C

Review Test E

1. A
2. C
3. B
4. C.
5. D
6. C
7. A
8. A
9. C
10. A
11. B
12. C
13. D
14. B
15. D.
16. A
17. C
18. B.
19. A
20. B
21. B
22. B
23. B
24. D
25. D

EXERCISE 23.1

1. X its
2. X it
3. X it
4. C
5. X its
6. X it
7. C
8. X those
9. X their

EXERCISE 23.2

1. X her
2. X them
3. C
4. X our
5. X themselves
6. C
7. X his
8. X its

EXERCISE 23.3

1. its (their)
2. they are (are)
3. themselves (them)
4. these (those)
5. them (themselves)
6. she helped (helped)
*7. Almost (Most)
8. its (their)
9. their (its)
10. they are (are)
11. himself (itself)
12. that (this)

EXERCISE 24

1. mammal (mammals)
2. humans (human)
3. automobiles (automobile)
4. years (year)
5. source (sources)
6. percents (percent)
*7. All college (All colleges)
8. thousand (thousands)
9. 500-pages (500-page)
10. man (men)
11. underwriter (underwriters)
12. appliance (appliances)
13. foot (feet)
*14. growth (grown)
15. farms (farm)
16. medicines (medicine)
17. more (most)
18. woman (women)
19. trillions (trillion)
20. sunlights (sunlight)

EXERCISE 25.1

1. in on of
2. For against within of
3. of to since into
4. At of of along between
5. of in of on in
6. at on to of
7. of in by with on
8. off of for of
9. In for from to
10. In at to on
11. In on of of at
12. to of by in of in
13. In of by of in through
14. on of to on
15. in for of in since

EXERCISE 25.2

1.	O	According polls to	11.	O	related the to
2.	O	Thanks improved to	12.	O	expert the on
3.	C		13.	C	
4.	I	of	14.	I	by
5.	I	on	15.	O	away the from
6.	O	regardless the of	16.	I	in
7.	C		17.	I	of
8.	O	aware the of	18.	O	side the of
9.	O	attached bones to	19.	O	familiar people to
10.	I	to	20.	I	in

EXERCISE 25.3

*1. Each
2. with a device
3. in which (which)
4. In
5. in the
6. Many of (Many)
7. Across
8. in its (on its)
*9. live (life)
10. with age
11. during (from)
12. with
13. on (in)
14. belongs one (belongs to one)
15. under the leadership of Samuel Gompers
16. are examples of
17. native of (native to)
18. There are some
19. on (in)
20. Since (For)
21. in use
22. thousands eggs (thousands of eggs)
23. In nowadays (Nowadays)
24. In (Since)
25. in width

EXERCISE 26.1

1. one the water fresh
2. The mineral the most fertilizers
3. The a electrical
4. Humor American the earliest the present
5. The ozone an most the Sun's
6. the early a Cherokee the a North
7. The Goddard New the the United the eighteenth
8. Popcorn the corn
9. the most research the social a well
10. the American the the twentieth its the a hundred
11. The nineteenth of his
12. The Hawaiian the most the world

EXERCISE 26.2

1. The most (Most)
2. the (their)
3. an attention (attention)
4. a underwater (an underwater)
5. young (the young)
6. an only (the only)
7. the third (a third *or* one third)
8. the customers (their customers *or* customers)
9. imaginary (an imaginary)
10. the beef (beef)
11. the career (her career)
12. first (the first)
13. a honor (an honor)
14. a highest (the highest)
15. a human (the human)
*16. record (recording)
17. the history (history)
18. At beginning (At the beginning)
*19. open (opened)
*20. lose it (lose them)

EXERCISE 27.1

1. X   chief source
2. X   brightly colored
3. C
4. X   is the Earth
5. X   the Earth is
6. C
7. X   miles longer
8. X   they are
9. X   natural habitats
10. X   it possible
11. X   dense enough
12. C
13. X   almost entirely
14. C
15. X   much too
16. X   children's books
17. X   Of all
18. X   too much
19. X   each second
20. X   All of

EXERCISE 27.2

1. extremely interesting features of
2. barrier major (major barrier)
3. is light (light is)
4. The most famous form
5. enough large (large enough)
6. did anyone even attempt
7. a crop grown primarily
8. much more efficiently than
9. benefit both (both benefit)
10. that are embedded in it
11. were primary schools free
12. moving slow (slow moving)
13. in such diverse occupations as
14. is it (it is)
*15. minerals grains (mineral grains)
16. original highly (highly original)
17. Perhaps the greatest triumph
18. one only (only one)
19. long feet (feet long)
20. corporations hardly ever introduce
21. lies Maryland's Eastern Shore
22. surrounded is (is surrounded)
23. those that grow best
24. satisfaction workers' (workers' satisfaction)
25. center trading (trading center)
26. Of the four types of
*27. lonely (loneliness)
28. for even small boats to navigate
29. none almost (almost none)
30. is international trade today

REVIEW TEST F

1. on one time — The wrong preposition is used; the phrase should correctly read *at one time*.

2. For her — Of the four choices, only a prepositional phrase correctly completes the sentence.

3. a third — Before an ordinal number (*third*), a definite article must be used: *the third*.

4. do redwood trees grow — After a negative adverb such as *rarely*, question word order must be used.

5. on — The preposition *in* is used before months.
6. instead a — The preposition *of* has been omitted from the phrase *instead of*.
7. are the most complex cells — Only this choice employs the correct word order.

8. a enormous — The article *an* must be used before words that begin with a vowel sound (*enormous*).

9. themselves — The correct pronoun is *them*. (The animals couldn't carry themselves!)
10. psychology human — The correct word order is *human psychology*.
11. a naturally occurring magnet — Only this choice uses the correct word order.

12. railroads — Only the second noun of a compound noun is pluralized: *railroad workers*.

13. furnitures — *Furniture* is an uncountable noun and cannot properly be pluralized.
14. long been known as — Of the four choices, only this one uses the correct word order.
15. itself — The pronoun must be plural (*themselves*) to agree with its referent, *flying squirrels*.

16. result of — The verb *result* is used with the preposition *in*. (The noun *result* is followed by the preposition *of*.)

17. all almost — The correct word order is *almost all*.
18. depend insects — The preposition *on* must be used after the verb *depend*.
19. enough safe — The correct word order is adjective + *enough: safe enough*.
20. With its — A prepositional phrase is needed to complete this sentence.

EXERCISE 28

1. both (either)
2. or
3. but also
*4. not longer (no longer)
*5. made
*6. it
7. and also (but also)
8. and
9. or (nor)
10. and (or)
11. either
*12. are used to (used to)
*13. produces (produce)
14. so
15. and (but)
*16. rust corrodes (does rust corrode)
17. or
*18. their (its)
19. as well as (but also)
*20. not the only substance
*21. require (requires)
22. but when
23. both frogs (frogs)
24. both
25. but

EXERCISE 29

1. like (alike)
2. not as sweet as
3. the most easiest (the easiest)
4. more strong (stronger)
5. are larger than
6. the more commonly (the most commonly)
7. than trains do
8. as (than)
9. the higher its
10. Unlike
11. worst (worse)
12. alike (like)
13. saltier than
14. like (as)
15. more serious than
16. more heavy (heavier)
17. bitter (more bitter *or* bitterer)
18. as that of honeybees
19. better known (best known)
20. the same as
21. less (least)
*22. contribution (contributions)
23. slender (more slender *or* slenderer)
24. largest (larger)
25. differs from

EXERCISE 30

1. the Republican party
2. Peer group relations, the
3. the first
*4. which is a part of the Rocky Mountains,
5. The dancer
*6. The Internet is
7. a method
8. members of a strict religious sect,
9. the term
10. a
11. a tropical plant of the orchid family,
12. taste buds, groups of cells

EXERCISE 31

1. many New Englanders emigrated to the Midwest in the 1820s
2. pecans are the most important nut crop in the southern United States
3. Pluto was discovered by the astronomer Clyde Tombaugh in 1930
4. the accordion has played only a limited role in classical music
5. vultures do not have feathers on their heads and necks
6. Ansel Adams' photographs depicted the Western wilderness
7. a tangerine is easy to peel and its sections separate readily
8. state and local governments obtain most of their funds through taxation
9. Hawaii received its first European visitor in 1778, when Captain James Cook landed there
10. Robert Frost wrote poems that were
11. Cornell University was established in 1865 by Ezra Cornell
12. Kate Chopin wrote *Bayou Folk*, a book about the folklore of

EXERCISE 32

1. no
2. not
3. not (no)
4. not
5. without
6. none
*7. alike (like)
8. not
9. no (not)
10. no
11. No
12. without
13. Not (No)
14. never
15. no longer

REVIEW TEST G

1. **The Welland Ship Canal,**   A noun phrase is needed to serve as subject of this sentence. (The phrase *one of Canada's . . .* is an appositive.)

2. **most highest**   The correct form of the superlative is *highest*.

3. **and**   The conjunction *but* is used before the word *rather* to show contrast.

4. **almost as old as**   The correct pattern is "*as* + adjective + *as . . .*"

5. **and**   The correct pattern is "whether A or B."

6. **the farther away it was**   This is a proportional statement; only this choice follows the pattern "The more A, the more B."

7. **D. W. Griffith's epic film *Birth of a Nation* was about the Civil War**   The participial phrase *Released in 1915* can logically modify only the title of a movie. For the first, second, and fourth choices, this is a misplaced modifier. Only in the third choice is the subject the title of a movie.

8. **like**   The correct pattern is "A and B are alike."

9. **None of**   The pronoun *none* means *not any* and is the only one of the choices that fits with the rest of the sentence. *No* and *Not* cannot be used before the article *the* and *Not one* must be used with *of*.

10. **like**   After certain verbs (including *serve*), the word *as* is used.

11. **a**   Of the four choices, only a noun phrase (an appositive) correctly completes the sentence.

12. **no**   Before a verb, the negative word *not* is needed.

13. **and**   There is a contrast between the information in the two clauses, so the conjunction *but* should be used.

14. **drugs can be used to treat the symptoms of many mental illnesses**   The modifying phrase *Properly administered* can logically only go with the subject *drugs*. Used with any of the other subjects, this is a misplaced modifier.

15. **alike**   The correct pattern is "A looked like B."

16. **or**   After *neither*, the conjunction *nor* should be used.

17. **A**   Only an appositive (which precedes the subject) correctly completes this sentence.

18. **just like**   The phrase *just as* should be used before a clause.

19. **No**   Before a noun, the negative adjective *no* should be used.

20. **much rare**   The comparative *rarer* is required.

21. **without**   The negative word *without*—meaning *not having*—is the only one that fits in this sentence.

22. **but**   Because of the contrast between the two clauses, the conjunction *but* must be used.

23. **either**   The correct pattern is "either A or B."

24. **most closest**   The correct superlative form is *closest*.

25. **Like**   The correct pattern is, "Like A, B . . ."

Section 3

READING

PREVIEW TEST 3: READING

1. **The correct answer is (B).** The passage discusses the plentiful supply of wood in the colonies and the advantages and disadvantages this involved.

2. **The correct answer is (B).** Strikingly means *dramatically*.

3. **The correct answer is (D).** Paragraph 2 states, "The first colonists did not, as many people imagine, find an entire continent covered by a climax forest."

4. **The correct answer is** abundant. Plentiful means *abundant*.

5. **The correct answer is (C).** Paragraph 2 states, "By the end of the colonial era, the price of wood had risen slightly in eastern cities . . ."

6. **The correct answer is (D).** Paragraph 3 indicates that, in the colonies, ". . . buildings were made of wood to a degree unknown in Britain." Therefore, many British houses must have been made of materials other than wood.

7. **The correct answer is (B).** According to paragraph 3, wood was the source of industrial compounds, and charcoal is given as an example. Charcoal is a component of gunpowder.

8. **The correct answer is (A).** The phrase follow suit means *do the same thing*.

9. **The correct answer is (A).** Paragraph 4 states that "Coke smelting led to technological innovations. . . ."

10. **The correct answer is** abandon. The opposite of cling to (which means *hold on to*) is *abandon*.

11. **The correct answer is** paragraph 4. The *X* should go by paragraph 4.

12. **The correct answer is (D).** The passage deals with the entire Peale family; the first and third choices are too specific, and the second is too general.

13. **The correct answer is** Charles Willson Peale. He refers to *Charles Willson Peale*.

14. **The correct answer is (A).** The passage indicates that the portrait was "so realistic" that Washington mistook the painted figures for real ones.

15. **The correct answer is** exhibits. The word displays is closest in meaning to *exhibits*.

16. **The correct answer is (D).** The author defines the term *mastodon* in paragraph 2 as "a huge, extinct elephant." The other terms are undefined.

17. **The correct answer is (D).** There is no information about when the museum was founded. All of the other questions are answered in the second paragraph: Charles Willson Peale found and prepared the animal exhibits; the museum was located in Philadelphia; its most popular exhibit, a mastodon's skeleton, was found on a farm in New York.

18. **The correct answer is (B).** The word unearthed means *dug up*.

19. **The correct answer is** fashion. In this context, rage means *fashion*.

20. **The correct answer is (B).** Charles Willson Peale painted over a dozen portraits of Washington (Paragraph 1); Rembrandt Peale also painted at least one (Paragraph 4).

21. **The correct answer is** His works show the same luminosity and attention to detail that the works of the Dutch masters show.

22. **The correct answer is (D).** Sarah Miriam Peale was Charles Willson Peale's niece (the daughter of his brother James Peale). Titian and Raphaelle are identified as Charles's sons in paragraph 1 and Reubens is identified as Charles's son in paragraph 3.

23. **The correct answer is (C).** The author praises the art and work of Charles Willson Peale and other members of the family; that, together with the absence of any critical comments, makes *admiring* the best choice.

24. **The correct answer is (A).** The main theme of this passage is the idea of transforming Mars.

25. **The correct answer is (A).** The word stark is closest in meaning to *harsh*.

26. **The correct answer is (C).** The word there refers to *Mars*.
27. **The correct answer is (A).** According to the passage, "The air there is 95% carbon dioxide."
28. **The correct answer is** Daytime temperatures may reach above freezing, but because the planet is blanketed by the mere wisp of an atmosphere, the heat radiates back into space.
29. **The correct answer is (B).** The passage states that "Daytime temperatures may reach above freezing," but there is no mention that temperatures ever become dangerously hot. The other characteristics are given in the first paragraph.
30. **The correct answer is (D).** According to the passage, building up the atmosphere "could create a 'greenhouse effect' that would stop heat from radiating back into space." The author points out that it is the fact that heat radiates back into space that makes Mars so cold.
31. **The correct answer is** melted. The word thawed is closest in meaning to *melted*.
32. **The correct answer is** viable. The word feasible is closest in meaning to *viable*.
33. **The correct answer is (D).** According to scientist Christopher McKay, the project could be started "in four or five decades"—forty or fifty years.
34. **The correct answer is (B).** The passage indicates that the possibility of transforming Mars comes from a "more profound understanding of how Earth's ecology supports life."
35. **The correct answer is** they. The word they refers to *researchers*.
36. **The correct answer is** astonishing. The word staggering means *astonishing*.
37. **The correct answer is (C).** The first paragraph indicates that age is "another" factor in susceptibility to colds; therefore, it is logical that a previous paragraph must deal with some other factor.
38. **The correct answer is** particulars. *Specific facts* is closest in meaning to the word particulars.
39. **The correct answer is (D).** Paragraph 1 states that the study "revealed particulars that seem to hold true for the general population."
40. **The correct answer is (A).** Paragraph 1 indicates that "Infants are the most cold-ridden group" and that infant boys have more colds than infant girls.
41. **The correct answer is** rate. The word incidence is closest in meaning to *rate*.
42. **The correct answer is (B).** No matter what age they are, parents of young children show an increase in cold infections; it is reasonable to assume that these parents are infected by their children.
43. **The correct answer is** people in their twenties. The phrase people in this age group refers to *people in their twenties*.
44. **The correct answer is (D).** This paragraph deals with the influence of economics on incidence of colds.
45. **The correct answer is** crowded. The word cramped means *crowded*.
46. **The correct answer is (3).** The study also found that economics plays an important role. **(1)** As income increases, the frequency at which colds are reported in the family decreases. **(2)** Families with the lowest income suffer a third more colds than families at the highest end. **(3)** Lower income generally forces people to live in more cramped quarters than those typically occupied by wealthier people, and crowded conditions increase the opportunities for the cold virus to travel from person to person. **Low income may also have an adverse effect on diet.** The degree to which deficient nutrition affects susceptibility to colds is not yet clearly established. **(4)** However, an inadequate diet is suspected of lowering resistance generally.

    The sentence beginning "The degree . . ." involves nutrition. This connects with the missing sentence, which introduces the relationship between economics and diet.
47. **The correct answer is** inadequate. The word deficient is closest in meaning to *inadequate*.
48. **The correct answer is (A).** This is an objective, scientific report about factors that influence the rate at which people get colds.
49. **The correct answer is (B).** The passage explores what can be learned by growing roots in isolation.
50. **The correct answer is (D).** The word themselves is a reference to *roots*.
51. **The correct answer is (A).** According to the passage, ATP is a "high-energy compound . . . which drives the biochemical reactions."
52. **The correct answer is** intact. The word intact means *whole*.
53. **The correct answer is (A).** The phrase comes in handy means *is useful*.

54. The correct answer is (D). The fact that roots provide organic nitrogen compounds is useful for "the growth of buds in the early spring when leaves are not yet functioning."

55. The correct answer is (C). The passage discusses an experiment involving plant roots and the significance of that experiment.

Exercise 33.1

1. (A) S
   (B) C
   (C) X
2. (A) G
   (B) S
   (C) C
3. (A) X
   (B) S
   (C) C
4. (A) X
   (B) C
   (C) I
5. (A) G
   (B) C
   (C) S
6. (A) G
   (B) S
   (C) C
7. (A) G
   (B) C
   (C) X
8. (A) C
   (B) X
   (C) I

Exercise 33.2

1. A
2. B
3. D
4. A
5. C
6. C
7. B
8. D
9. A
10. D
11. D

Exercise 33.3

1. C
2. A
3. D
4. B
5. C
6. C
7. A
8. A
9. C
10. A

Exercise 34.1

1. **The correct answer is** Deer use their antlers chiefly to fight for mates or for leadership of a herd.
2. **The correct answer is** The velvety skin dries up and the deer rubs the skin off by scraping its antlers against trees.
3. **The correct answer is** On most deer, the first antlers are short and straight.
4. **The correct answer is** In spite of his failings, he did succeed in bringing the traditions of Native Americans to the attention of the American public.
5. **The correct answer is** Their aim was to achieve complete accuracy in creating a record of Native American life.
6. **The correct answer is** This coating had to resist salt corrosion as well as protect launch structures from hot rocket exhaust.
7. **The correct answer is** The first attempt lasted only twelve seconds and covered a distance of less than the wingspan of the largest airplanes of modern aircraft.
8. **The correct answer is** The dominant features of supermarkets are large in-store inventories on self-service aisles and centralized checkout lines.
9. **The correct answer is** It permits the supermarket, as well as other types of retail stores, to sell items that carry a higher margin than most food items.

10. **The correct answer is** By not offering delivery and by hiring cashiers and stockers rather than true sales personnel, supermarkets are able to keep prices at a relatively low level.

11. **The correct answer is** Since argon is extremely dense, there is less movement of the gas between the glass panes and therefore, less heat is lost.

Exercise 34.2

1. **The correct answer is (B).**
2. **The correct answer is (B).**
3. **The correct answer is (B).**
4. **The correct answer is (A).**
5. **The correct answer is (C).**
6. **The correct answer is (A).**
7. **The correct answer is (B).**
8. **The correct answer is (C).**
9. **The correct answer is** paragraph 5
10. **The correct answer is (A).** The passage states that the dulcimer "is classified by musicologists as a box zither."
11. **The correct answer is (B).** The answer can be found in the eighth sentence.
12. **The correct answer is (A).** The passage states that dulcimers "are shaped like teardrops or hour-glasses."
13. **The correct answer is (A).** According to the passage, "most performers play the instruments while seated."
14. **The correct answer is (C).** See the last sentence.
15. **The correct answer is** Appalachian dulcimers are painstakingly fashioned by artisans in the mountains of West Virginia, Kentucky, Tennessee, and Virginia.
16. **The correct answer is (C).**
17. **The correct answer is** In 1841 Dix accepted an invitation from the state legislature to teach classes at a prison in East Cambridge, Massachusetts.
18. **The correct answer is (B).**
19. **The correct answer is (D).**
20. **The correct answer is** Dix's success was due to her independent and thorough research, her gentle but persistent manner, and her ability to secure the help of powerful and wealthy supporters.
21. **The correct answer is (D).**
22. **The correct answer is (A).**
23. **The correct answer is (C).**
24. **The correct answer is (C).**
25. **The correct answer is (C).**
26. **The correct answer is** These divers get their air from a hose connected to compressors on a boat.

Exercise 35.1

1. B
2. C
3. C
4. C
5. A
6. A
7. A
8. C
9. C
10. A
11. B
12. A

Exercise 35.2

1. D	12. C
2. D	13. B
3. D	14. B
4. C	15. A
5. B	16. D
6. B	17. B
7. C	18. C
8. B	19. B
9. B	20. B
10. B	21. C
11. D	

Exercise 36.1

1. **The correct answer is** drab
2. **The correct answer is** garbage
3. **The correct answer is** carries
4. **The correct answer is** freight
5. **The correct answer is** captures
6. **The correct answer is** initiated
7. **The correct answer is** course offerings
8. **The correct answer is** stressed
9. **The correct answer is** elective
10. **The correct answer is** group
11. **The correct answer is** haze
12. **The correct answer is** alone
13. **The correct answer is** clear
14. **The correct answer is** hunted
15. **The correct answer is** fearful
16. **The correct answer is** advantages
17. **The correct answer is** responsible
18. **The correct answer is** disagreements
19. **The correct answer is** afflict
20. **The correct answer is** terminate

Exercise 36.2

1. **The correct answer is** (A).
2. **The correct answer is** (C).
3. **The correct answer is** (C).
4. **The correct answer is** recent immigrants.
5. **The correct answer is** (D).
6. **The correct answer is** (B).
7. **The correct answer is** (D).
8. **The correct answer is** position.
9. **The correct answer is** (B).
10. **The correct answer is** (B).
11. **The correct answer is** competed.
12. **The correct answer is** (A).
13. **The correct answer is** unique to.
14. **The correct answer is** (C).
15. **The correct answer is** (A).
16. **The correct answer is** broad.
17. **The correct answer is** (C).

18. **The correct answer is** (D).
19. **The correct answer is** startling.
20. **The correct answer is** (B).
21. **The correct answer is** (A).
22. **The correct answer is** (A).
23. **The correct answer is** (D).
24. **The correct answer is** (C).
25. **The correct answer is** (B).
26. **The correct answer is** (B).
27. **The correct answer is** superbly.
28. **The correct answer is** primitive.
29. **The correct answer is** (D).

Exercise 37.1

1. **The correct answer is** paintings.
2. **The correct answers are** The anemone **and** its nest
3. **The correct answer is** (B).
4. **The correct answers are** a flat kite **and** tail.
5. **The correct answer is** Water.
6. **The correct answer is** (C).
7. **The correct answer is** smaller pieces.
8. **The correct answer is** Leaves.
9. **The correct answer is** (D).
10. **The correct answer is** mushrooms and other fungi.
11. **The correct answers are** Hamlin Garland **and** William Dean Howells.
12. **The correct answer is** The strange formations.

Exercise 37.2

1. **The correct answer is** the pieces.
2. **The correct answer is** trucks.
3. **The correct answer is** (D).
4. **The correct answer is** Water.
5. **The correct answer is** The metal particles.
6. **The correct answer is** (C).
7. **The correct answer is** the ore particles.
8. **The correct answer is** The mountain's summit.
9. **The correct answer is** glaciers.
10. **The correct answer is** (C).
11. **The correct answer is** The Wonderland Trail.
12. **The correct answer is** Their tracks.
13. **The correct answer is** (A).
14. **The correct answer is** The males.
15. **The correct answer is** (B).
16. **The correct answer is** tiny plants and animals.
17. **The correct answer is** Designers.
18. **The correct answer is** importance.
19. **The correct answer is** A circle and an oval.
20. **The correct answer is** a triangle.
21. **The correct answer is** (A).

Exercise 38

1. When a mammal is young, it looks much like a smaller form of an adult. **(1)** However, animals that undergo metamorphosis develop quite differently from mammals. **(2)** The young of these animals, which are called larvae, look very little like the mature forms and have a very different way of life. **(3)** Take the example of butterflies and caterpillars, which are the larval form of butterflies. **(4)** **Butterflies have two pairs of wings and six legs and feed on the nectar of flowers. (5)** Caterpillars, on the other hand, are wingless and have more than six legs. They move by crawling and feed on leaves. **(6)** To become adults, the larvae must radically change their forms. **(7)**

2. To accomplish this change, a larva must go through the process of metamorphosis. **(1)** It does this in the second stage of life, called the pupa stage. **(2)** When they are ready to pupate, caterpillars settle in sheltered positions. **(3)** Some spin a cocoon around themselves. **(4)** The caterpillar then sheds its old skin and grows a protective pupal skin. **(5)** Inside this skin, the body of the caterpillar gradually transforms itself. **(6)** The wingbuds, which were under the caterpillar's skin, grow into wings. **(7)** When the change is complete the pupal skin splits open and the butterfly emerges. **(8) At first it is damp and its wings are curled up. (9)** But soon it dries out, its wings unfurl, and it flies off. **(10)** Now it is ready to mate and to lay eggs that will develop into larvae. **(11)**

3. The process of miniaturization began in earnest with the transistor, which was invented in 1947. **(1)** It was much smaller than the smallest vacuum tube it was meant to replace and not needing a filament, it consumed far less power and generated virtually no waste heat. **(2)** There was almost no limit to how small the transistor could be once engineers had learned how to etch electronic circuits onto a substrate of silicon. **(3)** In the 1950s the standard radio had five vacuum tubes and dozens of resistors and capacitors, all hand-wired and soldered onto a chassis about the size of a hardbound book. **(4) Today all that circuitry and much more can fit into a microprocessor smaller than a postage stamp. (5)** In fact, the limiting factor in making appliances smaller is not the size of the electronic components but the human interface. **(6)** There is no point in reducing the size of a palm-held computer much further unless humans can evolve smaller fingers. **(7)**

4. It is believed that the first Americans were hunters who arrived by way of the only link between the hemispheres, the Siberian-Alaskan land bridge. **(1)** This strip of land remained above water until about 10,000 years ago. **More recent arrivals no doubt took the same route, crossing on winter ice. (2)** These migrants unquestionably brought with them the skills to make weapons, fur clothing, and shelters against the bitter cold. **(3)** It seems safe to assume that they also brought myths and folktales from the Old World. **(4)** But which myths and which folktales? **(5)**

5. Among myths, the most impressive candidate for Old World origin is the story of the Earth Diver. **(1)** This is the story of a group of water creatures who take turns diving for a piece of solid land. **(2)** The duck, the muskrat, the turtle, the crawfish, or some other animal succeeds but has to dive so deep that by the time it returns to the surface, it is half-drowned or dead. **But in its claws, the other animals find a bit of mud. (3)** The animals magically enlarge this tiny piece of solid land until it becomes the Earth. **(4)** Not every Native American tribe has a myth about the creation of the world, but of those that do, the Earth Diver myth is the most common. **(5)** It is found in all regions of North America except the Southwestern United States and the Arctic regions, and is also found in many locations in Asia and the Pacific Islands. **(6)**

6. Another common myth is that of the Theft of Fire. **(1)** In this story, a creature sets out to steal fire from a distant source, obtains it, often through trickery, and carries it home. **(2)** The best known version of this story is the Greek myth of Prometheus. **(3)** Other Old World versions of this story are told in Central Asia, India, and Africa. **In the New World, it appears among many Native American tribes west of the Rocky Mountains and in the American Southeast. (4)** In some New World locations it is replaced by Theft of the Sun, Theft of Daylight, or Theft of Heat stories. **(5)**

7. When drawing human figures, children often make the head too large for the rest of the body. **(1)** A recent study offers some insight into this common disproportion in children's illustrations. **(2)** As part of the study, researchers asked children between four and seven years old to make several drawings of adults. **(3)** When they drew frontal views of these subjects, the size of the heads was markedly enlarged. **However, when the children drew rear views of the adults, the size of the heads was not nearly so exaggerated.** The researchers suggest that children draw bigger heads when they know they must leave room for facial details. **(4)** Therefore, the distorted head size in children's illustrations is a form of planning ahead and not an indication of a poor sense of scale. **(5)**

8. It has been observed that periods of maximum rainfall occur in both the northern and southern hemispheres at about the same time. **(1)** This phenomenon cannot be adequately explained on a climatological basis, but meteors may offer a plausible explanation. **(2)** When the Earth encounters a swarm of meteors, each meteor striking the upper reaches of the atmosphere is vaporized by frictional heat. **(3)** The resulting debris is a fine smoke or powder. **(4)** This "stardust" then floats down into the lower atmosphere, where such dust might readily serve as nuclei upon which ice crystals or raindrops could form. **Confirmation that this phenomenon actually happens is found in the observed fact that increases in world rainfall come about a month after meteor systems are encountered in space. (5)** The delay of a month allows time for the dust to fall through the upper atmosphere. **(6)** Occasionally, large meteors leave visible traces of dust. **(7)** In a few witnessed cases, dust has remained visible for over an hour. **(8)** In one extreme instance—the great meteor that broke up in the sky over Siberia in 1908—the dust cloud traveled all over the world before disappearing. **(9)**

9. Lawn tennis is a comparatively modern modification of the ancient game of court tennis. **(1)** Major Walter C. Wingfield thought that something like court tennis might be played outdoors on the grass and in 1873 he introduced his new game under the name *Sphairistikè* at a lawn party in Wales. **It was an immediate success and spread rapidly, but the original name quickly disappeared. (2)** Players and spectators soon began to call the new game "lawn tennis." **(3)** In 1874 a woman named Mary Outerbridge returned to New York with the basic equipment of the game, which she had obtained from a British Army store in Bermuda. **(4)** The first game of lawn tennis in the United States was played on the grounds of the Staten Island Cricket and Baseball Club in 1874. **(5)**

10. The game went on in a haphazard fashion for a number of years. **Then in 1879, standard equipment, rules, and measurements for the court were instituted.** A year later, the U.S. Lawn Tennis Association was formed. **(1)** International matches for the Davis Cup began in 1900. **(2)** They were played at Chestnut Hill, Massachusetts between British and American players. **(3)** The home team won this first championship match. **(4)**

11. Photosynthesis is the process by which plants capture the Sun's energy to convert water and carbon dioxide into sugars to fuel their growth. **This process cannot take place without chlorophyll. (1)** In fact, chlorophyll is so essential to the life of plants that it forms almost instantly in seedlings as they come in contact with sunlight. **(2)** A green pigment, chlorophyll is responsible for the green coloring of plants. **(3)** But what turns the leaves of deciduous plants brilliant red and orange and gold in the autumn? **(4)**

12. Trees do not manufacture new pigments for fall. **(1)** Orange, red, yellow, and other colored pigments are present in the leaves throughout the spring and summer. **(2)** However, these are masked by the far greater quantity of chlorophyll. **(3)** When the days grow shorter and temperatures fall, trees sense the onset of fall. **(4)** They form an "abscission layer." **(5)** This layer is a barrier of tissue at the base of each leaf stalk. **It prevents nourishment from reaching the leaf and, conversely, prevents sugar created in the leaf from reaching the rest of the tree. (6)** Thus, sugar builds up in the leaf, causing the chlorophyll to break down. **(7)** The greens of summer then begin to fade. **(8)** The orange, red, yellow, and brown pigments now predominate, giving the leaves their vibrant autumn colors.

REVIEW TEST H

1. **The correct answer is (C).** The passage generally concerns the advantages of biological agents and the disadvantages of chemical agents.

2. **The correct answer is (A).** The word *marring* means *spoiling*.

3. **The correct answer is** impede. The word *hamper* is closest in meaning to the word *impede*.

4. **The correct answer is (C).** The author defines *weeds* as "any plants that thrive where they are unwanted" (sentence 2). No definitions are offered for the other terms.

5. **The correct answer is** injure. The word *harm* is closest in meaning to *injure*.

6. **The correct answer is (D).** Paragraph 2 says herbicides are sometimes necessary.

7. **The correct answer is (C).** Choice (A) is given in paragraph 4, which says that biological agents "leave crops and other plants untouched." Choice (B) is also given; chemical agents "harm workers who apply them." Choice (D) is given in paragraph 4; "biological agents can be administered only once," while chemical agents "typically must be used several times per growing season."

8. **The correct answer is (A).** According to the passage, the living organisms used to kill weeds are "primarily insects and microorganisms."

9. The biological agents now used to control weeds are environmentally benign and offer the benefit of specificity. **(1)** They can be chosen for their ability to attack selected targets and leave crops and other plants untouched, including plants that might be related to the target weeds. **In contrast, some of the most effective chemicals kill virtually all the plants they come in contact with. (2)** They spare only those that are naturally resistant or those that have been genetically modified for resistance. **(3)** Furthermore, a number of biological agents can be administered only once, after which no added applications are needed. **(4)** Chemicals typically must be used several times per growing season. **(5)**

   The phrase *In contrast* indicates that the missing sentence must follow a sentence that expresses an opposite idea. The main point of the missing sentence is that chemicals kill all the plants they come in contact with. The previous sentence talks about how biological agents are selective in the plants they kill.

10. **The correct answer is (C).** In this context, *applications* means *treatments* (with biological agents).

11. **The correct answer is** biological approaches. The word *they* refers to *biological approaches*.

12. **The correct answer is** conventional. The word *standard* is closest in meaning to *conventional*.

13. **The correct answer is (C).** The problem is the need to control weeds; the possible solutions are the use of chemical or biological agents.

14. **The correct answer is (A).** The author refers to the fact that Bernstein's score is "brilliant," that Stephen Sondheim "revealed a remarkable talent," and that Jerome Robbins' choreography is "electrifying." All of these positive factors, and the absence of negative ones, add up to a favorable attitude.

15. **The correct answer is (B).** Paragraph 1 says the play "is set in the early 1950s."

16. **The correct answer is (A).** Paragraph 1 mentions "The Montagues and Capulets of Shakespeare's play" and compares them with the Jets and Sharks in *West Side Story*.

17. **The correct answer is** opposing. The word *rival* means *opposing*.

18. **The correct answer is** The plot tells the story of Maria, a Puerto Rican whose brother Bernardo is the leader of the Sharks, and of Tony, a member of the Jets.

19. **The correct answer is (D).** Paragraph 2 states: "Stephen Sondheim . . . revealed a remarkable talent for writing lyrics."

20. **The correct answer is (B).** A score is the written form of a piece of music.

21. **The correct answer is** thrilling. The word *electrifying* is closest in meaning to *thrilling*.

22. **The correct answer is** Academy Awards. The word *ones* refers to *Academy Awards*.

23. **The correct answer is (B).** The second paragraph says that "Before *West Side Story*, no one thought that dance could be as integral to a narrative as the music and the lyrics. But the dances in *West Side Story* are among the most thrilling elements of the play."

24. **The correct answer is (D).** Paragraph 3 indicates that, after it first opened, the play ran for 734 performances in New York.

25. **The correct answer is (A).** Paragraph 1 states that "the black tie [i.e., very formal] audience treated the occasion . . . as a social affair."

26. **The correct answer is (A).** Paragraph 2 states that "German engineer Karl Benz built what are regarded as the first modern cars in the mid-1880s."

27. **The correct answer is** But the United States pioneered the merchandising of the automobile.

28. **The correct answer is (B).** 8,000 There were about 8,000 people at the 1900 National Automobile Show, according to paragraph 1. By coincidence, this was the same number of automobiles as there were in the United States in 1900 (paragraph 3).

29. **The correct answer is (C).** By happenstance means *Coincidentally*.

30. **The correct answer is (B)** According to the passage, only around 4,000 cars were assembled in the United States in 1900, and only a quarter of those were gasoline powered (paragraph 3). One quarter of 4,000 is 1,000.

31. **The correct answer is (A).** Paragraph 4 states that "the show's audience favored electric cars because they were quiet."

32. **The correct answer is** smelly. The word *fragrant* is most nearly opposite in meaning to the word *smelly*.

33. **The correct answer is (C).** According to the passage, "The Duryea Motor Wagon Company . . . offered a fragrant additive designed to mask the smells of the naphtha that it burned."

34. **The correct answer is (A).** The word is closest in meaning to *clumsy*.

35. **The correct answer is (B).** Paragraph 4 indicates that the Gasmobile, Franklin, and Orient steered with tillers (devices used to steer boats); the Duryea probably used a steering wheel.

36. **The correct answer is** wealthy. The word *well-to-do* is closest in meaning to *wealthy*.

37. **The correct answer is** These early model cars were practically handmade and were not very dependable. (1) They were basically toys of the well-to-do. (2) In fact, Woodrow Wilson, then a professor at Princeton University and later President of the United States, predicted that automobiles would cause conflict between the wealthy and the poor. (3) However, among the exhibitors at the 1900 show was a young engineer named Henry Ford. **The cars he exhibited at the 1900 show apparently attracted no special notice.** (4) But before the end of the decade, he would revolutionize the automobile industry with his Model T Ford. (5) The Model T, first produced in 1909, featured a standardized design and a streamlined method of production. (6) Its lower costs made it available to the mass market. (7) The missing sentence clearly refers to the exhibitor, Henry Ford. The first word in the following sentence is *but*, indicating contrast. The contrast involves the fact that, at the 1900 show, Ford's cars were not especially noticed, but in a few years, he would completely change the industry.

38. **The correct answer is (B).** Paragraph 6 indicates that the highest-priced cars at the show sold for $1,500 in 1900 dollars.

Section 4

ESSAY WRITING

EXERCISE 39.1

Answers will vary. These analyses are given as samples.

TYPE A

Prompt 1

This prompt says that there are two opinions regarding basic educational philosophy. Education can emphasize either competition or cooperation. I have to decide which of these I want to support.

 If I choose to support cooperation, I need to show how learning to cooperate will be useful in later life—for example, being able to work with one's colleagues. If I choose to defend the opposite idea, I can show the advantages of being a competitive person—in sports, in business, and so on. Or I might say that a good education should teach people that at times they must cooperate well and at times they must be strong competitors.

Prompt 2

When writing this essay, I have to show the benefits of either on-campus living or off-campus living. One advantage of dorm living is convenience. Another is that it provides opportunities for making friends. I could support this by giving examples of how dorm living makes life easy for students and encourages them to interact with other students. The main advantages of off-campus living are independence and privacy, I suppose. If I choose to take this side, I'll need to think of ways that living off-campus can make someone a better student and better prepared for adult life.

TYPE B

Prompt 3

There are two possible approaches to writing this essay. I can give a number of reasons why athletes and entertainers make far too much money for what they do, especially when compared with people who contribute much more to society than they do. If I choose to defend the other point of view, I have to justify these large salaries. I could say that, like any other workers, they are simply getting the salary that people are willing to give them for their services, and also that they bring a lot of entertainment and enjoyment to people.

Prompt 4

I could choose to agree with this statement. If I do, I have to show how taking a wide variety of classes makes a person well-rounded and better informed. I might say that it is fine for graduate students to specialize, but that undergraduates need to be generalists with some knowledge of history, science, math, art, and all the other important fields. On the other hand, if I take the opposite side, I have to give reasons why it is a good idea to concentrate only on one field of interest.

 I might say, for example, that for students in scientific and technical fields, there is so much to learn in four years that it is impossible for them to take many electives.

Type C

Prompt 5

For this prompt I must choose a figure from the past that I want to talk to. It could be someone internationally famous, such as Julius Caesar, Simón Bolívar, Abraham Lincoln, or Mahatma Gandhi. Or I could choose to speak to someone who is important to me personally, such as my great-great-grandfather. It will probably be best if I choose someone I know quite a bit about, and preferably someone in a field that I am interested in. I could choose Pele, for example, because I'm interested in football, or Adam Smith because I'm interested in economics. The most important things are to have good reasons why I want to talk to the person that I choose and to have some specific questions I'd like to ask this person.

Prompt 6

The prompt says that I can fund any one of a variety of city services. To write this essay, I need to decide what kind of service my hometown needs most. For example, if there is a high crime rate, then I could make a good case for funding the police department. It would probably be easy to explain why funding should go to schools or hospitals, because almost any community needs improvements in education and health care.

Exercise 39.2

Answers will vary.

Exercise 39.3

Answers will vary.

Exercise 40.1

Answers will vary.

Exercise 40.2

Answers will vary.

Exercise 40.3

Answers will vary.

Exercise 41.1

There may be several ways to join some of these sentences.

1. One of the most important holidays in my country is Independence Day, **which** is celebrated on September 16th.
2. Young children have a special talent for language learning, **so** they should be taught other languages at an early age.
   Because young children have a special talent for language learning, they should be taught other languages at an early age.
3. **Since** my brother began studying at the university, he has taken several large classes.
4. **Even though** some forms of advertising serve a useful purpose, many other forms do not. Some forms of advertising serve a useful purpose, **but** many other forms do not.
5. A friend is an acquaintance **who** will help you whenever possible.
6. I believe corporations should do more to recycle materials **and** to reduce air pollution.
7. Small classes are the best environment for learning, **but** sometimes universities must have large classes. **Although** small classes are the best environment for learning, sometimes universities must have large classes.

EXERCISE 41.2

Answers will vary for sentences 1–4.

5. In small classes, students get more personal attention.
6. If I needed to get in touch with a business associate, I would use e-mail.

EXERCISE 41.3

(Introduction 2)

Many students believe that small classes offer better educational opportunities than large ones. **However**, in my experience, that is not necessarily true. I believe that, with a good teacher, a large class can provide as good a learning opportunity as a small one.

(Body 1)

However, other people believe that space research has provided many benefits to humankind. They point out that hundreds of useful products, from personal computers to heart pacemakers to freeze-dried foods, are the direct or indirect results of space research. They say that weather and communication satellites, which are also products of space research, have benefited people all over the globe. In addition to these practical benefits, supporters of the space program point to the scientific knowledge that has been acquired about the Sun, the Moon, the planets, and even our own Earth as a result of space research.

(Body 2)

When I was an undergraduate student, most of the large classes I took were introductory classes for first- and second-year students. For example, I took classes in world history and economics that had more than 100 students and met in large lecture halls. I think these classes were as good as some of the small classes I took later. At the basic level, the lectures that a professor gives are basically the same no matter what size the class is. **Moreover**, the professors who taught these classes seemed more enthusiastic and energetic than the teachers I had in smaller classes. **Personally**, I think they enjoyed having a large audience! One supposed advantage of small classes is that there is usually a lot more interaction among students and between the teacher and the students than in large classes. **However**, in the large classes I took, there were discussion sessions held every week with a graduate teaching assistant in which there was a lot of interaction. **Besides**, the teachers for these classes had long office hours, and they were always willing to answer questions and talk over problems.

(Body 2)

The most obviously important characteristic of jet travel is the high speed involved. A hundred years ago, it took weeks to cross the Atlantic or Pacific Oceans by ship. **However**, today, those same trips can be completed in a matter of hours. One can attend a meeting in Paris and have dinner in New York the same day. These amazing speeds have changed people's concepts of space. Today the world is much smaller than it was in the past.

Another important aspect of jet travel is its relatively low cost. An international journey one hundred years ago was extremely expensive. Only wealthy people could afford to travel comfortably, in first class. Poor people had to save for years to purchase a ticket, and the conditions in which they traveled were often miserable. Today it is possible for more and more people in every country to travel in comfort. **Thus** it is possible for business people to do business all over the world, for students to attend universities in other countries, and for tourists to take vacations anywhere in the world.

(Conclusion 1)

I agree with those people who support space research and want it to continue. Space research, as shown, has already brought many benefits to humanity. Perhaps it will bring even more benefits in the future, ones that we can't even imagine now. **Moreover**, just as individual people need challenges to make their lives more interesting, I believe the human race itself needs a challenge, and I think that the peaceful exploration of outer space provides just such a challenge.

(Conclusion 2)

In conclusion, I don't think that the size of a class is very important. I think that learning depends more on the quality of the teaching than on the number of students in the class.

(Conclusion 3)

To summarize, the speed and low cost of international jet travel have changed the world.

Individual nations are not as isolated as they were in the past, and people now think of the whole planet as they once thought of their own hometowns.

EXERCISE 41.4

1. I believe that women should have the right to serve in the military. **However**, I don't believe that they should be assigned to combat roles.
2. Many actors, rock musicians, and sports stars receive huge amounts of money for the work that they do. **For example**, a baseball player was recently offered a contract worth more than twelve million dollars. **Personally**, I feel that this is far too much to pay a person who simply provides entertainment.
3. The development of the automobile has had a great impact on people everywhere. **Likewise**, the development of high-speed trains has had an impact on people in many countries, including my home country of France.
4. I used to work in a restaurant when I was in college. I realize what a difficult job restaurant work is. **Therefore**, whenever I go out to eat, I try to leave a good tip for my waiter or waitress.
5. Many people would agree with the idea that the best use for the open space in our community is to build a shopping center. **On the other hand,** there are other people who feel we should turn this open space into a park.

EXERCISE 41.5

There are a number of ways to correctly rewrite this essay.

There are certain people who always like to take their vacations in the same place. They return from a vacation and ask themselves, "When can I go back there again?" There are other people who like to go many places. They like to do many different things on their vacations.

When they return from a vacation, they ask themselves, "Where can I go next?" My parents are perfect examples of the first kind of people. They always like to go to a lake in the mountains where they went on their honeymoon. They bought a vacation cabin there several years after they were married. They have gone there two or three times a year for over twenty-five years. My parents have made friends with the people who also own cabins there. They enjoy getting together with them. Both my parents enjoy sailing and swimming, and my father likes to go fishing. My parents enjoy variety, but they say they can get variety by going to their cabin at different times of the year. They particularly like to go there in the autumn when the leaves are beautiful.

I am an example of a person who likes to go to different places for her vacation. When I was a child, I went to my parents' cabin, but when I got older, I wanted to travel to many different places. I spent a lot of time and money learning how to ski, so I wanted to travel to places where I could ski, such as Switzerland. I was interested in visiting historic places, so I went to Angkor Wat in Cambodia, even though it was difficult to get there. I would like to go to Egypt, because I want to see the pyramids, and to Rome to see the Coliseum.

Although I enjoy going to familiar places, I find that going to strange places is more exciting. The world is so huge and exciting that I don't want to go to the same place twice. Still, I understand my parents' point of view. They believe that you can never get to know a place too well.

EXERCISE 41.6

Answers will vary.

EXERCISE 42.1

There are several ways in which some of the errors in these paragraphs can be corrected.

Paragraph 1

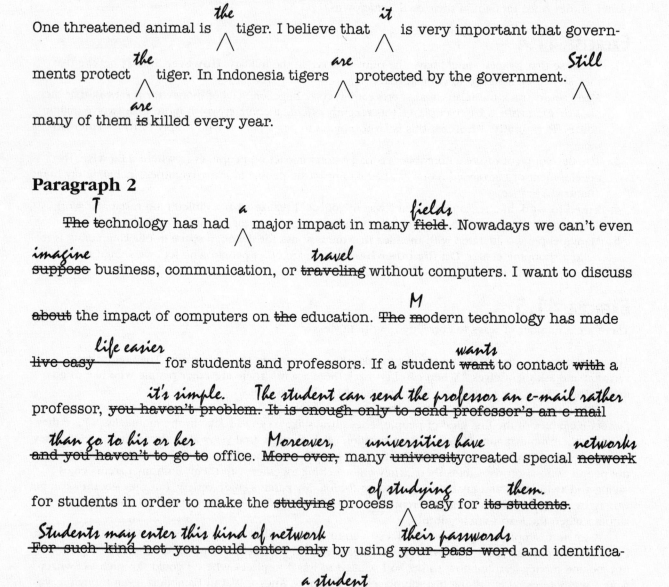

There ~~is~~ *are* many species of animals in the world threatened with extinction.

One threatened animal is ^*the* tiger. I believe that ^*it* is very important that governments protect ^*the* tiger. In Indonesia tigers ^*are* protected by the government. ^*Still* many of them ~~is~~ *are* killed every year.

Paragraph 2

~~The~~ *T*echnology has had ^*a* major impact in many ~~field~~ *fields*. Nowadays we can't even ~~suppose~~ *imagine* business, communication, or ~~traveling~~ *travel* without computers. I want to discuss ~~about~~ the impact of computers on ~~the~~ education. ~~The~~ *M*odern technology has made ~~live easy~~ *life easier* for students and professors. If a student ~~want~~ *wants* to contact ~~with~~ a professor, ~~you haven't problem. It is enough only to send professor's an e-mail~~ *it's simple. The student can send the professor an e-mail rather* ~~and you haven't to go to~~ *than go to his or her* office. ~~More over,~~ *Moreover,* many ~~university~~ *universities have* created special ~~network~~ *networks* for students in order to make the ~~studying~~ process ^*of studying* easy for ~~its students~~ *them*. ~~For such kind net you could enter only~~ *Students may enter this kind of network* by using ~~your pass word~~ *their passwords* and identification number. There are many categories ~~you~~ *a student* can choose to enter, such as "student tools" or "assignment box" ~~where you can know about your homeworks~~ *which contains homework assignments.*

~~Also is~~ *It is also* possible to access ~~to~~ the university library to ~~make~~ *do* researche~~s~~.

Computers also give students *the* opportunity to gather information~~s~~ about various

topic*s* from the ~~internet~~. ~~It~~ *This* is one of ~~most~~ easiest ways ~~of making~~ *the* research *for students to do*.

One other way that computers can help students, especially those from ~~another~~

countries, ~~to stay~~ *is to allow students to stay in* touch with their ~~freinds~~ *friends* and family at ~~their~~ home~~,~~ *.* ~~personally~~ *P*

I could not study in ~~usa~~ *the USA* if *I were* not *in* contact with my family, because I am

both *a* student ~~as well as work as~~ *and* a manager in my ~~families~~ *family's* business so I must

stay *in* touch with my ~~assistents~~ *assistants*.

Paragraph 3

One of the most interesting ~~book I am reading~~ *books I have read* recently was a biography

of ~~winston~~ *W* ~~churchill~~ *C*. ~~he~~ *H* was *the* prime minister of ~~the~~ ~~great~~ *G* ~~britain~~ *B* during

~~the~~ *W* ~~world~~ *W* ~~war~~ *O* II. ~~of~~ *O* course many ~~peopel~~ *people* know what a great ~~leadership~~ *leader* he was

during the war. ~~but~~ *B* I found his life before and after the war ~~were~~ *was* also very

interesting.

Paragraph 4

Some people ~~are believing~~ *believe* that *it* is impossible ~~falling~~ *to fall* in love with someone

"at first sight." ~~In~~ *On* the other hand, there are ~~others~~ *other* people who ~~are believing~~ *believe* that

you ~~recognition~~ *recognize* a person that you love immediately. I know ~~its~~ *it's* possible ~~falling~~ *to fall* in

love at first sight ~~Because~~ *b*ecause this happened to my wife and ~~I~~ *me*.

Paragraph 5

If you are ever in ~~thailand~~ (T) in *the* month of ~~may~~ (M) I suggest you ~~to~~ go to the Rocket Festival. It *is* held every year in a small town called ~~yasothon~~ (Y) about 300 ~~mile~~ *miles* from ~~b~~ (B)-angkok. ~~bangkok has many beautiful temples, including the temple of the dawn.~~*

This festival is well known ~~and famous~~ in Thailand. People from all over the country join the local people in ~~celebrate~~ *celebrating*. The local farmers launch ~~hundred~~ *hundreds* of colorful rockets ~~for gaining~~ *to gain* the favor of spirits ~~who~~ *whom* they believe will bring rain to their rice crops. However, if you go, you need ~~being~~ *to be* careful. Both farmers ~~or~~ *and* tourists ~~sometime injure~~ *are sometimes injured* or even ~~kill~~ *killed* by rockets that ~~goes~~ *go* out of control.

Paragraph 6

When I was *a* child I ~~live~~ *lived* in the town of Sendai, the biggest city in the ~~north~~ *northern* part of Japan. My grandmother ~~live~~ *lived* in Tokyo, ~~W~~*w*hich is in the ~~center~~ *central* part of ~~japan~~ (J). While I was ~~live~~ *living* in Sendai, I often went to see my grandmother, but it ~~takes~~ *took* five hours to get to ~~tokyo~~ (T) by local train. ~~Since~~ *In* 1983, the high-speed express train called the "Shinkansen" *was* built, and connected ~~between~~ Sendai and Tokyo. For me personally, this was *the* most ~~important~~ *important* development in transportation. It now takes only ~~a~~ *an* hour and *a* half to travel to Tokyo from Sendai. The trip ~~become~~ *became* very easy. It also ~~was~~ *had* a great impact on Sendai. ~~Economics~~ *Economic* development there increased. ~~In~~ *On* the negative side, prices for housing and other things went up. ~~In~~ *On* the whole, however, this development was very ~~big benefit~~ *beneficial* for the city.

EXERCISE 42.2
Answers will vary.

*This whole sentence is irrelevant to the paragraph.

Practice Test

SECTION 1: LISTENING

Part A

1. C
2. A
3. A
4. A
5. D
6. D
7. B
8. C
9. D
10. C
11. D
12. A
13. B
14. A
15. A

Part B

16. C
17. B
18. B
19. D
20. C, A, B
21. A
22. A
23. A, D
24. C
25. A
26. C
27. D, A, B
28. A, D.
29. B, C, A
30. B
31. A
32. C
33. D
34. C
35. C
36. C
37. B, D
38. A

AUDIO SCRIPT

Part A

1. F1: Excuse me—do you know which apartment Sally Hill lives in?
    M1: Sally Hill? As far as I know, she doesn't live in this apartment complex at all.
    M2: What does the woman imply about Sally Hill?

2. F2: Mary, may I use your phone? I think mine is out of order.
    F1: Feel free.
    M2: What does Mary tell the woman?

3. F1: Is Lillian still planning to study overseas?
    M1: No, her parents threw cold water on that plan.
    M2: What did Lillian's parents do?

4. M1: Uh, oh. Your roommate's making dinner again. Your kitchen is going to look like a tornado hit it.
    F1: Maybe not. Last night she cooked dinner and left the kitchen spick-and-span.
    M2: What does the woman say her roommate did last night?

5. F1: That's a beautiful old oak tree over there, but it needs to be sprayed—it has a parasite, I think.
    F2: How did you learn so much about trees?
    F1: Mostly from my father—he studied forestry in college.
    M2: How did the woman mainly learn about trees?

6.   *(Ring . . . Ring . . . Sound of phone being picked up)*
    M1: Hello.
    F2: Hi, Tom, this is Brenda. Since you didn't go to class today, I just thought I'd call to tell you that Professor Barclay said we're going to have to write a research paper for his class.
    M1: Really? And how long do we have to finish it?
    M2: What does Tom ask Brenda?

7.   M1: Julie certainly seems to like classical music.
    F2: She doesn't like just *any* classical music.
    M2: What does the woman imply about Julie?

8.   F1: How did you do on Professor Dixon's history test?
    M1: Probably not too well. I skipped a couple of questions and I didn't have time to go back to them.
    M2: What does the man say about the history test?

9.   F2: How do you like this desk I just bought?
    M1: It's beautiful. It must be an expensive antique.
    F2: It may look like that, but I got it for next to nothing.
    M2: What does the woman say about the desk?

10. M1: Hi, Emma. On your way home?
    F1: I wish I were. I still have two more classes today. I'd much rather be out there enjoying the sunshine.
    M1: Yeah, it's nice for a change, isn't it?
    M2: What can be inferred from the conversation?

11. M1: Gary's using that old tape player of yours.
    F2: He's welcome to it.
    M2: What does the woman mean?

12. F2: Who are you going to vote for to be president of the Student Assembly?
    M1: I think Ed Miller is the best choice.
    F2: So do I—now that Margaret Ling has dropped out of the race.
    M2: What does the woman mean?

13. F1: I'm going to Stephanie's house. I have an assignment to complete, and I need to use her computer.
    M1: Why don't you buy one of your own? Think how much time you could save.
    M2: What does the man suggest the woman do?

14. M1: I just ran into Shelly at the Recreation Center—she said to say hello to you.
    F2: How is she? The last time I spoke to her, she said she hadn't been feeling too well.
    M1: Well, when I saw her this morning, she was the picture of health.
    M2: What does the man say about Shelly?

15. F1: I'm really excited about going camping this weekend.
    M1: You're going camping? Then you don't have to study for that physics test after all?
    M2: What had the man originally assumed about the woman?

Part B

Questions 16–18

    F1: Walter, I know you signed up for Professor Crosley's anthropology class. Why haven't you been coming?
    M1: What do you mean? I've been there every morning!
    F1: Every morning? I don't understand. Oh, I get it—you must be in her morning class in cultural anthropology. I'm in her afternoon class in social anthropology. So tell me, how do you like the class?
    M1: Oh, it's pretty interesting. So far, we've been studying the art, the architecture, and the tools of different cultures. And Saturday, our class is going down to the local museum. There's going to be an exhibit of the artifacts of the early inhabitants of this area.
    F1: Your class has quite a different focus from mine. We're studying social relations in groups. For example, this week we've been talking about marriage customs and family life in lots of societies—including our own.

16. What do the two speakers have in common?
17. When does the woman's class meet?
18. Which of the following topics would most likely be discussed in the man's class?

Questions 19–23

M2: Listen to part of a lecture in an engineering class. The class has been discussing various types of aircraft.

M1: How many of you were at the football game Saturday night? Did you notice the blimp circling the stadium? That was the blimp *Columbia*. Today's blimps are much smaller descendants of the giant airships that were used in the early twentieth century.

There are really three types of airships. All of them are lighter-than-air balloons that use engines for power and rudders for steering. Rigid airships contained a number of envelopes or gas cells full of hydrogen. Their shape was determined by a rigid framework of wood or metal. The first rigid airships were flown in Germany by Count Zeppelin in the early 1900s, so they are sometimes called zeppelins. They were used in military operations in World War I. Afterwards, they were used to transport passengers, even taking them across the Atlantic. Another type was the semi-rigid airship, developed in the 1920s. They looked much like rigid airships, but their shape was maintained by a combination of gas cells and a longitudinal frame made of metal.

They were also used for passenger service, military operations, and exploration. The Italian semi-rigid *Norge* was the first airship to fly over the North Pole. Non-rigids were the last type of airship to be developed, and the only kind still flying. They are much smaller than the other two types, and their shape is maintained only by the pressure of gas inside the balloon. They are also much safer because they use helium instead of hydrogen, which burns very easily. They are sometimes called blimps. The blimp *Columbia*, which was flying over the football stadium Saturday night, is non-rigid.

As you may know, the era of the large airships came to an end in Lakehurst, New Jersey, in 1937. The famous German rigid airship, *Hindenburg*, full of hydrogen, caught fire and exploded while on a trip to the United States. After that, only a few non-rigid blimps such as the Columbia have been built. They are mainly used for advertising, aerial photography, and sightseeing trips.

Some engineers, though, hope that large rigid airships will someday fly again. These airships of the future would be equipped with jet engines and filled with helium. They could be used to transport either passengers or cargo. They would not be as fast as today's jet airplanes, but they would be much more fuel-efficient.

19. What is the main subject of the lecture?
20. Match the type of airship with the category in which it belongs.
21. What does the speaker say about the Italian airship *Norge*?
22. What event in the history of airships took place in Lakehurst, New Jersey, in 1937?
23. What can be inferred about airships of the future?

Questions 24–26

M2: Listen to a conversation between two students.

F1: Hi, Ted. I just read in the campus paper that your creative writing class is going to be giving a public reading Friday.

M1: Yes, in the ballroom at the Student Union building.

F1: Are you going to be reading some of your poems? You know, I love that poem you wrote about growing up in Alaska.

M1: Thanks. No, I haven't been writing poetry lately. I've been working on a novel, so I'll read from that on Friday.

F1: A novel? What's it about?

M1: It's about working on a commercial fishing boat.

F1: Really? Do you know much about that?

M1: Well, my grandfather owned a fishing boat, and when I was in high school, I worked on it during the summers. And he told me a million stories about fishing. Of course, I've changed the stories somewhat and fictionalized all the characters for my novel.

F1: Wow, that sounds like it might be an interesting book. Well, I'll try to be there on Friday for the reading.

24. What will Ted be doing on Friday?

25. What has Ted been writing most recently?

26. What is the subject of Ted's most recent writing?

Questions 27-32

M2: Listen to part of a lecture in a geology class.

M1: Good morning, class. As I said at the end of Wednesday's class, today we're going to talk about glaciers. Glaciers begin with ordinary snow. Normal snow is about 80 percent air space and about 20 percent solids. Now, when snow doesn't melt, it compacts. Much of the air space disappears, and the snow becomes granular ice called *firn*. Then, as the glacier becomes larger, deeply buried ice becomes even more compressed—about 90 percent solid-and becomes glacial ice. As the pressure from the weight of accumulated ice builds, the ice on the underside of the glacier becomes pliable enough to flow—usually only a few centimeters a day—and a glacier is born. There are three main types: valley glaciers, piedmont glaciers, and continental glaciers. Valley glaciers are small glaciers that are confined to a mountain valley.

Piedmont glaciers are formed where one or more flow out of their valleys and join together. Continental glaciers are giant, thick, slow-moving sheets of ice. Today, there are only two continental glaciers, one in Antarctica, one in Greenland, but during the Ice Ages, continental glaciers covered most of the northern hemisphere. By definition, continental glaciers cover at least 10,000 square kilometers. The average continental glacier was about the size of the entire state of West Virginia.

At some point, glaciers become stationary. In other words, they appear to stop moving. That's because they are melting at the same rate at which new ice is being added. Then they begin to recede. When they recede, glaciers actually appear to be moving uphill. However, what's really happening is that they are melting faster than they are adding new material.

Because glaciers are so heavy, they can cause large-scale erosion and create interesting features in the process. I'll just mention a couple of those for now. One is called a *cirque*, which is an amphitheater-shaped hollow, carved out of a mountainside. When a single mountain has cirques on at least three of its sides, the peak of the mountain takes on the shape of a pyramid. This peak is called a *horn*. I'll talk about some of the other features glaciers create in a minute, but first, anyone have any questions about glaciers so far?

27. The speaker mentions three types of materials that make up glaciers. Give the order in which these materials appear.

28. Where can continental glaciers be found today?

29. Match the type of glacier with its description.

30. What does the speaker say about receding glaciers?

31. Which part of the picture represents a *cirque*?

32. Which part of the picture represents a *horn*?

Questions 33-38

M2: Listen to a discussion that takes place in a history class.

F1: Well, we have only a few more minutes of class left today. Be sure to read Chapter 8 about the causes of the Civil War for Monday. Oh, and don't forget: On Saturday night, reset your clocks or you'll be an hour late for class on Monday.

F2: Oh, that's right—daylight saving time starts this weekend, doesn't it?

M1: I always forget—do we turn our clocks backwards or forwards?

F2: Don't you know that little saying: spring forward, fall back?

F1: That's right, Linda—in April, we move our clocks forward an hour from standard time to daylight saving time. We reverse that in October, when we turn the clock back an hour to standard time.

M1: So where did the idea of daylight saving time come from anyway, Professor?

F1: Apparently, the first person to propose the idea was Benjamin Franklin, way back in the 1790s. At the time, it was such a novel idea that people thought he was just joking.

F2: When was it put into effect, then?

F1: Not for many years. During World War I, people realized what an innovative idea old Ben Franklin had had. The Sun comes up earlier in the spring and summer, of course, so by moving the clock up then, people can take advantage of the extra daylight.

M1: But what's the real advantage of doing this?

F2: I think I know. You don't need as much fuel for lighting and so on. It's a way to save energy, right, Professor?

F1: Exactly . . . and energy is an important resource, especially during wartime. So the United States first adopted daylight saving time during World War I and went back to it during World War II.

F2: So, we've had daylight saving time since World War II?

F1: Well, not exactly. After the war, some parts of the country went back to year-round standard times and some parts didn't. There were some groups that opposed daylight saving . . .

M1: Really? Who would be against it? It's so nice to have extra daylight in the evening.

F1: Well, anyone who wants more daylight in the morning . . .

F2: Farmers would like that, I suppose, since they get up early to work . . .

F1: Yes, farmers, and some parents who didn't want their children going to school in the dark. Anyway, things were pretty confusing until Congress passed the Uniform Time Act in 1966. That made daylight saving a federal law and standardized the process. Then in 1986, daylight saving time was lengthened by a few weeks, and some people have proposed that we go to a year-round daylight saving time.

33. What is the main topic of this discussion?

34. When are clocks in the United States set *back*?

35. According to the professor, how would most people probably have characterized Benjamin Franklin's plan for daylight saving time when it was first proposed?

36. When was daylight saving time first actually put into effect?

37. Which of these groups opposed daylight saving time?

38. What was the effect of the Uniform Time Act of 1966?

SECTION 2: STRUCTURE

1. All	The noun phrase *All team sports* provides a subject for the sentence.	
2. light	In order to be parallel with the other adjectives in the series (*harder* and *more resistant*), the comparative form *lighter* must be used.	
3. most largest	The correct superlative form is *largest*.	
4. a	Of the four choices, only this one, which forms an appositive noun phrase, can correctly complete the sentence.	
5. destruction	The adjective form *destructive* is required in place of the noun.	
6. which across	The correct word order is preposition + relative pronoun: *across which*.	
7. were	The singular form of the verb (*was*) should be used to agree with the singular subject *influence*.	
8. without	This is the only correct negative form.	
9. Through her research	A preposition (*Through*) is needed before the series of noun phrases that come before the subject. The third choice is incorrect because it lacks the word *her*, which is needed for parallelism, and because the noun *research* is more appropriate in this series than the gerund *researching*.	
10. they are	The pronoun subject *they* is used unnecessarily and should be omitted.	
11. when	The relative word *where* must be used to refer to a place.	
12. Wherever people	An adverb clause is needed to correctly complete the sentence; only this choice supplies an adverb clause marker and subject.	

13. <u>its</u>   In order to agree with a plural noun (*sharks*), the plural possessive word *their* should be used.

14. <u>enough dense</u>   The correct word order is adjective + *enough*: *dense* enough.

15. <u>so</u>   *Such . . . that* is used with an adjective + noun phrase (*different surgical skills*). (*So . . . that* is used when an adjective appears alone.)

16. <u>able</u>   The noun *ability* is needed in place of the adjective.

17. many of which   The correct pattern is quantifier + *of* + relative pronoun.

18. That all   A noun clause, which serves as the subject of the sentence, is required to complete the sentence correctly.

19. <u>chemists</u>   To be parallel with the other nouns in the series (*physics* and *mathematics*), a noun that refers to the name of a field (*chemistry*) is needed.

20. <u>experts</u>   The adjective *expert* should not be pluralized.

21. When   The only correct choice forms a reduced adverb clause.

22. to   The preposition *for* must be used with the adjective *responsible* in this sentence (*responsible to* is sometimes used with a person).

23. are spotted turtles   When a sentence begins with a negative adverbial (*Rarely*), the subject and verb must be inverted.

24. more energy it has   This is a proportional statement; it follows the pattern *The more X, the more Y . . .*

25. <u>them</u>   Both the noun phrase (*these craftsmen*) and the pronoun refer to the same persons, so the reflexive pronoun *themselves* should be used.

SECTION 3: READING

1. **The correct answer is (D).** The primary purpose of this passage is to detail the stages of the Sun's life in the future.

2. **The correct answer is (A).** The word fueled is closest in meaning to *powered*.

3. **The correct answer is** thermonuclear reactions. The word They refers to thermonuclear reactions.

4. The Sun today is a yellow dwarf star. **(1)** It has existed in its present state for about 4 billion, 600 million years and is thousands of times larger than the Earth. **(2)** The Sun is fueled by thermonuclear reactions near its center that convert hydrogen to helium. **(3)** They release so much energy that the Sun can shine for about 10 billion years with little change in its size or brightness. **It maintains its size because the heat deep inside the Sun produces pressure that offsets the force of gravity. (4)** This balance of forces keeps the gases of the Sun from pulling any closer together.

   The last sentence of the paragraph refers to a balance of forces. The missing sentence discusses this balance of forces (between heat and gravity), so it should be placed in front of the last sentence.

5. **The correct answer is (A).** The Sun has existed in its present state for about 4 billion, 600 million years and can shine for about 10 billion years (paragraph 1). It is expected to become a red giant in about 5 billion years (paragraph 2). Therefore, it is about halfway through its life as a yellow dwarf.

6. **The correct answer is** interior. The word core is closest in meaning to ***interior***.

7. **The correct answer is (D).** Paragraph 2 states that "the core of the Sun will shrink and become hotter."

8. **The correct answer is (C).** The second paragraph describes the process by which the Sun becomes a red giant star. The last sentence of that paragraph states: "Temperatures on the Earth will become too hot for life to exist."

9. **The correct answer is (B).** Paragraph 3 indicates that the Sun will be a white dwarf "after it shrinks to about the size of the Earth." Paragraph 1 indicates that the Sun today is thousands of times larger than the Earth. Therefore, the Sun will be thousands of times smaller than it is today.

10. **The correct answer is (C).** According to the passage, the Sun is now a yellow dwarf star; it will then expand to a red giant star, shrink to a white dwarf star, and finally cool to a black dwarf star.

11. **The correct answer is** throw off. The phrase throw off is closest in meaning to *eject*.

12. **The correct answer is** the Earth. The word there refers to *the Earth*.

13. **The correct answer is (D).** Although the passage describes the end of the Earth, that event is so far in the future that the author's tone is scientifically dispassionate.

14. **The correct answer is (B).** Washington was one of the first people to realize the importance of canals and headed the first company in the United States formed to build a canal.

15. **The correct answer is** possibility. The word feasibility is closest in meaning to *possibility*.

16. **The correct answer is** method. The word means is closest in meaning to the word method.

17. **The correct answer is (B).** According to paragraph 2, the canal linked Albany on the Hudson River with Buffalo on Lake Erie.

18. **The correct answer is** put an end to. The phrase halted is closest in meaning to the phrase put an end to.

19. **The correct answer is (B).** The phrase on-again-off-again is closest in meaning to the word *Intermittent*.

20. **The correct answer is (A).** According to the passage, the governor of New York "persuaded the state to finance and build the canal" (paragraph 3).

21. **The correct answer is (C)** The cost had been estimated at $5 million but actually cost $2 million more (paragraph 3), a total of $7 million.

22. **The correct answer is (D).** The word tolls is closest in meaning to the word *Fees*.

23. **The correct answer is (D).** According to paragraph 4, the canal "allowed New York to supplant (replace) Boston, Philadelphia, and other eastern cities as the chief center of both domestic and foreign commerce." The other effects are mentioned in this paragraph.

24. **The correct answer is (C).** Paragraph 5 indicates that the expansion of the canal would have been warranted "had it not been for the development of the railroads." (This means, "if the railroads had not been developed.") The railroads must have taken so much traffic away from the canal that expansion was no longer needed.

25. **The correct answer is (B).** The word warranted is closest in meaning to *justified*.

26. **The correct answer is (D).** The passage mainly deals with the distress signals of trees. There is no direct information about the other choices in the passage.

27. **The correct answer is (A).** The reference is to the word *trees* in the third sentence.

28. **The correct answer is** attracted. The word drawn is closest in meaning to *attracted*. The word drawn is the past participle of the verb *draw*, which sometimes means *pull* or *attract*.

29. **The correct answer is** drought-stricken. The word parched has the same meaning as *drought-stricken*. A *drought* is a time of no rainfall. *Drought-stricken* therefore means damaged by a lack of water. The word *parched* means very dry.

30. **The correct answer is (B).** The word plight is closest in meaning to *condition*. A *plight* is a dangerous or terrible condition.

31. **The correct answer is** They fastened electronic sensors to the bark of drought-stricken trees and clearly heard distress calls.

32. **The correct answer is (C).** The trees' signals are in the 50–500 kilohertz range; the unaided human ear can detect no more than 20 kilohertz (paragraph 2).

33. **The correct answer is** fractured. The word fractured is closest in meaning to cracked.

34. **The correct answer is (D).** The signals are caused when the water column inside tubes in trees break, "a result of too little water."

35. **The correct answer is** insects. The word they refers to insects.

36. **The correct answer is (A).** In the context of the passage, pick up means *Perceive*.

37. **The correct answer is (D).** The first and second choice are mentioned in paragraph 3; the third choice is mentioned throughout the passage; there is no mention of the fourth choice.

38. **The correct answer is (C).** Paragraph 3 says, "Researchers are now running tests," implying that, at the time the article was written, research was continuing.

39. **The correct answer is (B).** The purpose of the passage is primarily to describe Charlie Chaplin's movie, *Modern Times*.

40. **The correct answer is (D).** Paragraph 1 states that Chaplin "was motivated to make the film by a reporter" during an interview.

41. **The correct answer is** packed. The word jammed is closest in meaning to *packed*.

42. **The correct answer is (B).** According to paragraph 3, "Scenes of factory interiors account for only about one-third of the footage." Therefore, about two-thirds of the film must have been shot outside the factory.

43. **The correct answer is** gentle. The word is biting most nearly opposite in meaning to the word *gentle*. (*Biting* here means "sharply critical.")

44. **The correct answer is (C).** The phrase *going insane* could best replace the phrase losing his mind.

45. Scenes of factory interiors account for only about one-third of the footage of *Modern Times*, but they contain some of the most pointed social commentary as well as the funniest comic situations. **(1)** No one who has seen the film can ever forget Chaplin vainly trying to keep pace with the fast-moving conveyor belt, almost losing his mind in the process. **(2)** Another popular scene features an automatic feeding machine brought to the assembly line so that workers need not interrupt their labor to eat. **All at once, this feeding device begins to malfunction. (3)** It hurls food at Chaplin, who is strapped into his position on the assembly line and cannot escape. **(4)** This serves to illustrate people's utter helplessness in the face of machines that are meant to serve their basic needs.

   The word *It* in the sentence following the missing sentence refers to the feeding device. Also, this sentence describes the malfunction that is first mentioned in the missing sentence.

46. **The correct answer is** people's. The word their refers to people's.

47. **The correct answer is (C).** The last sentence of paragraph 3 states: "This (the scene) serves to illustrate people's utter helplessness in the face of machines that are meant to serve their basic needs."

48. **The correct answer is (B).** The word utter is closest in meaning to *complete*.

49. **The correct answer is** flaws. The word faults is closest in meaning to *flaws*.

50. **The correct answer is (A).** The film "does not offer a radical social message" (Paragraph 3) and so would not be considered "revolutionary." Paragraph 2 states that "Chaplin preferred to entertain rather than lecture," so it is "entertaining." Paragraph 3 mentions that people who have seen the film cannot forget certain scenes, so it is certainly "memorable." According to paragraph 2, the opening scene's "biting tone . . . is replaced by a gentle note of satire"; therefore, the author would consider the film "satirical."

NOTES

Your online ticket to educational and professional success!

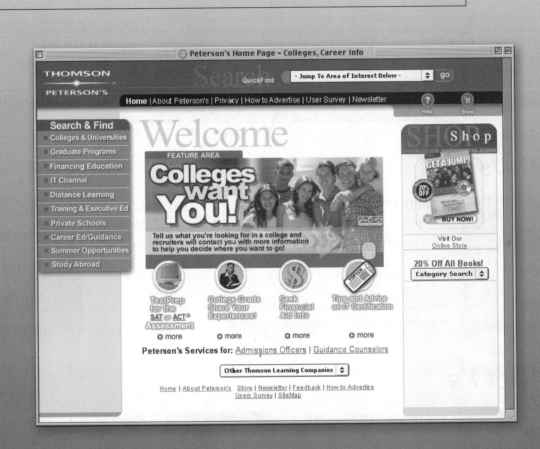

At petersons.com, *you can explore thousands of colleges, graduate programs, and distance learning programs; take online practice tests; and search the Internet's largest scholarship database and you'll find career advice you can use—tips on resumes, job-search strategies, interviewing techniques and more.*

www.petersons.com ■ tel: 800.338.3282

THOMSON
PETERSON'S

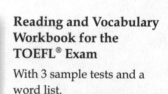